ELIZABETH ROBINS, 1862–1952

Elizabeth Robins, about 1904, with a portrait of George Parks by her side. (*Courtesy of the Fales Library. Reproduced with the permission of Mabel Smith, for the Backsettown Trustees.*)

ELIZABETH ROBINS, 1862–1952

Actress

Novelist

Feminist

Joanne E. Gates

The University of Alabama Press

Tuscaloosa and London

Copyright ©1994

The University of Alabama Press
Tuscaloosa, Alabama 35487–0380
All rights reserved
Manufactured in the United States of America

The paper on which this book is printed meets the minimum
requirements of American Standard for Information
Science-Permanence of Paper for Printed Library Materials,
ANSI Z39.48-1984.

Library of Congress Cataloging-in-Publication Data

Gates, Joanne E., 1950–
     Elizabeth Robins, 1862–1952 : actress, novelist, feminist / Joanne
E. Gates.
          p.   cm.
     Includes bibliographical references (p.) and index.
     ISBN 0-8173-0664-1 (alk. paper)
     1. Robins, Elizabeth, 1862–1952.   2. Novelists, American—20th
century—Biography.   3. Actors and actresses—United States—
Biography.   4. Feminists—United States—Biography.   I. Title.
PS2719.R4Z65   1994
813'.4—dc20
[B]   93-23813

British Library Cataloguing-in-Publication Data available

Contents

Illustrations

Acknowledgments

I AM GRATEFUL TO Judith Fryer for her advice and for her support of this work at a critical stage in its development. Her suggestions helped shape and focus my study of Elizabeth Robins. In addition, I thank all those who offered criticism and encouragement.

I am grateful to Ann Hagedorn at New York University for securing a grant to process the papers at the Fales Library. Frank Walker, curator of the Fales, was generous with his time and support of my work. I thank Sherlyn Abdoo and the archivists for the Robins project, Janet Evander and Marion Casey, also at the Fales Library. Dorothy Johnson of the Common Reader Bookshop was able to locate many out-of-print books by Robins. I also acknowledge cooperation of the staffs at the following libraries: New York Public Library, New York University (Tamiment Library), Washington State University (Pullman), City of Seattle, British Library, British Theatre Association, Fawcett Library (London), University of Sussex, City of Northallerton, Vassar College, University of Florida (Gainesville), University of Massachusetts (Amherst), and Wisconsin Historical Society (Madison). I benefited tremendously from interaction with fellow scholars at numerous professional conferences and from my discussions and correspondence with Robins enthusiasts, including Mel Heath, Katharine Houghton, Jane Marcus, Claire Tiley, Joseph Donohue, June Dwyer, Neil Salzman, Gay Cima, and Marcia Rock. In England, discussions with Mabel Smith, Tara Heinemann and Phillis Hartnoll contributed to my understanding of Elizabeth Robins. Lisa von Borowsky allowed me access to Chinsegut and guided me through its history and photographic record. I have also benefited from Victoria Joan Moessner's wisdom and collaborative instincts in our editing of Robins's Alaska diary (funded in its initial stages by the Alaska Humanities Forum). Grants from the New England Modern Language Association and fellowships from the American Society for Theatre Research and the University of Massachusetts facilitated research. Jacksonville State University provided travel funds for special collections research and conference presentations. I also thank Roy Gillespie and Norris Schneider of the Pioneer and Historical Society of Muskingum County

(Zanesville, Ohio), and the staff and administration at Jacksonville State University.

This work would not have been possible without the generous hospitality of friends, relatives, and gracious hosts, which made it possible for me to travel to sites important to Elizabeth Robins's residences in Yorkshire, Sussex, and London as well as in Zanesville, Ohio, and Brooksville, Florida. I thank also those many supporters who provided me with lodging while I visited special collections in England and the United States.

Marcia Brubeck was especially helpful in the copyediting of the manuscript. At the University of Alabama Press, thanks go to my editor, Nicole F. M. Mitchell, to Malcolm M. MacDonald, the Elizabeth Agee Prize Committee, and the readers, referees, and staff who guided the book through publication.

My deepest appreciation goes to my husband, Greg Halligan. He has very generously given encouragement and advice. His love and patience have enriched my life and supported me throughout the many stages of this project.

For permissions to use copyrighted material, I thank the following: Frank Walker, Fales Librarian, New York University, and the copyright holders, for permission to quote from material in the Elizabeth Robins Papers; Mabel Smith, on behalf of the Backsettown Trustees, for permission to quote passages from the Elizabeth Robins Papers, for the use of photographs in the Elizabeth Robins Collection (Fales Library, New York University), and for the quotation from the Methuen edition of *Votes for Women!* (1985); Mabel Smith for the passages quoted from Octavia Wilberforce's autobiography, "The Eighth Child" (typescript in the Fawcett Library, London); Richard Pankhurst for previously published remarks and letters of Emmeline Pankhurst; The Society of Authors on behalf of the Bernard Shaw Estate for quotations from the works of Bernard Shaw; the Random Century Group for quotations from Elizabeth Robins's *Ibsen and the Actress*, published by the Hogarth Press (1928); Hyperion Press for quotations from Elizabeth Robins's *Ancilla's Share: An Indictment of Sex Antagonism* (1924; reprint, Westport, Conn.: Hyperion, 1976); Virago Press for permission to quote from Dorothy Richardson's *Pilgrimage I* (London: Virago, 1979) and Jill Liddington and Jill Norris's *One Hand Tied Behind Us* (London: Virago, 1978); the University of Chicago Press for the quotation from Jane Gallop's "*Writing and Sexual Difference*: The Difference Within," anthologized in *Writing and Sexual Difference*, edited by Elizabeth Abel (Chicago: University of Chicago Press, 1982); and Lady Bridget Plowden for the quotations from a letter of her grandmother, Lady Florence Bell. Extracts from previously unpublished letters of John Masefield are quoted with permission, Copyright © The Estate of John Masefield 1991.

ELIZABETH ROBINS, 1862–1952

Introduction

MULTIPLE IDENTITY AND a sense of double duty were almost preconditions for Elizabeth Robins's artistic expression. At various stages of her life, she felt the simultaneous pull of competing obligations to her family and an acting career, to her husband and performances on tour, to commercial success as a performer and the goal of establishing higher standards for the theater. While she was still at her most active on the stage, she strove to establish her credentials as a writer of plays and fiction. In the early decades of the century, while she maintained her stature as a novelist, she devoted much energy to work for woman suffrage. The many volumes of her unpublished fiction reveal as much about her use of her own life in her fiction as do the published novels. Her work on behalf of woman suffrage rapidly involved her in a wide range of feminist issues. Had she persevered in any of her chosen fields—the stage, letters, or politics—her achievements might be more easily classified.

Robins left behind more than fifty years of diaries, voluminous correspondence, detailed drafts of most of her twenty-odd published books, and texts of many other titles in various states of completion. At age sixty-five, she was invited to speak about her experiences as an Ibsen actress; she spent much of her remaining twenty-four years working on autobiographical projects. During this time she completed three volumes of memoirs, numerous short portraits, and a novel (based partly on her father's record books), centered around her own youthful ambition to become an actress.

From her first years of accomplishment, she was conscious of the duality in her own voice. She relished the disguise of a pseudonym, and long after the identity of "C. E. Raimond" became known, was repeatedly tempted to publish anonymously. In March 1895, as she lay in bed, suffering from the influenza that took many lives in London, she composed her "will" and cautioned her future biographers: "Any account of the way I have spent my life must be more misleading than true. . . . In the first place I have a constitutional unwillingness to letting people know what seems to myself to be the real 'me.' I am afraid I have moods when I delight to darken counsel on this subject." Robins then expressed both her impulse to elude those who tried to uncover her most intimate confidences and her misgivings about her role-playing instincts. "I must content myself with trying to warn my relations and my friends that they will not find me or any explanation of me in any one's description or in any letter or diary of my own," she continued. "I have partly deliberately and partly unconsciously 'cooked my accounts.' " She made no attempt to record the most illuminating experiences of her life because she felt "these things should die with the person chiefly concerned," and yet she did preserve vast treasures of her private writing. Because she used so much of her own experience in her fiction, the material from her archive reveals her complex personality and the drives that motivated her. She identified her perhaps most conspicuous trait when she admitted, "I am conscious that in talking and writing to my nearest and most trusted friends I sometimes suppress and I sometimes embroider."[1]

Her ability—and her desire—to disguise her true self in her fiction shows that she had an artist's consciousness. The use to which she put evidence of her own life bears out this conclusion. If Robins did not "cook" her accounts in the process of setting down her sometimes sketchy, sometimes precisely detailed daily records, she certainly did so in the process of deciding which to preserve and which to destroy. She excised from her diary of 1887 the pages which record her thoughts between the disappearance of her husband, the actor George Parks, and the recovery of his body. Her later diaries show how often she sorted back through his letters and effects and consecrated them, with incense burning, to the flames. Gone from her archive are most of the letters that William Archer wrote to her over a period of ten years, which she turned over to him in 1915. She lamented in her diary, after learning that he was aghast at rereading these letters, that they must have been "burnt now I suppose . . . , all that gone up in smoke" (November 18). Her letters to John Masefield, if they had survived, might have given an account of her side of their brief affair, but Masefield was apparently carrying out her own wish to have her correspondence destroyed when he wrote her that he had translated her letters into his private combination of foreign languages and then set fire to the originals. Robins destroyed what she called "huge budgets" of her correspondence at frequent intervals.

Robins saved, and often "embroidered," masses of other correspondence and papers, much as an autobiographer makes mental notes of where certain documents should be placed. These annotated records provide a detailed account of her personal, political, and literary life. Her private life is a tale of passionate experience. Perhaps a dozen men and women at different times told her they could not live without her. Without forfeiting her independence, she reciprocated with restrained but genuine and deeply felt, judicious, mature, and often even motherly emotion, sometimes at great personal expense.

Indeed, it would be possible to write a biography of Robins that focused on her as a loved object whose irresistible attractiveness, intelligence, and personality were reflected in the statements others made about her. While her personal relationships do not lack significance, her public voice insistently asked why certain intimacies define a woman's life. The documents which she preserved show that there is much more to her life than the superficial aspects that appealed to admirers. In writing about Robins, I found myself absorbed by her multifaceted personality and by the achievements that attest to her literary and political influence. Elizabeth Robins was determined to transcend the limits imposed on women living in her times. It is indicative of the incomplete state of feminist scholarship that her very significant contributions to women's literature and to the women's rights movement remain largely unknown today. Robins herself was conscious—especially when she reminded fellow women writers of their opportunities—that without a biography, a life and a life's record could remain obscure.

If only because of their volume, her papers present her biographer with a great challenge. One must, by necessity, be selective and balance chronological narrative with attention to the significant recurring patterns. Robins herself used the imagery of fabric about her writing. That is, if she was not "embroidering" for strangers, she was mindful of the stitches that compose everyday records and the perseverance required to complete a design.

Each of my eight chapters accordingly explores a phase in Robins's life with a focus on her competing obligations and ambitions. I introduce each chapter with a dramatic episode taken directly from Robins's personal documents. These "dramatic episodes" carry the chronology forward and offer a cameo of her life during the time period represented.

My principal aim is to treat Robins's writing in the context of her developing feminist aesthetic. To do so, I draw on the details of her personal life, compare her with other writers of her day, and bring to bear the perspectives of contemporary feminist criticism. While several dissertations have dealt with her acting career or with her part in the suffrage campaign, no biographer to date has had full access to her private papers or has undertaken a comprehensive survey of her productive years and her writing in its entirety.[2] Too frequently, published material on Elizabeth Robins perpetuates factual errors and suffers from an incomplete examination of her papers and published work. *The Convert* alone, her suffrage novel written in 1907, ought to place her among the ranks of significant women writers at the turn of the century. Moreover, even her earliest unpublished novels and her least well received fiction illustrate the importance of silence as embodying female power and reveal that speech amounted to complicity with a patriarchal order. Several novels offer evidence that didactic writing can have artistic merit. Robins wrote about her part in a changing theater world with a sense of female difference, and what she wrote and did not publish about her stage experience is equally engaging. Her speeches and political essays remind us not only that the militant woman's suffrage movement in England depended upon commitments such as hers but also that one could formulate a feminist-pacifist critique of society based on daily headlines and everyday experiences. Elizabeth Robins's life invites analysis because it rests upon contradictions, failures to achieve, missed or denied opportunities, and the sometimes uneasy coexistence of actress, writer, politician, and a woman coming to terms with her past. Appreciation of her achievement—so long unrecognized—can only deepen our understanding of female experience and women's literature.

1 | "I Was Born in the Superlative"
Girlhood and American Stage Career, 1862–1888

> My disposition is made up of fragments from the mental organization of dead forefathers and each trait intensified by circumstances. . . . I can even trace this apparently new passion of mine for the stage. Our family are all fine readers, we are great *reciters* from Grandpapa Robins down to Raimond; Aunt Sarah wrote one play and read many a score, was thrilled by Rachel's acting; Mama was the finest reader in the Shakespeare Club and I have seen her worked up to that pitch of passion at home when her face was something to curdle men's blood, her gestures eloquent and noble and her voice bell-like, sonorous and such an intense expression of turbid passion, that I have looked at her and forgotten she was anathematising me for very wonder and admiration. This dark thread of Tragedy that has run through the daily lives and final fate of many of our house I will cut out of my personal experience and transfer to a profession where it will turn to gold.
>
> —Elizabeth Robins to her
> grandmother, January 14, 1882

THE SCENE: Zanesville, Ohio. May, 1881.[1] The recently opened Schultz's Opera House is the latest attraction for touring theatrical companies. Young Bessie Robins knew she had dramatic inclinations when she began to keep scrapbooks of the famous actresses of her day. At the age of twelve, she saw *Macbeth* performed in Louisville, Kentucky, the city of her birth. She recalled it later, when she attended the Putnam Female Seminary. As a child she organized theatricals among her younger siblings and her school friends. Later, at the seminary, she excelled in elocution.

VOICE OVER (YOUNG ELIZABETH ROBINS) [Describing the scene to her father]. Papa, I am writing this to you because no one here understands. You must be the first to know that our journey to New York and Washington and those many evenings spent in the theater last winter were not for naught.

Last night I went to the theater and heard Lawrence Barrett play "Richelieu" most grandly. While the curtain was down, between the acts, my thoughts turned from "My Lord Cardinal"—his plots and counter plots—to my own little drama and its still unknown *dénouement*.

Sitting there in the glare of the gas, and staring vacantly at the drop curtain, I formed a little new plot for this Drama of mine. I took a regret card and wrote "Will Mr. Barrett see a lady privately a few minutes? It will cost him little and will greatly oblige ——— ———."

[Shot of young Bessie Robins approaching "Ladies Entrance" of Zanesville's Zane House. Closeup of the neatly printed card with its two blanks. Zoom out to questioning expression on butler's face as he reads the card. The young girl gestures, indicating that she must gain entrance. With a shrug and a smile, the butler obliges and shows her into a parlor.]

VOICE OVER (YOUNG ELIZABETH ROBINS). "Enter Richelieu" with his stage step. He sat down. I launched into the subject.

[Overlap into dialogue of the scene:]

BESSIE ROBINS. . . . your opinion on . . . If you believed it possible for a young girl to become a fine actress without going through a course of dramatic training?

BARRETT. No great actress has ever been "made" by dramatic or elocutionary training previous to her appearance on the stage. . . . The famous actors train *themselves*—they begin at the lowest rung of the ladder.

BESSIE ROBINS. Mary Anderson was a success almost from the beginning of her career.

BARRETT. Yes, she has beauty and a sort of charm of manner but her acting is nothing to admire. You *have* finished school? You don't seem old enough to be ready for a life of touring.

BESSIE ROBINS. I received highest honors for my recitations at Commencement. I am nearly nineteen.

BARRETT (Looking at her more attentively). Eighteen is a good age to start. An actress must take subordinate parts, work and study, and then if in her prime at about thirty-five she had drawn the eyes of the world upon her and established her position, she will hold it.

BESSIE ROBINS. I think you make the actress too old before you give her success.

BARRETT. Charlotte Cushman died at sixty; she played constantly for twenty-five years before her death.

BESSIE ROBINS. Yes, but such horrid old women characters as Meg Merriles.

BARRETT (Counting on his fingers). Queen Catherine, Bianca. . . .

VOICE OVER OF YOUNG ELIZABETH ROBINS [As Barrett continues his lecture]. Oh, papa he must have talked to me for half an hour or more.

BARRETT. . . . I suppose you think I have influence—not so. Why, I once wrote a letter to the *New York Herald* advising that we must organize an association of American actors for the purpose of examining aspirants for the stage. This actress that is to be is not the beautiful Mary Anderson but some obscure girl now playing some subordinate part.

BESSIE ROBINS. She may not be doing so *yet*.

BARRETT (with a laugh at her directness). No, for it may be yourself.

VOICE OVER (YOUNG ELIZABETH ROBINS). Oh, papa—if I was intended for the stage I would reach it in spite of fate. I would overcome all obstacles, and as you would say, "being naturally selected and showing myself 'fit' I would survive." For youth there is no such word as "fail."

[Shot of Bessie Robins writing letter to her father, sealing and addressing it, and walking to post it. Superimposed over her journey are her images of herself in later life, first as a schoolteacher and maid, sternly drilling her pupils, shriveled and severe, and next as a bright and vibrant young performer.]

I have the choice of two lives: one is that of a single woman living much alone and reading with a sort of dogged pertinacity and gaining but little solace out of books in English and German. When this impoverished old maid must come out of her older fortress and go into some small school and lose her small stock of patience teaching the young not to shoot paper wads, I turn with a shudder to the alternative, brilliant by contrast:

A young girl calling herself—some assumed name—gets a promising subordinate part in a Theatrical Company, and has for her whole life an intense active interest in the Drama; unlike the school teacher she has constantly a great aim before her; her ambition has full sweep. It is limitless. Besides the interest such a life may have from an artistic point of view I do not think that woman will want bread. Papa *I am in earnest.* Just as soon as Grandma does not need me I will in some way get such a position as named. This shall be my life. It is not the fancy of a moment—but the only thing I feel fitted to undertake.

Notes on the Scene: The eighteen-year-old Bessie Robins had been struggling to find support for her dramatic ambitions long before her interview with Lawrence Barrett. She was the first child of Charles Ephraim Robins. Her mother was his first cousin and second wife, Hannah Maria Crow Robins. At age ten, young Bessie was sent from her first remembered home, on Staten Island, to her grandmother's house in Zanesville, Ohio, to attend the Putnam Female Seminary. After Bessie Robins became Elizabeth Robins, and after she took up her pen, which she did with an outlook influenced by the women's movement, she reflected upon the early years and playfully acknowledged her debt to Putnam Female Seminary with this brief composition:

In 1872, Susan B. Anthony went to the polls, voted, was arrested, tried and fined for her audacity.

In the same year Victoria Woodhull, a woman notorious for relations with men, ran for the Presidency and her equally disrespectable sister ran for Congress.

In the same year Elizabeth Robins, aged 10, left Staten Island to live with her grandmother and go to school.

Ergo, the year 1872 was one of considerable feminist activity in the U.S.A.[2]

Zanesville, in the decade between 1872 and 1881, was a smoky town in southeastern Ohio where the Licking River joins the Muskingum. The town's distinguishing feature is its "Y-Bridge," uniting Zanesville proper with the township of Putnam on the northern shore. Putnam, settled by Northerners who were outspoken abolitionists, boasted the Putnam Female Seminary and, a few short blocks away, a large brick residence, constructed in 1809 in order to lure the state legislature to Zanesville. It had been turned into the "Stone Academy" before becoming the Robins residence. A tunnel starting below the cellar stairs and running to the outside indicates that the house was a stop along the Underground Railroad.[3] This was her father's mother's house. Jane Hussey Robins, originally from Baltimore, had occupied the Stone House for several years when Elizabeth arrived to attend school.

Robins remembered scenes of her childhood, in Cliffwood, Staten Island, in poignant but incomplete impressions—of a mother who sang beautifully and a father who showed her the majestic sea. One of her earliest letters, addressed to her father, describes a birthday spent in Central Park. Her father would be away on business a great deal during her formative years, and Elizabeth in her later fiction would elaborate upon, and embellish, her one memorable experience with him.

Some time after Robins started school in Zanesville, the rest of the family followed her there. Charles Robins regretted the breakup of the Staten Island homestead, where he had formulated development plans and apparently took part in promoting the settlement of an ideal living community in Cliffwood. In Zanesville, Hannah's health wore out, quite possibly aggravated by marital difficulties. The young girl had watched her mother's mental and physical health decline as she gave birth to six additional children. Two babies died in infancy and were buried on Staten Island. Hannah fled from the Zanesville home of her aunt and mother-in-law, Jane Robins, to her married sister and their girlhood home in Louisville, Kentucky. Robins's next oldest brother, Saxton, was sent to Louisville, where Hannah was put under the care of her brother-in-law, Dr. James Bodine. Yet she lived, near poverty, in a public boardinghouse. Vernon, Eunice, and Raymond remained with Elizabeth at their grandmother's home in Zanesville. Recalling her mother's condition later, Robins focused, where possible, on her mother's positive influence and

Jane Hussey Robins, Elizabeth Robins's paternal
grandmother (and maternal great aunt), 1806–1885. Jane was
the primary caretaker for Elizabeth and her siblings. She warned
Elizabeth against marrying, fearing the perpetuation of the family
mental weakness. (*Courtesy of the Fales Library. Reproduced
with the permission of Mabel Smith, for the Backsettown
Trustees.*)

either forgave, suppressed, or subsequently fictionalized the struggles of a
family disrupted by Hannah's breakdown.

Several factors made up for the lack of a close bond with her mother. Her
grandmother and aunts, as well as the superior schooling she received at Putnam, were important forces in her life. She relished the confidential though
infrequent talks that she had with her father. The family could see that she
would make something of herself. Robins's grandmother, Jane Hussey Robins,

The "Old Stone House" in Zanesville, Ohio. The house was owned by Jane Hussey Robins and was Elizabeth Robins's residence between 1872 and 1881. Memorialized in Robins's novel, *The Open Question* (1898), as "The Fort," the building was constructed in Putnam (the northern riverbank of Zanesville) in 1809 to induce the state legislature to locate there. The house was subsequently converted to a school, the "Stone Academy," and then to a private residence. It is now the Pioneer and Historical Society of Muskingum County, Zanesville, Ohio. (*Photograph by the author.*)

deeply religious and wearied not only by the sad death of her artistically gifted daughter, Sarah Elizabeth Robins, but also from rearing a second generation of children, had seen the family fortunes wane. After witnessing the family's financial decline, Elizabeth Robins imagined that her own stage success could save the family from money worries. She also began to hope, as she paid visits to her mother, that money would make it possible to restore her mother's health, for she saw how Hannah suffered when she was away from the younger children.

Elizabeth was the oldest surviving child of Charles Robins. An older son, Eugene, by his first wife, Sarah Sullivan, had died in his teens while away at school. It was natural for Elizabeth to attract her father's attention, given his belief in the value of education. Charles Robins stimulated and encouraged his daughter's intellectual curiosity. Under his guidance, Elizabeth came to question religion freely. In this respect she contrasted sharply with her younger sister, Eunice, nicknamed Una, who, early in her stay with their grandmother, adopted a pious faith. Soon after Robins began regular stage employment in Boston, she wrote her father a summary of her views, which reflected not simply her rebellious instincts but also her exposure to many sermons and theological debates. As far as she was concerned, she told her father, God should spelled with two o's; "Man," she continued, "is doing the best he can; God isn't." She added: "Agnosticism to me is a gigantic trapeze upon which I may swing myself from theory to theory and from every Science to every 'ism.' I don't want to be *settled* anymore than I want to lie down in my grave" (ER to CER, September 12, 1883).

The Formative Years, 1862–1880

Bessie Robins had few memories of Louisville, Kentucky. She was born there, in the midst of a thunderstorm and at the height of the Civil War, on August 6, 1862. Her mother had been raised with a sense of Southern breeding, and her father had been a self-made man in the Northern business world. Charles wrote his mother of the happy occasion, but Jane expressed alarm for the health of the baby because she was informed that the birth was complicated by extra strong doses of chloroform. Although the abuses of chloroform were documented only later by medical historians, some of the family correspondence makes it plain that the effects of chloroform during delivery caused much concern. When the infant developed croup, Jane wrote to suggest the best remedy she knew, strong liquor. Later in her life, Elizabeth would be overly concerned about the nature of the relationship between her parents at the time of her birth. Robins allayed her anxiety by rereading her mother's diary of 1862; she was relieved to discover that her mother had been very much in love and looking forward to her birth. Charles's letters during the immediate months following Elizabeth's birth confirm his passionate love for his wife.

A number of Elizabeth's kin—including her mother, her mother's sister, and her father's poetically minded sister, Sarah Elizabeth—attended Putnam

Female Seminary before her. Several of Robins's early school compositions testify to her creative spirit. One, "The Herstory of a Button," composed in 1875 and published in the *American Voice* in 1990, is noteworthy as a playful feminist satire on schooling. With a perceptiveness that marked her later parodies as well, Robins narrates the adventures of a button through its escapades, first on the shoe of a schoolgirl and later after being left behind on the schoolroom floor. Young Bessie's love for the stage originated in such creativity as well as in the "family theatricals" that she arranged.

None of Elizabeth's immediate family understood or encouraged her drive to become an actress; so, as she excelled in elocution at school and directed family performances, she clung to the dream of being like the renowned Mary Anderson, herself from Louisville, who had achieved fame on two continents. Long before Elizabeth's graduation performance of Schiller's *Maria Stuart*, she filled scrapbooks documenting the accomplishments of Anderson and other American women who had proved successful on European and English stages. Through a distant relative in St. Louis, the philanthropic Wayman Crow, she claimed an association with the most respected actress of the previous generation, Charlotte Cushman. Cushman's nephew had married Wayman Crow's daughter. (The Wayman Crows not only built the St. Louis Art Museum but also paid for the European training of the sculptor Harriet Hosmer, the classmate of another Crow daughter.) At the time she introduced herself to Lawrence Barrett, Wayman Crow had just sent Bessie Robins a letter in which he told her that he could not help her financially.

During the previous summer, her father had attempted to distract her from the stage by taking Bessie to a goldmining camp in Summit, Colorado. There she could study nature firsthand and, under his tutelage, prepare for college. The summer adventure failed to achieve its intended purpose, however. Robins understood that her father had no money to send her to school, and after making a trip east to attend theatrical performances in New York and Washington, she reaffirmed her decision to pursue her schoolgirl dream in hopes of improving the family finances. In 1882, on the day after Elizabeth's twentieth birthday, her mother, Hannah, wrote from Louisville to inform her oldest daughter that she had succeeded in obtaining from her brother-in-law and doctor, James Morrison Bodine, a five-hundred-dollar loan to help finance Elizabeth's stage career in New York. In the letter her mother expressed the fervent wish that Elizabeth might one day be self-supporting.

When Elizabeth Robins was fifty, she sifted through her diaries and letters to her family and made them the source for a projected fictional trilogy about an actress's early years on the American stage. After the first volume had been rejected by a New York publisher, she continued to work at later parts of "Theodora: A Pilgrimage," but she never completed it. In particular she dwelled on the struggle of the young Theodora to find her first job. Robins seems to have been hindered in her effort to finish the story by her inability to resolve a romantic relationship in the life of her central character. She created a fictional lawyer, modeled upon her own actor husband, who begged Theodora to marry him and give up her career. In her autobiography as well, Robins focused on the obstacles and false leads that she had encountered in her pursuit of a theatrical career. The performance of *Hedda Gabler* in London, which Robins had intended as the climax of the first volume, had to be postponed to a never-published subsequent volume. Any biography that focuses in too great detail, as Robins did, on her formative years overlooks her real achievement. Essentially an expatriate artist and women's rights advocate, Robins did not come into her own until she reached English soil. Only abroad did she experience success, both as a novelist and as an actress of Ibsen. Accordingly, the brief account in this chapter of her American career outlines the events that were most essential to her personal and professional development.

First Stage Opportunities, 1881–1883

Elizabeth Robins's diaries and letters to her father and grandmother chronicle the struggle to earn enough to support her family. Despite innumerable setbacks, she was determined to remain independent. She gossiped freely with her father and his mother about the problems experienced by a young, unattached woman traveling with acting companies. Jane Robins, her grandmother, seemed more interested in one of her suitors than was Elizabeth, who sent her many letters demonstrating his respectability, which she ridiculed. Distant members of the Robins family misread or misreported the account of her sleigh accident during her tour with James O'Neill in Rochester, New York. She found it necessary to explain that it was *Mrs.* O'Neill, not Mr. O'Neill, who had accompanied her when their sleigh overturned. The sleigh's owner later appeared at the theater door to demand payment for damages.

Robins's actual relationship with the actor-manager was for the most part respectful and courteous. O'Neill and his wife roomed in a boardinghouse on East Twenty-fourth Street, where Robins moved in the fall of 1881. During Christmas week, O'Neill helped to get her a small part. Later in the season, he took her into the company that he had formed with himself as leading actor. O'Neill chided her for her lack of patience. She was, he said, in too much in a hurry to establish herself. Like Barrett, O'Neill advised her that patience was her best asset. On this first tour she was careful to take an assumed name, reasoning that she had best keep her activities secret from her

Zanesville friends and the more distant relatives. She decided upon Clara Raimond and then changed Clara to Claire. More than a decade later she used the pen name "C. E. Raimond."

To O'Neill Elizabeth Robins owed her biggest opportunities, and yet she recognized that by staying in this company she could only slow her progress. During the early O'Neill tour,[4] Robins met a few distant relatives, in Chicago, St. Louis, and elsewhere, who gave her practical support. Sometimes they offered her lodging on the road; each night in a relative's home saved her the $2.00 or $2.50 in hotel fare. Sometimes aid came in the form of cast-off gowns. Robins made costumes from many of them and recycled her used wardrobe by passing it on to her younger sister.

Lloyd Tevis, the president of Wells Fargo, was more forthcoming in his assistance than closer members of her family. Tevis, who had been lured to California by the 1849 gold rush, bought out Wells Fargo, after having amassed a fortune in mines and having established a rival transport company. His mother and Edward Crow, Hannah Robins's grandfather, were brother and sister. Tevis was approaching sixty when he met Robins in the first years of her stage career. With some pride, he reported to Robins the apparent success of Eleanor Calhoun, his earlier protégé, in London. Soon he was offering to pay for Robins's lessons in French and singing. Robins did not accept this offer, but she repeatedly accepted other financial support from Tevis.

Robins's first important notices came when she acted (for the first time under her own name), in H. M. Pitt's company in the spring of 1883. The company performed *Two Roses* and *Forgiven* in Boston and Brooklyn before it disbanded for lack of funds. The family correspondence suggests that Lloyd Tevis funded Robins—and possibly Pitt himself—and that he lost this considerable investment in Elizabeth's training. In Boston, however, Lloyd Tevis introduced Elizabeth to R. M. Field, manager of the Boston Museum Theatre, and before the summer was over, she had signed a three-year contract to perform with the Museum Company.

At the Boston Museum Theatre, 1883–1885: Courtship and Marriage

Robins spent the summer of 1883 in Zanesville, preparing for her new position. As soon as she reached Boston and had begun drawing a regular salary, she began to send two dollars a week back to her grandmother. The money covered expenses for the maid whose help Jane Robins needed to manage the large household. Robins had risen in the ranks of O'Neill's company, becoming leading woman when O'Neill took over *The Count of Monte Cristo* from another touring manager. In the same fashion, ever so gradually, time brought her better opportunities at the Boston Museum Theatre. She meticulously recorded her progress and saved the theater programs which documented the weekly offerings of the Boston Museum. The company, though based in Boston, made frequent tours. Seniority and the terms of her contract prevented Robins from rising rapidly within its ranks. Nevertheless, she played Julia in *The Rivals*, Grace Hardcastle in *London Assurance*, and Miss Neville in *She Stoops to Conquer*. Edwin Booth often performed as guest artist with the regular Boston company. Robins was his Player Queen in *Hamlet*, Jessica in *The Merchant of Venice*, Goneril in *King Lear*. In plays that have not survived the test of time, Robins had more substantial parts than in Shakespeare's classics; she played Ginerva in *The Fool's Revenge*, Margaret Overreach in *A New Way to Pay Old Debts*, and Blanche in *The Iron Chest*.

Later in life, Robins estimated that she had learned more than three hundred roles during her American tours. Her letters to her family afford occasional glimpses of the critical and technical aspects of her craft. Her grandmother was her chief confidante and adviser. Robins remembered her grandmother as her "touchstone." *The Open Question*, her roman à clef, eventually fictionalized her rebellion against her grandmother's strict moral principles while also acknowledging in its introduction the important role played in her life by the woman who had raised her strictly.[5] In early December 1883, Robins faced the first real crisis in her life, when she confronted George Parks, a fellow actor in the Museum Company who had begun to pay her attention. Robins pulled away from Parks's advances almost instinctively, with a reflex action perfected by the years of self-restraint. Equally instinctive was Robins's resort to her pen, first to explain herself to Parks and later to ask for her grandmother's advice.

To Jane Robins she wrote: "After some vacillating and several scenes I rose Friday night about 12 o'clock and wrote a long letter to Mr. Parks. I had learned by experience that I could not *say* such things to him as it were best he should hear—my only recourse, my only weapon was the pen—there I was master of the field and he without defense of eager words and looks that took the edge from all my cooler argument" (ER to JHR, December 10, 1883). With the firmness of spirit that consistently impelled Robins toward her artistic goal, she clarified her rejection of Parks: "*I do not intend ever to marry. I have always said so and unlike most girls have meant it*" (ER to JHR, December 10, 1883).

Not until Saturday evening did she mail the letter, as she went to the theater with a servant. On this night, there was a special performance of *Macbeth* to benefit the distinguished Boston Museum actress Annie Clark. In this performance Parks, but not Robins, had been cast for a part. Robins reminded her grandmother that *Macbeth* had given her her "first glimpse of that weird world beyond the footlights, on another Saturday evening nine years ago" (ER to JHR, December 10, 1883). Not only had the outer circumstances changed drastically, but the little girl of twelve who saw nothing but the weak and wicked Scot now focused on other faces and other scenes. At the end of the play, Parks, who had played Banquo, managed to dismiss Robins's servant so that he might escort her home. At her doorstep he pressed her for a response to his demands. Robins was evasive but resolute: "You will get a letter Monday. It will tell you all you want to know, answer all questions" (ER to JHR, December 10, 1883).

Parks replied, "What have you to tell me that you cannot *say?*" Robins answered him. "Nothing that ought to surprise you; either unlock the inner door or else give me the keys." "I was at a disadvantage," Robins wrote her grandmother as candidly as she could, "because I did not dare to make a noise and he would not give up the keys." To her relief, a couple whom she knew approached to enter the boardinghouse. Loudly enough for them to hear, she said good night. Under her breath she whispered, "*Goodbye*" (ER to JHR, December 10, 1883).

She wrote her grandmother as if the troublesome episode had ended. The following Monday she started a letter in which she proposed that her next younger brother Saxton come live with her in Boston. After sealing this letter, however, she reopened it to report a disturbing development. Parks had returned her letter to him with a note saying that he in no way considered her words final; they seemed only to have "added fuel to the flame" (ER to JHR, December 10, 1883). She told her grandmother she had once again sent him her last word on the subject. At the same time, she felt incapable of predicting his next move.

For her part, Jane Robins overreacted to the difficulty in which her granddaughter found herself. She forwarded the letter to Charles Robins, insisting that he write Parks directly, exhorting him to cease his romantic attentions to Elizabeth. Jane had already written several letters to Elizabeth. After stressing that matrimony would keep her from pursuing her career, she asked: "What do you hear from Louisville? Has your papa written you that he has been there recently by Dr. Bodine's summons? . . . Have you received letters from your mother lately? *I hope not*" (JHR to ER, December 7, 1883). Jane proceeded to lay out the events of Hannah's most recent abandonment of her residence. She had left the boardinghouse where she was staying and fled with Saxton and Raymond to her sister and brother-in-law, the Bodines. Jane wrote to Elizabeth emphatically, "*Her mind is much disordered*" (JHR to ER, December 7, 1883), and quoted from the doctor's letter to show that there was little chance of improvement. She added:

I would on no account have written this to you—but as *a warning*—Sh! It is a thing of heredity—Do not, I beseech you, my darling child, rush into matrimony which may plunge you into a sea of difficulty where you may sink to rise no more!

Never mind sentiment, feeling, preference, and all that—do not commit yourself—if you think you have encouraged hope, never mind, it is a woman's privilege to reconsider—to change her mind. [JHR to ER, December 7, 1883]

Elizabeth had encountered family illness before. Hannah had spoken of infirmities on the male side of the family, and illness and premature death among Robins's aunts and an uncle were generally ascribed to weakness of constitution. But forever afterward, Robins connected passion and the consequences of passion with her mother's deteriorated mental state. After watching her mother's decline, Robins concluded that marriage was not for her.

George Parks's courtship continued for more than a year. Robins returned to Zanesville in the summer of 1884 to recover from what is described in family correspondence as severe heart fatigue. Back in Boston in the fall, she resolved to hire a private maid who would serve as chaperone (and who would also protect her from encounters with Parks). On the Museum Company's tour to northern New England and Canada, Robins found herself unable to pay for the maid's travel and was forced to send the woman home. When she did so, Parks immediately volunteered to serve as escort. George Parks's ultimatums and her fears might well have prompted Robins to acquiesce. Perhaps, though, the letter she wrote her family merely masked her real feelings; for Parks, despite his excesses, was elegantly chivalrous and passionately in love. On January 12, 1885, with only a single witness, the two were married in the Episcopal church in Salem, Massachusetts. That evening, Robins stayed to play in the touring company, and Parks returned to Boston for a different performance.

Robins had her reasons for keeping the ceremony a secret. As soon as R. M. Field learned of the marriage, he informed her that he would not honor her three-year contract and would drop her at the end of the season. Robins learned more about Parks's precarious finances. He was supporting a widowed mother, a sister, and a younger brother. Apparently Parks had initially accepted the fact that his wife would continue with her profession, but he may not have understood how committed she was to her career. At any rate, she realized that her acting was necessary for their financial security. In its early period their marriage was certainly tranquil, even deeply romantic. Parks had, however, a tragic temperament and a possessive nature. In one of her more telling letters to her father, written six weeks after her marriage, Robins dismissed the changes her marriage had brought and understated Parks's expectations of her as his wife: "In truth, my marriage has been but a ripple in my life—so much together before and he had come into my life so inevitably at every turn that it is less a change to me than to most girls—to have him always" (ER to CER, March 19, 1885). Although Elizabeth tried to reassure her father, her report exposed the tension between her and her husband: "He hates to see me poring over books and gets a 'cross boy' when I want to read German. . . . we have *awful* times when I want to read at night after the theatre. In a rash moment I told him once that Mrs. Longstreet advised me to write a book—how he blazed!" Parks had warned her, she said, that a wife who wrote a book was giving "grounds for a divorce"; he offered "a horrible warning to all daring wives—how the writing of a book was the alienation of a mother from her children and finally a separation of husband and wife— the ruin of a home." Robins dismissed the threat with a lighthearted joke about the possibility that her writing would break up the "boarding house" where the couple rented rooms. She promised, "I'll run no risks and will not attack literature this season" (ER to CER, March 19, 1885).

On Tour with O'Neill, 1885–1886

Upon release from her Boston Museum contract in early 1885, Robins searched for improved opportunities. Failing other employment, she returned, almost as last resort, to her old manager, James O'Neill, this time as the female lead, Mercedes, in his recent successful melodrama, *The Count of Monte Cristo*. Her role was the only large female part, but the play was a vehicle for the actor-manager, and Robins saw more quickly than O'Neill himself that her artistic development was being stifled by the repetition of a single role.

On December 1, 1885, Robins made a triumphant return to her home town of Zanesville, Ohio, performing Mercedes opposite O'Neill in Schultz's Opera House. The performance was sold out (for the first time since the theater had opened), and the standees were several rows deep. Acclaim for Robins was capped with ovations and bouquets. *The Courier* of Zanesville showed pride in their hometown heroine, as it proclaimed for its headline, "RIGHT ROYALLY / Did Mrs. Bessie Robins Parks Acquit / Herself as Mercedes in Monte Cristo / at the Opera House Last Night." Robins was called out in front of the curtain at the conclusion of the fourth, penultimate act, in which she had her most stirring scene, and was presented with bouquets. The reviewer predicted the actress would "take a commanding position in tragedy."[6] Another paper spoke of the quality of the play and the scenery and also paid tribute to Robins alone.

The public excitement over her performance contrasted sharply with the tone of her conversation with her father that night. She heard of his sad journey to place her mother in the care of a mental sanitarium in Jacksonville, Illinois. Her father also gave her, as a belated wedding present, unalloyed gold from the mining trip they had taken together in 1880.

Parks and Robins, though married, continued the exhausting routines of their separate tours. Parks joined Robins wherever he could. They spent vacations together. He worried about finding an engagement for the following season but was able to secure one. Robins prepared, reluctantly, and as a last resort, to rejoin O'Neill. She knew she would not enjoy performing the same role again and again, at little salary and with very little challenge. When she attended Parks's successful opening in *Held by the Enemy*, in New York in the fall of 1886, she learned that she could have had a good part with his company. This information may have provoked their first serious argument. She asked whether Parks did not want her to be with him. He would rather, he said, that she retire from the stage, and she could not explain how impossible it was for her to do so.

Robins had rejoined the Monte Cristo company in the fall of 1886, but a succession of misfortunes kept her in the company only through the fall. As she continued to tour with O'Neill, Parks's letters of complaint to Robins grew more and more shrill. Finally, he wrote that, if she did not give up her work and join him, he would do something desperate. Meanwhile, her father had written to tell her that his finances were failing. He had attempted to take his other children to a remote settlement in southern Florida, and Robins's younger sister was sick with malaria. Robins had finally been able to afford newly constructed stage gowns, which had required numerous fittings during the last part of the summer. All these costumes were ruined during a flood in the theater in which the company was performing in Providence. This blow prompted Robins to comply with George's request that she give up her contract. No sooner had she turned in her resignation to O'Neill, however, than she heard from her father in Florida that her younger sister had died. She resolved to join her father in Florida.

Suicide of George Parks, 1887

In Florida, she helped to set the cabin in order, did the baking and cooking, and sewed mosquito nets for all the family. With her brothers, she took a boat up the Alva River as far as Lake Okeechobee. Robins herself contracted malaria and struggled to recover. Parks wrote her that he was now quite ill;

George Richmond Parks, fellow member of the Boston Museum Company. Parks courted Robins from their first theatrical season together in 1883, married her on January 12, 1885, and committed suicide in June 1887. (*Courtesy of the Fales Library. Reproduced with the permission of Mabel Smith, for the Backsettown Trustees.*)

he had lost his voice and much weight, was taking many different medicines, and was barely able to perform. Quite possibly he was drinking heavily.

When she returned to her Staten Island friends in late spring 1887, Robins was laid up with a more severe case of the malaria she had contracted in Florida. She spent most of that spring recovering. Parks visited, then sent desperate letters from his engagement in Boston. As soon as Robins was well, she resolved to do all she could to improve their financial situation. From her first stage idol, Lawrence Barrett, she learned that she could probably have a position in Booth's and Barrett's joint tour across the continent, scheduled for the fall. In Manhattan, in mid-May, she learned that Booth was playing in Hartford, Connecticut, that evening; impulsively she traveled there the same day and made her way backstage during the performance. Booth was impressed with her initiative and promised her the position. Another interview, with Barrett in New York, secured her contract. Her father agreed to help her and Parks through the summer and promised to send more money. She records few specific details in her diary, but her entries suggest that she decided not to tell Parks of the reasons for her plans, quite probably because of his attitude toward her working. On May 24, she wrote her father about the gold he was transferring to her, then lunched with Parks, "but conclude[d] to hold it awhile" (Diary, May 24). Possibly Robins was pregnant or had terminated a pregnancy with an abortion. There is too little evidence to let us know for certain. There are a few indirect later clues that Robins had at some point carried his child. But we can only conjecture that she may have had an abortion before their marriage or in the early months of 1887.

On June 1, 1887, Robins received Parks's delirious note in which he revealed his plan to commit suicide. The Boston papers gave his subsequent disappearance extensive coverage. A week later his decomposing body was recovered from the Charles River. It had worked free from the heavy weight of his chain mail armor, which he had strapped to his waist.

Robins alternated between exhaustion and raving grief. She recorded severe headaches and periods of uncontrollable sobbing. When, a day or so after his burial service at St. Andrew's Church, in Richmond, Staten Island, she was brought a packet of the possessions found with his body, she "spread his dear possessions out on my bureau to dry. The room is filled with the salt sick smell" (Diary, June 16, 1887). She apparently read and reread the sensational accounts of his death. On June 30 she wrote in her diary, "Mrs. Longstreet makes me promise I will not read the accounts of the finding of my darling's body for six months. . . . I commit myself and she keeps the papers." The next day was the first of the many anniversaries she marked, "just a month today" since his disappearance. She had a friend accompany her to the pier where she threw back to sea the packet with "my darling's watch, scissors, etc., etc." (Diary, July 1, 1887).

Her diary records her fitting for her mourning, in layers and layers of black, capped by a heavy veil. Behind it she hid, stunned and pale, often dissolved in tears. She learned to conceal her grief at times, but she did not overcome it. Some of her closest friends were spiritualists, and they seemed to challenge her lack of faith in the afterlife. She commented that "Mrs. Longstreet thinks I *wish* to disbelieve—how little she knows. . . . she thinks my ideas are low because I call them sensible names" (Diary, June 17, 1887). In July, she recorded in diary entries only the summary effect of two dreams of Parks, "some little tantalizing comfort" (July 3) and, a week later, "delicious dream that is like reality—that I accept as *real* comfort" (July 10). Yet she would never be free of the internal despair. Brief reminders, such as "Happiness of a year ago" (July 5), indicate the poignancy of her emotional trauma. Months later, she still found it hard to keep her composure. In Milwaukee, watching Booth play Hamlet, "Mad scene breaks me down" (Diary, October 1, 1887).

Across America with Booth and Barrett, 1887–1888

In the fall of 1887, Robins began to travel with Edwin Booth and Lawrence Barrett on the Pullman car that had been specially equipped for the company. Although Robins was able to share in the two stars' lively talk about the history of the profession and tales of earlier acting days, her role in the company was too minor to satisfy her. The play most often performed was *Othello*, in which she was not cast. At such times she spent long evenings either in the audience or in the Pullman car. Friends had told her that she could earn something by writing of her experiences as an actress, and Robins formed a resolution to write about traveling with Barrett and Booth.

Just as she was beginning to take more control of her circumstances, however, she was let go from the company. In San Francisco, she learned that the troupe needed to economize. Lloyd Tevis was again on hand to urge that the company keep her on. He had no success, and Robins elected to return to the East Coast by way of Panama. As she traveled through Central America, a Chilean traveler made advances and probably attempted to seduce her. Her experiences on this trip became a source for the first novel she began to write in England, which she completed in 1899 and published several years afterward as *Under the Southern Cross*.

An Opportunity to Visit England, 1888

Shortly after Elizabeth Robins's arrival on Staten Island, her Boston friend, Sara Bull, widow of the composer Ole Bull, invited her to serve as a companion to Sara's young daughters on a trip to Norway. Because the trip would involve stopovers in England and the chance to see theater in London, Robins thought it might help her realize her dream of acting in England.

If Robins had not had a great capacity for putting difficult experiences

ambition

behind her, she might have been less persistent in her determination to act. She had a certain amount of blind faith and studied optimism, of course. She also believed that the commercial American theater had not allowed her to demonstrate her dramatic talents fully. England, she trusted, would be a place where women could practice their profession and where artistic concerns, and not business, set theatrical standards.

2 | The Coming Woman
Early Years in London, 1888–1892

Miss Hamam (dresser) tells me she overheard some people coming out of the Theatre last night say, "Miss Robins is the best artist there. She's the coming woman!"

—Elizabeth Robins,
Diary, October 21, 1890

I will try Literature, loving The Stage ever the best. I will take up my new work with no illusions. It is to be for a *purpose* and that end must consecrate my work.

—ER Diary, February 1890

T*HE SCENE*: Early February, 1891, home of Edmund Gosse.[1]

Several years of struggle and hardship have marked Elizabeth Robins's life in London. Although the ordeal of finding her bearings as a stage performer is relieved by remarkable friendships with the leading personalities of the English stage, she has found only sporadic work and has overcome disappointments only through sheer perseverance and determination. Now everything depends upon the interview that Marion Lea and Robins will have with Edmund Gosse.

The two American actresses proceed with caution because they are all too aware of rival claimants to the stage rights to *Hedda Gabler* and the translation dispute which erupted when William Archer charged in print that Gosse's translation "reproduces the terse and nervous original about as faithfully as a fourth-form school boy."[2] Archer's own translation has gone unpublished because Gosse's publisher, William Heinemann, won from Ibsen the sole rights to the play. The actresses have Archer's admission that he will work secretly with them to produce a speakable and more accurate translation—if Gosse and Heinemann do not find out that Archer is assisting the women. They have Heinemann's encouragement to approach Gosse, because Gosse authorized an adapter, Justin Huntly McCarthy, to distort the text even further.

Lea and Robins have been talking for months of their plans to manage their own theater company. They regard Ibsen's previous plays as having

24

promise and have approached managers with plans to do *The Lady from the Sea*. No manager is interested. Then *Hedda Gabler* arouses their determination as nothing has before. "Here is Our Play," they declare after reading the first available copy of Gosse's translation. All they need is to convince this respected man of letters, angered by Archer's treatment of him, that he should feel as they do.

[ELIZABETH ROBINS and MARION LEA signal to each other nonverbally whenever they feel the need to reconfirm their strategy. All their planning and the urgency of their mission prompt them to finish each other's sentences, to speak in the kindest euphemisms, to compliment when they are in fact suspicious of their adversary.]

ELIZABETH ROBINS. Might we tell you our plans—

MARION LEA. —Our hopes, rather—with your permission, of course.

ELIZABETH ROBINS. Yes, our *hopes* for staging the play?

EDMUND GOSSE. Yes, of course.

ELIZABETH ROBINS [with barely controlled fervor]. Then perhaps we can tell you what excitement we felt [touching on the new subject as lightly as she can] about the play itself, when we first read it—

MARION LEA. —With such great excitement.

EDMUND GOSSE. *You*, then, weren't . . . repelled by . . . a . . . by . . . the *character* of the woman?

ELIZABETH ROBINS. Repelled! Hedda is one of the greatest parts ever written. We speak merely as actresses, of course. We leave the interpretation of Ibsen to the critics.

MARION LEA. Yes, speaking as actresses, may we venture to point out the . . . the need. . . .

ELIZABETH ROBINS. —The special needs as well as the limitations of the Theatre.

MARION LEA. Perhaps you've not had the time to go into the . . . peculiar demands made by the Stage.

EDMUND GOSSE. No, I assure you, I've other occupations besides—

MARION LEA. That is exactly what we were afraid of, in view of the concessions you've made to your adapter, Mr. McCarthy.

EDMUND GOSSE. Concessions?

ELIZABETH ROBINS. We gathered, Mr. Gosse, rather than seeing your *translation*, here and there a little *modified*, to meet the exigencies of the stage, you would prefer to see Mr. McCarthy's *adaptation* of your translation.

[Slight displeasure from GOSSE.]

MARION LEA. Mr. McCarthy has been unresponsive to our requests to see him, but if you *prefer* his adaptation, then perhaps you could endorse our negotiating with him for the rights to stage his adaptation?

EDMUND GOSSE. McCarthy's rights?

ELIZABETH ROBINS. We assumed he would have the rights to the adaptation.

EDMUND GOSSE. Why then, of course, if you feel it will help you, I'll tell Heinemann to arrange the meeting. McCarthy will be interested.

MARION LEA. But how soon?

ELIZABETH ROBINS. After all, an adaptation may mean . . . practically rewriting the play.

[GOSSE's irritation grows to polite anger. He glares through his spectacles.]

MARION LEA. It is Mr. McCarthy's reputation at stake.

ELIZABETH ROBINS. Yes, he is the person, the only person, responsible for the Adaptation.

EDMUND GOSSE [a bit grave]. I am not aware of the general practice.

MARION LEA. About that we can tell you; we have just performed in the stage adaptation of Dostoevsky's *Crime and Punishment.*

[GOSSE searches his memory, trying to recall notice of it.]

ELIZABETH ROBINS. Retitled by the adapter, Mr. Robert Buchanan, *The Sixth Commandment*?

EDMUND GOSSE. Ah, yes.

MARION LEA. Well, then, the Adapter's name always appears on the bills and programs. . . .

ELIZABETH ROBINS. And in the newspapers.

EDMUND GOSSE [with sudden haughtiness]. I know nothing of these matters. I wash my hands of the newspapers.

ELIZABETH ROBINS [privately to MARION LEA]. Oh no, he means William Archer's attack on him. Here it comes.

[The actresses quickly steer him off the subject.]

MARION LEA. What do you think of Mr. McCarthy's adaptation?

EDMUND GOSSE. I'm afraid I have not seen it.

ELIZABETH ROBINS [feigned surprise]. Not seen the adaptation of your own translation?

EDMUND GOSSE [in another effort to dismiss them]. *He* knows I am a busy man.

MARION LEA [taking up her fellow actress's amazement]. And you would prefer we should do the adaptation, whatever it's like, rather than allow us the privilege of acting your version?

EDMUND GOSSE. You're suggesting you would prefer to do my translation?

ELIZABETH ROBINS and MARION LEA [together]. Yes, yes.

MARION LEA. Allowing, of course, for such changes, as—

ELIZABETH ROBINS. —As, from the actors' point of view, would get the effect you mean to produce across the footlights.

MARION LEA. The exigencies of the stage, Mr. Gosse—

ELIZABETH ROBINS. —Require so different a touch than even the literary masters—Tennyson, Swinburne, Wordsworth—were prepared for.

MARION LEA. Their stage ventures ended in failure.

ELIZABETH ROBINS. And we want Hedda gloriously to succeed, and she *can*!

MARION LEA [more soberly]. If *we* had *Hedda Gabler*, we would of course submit any and all the suggested changes to you for approval.

[Long pause. Fate hangs in the balance.]

EDMUND GOSSE [evenly]. I *could* of course tell Heinemann to let you have two sets of page proofs to work on. [Another silence. Then to the prospective Hedda.] You would feel free to write in your . . . ah . . . alternative suggestions. [And to MARION LEA.] And you free to object—

ELIZABETH ROBINS [covering her triumph with a lightly tossed suggestion]. And you free to object to our suggestions—[She telegraphs silently to MARION: And I free to die for mine!]

EDMUND GOSSE. Then, all there is to do is for me to write to McCarthy suggesting there may not be a need for his adaptation.

[General agreement and great enthusiasm on everyone's part. The two actresses continue to signal their triumph to each other as they take their polite leave.]

Notes on the Scene: Elizabeth Robins's drive to determine the course of her own career is illustrated in the two months' effort to stage *Hedda Gabler*. She succeeded in making the production the one that influenced more remarkably than any other Ibsen's reception in England. The two actresses recognized the need to control the production; according to Robins's later memoir, they each put up their jewelry as collateral for a loan to rent a theater. Archer had persuaded them of the need for a more speakable, more accurate translation and welcomed their conspiracy to deceive Gosse and Heinemann. Besides the actresses' success with Gosse, and then McCarthy, Robins could boast of winning support from William Archer, William Heinemann, and, when the production opened, Henry James and Bernard Shaw. Learning from the press's failure to notice her earlier appearances, she arranged for several pre-performance articles to arouse interest in her project.

Before *Hedda Gabler*, Robins's attempts to establish herself on the London stage had been plagued with difficulties. She discovered that breaking into the ranks in the London theater involved establishing connections through money and influence. The actor-manager system militated against both the rise of young talent such as hers and the intellectual drama to which she was immediately drawn. She came to England determined to leave behind her the memory of her marriage and her husband's suicide. Instead she encountered men who thrust themselves upon her. Her relationships with them left her feeling that romantic involvement would compromise her career.

She turned to writing as a second occupation in part to console herself because she was not acting enough, in part because she was critical of the theater as it existed, and in part to earn money to help support her family. Gradually, as she developed her style and reflected upon her own circumstances, her commitment to this second profession consolidated her feminist stance. Much of her autobiographical fiction of the early 1890s remains unpublished, but her unfinished novella, "The Coming Woman," together with her journals, letters, and the memoir she published of these years, convey her sense of the injustice of male domination of the theatrical profession.

Her own ambitions reflected both her inner strength and her sense of family obligations. She clung to the hope that her experience in England would far surpass any she might gain in America. The late 1880s marked a renewal of concern for dramatic excellence and a proliferation of theaters and theater companies. On the one hand, Henry Irving was mounting lavish productions of Shakespeare. On the other, new plays, many presented in trial afternoon performances that occasioned lively debate, abounded. In short, Robins had every reason for optimism as soon as she stepped on English soil.

Arrival in London, 1888

All her life Elizabeth Robins had wanted to act. London, in September 1888, was surely the place to try her talent in earnest. Elizabeth Robins's ambition had carried her through school and away from her family, had sent her across America, first with the touring company of James O'Neill, then with Lawrence Barrett and Edwin Booth. Her professional commitment had helped her cope with the trauma of her actor husband's suicide. Now, in London, she was free to seek introductions and offers of assistance. At the close of the theater season in the United States, she had been invited to serve as companion to the daughters of Mrs. Sara Bull as they revisited Norway, the homeland that Mrs. Bull wanted her half-Norwegian daughters not to forget. As the summer journey neared its conclusion, only three days before her steamer sailed to America, Elizabeth Robins, just turned twenty-six, weary from her elaborate mourning dress and veil, sat in London "plunged in gloom and writing a story."[3]

Thus began her double existence. The desire to act would henceforth compete with her need to write. Frequently, the two careers would complement each other. Just as often, however, the theater projects came when she was midstream in a piece of writing.

She had, in the short space of time since she had arrived in London, been offered a part in a matinée. The offer came upon the recommendation of Eleanor Calhoun, an American actress once supported by Robins's wealthy cousin, Lloyd Tevis, and now established in London. Robins had also met and found enthusiastic support in Oscar Wilde. Wilde had been impressed by the young American widow. Her diary mentions his witty remarks about her country: "England . . . is a Garden. . . . Boston is an invention. . . . New York is a piece of 'dry goods' on a counter" (*BSC* 9). But Robins countered by reminding him that he had once praised the St. Louis Fine Arts Museum and added that she was related to Wayman Crow, its designer and builder. She was here in England, she explained when she was asked, because what she "wanted to do, was to act" (*BSC* 10). Wilde instantly offered more advice than Robins wanted: she should get up her own matinée; it would cost only a hundred pounds. The actress was suddenly stopped short; she had no funds of this kind. Later, when Wilde found out that Eleanor Calhoun had arranged an opportunity for Robins to debut, he told her to refuse the part because of his misgivings about the manager.

Robins heeded Wilde's warning, but more than ever she sensed that she had lost another opportunity. Her dream of standing on the London stage seemed far off indeed, but she had fallen in love with the country and its culture. Before she left for Norway, she had received a respectable offer from the New York manager Augustin Daly. She knew she could return to his company and have the promise of a year's employment. Still, England's attraction for her was forceful enough to prompt her to take up an alternative existence. Her thoughts, she wrote in retrospect, had "taken a direction not unusual in moments of deepest gloom. Since all else had failed perhaps I'd better become an authoress" (*BSC* 21).

Robins's first literary effort in London was a reworking of a piece she had completed and submitted in longhand to the *Home Journal* before she left America. With an editor's rejection letter came also a comment that her writing was full of promise and that her "vivid impression of real child life" was "literature and not a recital of the case." Most helpful of all was the indication that other magazines might take her piece.[4]

Robins admitted in her memoirs that she based her story, "Him and Her," on an event in her mother's life. The main part of the story is told in the form of a woman's letter to her daughter, Helen (a character based on Elizabeth), telling the girl of the circumstances surrounding her husband's—Helen's father's—estrangement from his first wife. Largely to account for the father's strong love for his son, Helen's mother explains what she learned on her marriage day, that her husband's first wife committed flagrant adultery. Helen's father had had to endure his wife's behavior and had initiated court proceedings to gain custody of the boy. Young Helen, having read the letter, and having some acquaintance with the much-loved son, is filled with awe at the meaning behind the phrase used by the servants to express the boy's misfortune at the first wife's death: "Him and her is parted." Then suddenly, while he is away at school, her older half brother becomes ill and dies. Learning the news, twelve-year-old Helen remarks, "Him and her are not parted any more." Like the girl in the story, Elizabeth Robins experienced the death of her older half brother. She realized that her father had transferred to her his hopes for his bright young son, Eugene. Charles Robins had wanted Elizabeth to attend college; he had hoped that she would study science or medicine.

In London, Robins sought to compensate for the transgression against family honor that she had caused by going onto the stage six and a half years earlier. She had promised herself and her family that she would help pay for the education of her younger brother, Vernon, who had his hopes set on a medical career. She also wanted to earn enough money to finance her mother's release from the Oak Lawn mental asylum in Jacksonville, Illinois. Robins later explained that she had thought of writing not as a "way in, or a way up" but as a "way out" (*BSC* 21). Having decided to prolong her stay in London while she waited for the ideal acting opportunity, she tried to support herself by writing.

Her early writing career was strictly a way out, however, an expedient to be avoided if stage prospects seemed imminent. Oscar Wilde got her a seat at the Haymarket's *Captain Swift* and arranged for her introduction to its actor-manager, Herbert Beerbohm Tree. The introduction was supposed to take place on the night before her departure from London, but after being "swept away" by Tree's mesmerizing performance and spurred on by his words about the need for quality actresses—"There are *plenty* of opportunities. . . . There are never enough clever people to go round"—Robins committed what she called "the rashest act of my life" (*BSC* 28). She canceled her return passage and hoped that Tree could add substance to his promises.

Robins saw two sides of the renowned actor-manager in the next several weeks and months. Tree fell into the habit of making box seats available for her. She saw him play a wide variety of characters. Aware herself of the dangers of being type cast and recognizing that Tree's success depended on his versatility, she told herself she wanted "to be the actress doing that" (*BSC* 249). She also received him in the public drawing room at her boardinghouse on Duchess Street. There Tree appeared to her without makeup, fighting a bad head cold, and probably unaware of the extent of her need for his assistance.

Outside her box at the Haymarket, Tree mentioned that he needed a leading lady for *Judah*, a new play by Henry Arthur Jones. When he appeared at Robins's Duchess Street lodgings several days later, he informed her rather casually that, after reading the whole play, he had decided not to do it. For the actress, "A chasm opened." She was still to learn the reason for Tree's refusal: "he thought the 'unconventional woman's part' was better than the hero's" (*BSC* 51). Tree, she was to discover, had a pride and arrogance that was common in the actor-manager theater: no female part must overshadow that of the leading man.

Tree sexist X

In the end, Robins's first appearances had nothing to do with Tree. She accepted an offer to appear in William Poel's *Cheiromancy*, and her London debut in October 1888 at his semiprivate single matinée went unnoticed in the press. In early December she joined F. R. Benson's Shakespeare company in Exeter to perform Portia in *The Merchant of Venice*. By Christmas, she had been offered the chance to replace Mary Rorke on Saturday afternoons as the American widow in Mrs. Oscar Beringer's production of *The Real Little Lord Fauntleroy*. She contacted Genevieve Ward, an older and well-established American actress, who offered her a part. Robins, however, had asked to read the play before she accepted, was not impressed by the role, and ultimately refused the offer. Ward must have been surprised, for an actress did not usually decline a role.

Searching for Opportunity

When Robins looked back over the diaries she kept during her early months in London, she realized how inept her first efforts had been. On the day of her interview with Mrs. Beringer in Bath, she had passed up an opportunity to watch a performance of *Lord Fauntleroy* so that she could visit the abbey church. She wrote Benson, asking him to postpone her first rehearsal as Portia so that she could meet Mrs. Kendal, manager of the Beringer company. Robins had to put off her meeting with Genevieve Ward because she mistook ammonia for mouthwash and burned her throat. Invariably, she found herself walking in wrong directions when she set out for appointments or tried to save money getting home. She wore a hole in her shoe and had no money to buy a new pair.

Her writing kept her occupied in the long intervals between prospective engagements. She proposed a series of "Letters from an American Actress Abroad" to a periodical in Washington, D.C. For this purpose she took notes on the Lord Mayor's Show in early November. In December the rejection of her first "letter" arrived, and she plunged into work on a novel, a story again based on real life.

This story, "The Peruvian," was rejected by a publisher in early 1889. It dealt with a woman's escape from attempted seduction during an excursion through Central America. Robins reworked the story for *Under the Southern Cross*, which was accepted by Frederick A. Stokes in the United States in 1900 and was finally published in 1907. She stressed in her memoirs that strange men in London also made advances. Though she always felt able to take care of herself, she vowed that she would make use of the "Nature of Man" in her fiction (*BSC* 244).

Determined to use her writing to advance her acting career, Robins secured interviews with Henry Irving and Ellen Terry; if she could not obtain a position in Irving's company, she could at least use their conversation for an article. Irving abruptly judged her too impatient: "Miss Robins, I waited ten years for the opportunity you have now" (*BSC* 189). Ellen Terry, who was imposing in a different way, made Robins feel as if *she* were being interviewed. The leading lady of the Lyceum quickly dismissed the possibility that she could supply her interviewer with a story. Terry asked, "Do you play to-night? Oh, how *wicked* of you to be running about tiring yourself in the afternoon. I never do. I always stay home and rest." The novice interviewer felt mesmerized: "I looked into her wonderful face and was too Terry-fied not to believe anything she chose to tell me" (*BSC* 236). Though it appears that nothing came of the meeting, Robins apparently recalled Terry's manner in a later satire. "A Highly Respectable Heroine" pokes fun at a leading actress with a reputation to maintain.

By degrees Elizabeth Robins's stage opportunities increased. Playwright Arthur Wing Pinero remembered the woman he had seen dressed in widow's weeds for her role in *Little Lord Fauntleroy* and offered her three pounds a week as a regular understudy for his play, *The Profligate*, at the Garrick Theatre under John Hare's management. When Robins and Pinero first met, he had complimented her on her characterization of Mrs. Errol in *Fauntleroy*. As he listened to Robins describe the other parts she had played, he commented, "I see . . . your line is sympathetic Outcasts." He regretted that a company for his own play had already been hired; Robins introduced herself to him as someone needing "instant work" (*BSC* 176).

The once-a-week replacement opportunity in *Little Lord Fauntleroy* ended abruptly when Mrs. Beringer decided to replace Robins with a woman who could draw a bigger audience. Marion Terry, Ellen's sister, took over the role. Robins's brief connection with the Beringer company would later help her secure the part of Martha in Ibsen's *The Pillars of Society*, which was performed as a benefit matinée for the young Vera Beringer. The play and the part of Martha gave Robins her first personal contact with Ibsen. A month earlier, she had admired Janet Achurch's performances in *A Doll's House*; but for the moment, despite a few complimentary notices and the sense that her Ibsen role was "something alive, that called to me" (*BSC* 208), Robins was "as unconscious of the nature of my rescue as a blind swimmer who has been picked up by a battleship" (*BSC* 209).

Robins similarly failed to exploit a greater demonstration of her talent. She had been introduced to the playwright-physician, Dr. Dabbs, in September 1889, during the last hours she visited the Isle of Wight as a guest of Genevieve Ward. On November 6, Robins starred in the trial matinée at the Haymarket of Dr. Dabbs's *Her Own Witness*. This time she received enthusiastic notices. Clement Scott, a leading critic, took the occasion of Robins's splendid playing to lament the rigidity of the actor-manager system. He claimed that her talent should have earned her a long-term contract, but he predicted, "Probably she will remain on the shelf until she becomes heart-broken."[5] Because the play "was, fatally, a woman's play," no actor manager wanted it (*BSC* 217). Neither Dabbs, who had financed the matinée, nor Robins could afford to give it a regular run. Robins fell back on her surer income as understudy, this time at the Haymarket and with a slightly higher salary.

Although neither of her positions as understudy gave her much of a chance of replacing a leading actress, Robins enjoyed the special atmospheres of both theaters. The Garrick brought her its luxurious green room and pleasant company. At the Haymarket, the Trees welcomed her. Tree expressed an interest in looking at an article she was writing on her experience touring with Lawrence Barrett and Edwin Booth. When it was eventually published, she called it "Across America with 'Junius Brutus Booth,'" the 'Junius Brutus' a reference to the name Edwin Booth had given (in honor of his actor father) to the custom-built Pullman car that housed his traveling company. Between the time Robins first drafted the article and its appearance in the July 1890 *Universal Review*, several experiences determined that writing would have a permanent place in her life.

The most telling event occurred when Robins accepted from George Alexander a position in his newly formed company and a role in his production of *Dr. Bill*. Real opportunity seemed to have come her way at last. Robins, however, was to learn much about the tyranny of actor-managers in the course of her stay with Alexander. She needed an independence which Alexander, in his first venture as actor-manager, could not accommodate. She assumed she could maintain her understudy position at the Haymarket until she started to perform in the evenings for Alexander. Her relationship with the manager was further compromised by her refusal to wear a hat that she found ridiculous; the hat proved to have been trimmed by Mrs. Alexander.

Moreover, Robins committed herself to performing in a private theatrical directed by William Poel during the week that Alexander's production opened at the Avenue. In her diary, she reacted to the absurdities she found in such an engagement: "For the first time in my life I have a sensation that this dressing up and affecting passion for the amusement of a lot of stupid people is unworthy acting. . . . I came up stairs in a great rage at my own ignorant stupidity in doing such a thing—and vowing no more paltry drawing room performances for me."[6] In the initial days of *Dr. Bill*, Robins made a further resolution. She declared in her journal, "I must not depend upon the precarious living afforded me by the stage. I must write letters for the press if the opportunity comes; if not, novels." She continued her reasoning: "Lots of stupid women write books and make money. I shall not, *cannot* be worse than some and if I write a passable story and follow it with others and can make a home for my mother and take my brother through College . . . " She resolved, "so will I try Literature, loving The Stage ever the best" (as quoted in *BSC* 231, 232).

Despite her decision to make something more of her writing, Robins almost immediately found herself consumed by the theater. George Alexander had mounted a popular success in *Dr. Bill* and sought to keep it running for as long as possible. Robins found herself playing an "inane part in a play that would go on forever and ever" (*BSC* 239). Alexander made many demands: he insisted she change her costumes faster and required that she add to her duties the understudying of Fanny Brough's larger part. In a sudden move, he replaced his curtain raiser with a two-character sketch by Justin Huntly McCarthy, *The Will and the Way*, and cast Robins as one of the lovers. In response to her performance, he complained that she kept the curtain down too long with her costume change. One night when she arrived too ill to perform, he refused to let her turn her part over to an understudy. Alexander insisted that she present a doctor's certificate, but Robins had taken ill on the way to the theater. She promptly gave the manager—in writing—her two weeks' notice. Alexander failed to grasp that she meant to leave and asked her to stay longer. When the final rupture came, Alexander let loose a tirade, claiming that she was "always wanting to mix up other work with mine." Clearly, Alexander resented Robins's independent ventures, such as her attempt to revive *Her Own Witness* for two weeks of matinées. At last he exploded: "I hope you'll get another engagement when you leave here for I'll never have you in *my* theatre again!" (*BSC* 277).

It was an empty threat to an actress who was glad to have been released. But another worry loomed ahead. Robins had sent her article on touring with Booth to the writer Oswald Crawfurd. Crawfurd sent it to Reverend John Verschoyle, editor of the *Fortnightly Review*. Verschoyle listened sympathetically to Robins's complaints that management wasted performers' potential when it gave them long runs and a single character line. He wrote her that he was enthusiastic about her proposal to expose "this latter day slavery of women on the stage," but rather than a story, he preferred a direct, "trenchant and telling article" (*BSC* 253). Robins declined the opportunity. She knew her stage career would be ruined if she attempted such an exposé. She did not altogether abandon the idea of a fictional indictment and gradually, over the next several years, managed to write several brilliant satires of stage conditions, always behind a pseudonym.

For the moment, Robins was finding her way to self-expression in her vision of what she wanted the stage to be. She was keeping a diary faithfully. In early June she finished reading *The Journal of Marie Bashkirtseff*, which included after the last entry the words "Marie Bashkirtseff died eleven days after." Robins wrote in her own journal: "I turned my head face down in the pillow and cried." No fictional character had captured her sympathy more than "this strange life." This other struggling artist had expressed herself completely; Robins found the artist's journal "strange because so startlingly true and horribly frank, fascinating because so modern and minute." The American actress thought it "astonishing" that she and the Russian woman struggling in France, "so radically different from me in nationality, breeding and environment," could "yet be so alike" (as quoted in *BSC* 261). *Both Sides of the Curtain*

Over several days, Robins's sense of closeness to this other compulsive journal writer took on a new dimension. She recognized that she was a writer herself but not one who would turn over her personal diaries to public view. After enumerating her own planned writing projects, all based on personal experience, she marveled: "Marie Bashkirtseff boasts she tells all; I tell not a hundredth, and I tell that little to remind myself of what I do not tell." She described her own diary as a "storehouse of ideas and sensations accessible to myself alone, in cipher." She declared, "I find the same delight in truth that Marie Bashkirtseff did only I don't want that white light turned on *me* for the benefit of others' amusement or pity any more than I would stand naked in the market place" (ER Diary, 1890, as quoted in *BSC* 262).

Robins's revelation that she was prone to self-suppression and self-censorship reflects her conviction that some form of daily record would be useful for a novelist. Just as the consummate performer puts everything of her experience into creating a role yet maintains her private being, so also did Robins hide her true self from her reading public. Robins's choice of anonymity and a pseudonym were more than mere tactics or devices by which to separate her theater reputation from the reception of her fiction. Her whole actor's being depended upon the separation of the performer from her created role. For Robins, anonymous authorship was necessary as a means of enabling her, in her writing, to pursue art and to profess to be an artist.

Robins used her diary sketchily. The first-person account, "Across America with 'Junius Brutus Booth,'" is effective only as a piece of travelog. Robins was promised seven pounds for the seventeen-page article as long as she also supplied photographs of the actors, which she did. It could hardly have seemed to be evidence that her career as a writer was off to a successful start. Beerbohm Tree took some interest in wanting to review the article with her, but if he did, he learned nothing more about how Elizabeth Robins saw herself as an actress nor what she thought of the way Booth and Barrett performed.

The actress's first article takes us inside the Pullman car in which the company lived during its journey from Richmond to San Francisco, January to March 1888, but she keeps her readers outside her own mind and not privy to her emotions and thoughts as she performed with Booth. She says little of their performances of *Othello* except that, in Charleston, "The house is crowded, the enthusiasm boundless."[7] Although she gives few details, she makes clear that Booth and Barrett shared their meals and their reminiscences with the company. To the extent that she describes herself, she appears as an avid hiker, as a tourist interested in all the sights (including Confederate graveyards and the Alamo), and as an actress very much used to one night stands under conditions not as comfortable as those on the specially furbished Pullman car.

Most of Robins's notations were the comments of a tourist, not a performer's analysis from behind the footlights. Her very next journalism project was an account of the Passion Play in Oberammergau, however, and it reflected her stage impressions. She realized how different her ambitions were from those of other actors when she told fellow players of her real reasons for leaving the Alexander company. One of her staunchest friends from America, Mrs. Erskine Clement Waters, had invited her to attend the Passion Play in Oberammergau. Her interest having been sparked by W. T. Stead's published account of the experience, Robins resolved to make good use of the excursion. She arranged a meeting with Stead in order to calculate exactly how much (for she was only a struggling actress) she might have to spend. Her purpose in attending, as she explained to Stead, was to write something on Oberammergau from the viewpoint of a fellow performer. Stead, a great Christian reformer, had written of his moving experience in religious terms; he had never seen a play and vowed never to enter a commercial theater. This first meeting initiated a lasting friendship. Fourteen years later, Robins escorted Stead on a series of theater excursions and edited his "Impressions of the Stage" for Stead's journal, the *Review of Reviews*. During their first meeting, however, he scoffed at Elizabeth Robins's purposes and encouraged her to drop her stage career at once. When he saw that she was still determined, he sent her home with books to read and the promise of an introduction or two. Stead's endorsements gave Robins unusual opportunities.

She returned to London thoroughly transformed. From her talks with performers and her observations at rehearsals she realized that the spirit of the Oberammergau people came from the fact that they performed, not once a decade, but every summer, a wide variety of classical and biblical plays in which almost every town resident participated. Though it was strictly forbidden, she was able, because she was an actress and because of her connection with Stead, to gain admittance backstage. Robins realized that German actors had the same problem she did: the cues written into a part to indicate the last phrase of the previous speaker were much too short. She also felt a bond with Johann Diemer, her guide, when he declared Shylock his favorite role. Diemer, who had decades of experience, was to play Herod this year. Robins earned his friendship when she let it be known that she had often performed in *The Merchant of Venice*. Before she left, Diemer inscribed his "role" and presented it to her as a memento.

The Higher Purpose of the Theater

Throughout that fall in London, Elizabeth Robins felt buoyed by the Passion Play. Not only had her trip given her a new way of seeing herself in her profession, but she was also writing up her account of her actress's look at Oberammergau. In identifying what acting meant to these villagers, Robins expressed something that is true universally for the performer and that confirmed as well her own passion for performing. In her study of Ibsen actresses, Mary Heath identifies Robins's Oberammergau experiences as crucial to a change in her outlook: she ceased to regard the theater as the unholy profession that it was in the eyes of her puritanical family and came to see it instead as a mission with a religious purpose.[8] Stead had brought back the message that Christianity was nowhere better felt; Robins brought back a faith dedicated to the moral purpose of a truly artistic theater.

Robins's identity as an actress might further be understood by what Juliet Blair postulates as the actress's need to develop a sense of "public usefulness" in a profession which requires the expression—and exposure—of her most private self, including her emotions, her body, and her sexual identity.[9] In fact, Robins had long before come to a sense of personal mission about her own life on the stage. The experiences of Oberammergau, however, prompted Robins to extend her belief in the theater so that it encompassed relationships with others. At Oberammergau and in subsequent experiences in England, Robins saw the need for a *collective* dedication to the higher goal of theater and concluded that collaborative working relationships were more important than private sexual fulfillment. According to Blair, an actress reveals herself emotionally and, since the 1970s, sexually in order to communicate a higher purpose. In contrast, Robins forfeited her private self to a public goal, living wholly by her "passion" for a collective artistic enterprise.

Robins's article "An American Actress at Oberammergau" was much more substantial than her sketch of Booth and Barrett. Much later in her career, the piece was for some time in the hands of her agent in America, Paul Reynolds. It was never accepted for publication. Before she left London to attend the Passion Play, she had signed a contract to appear in Mrs. Lancaster Wallis's production of *The Sixth Commandment*, the Robert Buchanan adaptation of Dostoevsky's *Crime and Punishment*. The surer income (ten pounds a week) enabled her to send for her brother Vernon, and she devoted much time to arranging for his studies. Anticipating Vernon's arrival, Robins took possession of a new flat at 28 Manchester Square Mansions, which she painted and decorated herself. It was a two-bedroom apartment with separate dining room and study, on the top floor of a building, reached by climbing seventy-four stairs. She occupied 28 Manchester Square Mansions until 1900. In a letter to her former school friend, Emma Blandy, Robins spoke with delight of the "strict simplicity" of her living arrangements. A dependable maid kept the place while she was away. Robins enjoyed serving afternoon tea to friends. Her new home had two growing palms and fresh-cut flowers. She treasured most of all her "little nook *full* of books and plays in half a dozen languages," with a writing table "littered with papers."[10]

Robins had less time for writing than in her lonely first days in London because new and important friendships were occupying her time. In her conversations with fellow actors she spoke of her Oberammergau-inspired dreams. In her diary she noted:

> Been thinking much about a society for Dramatic Study, an association of workers in Art for Art's sake. Our aim, the improvement of our knowledge and elevation of our aims by doing work of the highest kind without money and without other "price" than an earnest spirit and a generous love of our calling, and one another. We could explore the wide field of classical poetic Drama. . . . We would get the practice we lack in these times of "long runs." We would quicken our artistic perceptions and by all in turn playing "little parts" and lifting higher the standard of dramatic work, we should help actors, the Stage—the World.[11]

Robins's plans for an ideal theater do not differ from the goals of a modern repertory theater. Robins's first completed novel explores the same theme and in fact occasionally echoes the lofty hyperboles of her diary. A full year and a half would pass, however—most of it crammed with theater productions and plans for theater ventures—before Robins would begin work on her stage novel. When she did, the story took its title from a diary entry she made

Elizabeth Robins at the start of her career on the London stage. The photograph dates from 1890, when she took her apartment in Manchester Square Mansions, where she lived until 1900. (*Courtesy of the Fales Library. Reproduced with the permission of Mabel Smith, for the Backsettown Trustees.*)

in October 1890, when she repeated a remark quoted by her dresser: "Miss Robins is the best artist there. She's the Coming Woman!" (ER Diary, October 22, 1890).

Twenty months later, Robins put pen to paper and began her novel, "The Coming Woman," the story of Katherine Fleet, the rising actress who has a dream of a theater founded on artistic, and not commercial, lines. In those twenty months she gained fame by creating a new Ibsen heroine. In the process, however, she learned just how limited the opportunities were for an actress who had higher standards for the drama and who was so independent that the managers grew wary of her. Although Robins herself and others have written about those months as they relate to her acting career,[12] a brief account of her activities—and her lost opportunities—in late 1890, 1891, and the first half of 1892 will shed light on "The Coming Woman," which Robins wrote almost directly from her own experience.

More than any of her stage appearances, either singly or collectively, the friendships Robins established and the working projects that grew from them made her artistic visions worthy of pursuit. Robins had working relationships with fellow American actress Marion Lea and the writer and adapter of plays Florence Bell. Mrs. Patrick Campbell, after she performed with Robins in an 1891 production, shared with Robins her problems finding work and craved support and intimacy. Henry James, William Archer, Bernard Shaw, and William Heinemann, each prominent in his respective field and each vitally attracted to Ibsen's drama, admired Elizabeth Robins in various ways. While Robins's public success is not to be underestimated, the full meaning of her struggle to establish herself can hardly be explained without primary focus upon the interpersonal relationships Robins developed during these months. As she later demonstrated in "The Coming Woman," the competing bids for attention and intimacy, the threats to an actress's independence, and the plans for a working collaboration among artists were the operative forces during these formative months. Most important, the conflict between the life men said they wanted to provide for her, on the one hand, and artistic fulfillment, on the other, prompted Robins to declare that her profession took priority.

Theater and Friendships: Marion Lea

In the same October entry which records Robins's comment that people were calling her "the Coming Woman," she noted that "Marion Lea talks her Ibsen scheme, *The Lady from the Sea*, and I encourage her." Marion Lea's friendship was important in these months, for she helped turn Elizabeth Robins's aspirations into concrete plans. Like Robins, Lea was an American actress who hoped to make a name in London. She lived with her half sister

Anna Lea-Merritt, the painter who knew most of the American expatriates in London. The only role for which Lea had received high praise was her rustically comic Audrey in *As You Like It*. She confided to Robins that she carried with her the worst review she had ever gotten as a reminder of the capricious standards in the theatrical world.

While the two American actresses were engaged together in *The Sixth Commandment*, they turned their discussions of *The Lady from the Sea* into a serious proposal they took to managers. When one after another of London's actor-managers rejected the idea, Robins recalled, "We arraigned the managers, we raged, dreamed, and then more or less awake, began to consider ways and means" ("WH," chapter 41, p. 8). At that time they resolved to form the "Robins-Lea Joint Management" for the purposes of mounting their own productions.

[handwritten marginal notes: "Jet?" / "Ibsen?" / "the Actress" / "Whither?" / "How"]

Just when prospects seemed most dismal, they heard that Ibsen's new play, one with a woman's name for its title, *Hedda Gabler*, had been printed in Copenhagen. They also learned that a dispute over the English rights to translate the play threatened to delay its availability for production. Nevertheless, Robins counted it a "great moment" when in mid-January Marion Lea brought to her "the earliest obtainable copy of Mr. Gosse's Hedda. . . . We fell upon it with unforgettable eagerness. We read with bewilderment, we declaimed bits with jeers, we rolled with irreverent laughter; then, brought up short by a thrust at our vitals from the Ibsen rapier, blinked, stared at each other and ended in a state of demoralised excitement" ("WH," chapter 43, p. 8).

Lea's assistance was invaluable in the negotiations to convince Archer, then Heinemann, and later Edmund Gosse, that their independent effort could promise a faithful performance of the text. Though Lea's role as Mrs. Elvsted was a small part, critics drew attention not only to the producers' initiatives but also to their combined acting talents. Before they had begun regular rehearsals with the cast, they had assisted in a new collaborative translation and had prepared their own scenes thoroughly.

In April and May 1891 the Robins-Lea *Hedda Gabler* emerged as a significant dramatic event, one that stirred up controversy, forced reexamination of Ibsen, and caused London writers to discuss their own society in terms of Ibsen's themes. A woman trapped in a dull marriage spoils a desperate attempt to sanctify her former would-be lover's debauched idealism. A third man has evidence that she gave to Løvborg, the former lover, the dueling pistol with which he killed himself. When she knows she has no other means of release from a compromising relationship with this third man, Hedda kills herself with the other pistol. Late Victorians repudiated the play's morality; decadents applauded it. Primarily because it was so well presented, the papers were full

Elizabeth Robins and fellow American actress Marion Lea in Ibsen's *Hedda Gabler*, London, 1891. Robins boasted in her memoir, *Ibsen and the Actress*, that the Robins-Lea Joint Management funded this first production by putting up their jewelry as collateral for a loan. (*Courtesy of the Fales Library. Reproduced with the permission of Mabel Smith, for the Backsettown Trustees.*)

of commentary. Much of the criticism denounced the play while acknowledging that Ibsen should be taken seriously as a dramatist. Most important, even the leading anti-Ibsenite, Clement Scott, felt compelled to praise Robins's talent: "She has made vice attractive by her art. She has almost ennobled crime. She has made a heroine out of a sublimated sinner. She has fascinated us with a savage."[13] The play's single week of matinées was extended to a second. Then the play replaced the night bill at the Vaudeville Theatre; the profits from the evening performances paid the salaries of the company that had been displaced.

With the success of the Joint Management firmly established, Robins and Lea considered a wide range of plays for their next ventures. In the course of their planning, Lea married the American playwright Langdon Mitchell, and Mitchell cast his wife in his own play, *Deborah*. Robins described in letters to Florence Bell, another friend, her sense that Mitchell's playwriting was inferior to Lea's acting and finally her conviction that Lea's talent was being wasted. In July, Lea, pregnant with her first child, returned to America with Mitchell. Robins wrote of the departure of her co-worker: "The wrench was quite terrible and I was a bit shaken to see how hard *she* took it. . . . all over again I felt the ghastly eternal inequality between those two" (ER to FB, July 31, 1892). If Robins had not been convinced before this experience of the incompatibility of marriage and a career on the stage, Lea's retirement confirmed her need for her own independence.

Theater and Friendships: Henry James

By this time, however, Robins was no longer alone in her quest to "lift higher the standard of drama." Through Marion Lea and her sister Mrs. Lea-Merritt Robins first met Henry James in early 1890. James himself had recently turned dramatist following his completion of his novel of art and the stage, *The Tragic Muse*. His stage adaptation of his novel *The American*, under Edward Compton's management, had a trial production in Southport. James had been so moved by the spontaneous ovation after the première that he wrote to his brother, "I feel at last as if I had found my *real* form."[14] Compton and James were looking for a strong cast for a London production. James had seen Robins's performance as Mrs. Linden in *A Doll's House* on January 27, and the two had been introduced. Robins gained so many superlative notices that when James invited the two actresses to dinner two weeks later for the purpose of talking about a role in his dramatization, she could look forward to it only as a great step forward for her career. Lea sent Robins a copy of *The American*, and she read with studied interest the part of the heroine, Claire de Cintré. Because negotiations over the translation rights to *Hedda Gabler* were deadlocked, her plans to produce the new Ibsen play were temporarily on hold. She knew that the Robins-Lea Joint Management could only benefit if James offered her the chance to play his leading lady.

Henry James had different expectations, Robins was to discover. She wrote that they skirted the main reason for his invitation all through the meal and then were ushered into another room for coffee, "where I remember feeling swallowed up in the armchair, glancing over the deep arms with a vague consciousness of books, books, and of pictures I did not verify or even glance at" ("WH," chapter 46, p. 4).

When James finally raised the subject of Compton's interest in her acting, he did so "hemming, halting, and going heavily on with a hundred kind and more than considerate qualifyings and apologies 'for suggesting to a young woman, a . . . (a young woman who . . . who . . . a . . .).'" As Robins waited for him to phrase what he wanted to say, she thought of him trying to "balance himself, carefully holding on to the arms of protective parenthesis." What James was saying, Robins was surprised to learn, was that he had seen her play Mrs. Linden in *A Doll's House* and assumed she would be interested in playing the part of his elderly American housekeeper, Mrs. Bread, and not the heroine: "I took it full in the face. He wanted me for his old Housekeeper. The small fraction of my vast astonishment that succeeded in reaching him was yet enough to bring him down from his native altitude a little nearer to my level. He looked at me. More, I felt he examined me with an effect of seeing me for the first time, during that interview, as other than Mrs. Linden" ("WH," chapter 46, pp. 4–5; ellipsis points in the original).

Robins realized that James had taken all too seriously her earlier comments to him about the need for versatility, specifically her ambition to play characters of any age; he remembered her not so much as an accomplished actress in the role of Mrs. Linden but *"as the part"* of the older woman. "It was dreadful," Robins recalled. "To myself I wondered: Couldn't I perhaps fit Mrs. Bread in?" ("WH," chapter 46, p. 7). What surprised Robins about this first meeting was something else, however: James so impressed her as a man who cared for her career that she probably would have accepted even this offer —which she found almost insulting—except "for the light already projected across my path by that singular contrast to Mrs. Bread, the lurid Hedda" ("WH," chapter 46, pp. 7–8).

To some degree it is possible to envision Robins as the heroine of first one and then another James novel. Robins arrived in England an Isabel Archer, in full mourning dress, searching for some life beyond her previous existence and susceptible to the affections of men who promised her fulfillment. Her experience of the pull between marriage and public life for a great cause likens her to the gifted Verena Tarrant of *The Bostonians*. On the other hand, the direction she chose for herself invites comparison with Miriam Rooth's vision of herself in *The Tragic Muse*. More significantly, Robins searched for an image of herself that went beyond men's need of her, beyond the condition of muse and inspirer. She wanted to be a woman who could be a creative talent in her own right. Miriam, of course, serves James's plot by charting a course that prompts a portrait painter and a diplomat to discover their own relationships to art. *The Tragic Muse* served James especially, for the act of writing it determined his relationship to the theater for several years to come. He signed a contract for his novel's publication in 1889 and again realized he would earn very little income from fiction. Almost immediately thereafter he committed himself to a career as a dramatist. There was nothing he needed more than an actress who could validate his choice and turn his plays into artistic and public triumphs.

Robins's success as Hedda enhanced James's opinion of her talents. His essay, "On the Occasion of *Hedda Gabler*," credited Robins's acting ability *the muse* with having improved his opinion of Ibsen as a dramatist. Although he was careful not to label himself a converted Ibsenite, James observed, "If we possessed the unattainable, an eclectic, artistic, disinterested theatre, to which we *hats off* might look for alternation and variety, it would simply be a point of honor in *to Ibsen* such a temple to sacrifice sometimes to Henrik Ibsen."[15]

A few weeks later, when Robins signed the contract to perform in London as Mme. de Cintré, James espoused a different cause, namely that of Elizabeth Robins, actress with a mission to lift higher the standard of the drama. James wholeheartedly supported Robins's request for a clause in her contract which would allow her, during the run of *The American*, to perform in trial matinées *pioneer of* at other theaters. These matinées, sometimes performances of new plays on a *new drama* single afternoon, were the chief route by which the new drama was finding its way to the London public. Robins had resented the usual form of a contract which "stipulated that even when the actor was not needed at his own theatre, under no circumstances should he appear professionally in any other" (*T&F* 32). Her casting for *Hedda Gabler* had suffered from this restriction, for many actors willing to take on the extra work were prevented by their managers from performing.

The American ran for seventy performances (and would be the longest running of James's London plays). Robins appeared in the production "on leave" from her main engagement, *The Trumpet Call*, at the Adelphi. Eventually, she lost the chance to return to that play. James spoke of her kindness in acting in his play, noted her forfeit of the better-paying role that reached wider audiences, and found his play almost undeserving of the honor she paid it. Over the next months he was all the more her servant in his attempts to locate other plays which would suit the Joint Management. He scoured the French drama and worked to secure *Denise* for Robins and Lea. Most significant, he became more serious about his own writing for the stage. In mid-June 1891, he asked Robins to set "any day next week" for his reading of his first two acts of his new comedy (HJ to ER, June 16, 1891, in *T&F*, 36). Robins confided to her schoolgirl friend in America that "our beloved Henry James is going to write a play *for me*" and swore her friend to secrecy.[16] Early in the fall he forwarded to her a French play he had obtained. Their meetings to discuss the drama grew more frequent. The following spring he wrote, "I *yearn* for another dramatic evening—with a couple of acts under my arm." Again he encouraged Robins to name the day and the time (HJ to ER, March 22, 1892, quoted in *T&F*, 67).

Although Robins kept from James her secret literary career, her friendship with him flourished at the most critical time in Robins's career as both an actress and an aspiring writer. Robins's long dramatic evenings with James no doubt led to his short story, "Nona Vincent," in which a novice playwright transfers his affections from an older woman who is his literary confidante to the young actress chosen to play the character he had invented with the help of the older woman. In the story, the playwright marries the actress, Violet Grey, ending her career. In real life, James and Robins had too much in common to compromise their individual professional careers. Robins stepped out of James's frame, out of his portrait of muse, to become a fellow creative presence. Those evenings during which the two discussed his latest play or the prospects of one or another adaptation from the French that suited Robins's acting requirements must also have contributed to Robins's later determination to write plays.

Theater and Friendships: Florence Bell

Through James, Robins became friends with Florence Bell, wife of the Yorkshire ironmonger, Hugh Bell, and daughter of Sir Joseph Olliffe of the English aristocracy. Bell shared with James a familiarity with the Parisian theater. When Bell at the insistence of her family relinquished her ambition to study music professionally, she devoted herself to writing. She composed in French as easily as in English and had the distinction of having one of her plays (*L'Indécis*, 1887) performed by the great French actor Coquelin. It was to Florence Bell that Elizabeth Robins poured out her remorse over Marion Lea's departure for America. She had visited Bell for a second time at Bell's home, "Red Barns," a sprawling red brick townhouse comfortably nestled a few blocks from the sea in Redcar, on the North Yorkshire coast, just before she returned to London to say farewell to her acting partner; and she knew that she had gained in that visit a close friendship with a woman who understood her ambitions.

The Joint Management's production of Bell's translation of the play *Karin* from the Swedish of Alfhild Agrell reflected this new relationship. Robins also spoke to Bell of the tribulations of working with Charles Wyndham. Wyndham, manager of the Criterion, was anxious to secure Robins for his next new play, *The Fringe of Society* (rumored to be an English version of the celebrated *Le Demi-Monde* of Alexandre Dumas *fils*). Before her performances in *The American* had ended, he had begun to pay her a retainer fee. During her wait, and while Wyndham had another play in performance, Wyndham prevented Robins from recreating even for a "few nights" the role of Mrs. Linden in the Janet Achurch revival of *A Doll's House*, even though Robins was well rehearsed in his play and was merely waiting for the performances to begin. In addition, just before *The Fringe of Society* was ready to open, Wyndham insisted that Robins sign a clause in her contract that obligated her if he decided to take the play to America. The clause provided, specifically, that her services during the engagement belonged "exclusively and absolutely to the said Charles Wyndham whenever and wherever the same may be required" (as quoted in *T&F* 69).

Robins refused to sign. Her freedom was not to be bought; she had worked too hard to establish herself in London. Wyndham released her immediately and telegraphed Mrs. Lily Langtry to return from Nice to take her place. The play was, according to Robins, "roundly hissed," taken off after a brief run, and "consigned to oblivion" (*T&F* 71).

At the time, Robins felt only exasperation. To Bell she wrote: "I am left here gasping—high and dry like a creature of the sea whom the sea has cast ashore" (ER to FB, April 16, 1892). After an escape to the country to "get back my breath," Robins reflected on what her release meant. She was relieved that "my friends do so much to make the matter tolerable," and she reported to Bell that she had had a "beautiful gentle letter from Mr. James which almost made me cry." Robins later explained how much her independence worked against her: "I had yet to learn the solidarity of Managerial Trade Unionism" (*T&F* 71). Her refusal to tie herself exclusively to one manager eventually contributed to her reputation for being strong-willed.

As Robins rehearsed *Karin* later in April, she wrote to Bell, "I quite fancy at times she [Karin, defiantly rebellious because of a disastrous marriage] is the 'Ugly Duckling' of my life and that no one else will ever care a bit for her and so with a half unconscious perversity I must e'en love her the more" (ER to FB, April 26, 1892). Robins might as readily have said that she felt herself the ugly duckling actress, unappreciated by every manager. On May 10 and 12 at the Vaudeville, the Joint Management presented both *Karin* and the curtain raiser by Musset, *A Caprice*, in which Marion Lea "scored handsomely" (*T&F* 71). The reviewer for the *Star* was amazed that Robins had taken the difficult play so to heart and claimed that she had surpassed her performance as Hedda Gabler. He went on:

> She has evidently "lived with" the character of Karin, made it part of herself, felt it in every nerve and fiber; and so makes you feel it. It is not only in her big outbursts of emotion, in her distraction over her child's death . . . , but in the quiet, subtle touches that you perceive the artist. . . . Ibsen apart, it is a long time since we have had anything in London on the same intellectual plane as Karin.[17]

Despite her widespread favorable notices, Robins received no concrete offers, neither financial proposals to support *Karin* with a regular run nor contract offers to play in another manager's theater.

Just a week after she appeared as Karin, Oscar Wilde paid another visit. Over "tea and cigarettes" they discussed their "visions of the theatre of the future" (EBook, May 17, 1892). She wrote to Bell the next day: "Had a royal good time talking to or rather listening to Oscar Wilde! . . . As he went he said laughing, 'Well we've had a profitable time, we've built a Theatre, written several plays and founded a school!'" Robins encouraged Wilde to give his ideas to the world "in practical permanent form," and he promised her he would "speak for it at the Fund Dinner" and "'Crystallize the subject' later in an essay" (ER to FB, May 18, 1892). Robins expressed her delight. It seemed to be the first time that some of her long-held ideas had encountered the real possibility of a collaborative venture. Much of the new enthusiasm Wilde aroused she would transfer to her novel's heroine, Katherine Fleet.

Over the next few weeks, Robins's life was full of social engagements. She saw Coquelin perform in London several times in the company of Henry James and attended Sarah Bernhardt's *Leah*, subtitled *The Forsaken*. She was regularly at Florence Bell's "at homes" on Tuesdays; she dined with the Crackanthorpes, the Edmund Gosses, Marion Lea, and Langdon Mitchell. She saw William Archer regularly. Possibly they were continuing the work that she described on April 19: "Mr. Archer and I are going over and editing *Rosmersholm*" (ER to FB, April 19, 1892).

As a result of Bell's successful assistance of Robins's career with her translation of *Karin*, the two looked for a London manager who would accept Bell's own play, *Stella*, and would cast Robins as the heroine. In a telling letter on July 3, Robins expressed to Bell her concern lest *Stella* fall prey to the unpredictable management of Charles Charrington and his wife, Janet Achurch. Robins saw clearly the difficulty that her holding on to the part would cause her playwright friend: "I assure you these managers are not pining for me. The better ones find my point of view and my active policy antagonistic. The inefficient ones I loathe having commerce with" (ER to FB, July 3, 1892).

Two days later, Robins recorded in her engagement book, "Begin 'Katherine' in train." If she could not realize any of her ambitions in London theaters, either by performing coveted parts or reforming the theater, she would work them out on paper. During much of that summer, she wrote "The Coming Woman." The months continued to be full of other engagements as well. Most significant for her future course was that three times she visited the Bells' home, Red Barns, in Redcar for extended stays. She recorded in her engagement book on the first day of her second visit, July 13, "Redcar. Study Norsk." For the next week of days, she made ditto marks as the only entries. At the time of her third visit, August 18 to September 9, Robins and Bell retreated to a private location to pursue their studies. She marked her engagement book with all she was translating and reading. Mostly, she read the plays of Ibsen. Publisher William Heinemann offered to pay Robins for her translations of Björnson. She began on *Støv*, and reported in her memoirs that her translations paid her rent one year, but other evidence suggests that Heinemann was not initially forthcoming with his payments. When *Støv* was completed, Robins wrote to Bell and chided her for thinking that she saw James's influence in her style: "He hasn't seen a line of it—did you think he had? I don't think I *could* show him any work of this kind—he would be so unhappy and depressed at the spectacle of misplaced feminine energy" (ER to FB, September 28, 1892).

Robins's most important reason for learning Norwegian, however, was so that she and Bell could translate Ibsen's next play together. Heinemann was in Christiania in early August negotiating with Ibsen about rights to his current play. The reports Robins received were in the form of annoyingly familiar letters—Heinemann for over a year had expressed his infatuation with her—but she knew that she could have stage rights to the play if she wanted them. She discussed with Archer the plan she and Bell had for their joint translation, and on August 16 she reported Archer's response to her friend. Archer, she explained, encouraged their translation work but warned Robins not to have her name attached; that "would unnecessarily emphasize my Ibsenite proclivities." Robins seemed content with this anonymity: "Just so that I may help with the work and keep the play from Gosse and other incompetents I'm con-

·ed "deep dark secret."
he time William Heine-
nd Gosse and William
ιe Coming Woman." She
1 production of the new
her as the leading actress
and translations for hire,
ξton and Achurch to per-
Ͻctober, Robins was able

forts of a young noncom-
n a melodramatic role and
vrights. Their joint efforts
:heater dedicated to higher
ιeme to found a new theater
:st leading talent of London

depend upon the associations and relationships developed by Katherine. The poet Maurice Neill is a thinly disguised Oscar Wilde. A friendly critic, Mc-Bride, often resembles William Archer. The imposing Brazilian, Matzala, is partly based upon William Heinemann, who was infatuated with Robins. The well-known playwright Patterson, whose play is to inaugurate the new theater, has many of Pinero's characteristics.

Most striking of all, however, is the portrait of Della Stanley, Katherine Fleet's opposite self, the actress born to the profession, a self-appointed "savage" with her language and manners, openly rebellious when managers or playwrights interfere with her craft yet possessed of passionate feelings, hungrily affectionate, and in need of Katherine's kindness. The fictional Della Stanley is undeniably modeled on Stella Campbell, known on the professional stage as Mrs. Patrick Campbell, or more economically, as "Mrs. Pat." Robins and Campbell met in circumstances strikingly similar to those that Robins describes in "The Coming Woman." A few short weeks after her extended run of *Hedda Gabler*, Robins had signed a contract to perform in the Adelphi melodrama *The Trumpet Call*. Mrs. Pat was hired, in her first London role, as the antiheroine, Astrea, the gypsy-blooded first wife of the hero, to whom Elizabeth Robins, as Constance, is now married. Katherine Fleet, Robins's fictional heroine, renowned for her exquisite performances in private theatricals, accepts an offer to play professionally in a popular theater, and Della Stanley is cast as the peasant woman whose role is nearly as significant. The two actresses meet at the first rehearsal, and their relationship stresses their opposite natures and similar needs. They are both women in the male-dominated world of the theater and need each other's support to survive.

Although the women are based in broad terms on the real life actresses who met backstage at the Adelphi, Robins in her fiction sharpened the contrast between them. Katherine Fleet is refined, deliberate; Stanley, impulsive, with genuine emotive talent. They might almost be different facets of a single actress who finds her creative talent stifled at every turn. At their first rehearsal Katherine hears Della promise her friends, "I'll wipe up the stage with that noble heroine."[18] The competitive edge between the two actresses dissolves as Della pleads for attention and develops her role. After each has played her first scene in the first rehearsal—Katherine's memorized and with added animation, Della's sloppy and lackluster—Della praises Katherine: "This ain't good enough for you" ("CW," 22). She mentions Katherine's reputation as a society actress, popular at charity performances, invited by Coquelin to recite. When Della comments upon Katherine's clever habit of dressing, Katherine starts to leave and Della Stanley begs, "Don't go 'way! . . . I like you awfully—Don't mind anything I say—I'm a savage" ("CW," 23).

Through Della's admiration, Robins contrasts the two actresses' positions. Katherine, Della maintains, should not have accepted the part. She tells Katherine that she's the kind of actress who "if you just got up and said the multiplication table people would like it better than Shakespeare" ("CW," 25). Della, however, counts herself fortunate to have gotten the lower-paying part. "I ain't like you. I have to take anything that comes along" ("CW," 26).

Robins's next chapter begins with the description of their dependence, one upon the other: "This day was the beginning of an odd friendliness between the two." Each held a fascination for the other: "The child of gentle breeding and long conventional training found a tonic, an acute exhilaration in the sheer unexpectedness and audacious unreserve of this keen-witted, unkempt creature from God knows where" ("CW," 26).

Katherine finally does, on the advice of more professional associates, withdraw from her part. She concludes that her debut in a potboiler is not the best opportunity for the actress whose dreams for a "Theatre of the Future" are beginning to produce concrete plans, with backers, advocates—everything but a play worthy of the theater's première. She comes to understand Della Stanley's circumstances as the product of a theater system that treats its dedicated performers like so much "grist for the mill." When Katherine meets Della backstage at the play's première, ready to congratulate her, Della informs her, "They've given me the sack . . . on account of a little difficulty with the manager" ("CW," 105). Katherine defends her instinct to support Della when she tells her associates that Della is the kind of actress whom few critics are willing to praise.

Katherine's pledge to help the unfortunate Della Stanley played itself out in real life a few months after Elizabeth Robins wrote these scenes. In the spring of 1893, Robins would forfeit an opportunity to create the title role in *The Second Mrs. Tanqueray* to Campbell. Like her heroine Katherine Fleet, moreover, she saw herself as organizer of a Theatre of the Future. As a writer, too, she saw a higher purpose in life, a higher position than that dictated by the constraints of the actor-manager system. When Robins withdrew from the role, her congratulations to Mrs. Pat included the mutually understood remark, "There is to my mind no woman in London so enviable at this moment, dear savage, as *you*."[19]

Pinero himself is portrayed in "The Coming Woman" as the balding playwright Patterson, who has just written his greatest play, and vows he will lock it away until he finds the perfect actress: an English Sarah Bernhardt who is young enough to play a twenty-year-old. Katherine Fleet's visit to playwright Patterson's out-of-town retreat convinces him that Katherine must play the part. Katherine is embarrassed that her trip on behalf of the New Theatre appears selfish. Patterson, immediately impressed by her talent, offers to give his play to the New Theatre if Katherine will play the heroine. Rather than accept his conditions, Katherine retreats from the scene.

Other problems highlight Katherine's evasiveness at the end. Katherine needs to escape from the Brazilian's advances and also from an aristocrat who is proposing marriage. Speaking to a young admirer of people whom she fears as enemies, she confides that she is really running away from herself. Robins's exploration of the problems of a woman constrained to avoid serious relationships with men has a clear feminist element. Although Katherine's association with Della Stanley figures as the dominant chord of the story, the various other appeals for Katherine's affections build to make the reader appreciate Katherine's sensation of entrapment. Each admirer longs for some stake in Katherine's future, and all offer to assist her with her new theater. In the final scene, a party, Katherine uses all her talent to play one man against the other in order to effect her escape from entanglements.

Robins knew Katherine's predicament well, for she understood that she paid for freedom from entanglements by forfeiting devotion that she easily might have had from a number of men. As early as 1890, when her friendships with the men in the company of *The Sixth Commandment* exhibited the potential of growing into something more intimate, she recognized that she was doomed to reject all gestures of affection. Partly this was her own nature. Partly it came from the trauma she still felt over the suicide of her husband, George Parks. She wrote in her diary in the fall of 1890 when visions of her life with Parks came back to haunt her present relationships: "I saw how I had missed, or rather had and lost the most blessed thing in life, Devotion. . . . When this gift drops at my feet, I am impelled to turn aside and leave it lying there" (ER Diary, October 20, 1890).

By late 1892, a number of men had been attracted to Robins and had pursued her. Two of these men were associates with whom she would continue to work professionally. From William Heinemann she received the most sustained appeals to her feelings. Heinemann proposed to Robins many times. Aware that she could never recommit herself to marrying, Robins eventually found his advances irritating. At one point she promised to stop mentioning his courtship in her conversations with Bell (ER to FB, July 18, 1892).

The relationship between Robins and William Archer was more complex and gave Robins greater reasons to conceal her feelings. On September 30, 1891, the two apparently shared an intimate evening that they remembered years afterward as a sort of anniversary. When Robins realized that Archer was "coming to demand too much of me of time and regard," she wrote in her diary,

It would not be hard for me to love this man not wisely but too well and I must guard my poor life against a curse like that. For soon after I had acknowledged him the one being in the world for me he would possess the supremest power to pain me, and unconsciously and inevitably he would use his power. Not that he would *wish* to, not that he wouldn't try to avoid it, but he would be as helpless as I.[20]

Robins's restraint was not as automatic as her account here suggests. When she began to record events in her engagement books with some regularity, she used the symbol of an ampersand for her frequent meetings with Archer. When Archer found documents Robins had entrusted to him, he destroyed them. Still, enough remains of his correspondence to demonstrate that he was much in love with her. Archer's own sense of propriety and his own dedication to a lasting creative relationship suggest that their intimacy was not sexual despite temptation to make it so in the early stages. On one occasion, however, Robins wrote, "No woman ever had greater power of control with such capacity for Passion as I."[21] She titled the meditation "Study for a woman of 30 who is loved and *resists* and what she thinks of herself," and carefully inked out or cut off any reference to names or dates. She did indicate that in this instance the man who had stirred her passions was a man she cared about. Perhaps she could rationalize preserving the piece only by calling it fiction. She searched her being to explain why, "when gladness and fruition stand at my door I frown unwelcome, while every nerve in my poor body cries Come, Come, Come in!" ("Study," 3). She credited "some dead ancestress . . . , some Puritan or maybe my own grandmother who reared me and whose spirit walks again in me" as the source of her resistance. Still, she refused to accept the fact that her victories against temptation made her course the right one: "Why if so [if it is weakness to submit] have men and women who have been so strong intellectually and artistically—why have they been the ones to obey this call most blindly? Why do those who fight against it lose their health and strength and peace? Why are the asylums filled with the wrecks of [those] who have *won* this sorry battle, and lost themselves?" ("Study," 6).

In an earlier passage in the same document, Robins suggests the future benefits of such turmoil and admits that it was one of her "supremest difficulties" that she could not look at any concern from "one side only":

And I end up discovering almost as much for as against any given course. One moment I cry out against the savage that sleeps and wakes within me, again I glory in it and believe profoundly that I am richer for being untamed—that it means strength and courage and even artistic capacity that I am mad to hold in leash until fretting and chafing it lies down to weary acceptance of its bonds. ["Study," 3]

Robins could not accept the possibility that sexual fulfillment enhanced artistic capacity. Ever conscious of herself as an aspiring artist, she studied her own dilemma and used it to the degree it furthered her artistic goals. Here, for instance, this double perspective enabled Robins to manage a sense of humor. When she added a section that confirmed that she "won the battle begun yesterday at 5 and ended at about midnight," she admitted that "some idiot would call me virtuous and a lot else intended to be satisfactory—I know I'm a purblind fool! . . . I *am master* of these red hot stirring times—but I'm getting damned ugly!" ("Study," fourth fragment).

Robins's fictional account of a woman's passions in "The Coming Woman" is hardly as graphic as her private "Study for a woman of 30." In fact, the end of the typed version of the story is ambiguous. Katherine temporarily deflects the men who vie for her allegiance. She departs for Paris to seek European plays suitable for her theater. (Robins, like Katherine, traveled to Paris, where she attended the French première of *Hedda Gabler*.) The strong implication is that Katherine will work through her personal difficulties and go on to work to improve the theater.

The ending leaves many questions unanswered, as was often the case in Robins's early fiction. However, in a later fragment, set months after Katherine and Della have gone their separate ways, Robins converts her personal struggle for control over her passions into the tendency of an actress to capitulate to men's control over her career. Della, who has been out of work and starving, shocks Katherine by admitting that she has allowed herself to be "kept" by a male patron. Katherine (and Robins herself, as she notes in *Both Sides of the Curtain*) also came close to a compromising alliance but escaped.

Robins's attack on the contemporary theater addresses other issues as well. According to Robins, the critics have too much power and do not use it in ways that advance the drama; the best writers have no incentive to write for the stage; the hack playwrights are only interested in making money; and there is no chance for an association of all artists—writers, performers, painters—to work together. Robins's first attempt at fiction, however, principally attacks the dependent status of women in the theater.

Robins expressed to Bell her regret that she had set aside her creative work while the Ibsen matinées with the Charringtons in Brighton had engaged her, determining to "pick up the loose threads . . . and go at the thing every day until it's finished—unless of course stage work puts a stop to it" (ER to FB, October 13, 1892). Soon after this resolution, Heinemann offered her a new translation project, Björnson's *Magnhild*.

An important new event interrupted this endeavor: piecemeal, or, as she described it, in "small, in very small, violently agitating spurts—or as one might say, in volts, projected across the North Sea in a series of electric

shocks," there arrived—a few sheets at a time—the text of Ibsen's next
play. [22] As she translated, James, Heinemann, Archer, and scores of other London literati visited her to explore the prospects for the play's performance.
Robins may not have shown much of her disappointment to them, but she
lamented to Bell of this play that would be named, when Gosse supplied the
title, *The Master Builder*, "So far the acting opportunities are all with Solness . . . but alas, the women." Two days later she wrote, "I am desolate.
. . . James . . . in his heart knows I'm not the one to play Hilda." And the next
day: "I am *amazed* at the radical unfitness of the play for the Theatre. . . . I
don't know what to do, or look forward to, now this Ibsen bubble bids fair
to burst." As an afterthought, she spoke of the status of her fiction: "Enclosed
from Macmillan received last night gives me a renewed spasm of interest in
the thing. I shall finish it one day and send it some where else" (ER to FB,
November 13, 15, 16, 1892).

It was to be the pattern of her life for a long while: Robins immersed
herself in her writing until the most precarious of prospects tempted her to set
it aside for stage work.

[handwritten marginalia: "(a) center stage of this at least"]

3 | # The Power of Anonymity
Free Choices and a Dual Career,
1893–1896

> There is a side of me unfitted for public life. . . . Don't you see I want to
> *act*. I don't want to vindicate Pinero and the English Drama and Elizabeth
> Robins. It's too much.
>
> —Elizabeth Robins to Florence Bell, October 13, 1894

> His wife was not long in realizing that she had found her mission. Yes,
> she had "oracles to deliver." She would be not only a novelist, but a teacher
> and leader of men. She would champion the cause of Progress, she would
> hold high the banner of Woman's Emancipation. She would not consent,
> however, to be criticized by the narrow standards applied in these evil days
> to woman's work. She was assured she had a powerful and original
> mind—she would not allow the soft veil of her sex to hide her merit from
> the public eye. She would call herself "George Mandeville": George, out of
> a sense of kinship with Madame Dudevant and Marian Evans, and because
> the lady novelist finds a mysterious virtue in George; Mandeville, because,
> by some obscure process of reasoning, she had come to consider herself
> allied to a noble English family of that name. And the names looked so
> well together! She printed them five times in large letters on a sheet of
> foolscap. Yes, she would be George Mandeville henceforth!
>
> —C. E. Raimond, *George Mandeville's Husband*

T*HE SCENE*: London, Rutland Gate, home of Montague and Blanche Althea
Crackanthorpe. Evening late in January 1895.[1] A fancy dress dinner party
amid lively company. In the foreground, Elizabeth Robins exchanges greetings
with Mrs. Crackanthorpe. In the background, Henry James entertains a bevy
of women, including Mrs. Yates Thompson. In gossiping tones, he remarks
that the theater and its audience will have to reform before he graces London
with another play. We see him catch sight of Robins, acknowledge her with
a nod, and turn his attention back to his group. Speaking animatedly, he begins a fresh anecdote, "Did I tell you the dream I had of Miss Robins?" His
voice drops as he continues, and his story does not carry to others across the
room.

From the outskirts of the gathering, we hear that James's play has suddenly closed at the St. James Theatre. Actor-manager George Alexander is busy readying Oscar Wilde's new play to replace it. Someone comments that the substitution will give Wilde two plays running concurrently. The focus on Robins and Mrs. Crackanthorpe catches part of their private conversation.

MRS. CRACKANTHORPE [lightly]. No, I swear to you, I have not told a soul. No one knows the real identity of C. E. Raimond. It is tempting, you know, for people to suspect that the author of *George Mandeville's Husband* is someone who knows of my literary avocations. Hubert was told the other day that his mother's ambition to write would stifle his own. Do you think I would neglect my children so deliberately as your "George Mandeville"?

ROBINS. Shhh!—please! You know nothing of C. E. Raimond, unless you want it said that I suspect Raimond is *you*.

MRS. CRACKANTHORPE. I've told you I thought your best protection of "your" Raimond was for you to convince Mr. Heinemann to publish *my* sequel to Raimond's *New Moon* as from Mr. Raimond's own pen. How else will anyone see anything in your superstitious "Milly"? Why, I've made her the most fascinating character in my version of your story. She knows full well those three sightings of the new moon signify that some Diana is tempting her husband. But come tell me about "The Poet." When will you be ready to show it to me? Is it dear Oscar Wilde, or that rascally Richard Le Gallienne, whom you plan to make fun of?

ROBINS. Hush, I tell you. I may never write again. I've abandoned "The Poet," thanks to altogether too many friendly critics. "Raimond" is dead. The only way you know Elizabeth Robins is as an actress who would like to get the opportunity to act something besides Ibsen. And that is that.

[The groups shift. James has approached Robins, apologizes for not greeting her sooner, and offers to tell her what she has missed. People gather around them as he speaks to her.]

JAMES. Yes, a vivid dream, Miss Robins. You and I were discussing something very intently, in a totally white room—I've no idea what *that* meant, do you?—something symbolic, no doubt—

ROBINS [thinking to herself]. His own "white parlor" in the third act of *Guy Domville*—is he putting *me* into his failed play?

JAMES. And *you*, Miss Robins, were standing in front of me as I sat by the fire, standing there calmly talking to me as I sat on the sofa. Yes, that sofa without a back. When, lo, as I looked beyond you a door opened in the wall where I did not know a door existed. And a little fantastic girl dressed in red came dancing up behind you. You were totally unconscious of the intrusion, and I thought to myself, "My goodness, this is the *third* time I've seen that girl. What can it mean?" She came right up behind you, and there was nothing to do but to utter a little cry of warning: "Miss *Robins*, I see a little girl in red!" At that, Miss Robins, you *shrieked* at the top of your voice, "*What!* I've seen her twice before!" And then, regaining your composure a bit, you whispered to me, "Oh please don't tell H—" But a sudden impulse made you turn—the little red demon vanished—poof—and well, your emotion so over-powered you, that you sank to the floor *ohnmächtig*—as we say—unconscious!

Now for the life of me, tell me what you meant by that—what were you doing in my dream, spoiling my pleasant chat with you in such a promising little room with such a—Lady Macbeth—of an attitude—? Why, Miss Robins, are we haunted by the same demons?

ROBINS. For the life of *me*, Mr. James, I could never guess. Perhaps we both ate something disagreeable at the same dinner party that night.

[General laughter. Mrs. Crackanthorpe catches Robins's attention. Silently Robins telegraphs, "Did you tell him I'd written a novel?" Mrs. Crackanthorpe signals back, "Whatever can you mean?"]

ROBINS [thinking to herself, a closeup on her]. Three times a curse—the very device of my pseudonymous novel—what *does* he know about my writing? And *if* he knew—what does he fear about me?

[The party scene dissolves to a scene of Robins at her writing desk. We see her composing a letter, with the substance of James's conversation just set down. She blots the ink and continues: "Dear F. B.: Will you please send me your interpretation by Monday morning!"]

Notes on the Scene: Florence Bell's letter in reply does not survive, but Robins's next letter indicates that James's nightmare of Elizabeth Robins entertained them, for she comments, "Tell Gertrude [Florence Bell's stepdaughter] if she's right about H.J.'s dream I trust he will die in blissful ignorance of the significance of 'the little girl in red'" (ER to FB, January 30, 1895).

In early 1895, Robins was expecting the publication of her second novel, *The New Moon*, and was at work on a satire dealing with the poet Richard Le Gallienne and his school. Robins's anonymity was crucial to her. Soon after this dinner, Robins abandoned work on "Valentine Cobb, or The Poet," and Crackanthorpe's correspondence to her shows that Crackanthorpe's knowledge of "Valentine Cobb" made Robins feel it was too risky to publish. Her association with the Crackanthorpes indicates that C. E. Raimond's anonymity was fragile indeed. Blanche Crackanthorpe's son, Hubert, would have been considered part of the Le Gallienne school; Hubert's affair with Richard Le Gallienne's married sister in 1896 precipitated the events which ended in Hubert's suicide.

Robins protected her pseudonym for many reasons, some of them complex. She did not want her fiction labeled "Ibsenish"; she feared that her reputation as an actress might diminish; she continued to regard her writing as an apprenticeship. Her mentor during these years was William Archer, who *Who was* had good reasons of his own to attack Le Gallienne and who had expectations *Le Gallienne* for Robins's abandoned novel, "Valentine Cobb," that differed greatly from her own.

Henry James remained a close personal friend, a theatergoing companion, an admirer of Robins's art, and himself a writer hoping during this period to establish his credentials as a playwright. James told his sister Alice that, next to the celebrated French actor, Benoît Constant Coquelin, Robins was the most intelligent artist with whom he had conversed about her art.[2] Yet it was most of all from James that she kept the secret of her writing. It was one thing to play the tragic muse—to be the inspiration for, the interpreter of, the man's own successful drama—and another to seem to trespass into the man's own medium. Robins herself had earlier remarked that James would think her effort an unhappy "spectacle of misplaced feminine energy." Robins began her secret career little supposing that she might be the red demon in James's dream; nevertheless, her pen name was the first of her fictions, the first step *what were* on a path which eventually led her to challenge male literary values. *those values*

Elizabeth Robins began to write in part simply to prove that she could finish a story, get it accepted, profit from its sale, and not have to justify her point of view. Her first pseudonymous novel, *George Mandeville's Husband*, captured the spirit of the early 1890s. Scribbling women were the staple of the publishers' lists. Many of them wrote under pseudonyms or—as the novelist Lucy Clifford admitted to Robins—wished they could.

Robins's own publisher, William Heinemann, spoke to her of the financial success of Sarah Grand, perhaps hoping to give Robins added incentive to write. Grand's *The Heavenly Twins* sold twenty thousand copies during its first week of publication, not simply because of its staunchly feminist message, but also because it dwelled on the sexually transmitted diseases that men passed on to innocent wives; in short, it moralized an immoral topic while also subverting, as Elaine Showalter has observed, the "conventions of the novel about female chastity and male sexuality by taking them seriously."[3] George Mandeville's mission as teacher and leader echoes that of Sarah Grand. The public also hungered for the moral fiction of Mrs. Humphrey Ward, whom Robins knew through Florence Bell and who was one of the few who knew the identity of C. E. Raimond.

Despite her penchant for secrecy, Robins was very much part of the literary scene. On at least one occasion, Heinemann's assistant, Sydney Pawling, depended on her to give advice on a novel the firm was considering.[4] She apparently told Cora and Stephen Crane that she had written her very first short story, "A Lucky Sixpence," although in speaking with others, she vehemently denied having written it.[5] If there is no single theme in her early writing, the reason was that she had the freedom of a pseudonym and was an impulsive role-player.

Robins defies classification as a purist; as an actress in London during the 1890s, she wanted both to elevate the reputation of her profession and to play the fallen woman in all her psychological complexity. Certainly, Robins asked herself whether the male dramatists and women writers had alternative views of women to present, and these questions, even subconsciously, directed her career. Recognized as an "intellectual actress," she could not be content with the roles that commercial theaters offered women. Her Hilda Wangel would continue to represent her artistic powers at their peak, but Robins could not rest satisfied that she was the leading interpreter of Ibsen. She strove hard to present Ibsen yet knew that her triumphs on stage achieved no lasting progress toward the realization of her hopes for the theater. *didn't they?*

The Master Builder, 1892–1893

More than any Ibsen play yet seen in London, *The Master Builder* was an actor-manager's play. Its success depended upon an actor who could bring both majestic self-worth and tragic depth to the part of Solness. Gradually, Robins began to see that this aspect, the one that she most deplored, was her greatest asset in arranging for the play's production. She saw, too, that Hilda Wangel was a remarkable role. Hilda's effect in the play is not so much what she does but how she thinks and whom she influences. She has a dream, planted in her by a younger Solness, that he would build her a castle in the air. When she returns to claim her promise, she literally shakes the foundations of Solness's impressive lifelong career. In the wider social context of the play's reception, moreover, Hilda represented the hopes for the next century, not merely for the other characters in the play but for all the young idealists of the late Victorian era. She was, in the image that recurs throughout the play, "youth knocking at the door."

Robins recognized the production value of both the play and the part and took it to the friend and manager she had admired from her first days in London, Herbert Beerbohm Tree. Two days after reading the play to him on December 18, she reported to Bell, "Tree is swept away by Solness—wants to play it but I don't see how he *can*. To give merely detached matinée performances of the new play would be a poor distinction for it." She explained that Tree would not allow the play to be performed in his theater unless he played the part and that playing *consecutive* afternoons, along with an evening production, was something he "can't stand" (ER to FB, December 20, 1892).

Robins recognized again the constrictions of the commercial theater. She wrote in retrospect that "the amazing alterations demanded by Mr. Tree" sent her elsewhere (*T&F* 90). In her account in *Ibsen and the Actress* Robins specified that Tree wanted the play rewritten for an English locale and that he wanted Solness portrayed as a sculptor.[6]

"One manager after another had been offered the chance to godfather the new Ibsen," she observed in *Theatre and Friendship* (88). She did not mention in this public account that, in early January, she had discovered from William Heinemann, the publisher who controlled the production rights, that Tree had been secretly imploring Heinemann to give the rights to Charles Wyndham, the actor-manager who had fired Robins. To her friend Bell she fumed and exclaimed:

> Tree used my confidence to do his best to betray me. He goes to my arch enemy and then after interesting him in this play he'd never seen but for me!—he urges William Heinemann to let Wyndham have it! I felt as if some one had stabbed me! It is quite clear the actor-managers are all leagued together—if Tree could serve Wyndham at my expense it seems he would not shrink. I am heart sick at the thought of such treachery—and I told him [Tree] the last time I saw him, "It was the knowledge that this Ibsen play was waiting for me in the future that gave me the strength to refuse Wyndham's villainous contract." Oh man, man! What stuff *is* the human heart *anyhow*! [ER to FB, January 11, 1893]

Her later reference to the incident revealed that Wyndham was prepared to offer Heinemann "cash down" for the play (ER to FB, January 27, 1894).

This competition for the rights to the production, however, simply made Robins all the more determined to strike out on her own. While Heinemann remained faithful to her claim on the play, she deemed it important not to accept any financial backing from him. By January 20, she had enlisted Herbert Waring (an actor with whom she had worked in *The Sixth Commandment*) to play Solness. Waring found a backer, R. G. Graham, and Robins signed a contract, still not sure she possessed a worthy project. "I am now the owner of this poor wretched bone of contention, the new Ibsen play," she wrote Bell the next day. Graham put up money toward the production costs, but the contract apparently demanded that Robins and Waring as co-producers repay all expenses. Henry James reported to Florence Bell that all her profits went to paying her investors, and she corroborates in her memoirs that she made no money on the production.

The preparation for the production was hardly smooth sailing. Toward the end of January, the husband-and-wife acting team, Janet Achurch and Charles Charrington, made her a "grotesque proposition" probably designed to involve them in the production. Robins was able to decline their proposal only by putting on "as good a bit of acting as I've ever found myself 'cast' for. . . . They're in too great *haste* to ruin me," she confessed to Bell and pleaded with her never to discuss the matter (ER to FB, January 25, 1893).

Bernard Shaw called on Robins with a proposal to puff the play by printing an interview with her. (He had made a similar offer previously, when Achurch and Robins were playing *Hedda Gabler* in Brighton.) During his visit, Robins was taken aback by his personal advances. Shaw later wrote wryly, "I have interviewed beautiful women before; but none of them were so noble as to threaten to shoot me."[7] Shaw may have been likening her rejection to Hedda Gabler's behavior toward Løvborg, but in any case, humor became his chief way of dealing with her determination to maintain her freedom. Once he had seen Robins's performance as Hilda, he was moved to congratulate her. "My critical troll is deeply grateful to your artistic troll," he wrote her upon seeing *The Master Builder* a second time. Admiration did not, however, prevent him from filling his letter with specific criticisms and reiterating his "unmitigated defiance, and resentment of the wounds you have dealt to my justifiable vanity" (GBS to ER, March 3, 1893, in *Letters* I, 385, 386).

Shaw was not alone in discovering an Elizabeth Robins he could not advise or flatter. Henry James became upset when he discovered at the dress rehearsal that Robins intended to follow Ibsen's directions and wear a simple traveling dress for Hilda's costume. At midnight, after the Friday dress rehearsal, he wrote her a letter that urged her to "Throw Ibsen's prescriptions to the winds if practically they betray you. . . . be *pretty*, be agreeable, in the right key. . . . And wear something else in Act II" (HJ to ER, February 17, 1893, quoted in *T&F* 99). Robins insisted on wearing Hilda's one short dress —not at all fashionable—and accompanied it with alpenstock, knapsack, and hob-nailed boots.

When the play opened on Monday, there was an obvious disparity between the first night critics, who were for the most part negative or almost wholly baffled by the play, and the public impression for which James had paved the way three days earlier in the *Pall Mall Gazette*. Unlike his essay on *Hedda Gabler*, which expressed his great reservation, "Ibsen's New Play"[8] was an enthusiastic endorsement which averred that the production's entrancing qualities overcame any of the play's difficulties. James announced that he had had the pleasure of seeing a rehearsal and wrote of Ibsen: "His independence, his perversity, his intensity, his vividness, the hard compulsion of his strangely inscrutable art, are present in full measure, together with that quality which comes almost uppermost when it is a question of seeing him on the stage, his peculiar blessedness to actors." Before he went on to describe enough of the story to allow *The Master Builder* to be a play to which a young lady might "properly take her mother," he called Ibsen "the master" and stated his conviction that even if the public entirely renounced the playwright,

Elizabeth Robins as Hilda Wangel in Ibsen's *The Master Builder*, 1893. Robins scorned Henry James's advice to wear something "agreeable" and change her dress for Act II. (*Courtesy of the Fales Library. Reproduced with the permission of Mabel Smith, for the Backsettown Trustees.*)

"players enamored of their art will still be found ready to interpret him for that art's sake to empty benches."

Those who agreed with James—those who were fascinated with the "hold" the play had on them—can be credited with keeping the play running for two weeks of matinées and three additional weeks of evening performances, February 20 to March 25, with the final performance presented just before Passion Week darkened all London's theaters. Many came back a second and third time. Robins certainly felt her power in the part. She wrote that no other role ever brought her "such a sense . . . of release, such conviction of having the audience with me, and at the same time such freedom from the yoke of the audience." She measured her accomplishment not by applause, but by "that unmistakable response" when her audience "took the 'points.'" Robins could feel that the response was "no less to the 'little devil' in Hilda than to her thrilling sense of the adventure of living; a response to that queer mixture of wildness and tenderness; that determination to have her own imperious way, crossed by the necessity to feel what other people were feeling."[9]

Robins created an aura of brilliance with her committed playing. A great number of people introduced or reintroduced themselves to the actress-producer and praised her interpretation. Robins's first manager, Mrs. Beringer, sent congratulations; and Lawrence Irving, son of Henry Irving, the famous Shakespearean actor-manager at the Lyceum, wrote to express his admiration, prompting Elizabeth Robins to marvel that the father had not trained the son to despise Ibsen. The novelist and aspiring playwright George Moore, whose play Robins had just declined to do, sent a note of praise and confided that he had returned to watch her perform three times.

Still, there were disappointments, too. Robins had hoped to add to the bill the fourth act scene from *Brand*. Probably because she was, near the end of the run, fighting off a cold, the attempt was abandoned after one rehearsal, and Robins privately lamented, "Alas! Alas!" (EBook, March 21, 1893). Later that week, she spent most days in bed so that she could save her strength for performance at night. When she got to the theater on Friday evening, she was too ill to play; and the performance was canceled. On the final Saturday she gave two performances and recorded in her diary, "Oscar Wilde raves over the play and Hilda" (EBook, March 25, 1893). On the following Thursday, the company performed a matinée in Brighton; and the *Sussex Daily News*, which reported a large house and many curtain calls, called Elizabeth Robins's Hilda an "inspiration."[10]

During the first two weeks of April, she went to be with the Bells in Redcar and there suffered a severe cold. By April 17, she was back in London rehearsing "Befraid," or *Alan's Wife*, a dramatization of the Swedish story by Elin Ameen, presented under the auspices of the Independent Theatre.

Alan's Wife, 1893

Perhaps the nearest real-life counterpart to Robins's fictionalized ideal theater of her unfinished novel was J. T. Grein's Independent Theatre. Grein's London version of the continental "free theatre" movement was never without controversy because the Independent's first production was Ibsen's *Ghosts*. This Ibsen play caused a furor early in 1891, not simply because its subject was hereditary syphilis, but also because Ibsen used the disease to expose moral decay. Robins had first encountered the Swedish short story "Befraid" in 1891 and showed it to William Archer as a possibility for a dramatic adaptation. He immediately drafted a scenario and suggested the names of several dramatists to whom she might take it to commission an adaptation. Instead, Robins and Bell coauthored the play version. Grein was enthusiastic when Robins read him the dramatized translation of "Befraid" on December 30, 1892. Shortly afterward he promised her an April production.

The play, like much of the New Drama, fed into the controversy surrounding realism in its relation to art and the presentation of ethical dilemmas. Jean Creyke, the Alan's wife of the title, is devastated when her husband's body is brought out of the works, having been crushed by the machinery. Later, when her son is born unhealthy, she sees that the child's only blessing will be a quick end to his suffering. She baptizes the infant herself, then smothers it. In the third scene, the incarcerated Jean is given a chance to confess that she was out of her mind when she killed the infant, but she endures the pleas of her mother, the warden, and priest with determined silence. The priest asks for a confession of faith so that her crime will be forgiven, and only then does Jean finally burst out in response, "Crime!" When the warden insists she hadn't the courage to bear the sight of his deformity, she continues: "I hadn't courage? I've had courage—just once in my life I've been strong and kind— and it was the night I killed my child!"[11] To her hysterical mother, she explains the difference between man's law, which condemns her to death, and a higher judgment, which will restore her to her son and her husband.

In something of a revolutionary spirit, Bell wrote Robins in the fall of 1892, proposing "Set Free" as a title for *Alan's Wife*. "Why not?" She added, "It's simple, it tells nothing, it isn't a name with a purpose and the last sentence of the play ends with it" (FB to ER, November 9, 1892). The phrase is also suggestive of the freedom of expression made possible by the coauthors' anonymity and the process by which Elizabeth Robins's private griefs were transformed into heroic acting.

During the summer the book was readied for publication in Heinemann's series "Independent Theatre Plays." In a lengthy introduction, Archer attacked the critic A. B. Walkley for condemning the play on what Archer insisted were false grounds. Walkley had complained in print that, by exposing Alan's bloody body to view, the production exploited sensationalism. Archer quoted Robins and the stage manager to undermine Walkley's claim and argued that Walkley had simply imagined the exposed body.[12]

Robins and Bell took the attitude that Archer's lengthy introduction smothered the printed text of the play. Public opinion agreed with them. A cartoon published to accompany a review of the book showed a diminutive *Alan's Wife* being led into the world by a towering Archer.[13] The introduction makes the book a curious theatrical artifact. Archer's commentary records many details of the play as it was acted and traces the history of the play's development but carefully preserves the adapters' anonymity. The published script highlights Jean's refusal to speak by printing her silent thoughts; the interior monologues seem to intensify the power of the play's text. Jean's unspoken replies become the defiant acts of a woman who *chooses* silence.

As both dramatizer and performer, Elizabeth Robins had more freedom in staging this play than she had had even with *Hedda Gabler*. Control of her artistic opportunities had become essential. Robins and Bell's dialogue, shown in the crisp repartee, in the climax of each scene, and in Jean's haunting muteness, offered a superb vehicle for Robins's abilities as performer. Still, Robins's critical success as Jean Creyke was short-lived, for the Independent Theatre's production consisted of just two matinée performances. Once more, Robins reaped no financial gain. As Henry James remarked, "Yet what a misery is 'again'—when again is only once or twice!" (HJ to ER [April 30, 1893], quoted in *T&F* 124). James maintained that Robins had not sufficiently seized on her commercial potential as an artist. "She sees her life in a certain way— and that's the end of it," he confided to Bell after he had tried to persuade her that her performance in *The Master Builder* would lead to better opportunities. Robins, he reported, thought her Hilda Wangel would lead to nothing. "She will be thought more remarkable, but be just as remarkably let alone" (HJ to FB, March 4 [1893], in *T&F* 104).

Unfortunately, however, Robins's talent and her willingness to play exceeded the opportunities available to her. Given its theme, *Alan's Wife* could have been presented in no setting other than the Independent Theatre's private subscription matinées. At length a first commercial offer arrived; Robins had a fleeting chance to create Paula Tanqueray at Alexander's St. James's Theatre. Like Hedda Gabler, Paula Tanqueray is a new wife who kills herself after discovering that she and her husband are incompatible. In contrast to Ibsen's heroine, Paula Tanqueray awakens upon realizing that, as her new husband's former mistress, she has no place in his life. On May 1, Robins noted in her calendar, Pinero's new play would be read at the St. James. On May 2, Pinero and Alexander asked her to give up the part. Mrs. Patrick Campbell had arranged for release from her Adelphi contract and announced that she would be available for the title role in *The Second Mrs. Tanqueray*. Alexander and Pinero preferred the more flamboyant Mrs. Pat. Robins immediately relinquished the part, no doubt motivated by her concern for Campbell as a fellow artist struggling with the desperation of a Della Stanley. Then, too, Robins could hardly claim favorable standing in Alexander's eyes.

Soon thereafter, Robins began pursuing the plans she had begun to formulate when she had begun rehearsals of Ibsen's *Brand* while performing in *The Master Builder*. This time, she organized a committee to collect subscriptions as she initiated preparations for presenting Ibsen in repertory. Not only could she revive the two Ibsen roles that had established her reputation, Hedda and Hilda, but she would also introduce two new roles, Agnes in *Brand* and Rebecca West in *Rosmersholm*.

Repertory

In mid-May, by the time her preparations for this Ibsen Repertory Series were well under way, Robins's situation had ceased to resemble that of an outcast. On May 12, she reported to Bell that John Hare had approached her with an offer to join his company for a year. Hare's current production of *Diplomacy* was doing such excellent business that there was no telling when he would change the bill. For Robins, the opportunity would mean recreating a part another actress had originated, and when Hare did mount a new play, there might not be a role for her. This opportunity to join a regular company was, however, far more promising than another offer that she received and quickly refused. Joseph W. Comyns Carr, a leading dramatist and manager, asked her to play the heroine in his new adaptation of Feydeau. She read the play, found it not to her taste, and declined the offer. Privately she remarked, "I think I shall refuse and refuse and refuse as long as offers come. In truth I pine to accept—but not this—oh, not this!!" (ER to FB [?May], 1893).

On May 22, Robins signed the contract to begin with Hare in September. In mid-June, just after her independent productions of four Ibsen plays, she began rehearsals at the Adelphi for *A Woman's Revenge*. It was ironic that she, who had enabled Campbell to escape the Adelphi, should now be starting work for the summer in this house that had built its reputation on melodrama of low quality. Some observers predicted that Robins would lose her Ibsen proclivities in her new position. Others merely commented that she had succumbed to an inferior kind of drama.

Quite different and very private circumstances made more plausible her decision to earn twenty-five pounds a week for the summer; the contract with Hare would guarantee her employment at least through December. Before the end of April 1893, Robins received word from her youngest brother that their father, Charles Ephraim Robins, had died. In her engagement book she recorded the dates of his death, the discovery of his death, and his funeral as April 5, 6, and 7. On the page for the last date she wrote, "How little I dreamed what was happening." On April 28, the day of the first matinée of *Alan's Wife*, Robins appeared dressed in black at a private viewing at the Royal Academy, as *Hearth and Home* reported the following week.

By this time, she had received a letter from her brother Raymond in Florida. It began, "Our father needs no eulogy" and set forth the family situation in detail. Raymond promised to send his sister twenty-five dollars a month toward her expenses in England and signed himself "Devotedly your brother to command." His financial support lasted only a few months, but his dedication to his sister spurred much of his subsequent initiative.[14]

Elizabeth was all too prepared for the news that her oldest brother Saxton sent her later in the month. Saxton's financial account of "C.E.R.'s remains" explained that the money in their father's bank account, less funeral expenses, amounted to $51.14 for each of the four surviving children. The idealism that had prompted her father to take up, then abandon, one business scheme after another had ruined a family fortune. Elizabeth had witnessed firsthand how Charles Robins had tried to persuade his mother, Jane Hussey Robins, to sell the last of her stock in the Baltimore & Ohio, to give up her home in Zanesville, Ohio, and to move south with him to his wilderness plantation in Florida. Jane had deeded the property to Elizabeth, and Elizabeth had prevailed upon her father to keep the property as long as she could pay taxes on it. Only because of this land did Elizabeth have any funds (ER to CER, February 24, 1884). Much earlier, Robins had learned that her father did not have enough money to send her to college as he dreamed.

In the midst of mourning for her father, then, and of contemplating his failed financial ventures, Robins prepared for the most ambitious acting venture she had yet attempted. In addition to revivals of *Hedda Gabler* and *The Master Builder*, Robins added *Rosmersholm* and the fourth act of *Brand* to her list of Ibsen plays offered in the Ibsen Repertory Series. Rebecca West and Agnes Brand were two roles that she had wanted to play for some time. The schedule of the series was itself a daring venture: two performances each of *Hedda Gabler*, *Rosmersholm*, and the double bill of *The Master Builder* and *Brand*, performed at matinées during the first week (May 29 to June 3), and the cycle repeated in the evenings of the week following. Established London theaters depended more and more upon the long run; *Charley's Aunt* and *The Second Mrs. Tanqueray* would run for months. Robins, however, took her model from visiting foreign troupes. When Coquelin, Eleonora Duse, and Sarah Bernhardt visited London, they performed, usually in the course of a few short days or weeks, a repertory consisting of several plays. These artists were Robins's inspiration. Something of Robins's missionary zeal in the promotion of Ibsen emerges in the financial arrangements for the Repertory Series: Robins returned to her subscribers all profits that remained after modest salaries had been paid.

After this sacrifice, Robins's well-paid roles in *A Woman's Revenge* and *Diplomacy* were like a respite from the theater projects that were closer to her heart. The commercial performances were not artistically as exacting as her independent productions; perhaps in compensation, she began again to write. Robins played the Countess Zicka in Clement Scott's *Diplomacy* with more realism than audiences were used to. Zicka, a very unsympathetic outcast, blackmails the new bride of a young English diplomat in order to prove that only her love for him keeps her alive. Although she is the villainess of the piece, she has a stirring scene in the fourth act in which she enumerates the injustices done her in pleading for forgiveness. The play began its tour in Liverpool and traveled to Manchester, Birmingham, Edinburgh, and Glasgow, gathering more and more favorable notices along the way. Hare was invited to give a special performance for the Queen and her court at Balmoral Castle; then the play reopened in London in November. Robins's letters to Bell at this time seem more concerned with the excitement of her travels and the enrichment of their friendship than with her acting ambitions. In 1895, she drew on her experiences with Hare's company to write an essay, "An American Actress at Balmoral Castle." For the present, she seemed to enjoy the tour as a holiday.

There was more keeping her occupied than the touring of *Diplomacy*, however. In Liverpool, she finished a short piece of fiction she called first "Hester," after its central character, a pitiable, lower-class servant girl, and soon afterward renamed "A Lucky Sixpence." From Manchester, she sent the story to William Archer; and on September 23, he sent back his praise. The following week, Bell joined her for two days in Manchester. Robins began a letter to her friend on the evening Bell left, concluding it two days later: "You are a very large part *of the good of living* and I don't see why I shouldn't tell you so now and then. . . . *Nobody* does for me what you do. You re-create me and send me bowling on with fresh vigour and capacity for joy" (ER to FB, September 30, October 2, 1893). Her friendship with Florence Bell was to be the central intimacy in Robins's life. Until Bell's death in 1930, Robins turned first to her for advice, critical response, support, collaboration, or a fresh idea.

good friends

"A Lucky Sixpence"

Elizabeth Robins spoke to Florence Bell of her desire to maintain her anonymity as the author of fiction. While she was attempting to place "A Lucky Sixpence," as she wrote her friend, she had told one editor that she "did not care to have any one else know that I was willing to affront Destiny in more ways than *one*" (ER to Frank Harris, quoted in ER to FB, October [?21], 1893). By December 7, Robins was able to report that the *New Review* had offered to publish "A Lucky Sixpence" in the January issue.

Two days afterward, she discovered the disadvantages of anonymity. William Archer warned her that the terms offered were "nonsensical" and that if she could not get at least ten pounds (it was worth fifteen or twenty, he hinted) she should ask for her manuscript back. She followed his advice yet feared that her story might never be published. Archer prodded her to adopt a more serious attitude toward her new occupation, telling her, as she confided to Bell, "What on earth is the good of *my* scribbling if I don't get decently paid for it!" (ER to FB, December 9, 1893). When the story appeared in January, it was published as the anonymous work of a new writer of fiction, one which the editors used to herald a new policy of selecting each month a short story "entirely on its merits."[15]

In "A Lucky Sixpence," Robins took up the themes which would mark much of her short fiction in the next few years. She drew many of her characters from the servant class. They were often foreign born, and their problems raised issues of class and sex. Robins credited the servants she knew and the months she spent in an English boardinghouse at 10 Duchess Street, where many foreigners roomed, as a source for her lively characters. In her first published story, the poor uneducated Hester confesses to a personal maid hardened by experience that Hester's master has made improper advances to her. The maid seems to befriend the girl but also informs Mrs. Baily of Mr. Baily's transgressions: "It's true, I tell ye, . . . and it ain't right for 'er to 'ave to shoulder all the blyme. Instead of treatin' 'er like a dog, you ought to try and 'elp 'er bear the trouble your own 'usband 'as brought on 'er."[16] When Mrs. Baily questions her husband, he denies any wrongdoing. He forces Hester to confess that she has lied, and in front of his wife, he suggests to her, "Someone has brought trouble upon you and you falsely accused me of it." With Hester's "Yes, Master," Mrs. Baily, "with a low, remorseful cry . . . threw her arms round her husband's neck." Hester watches unnoticed as her master soothes his wife with the same affectionate caresses that he had bestowed upon Hester. She is stupefied and helpless at the "sight of these two building the foundations of their future on her poor little trembling lie" ("Sixpence," 125).

Blindly, Hester still cherishes the lucky sixpence, one with a hole in it that her master had given her long ago, and thinks while she packs, "Oh, if I only had a common sixpence." This thought becomes, "Well, if I'm going to die, sixpence is enough," and then, "I'll have to spend it. . . . It's very hard to have to spend it" ("Sixpence," 125, 126). Robins takes her story only as far as the girl's departure. What happens when Hester is on her own remains unsettled, and the state she feared she would be left in, "without a character"—without references—now takes on double meaning. She will never have a chance to get another job; hereafter she will be among the lowest of women.

William Archer congratulated Robins for her achievement at the time the story appeared. His letters to her praised her writing as "masculine" and quoted L. F. Austin, the reviewer in the *Illustrated London News*, who guessed that the unidentified author was likely to be George Moore. Later, it became evident that Robins's motivation for writing extended beyond a concern to rival the best male writers.[17]

writing is "male" is a compliment

William Heinemann, principal editor of the *New Review*, announced in the issue in which the story appeared that the story "should stand on its own merits rather than be suspected of assistance from the considerable position occupied by its author on another platform."[18] Robins was upset that Heinemann had so broadly hinted at her professional identity. As it turned out, Heinemann, Edmund Gosse, and Clement Shorter confided to others that she had written the piece. Robins insisted that the three retract the attribution, which they did. She reported to Bell that she had denied the story "up hill and down dale and shall stick to my evil courses" (ER to FB, January [?], 1894). She even called on her talent as performer to keep up her pretense; she obviously delighted in misleading those she did not want to know of her authorship and enjoyed swearing to secrecy those she trusted. In doing so, Robins shared with her American literary cousins of earlier generations the passion for privacy which Mary Kelley identifies in *Private Woman, Public Stage*, her study of the female literary domestic.[19] Rather than fearing that her identity would be effaced, however, Elizabeth Robins perceived the woman writer as a being with many potential identities. Her pen was a powerful weapon against a theater system reluctant to allow women to realize their full potential.

The scant surviving evidence suggests that Robins was not yet prepared to launch a full-scale career as writer. She assured Bell in a letter in February, "No, I believe the author of 'The Lucky Sixpence' has no further designs upon the Public Morals. Indeed so long as any theatrical scheme is to the fore, the public is safe" (ER to FB, February 2, 1894). By this time, in fact, she had a theatrical project to engage her interests.

Although she drafted other stories, Robins continued to be chiefly preoccupied with seeking better acting opportunities for herself. During January, she lobbied John Hare—with whom she was still under contract, although she was not acting in his current bill—to accept a play written by Constance Fletcher. Robins confessed to Bell that her scheme involved first approaching Beerbohm Tree while all the time hoping that Hare would produce Fletcher's script: "I'm sure you understand if I'd not been here to hustle Hare with the phantom of another greedy manager the thing wouldn't have been settled yet" (ER to FB, January 27, 1894).

The condition on which Hare agreed to produce the play, which was provisionally entitled "The Other Woman" and was finally called *Mrs. Lessingham,* was that Fletcher rewrite the last act. In this work, Robins herself took a large part. She met with Fletcher and read aloud the new draft as they discussed revisions. Robins's assistance and encouragement gave her a certain claim to the play. In a letter to Bell suggesting she may also have been promised Oscar Wilde's new play, Robins wrote, "I should like to do the Fletcher play forthwith (Oscar writes me his own is not finished!!) and take it and Hedda and Hilda to New York next Autumn or Winter" (ER to FB, February 2, 1894). A week later she reported she had negotiated the contract between Hare and Fletcher and had secured for herself the American rights. For the next two months, she engaged herself almost exclusively with rehearsals. The role of Mrs. Lessingham gave Robins some difficulty because, as critics complained, it was not realistic. Mrs. Lessingham is a widow who causes a barrister, with whom she had an affair before her marriage, to end his engagement to a young woman. After marrying the barrister, Mrs. Lessingham realizes that her new husband is really in love with the younger woman, so she kills herself. Robins hinted that she was uncomfortable during rehearsals. To Florence Bell, she apologized for all the changes over which she had no control. More disheartening, she learned—just four days after her première—that Fletcher had withdrawn her permission for Robins to perform the play in America. It was the final signal that Robins's initial enthusiasm for Fletcher's talent had turned to disaffection: "I am too tired of the ignoble battle, to contest this or *any* demand she may be disposed to make in this connection" (ER to FB, April 11, 1894).

No doubt the loss of the play contract caused Robins to have "further designs upon the Public Morals," as she characterized her writing efforts. She may even have let her disappointment with Fletcher seep into the novel she began to write, a satire on a woman writer, who, like Fletcher, adopts a male pseudonym. Fletcher was George Fleming to the reading public, and Robins used her novel to ridicule the tradition according to which the woman of letters used a male signature. To draw further attention to the problem of gender affiliation, Robins entitled her book *George Mandeville's Husband.* Her pen name, C. E. Raimond, and her narrator's affinity with the husband of the writer helped readers to empathize with a presumably masculine viewpoint. Perhaps to counter the rumors that she had written "A Lucky Sixpence," Robins wrote both this longer work and her very next short story in a way that assured her of anonymity.

"Dedicated to John Huntley"

Robins reported on May 3 to Florence Bell that the story "Dedicated to John Huntley" had been accepted by the *New Review*. The piece describes, in the first person, a young novelist's destruction of his masterpiece when he realizes that his good friend, the well-known writer John Huntley, has appropriated the young man's own story and has turned it into a best-seller. Robins masked her identity as the writer in a number of ways: the story is told as the account of a nameless male writer, and the only public confirmation of Robins's authorship is in the alphabetical list of authors included in the bound volume 10 of the *New Review*, where "Author of 'A Lucky Sixpence' " is cited as having also written "Dedicated to John Huntley" for the July issue.[20] Upon discovering that Huntley has used his unfinished plot for Huntley's own popular novel, the younger writer does not divulge that he has completed his book. In an action that might be read as an echo of *Hedda Gabler*, the narrator burns his manuscript, page by page, until it is reduced to a charred fragment. The destruction of his own work does not lessen his attachment to it. He holds the leaf with the last words he has written, "Dedicated to John Huntley," and gropes among the ashes in a final effort to retrieve his proud creation. Although he knows that he may eventually write again, "the strongest and vitalest thing I could do was written on the charred fragments in the grate and on the hearth" ("DJH," 758).

Robins treated plagiarism satirically in a later story, but "Dedicated to John Huntley" is deadly serious. The narrator's last sentences convey the agony of a writer who maintains his integrity by destroying his masterpiece. Although the young writer finds the thought of life without his great work bleak, his sacrifice reflects his independence, as if he could say that from now on his writing was indebted to no man. The story has another aspect as well, however. Robins herself is lurking behind the persona of the writer in "Dedicated to John Huntley," and she was soon to effect a character transferal by means of her pseudonym. The story of the narrator's painful loss thus also embodies its author's admission of her own as yet unborn powers.

George Mandeville's Husband, 1894

George Mandeville's Husband reflected Elizabeth Robins's development as a writer even more than had her two anonymous stories. "George Mandeville" is the pen name taken up by Mrs. Ralph Wilbraham (née Lois Carpenter) when she determines that marriage and a child do not fulfill her creative impulses. Her literary ambitions and her arrogance toward her family devastate her husband and turn their daughter, Rosina, into a pathetic invalid. George Mandeville maneuvers for space in their modest apartment, seeks attention whenever criticism of her work threatens her security, and bids for control when she mounts her trial matinée of a play based upon her novel. In this central character Robins explores the arrogance of a woman who assumes that whatever she writes is the very best.

Ralph Wilbraham is forced to give up his hopes of becoming a painter (though he retreats to paint in secret), and he tells his devoted daughter that he wants her to have nothing to do with artistic expression. When Rosina asks of his painting, "Is that the very best?" Wilbraham replies bitterly, "No, but if a woman had done it, she'd think it was."[21] George Eliot looms large as a presence in the book. Ralph Wilbraham condemns her and her writing when Rosina speaks of her as a good model; Robins wryly alludes to George Eliot when she exposes George Mandeville's imperfections. Throughout the novel, Robins's treatment of George Mandeville's inflated opinions of herself as they wreak havoc upon her husband and daughter is satiric. The episodes in which the "authoress" invades the theatrical world in particular draw upon Robins's knowledge of independent productions and her experiences with Constance Fletcher.

In mocking female authors who establish their own circles, however, Robins also indicts the passive husband who can only lament the state of his family. The fact that the plot focuses upon Rosina's plight heightens the irony. In her mother's eyes, Rosina's plainness works against her. George Mandeville has entertained few hopes for her daughter since her illness as an infant. Rosina is even more unsettled by her father's overprotection than by her mother's neglect. Wilbraham endlessly explains to his daughter that it is unnatural for women to try their hand at any art form—writing or painting—and Rosina feels as if she were being scolded for something that she had not done. Wilbraham then forbids Rosina to enter a creative profession. Rosina feels closest to Wilbraham when they are secluded in the "box room," Wilbraham's private retreat, where he continues to paint without his wife's knowledge. Rosina, having discovered Wilbraham's secret activity, is so enraptured by his paintings that she begs for permission to join him. Wilbraham takes to sketching her in various poses and "felt conscious that with her for a subject he was doing his best work" (*GMH*, 55).

Father and daughter conspire to endure George Mandeville's idiosyncratic demands until, in the midst of her efforts to produce her play, the fourteen-year-old Rosina shows signs of fever and illness. The mother then steps in to take charge. When her father discovers that George Mandeville has left her daughter more distraught, Rosina confides in him, "About some things mothers shouldn't speak till they are spoken to. . . . I don't feel confidential with mamma. . . . I never tell her about everyday things, and why should she question and lecture me as she does about—about those 'facts of existence,' as she calls them? Ugh! she makes everything so ugly, *so ugly*" (*GMH*, 97–98).

Rosina resents her mother's indictment of her own sex. Robins portrays her as a girl reluctant to face womanhood because of the self-serving behavior of a mother, in her disclosure of the facts of menstruation. George Mandeville also expects her daughter to remain by her side at the public première, during its invitational dress rehearsal, although the play clearly means more to her than the health of her daughter. Overexposure during the long ordeal—made longer and more embarrassing for Rosina because her mother is constantly interrupting to direct and reprimand the actors and stage hands—causes Rosina, upon returning home, to take to her bed. After a night of feverish delirium with her father by her side, she dies of a sudden hemorrhage. George Mandeville sends Wilbraham into the drawing room to host her regular weekly gathering. When he returns to Rosina's room, he finds his wife "kneeling by the dead girl sobbing bitterly, kissing her hand, and calling her baby-names. The white bedclothes were bright with new-spilt blood" (*GMH*, 151).

The conclusion underscores the total insignificance of Rosina's life. As the years pass, people comment on Ralph Wilbraham as model husband, not knowing "that the particular virtue which they admire in him springs from apathy rather than conviction" (*GMH*, 154). At first he is angry that his wife has canonized Rosina by endowing her features with the romantic characteristics of her heroines, but even this resentment fades to nothingness. By closing on this note and stressing Rosina's total effacement, Robins turns her clever parody to biting satire. These darker aspects hint at the young woman's disorientation in a modern world, a theme that Virginia Woolf later explored insightfully in *The Voyage Out*. Both Rosina Wilbraham's and Rachel Vinrace's passages into womanhood are plagued by the frightening discoveries of the constraints operative on them as women in an adult world. In one important variation on the theme of woman as muse, Robins shows Wilbraham bringing out his paintings of Rosina to comfort her in her last feverish night. He is hoping the sight of the painting she has called for will allow her to sleep. Instead, Rosina grows more and more feverish, asks to see every portrait he has done, and finally collapses in a room filled with his artistic renderings of Rosina as Arachne, Themis, the Naiads, all the Fates, and finally Nemesis, the "terrible daughter of Nox" (*GMH*, 133). Her father's obsession with painting Rosina culminates when Nemesis, or Retribution herself, comes back to accuse the painter who uses his daughter as his muse, for his own self-expression. Robins's indictment of Wilbraham for insisting that his daughter lead a sheltered life is as strong as her burlesque of a presumptuous literary woman. Rosina is victimized by unnatural extremes in both mother and father.

As Robins completed *George Mandeville's Husband* in June, she sketched "Poppy and Mandragora," a story of the counterinfluences upon a captain and the woman he visits and to whom he reads. Although the story was never revised and was never published, it sheds light on Robins's next major effort, which was concerned with the private relationship between a married man and the young woman whose company sustains him.

The New Moon

Robins began writing *The New Moon* in the late summer of 1894. The novel is the confession, told in the first person, of an unhappily married doctor who falls in love with Dorothy Lance, the young and intelligent granddaughter and caretaker of one of his patients. The work is significant for Robins's development because it recalls earlier women's fiction, including *Jane Eyre*, and anticipates another novel that Robins wrote about a woman's relationship with her doctor, *A Dark Lantern*. Robins's portrait of the deep relationship echoes the tension at the core of her own life, moreover. Her use of a male narrator and a pseudonym freed her to explore the theme of greatest importance in her personal life, the battle between the claims of sexual passion and the sanctity of a chaste comradeship. The tension that animated *Hedda Gabler* would be Robins's recurring and most private theme. In this work, she explored it from the point of view of a character not unlike Charlotte Brontë's Rochester, whose adulterous passion overcomes him. A climactic fire causing both his invalid wife's and his lover's death gives the tale a grim ending in stark contrast to that of *Jane Eyre*. The anonymity Robins enjoyed because of her pseudonym, furthermore, prompted her to encourage her closest friends, Florence Bell and Blanche Crackanthorpe, to write analogues to *The New Moon* which were narrated in the first person by the two women in her story. Robins thus contrived a feminist deconstruction of her own text.

In the story, Dr. Geoffrey Monroe is setting down his confession, knowing that he has only a short time before death. He is haunted by events from which he knows he cannot be freed, and he recounts his sad years with his excessively dependent wife. He regains some interest in life after developing a friendship with the granddaughter of one of his patients. Geoffrey's growing attraction for Dorothy Lance is thrown into high relief by scenes revealing his wife's plight. He is forced to pamper and read aloud to his wife, Millicent Monroe. She grows more and more superstitious and visits mediums. Seeking

Dorothy's comforting cheer and intellectual companionship, Monroe arranges to call on her for tea every day.

Dorothy seems to know the doctor better than he knows himself. She surprises him when she predicts that his generosity and concern to respect his wife will always keep their own extramarital relationship chaste: "Shall I tell you what I sometimes regret most of all?" Dorothy proposes. "That you and I are so disgustingly good. . . . Quite good enough to spoil our lives" (*New Moon*, 115–16).

The climactic events which make Monroe's written confession an obligation on his part take place in the Swiss resort that Geoffrey has conveniently prescribed for both his invalid wife and Dorothy's grandmother. As Monroe's need to see Dorothy grows, so does his guilt toward his highly superstitious but unsuspecting wife. Milly predicts that if she sees the new moon for the third month in a row her life will be threatened. When she mistakes a lantern (which Dorothy hangs in her window as signal to Monroe) for the new moon, Monroe is frantic to calm her. He runs to Dorothy's lodgings in order to beg her to come to his wife and explain that she has put a lamp in the window. Their secret rendezvous suddenly changes character with this strange request that Dorothy introduce herself to his wife. Earlier in their relationship Dorothy had been devastated when Monroe, after months of friendly daily meetings, had first mentioned his wife to her. She responded on that occasion by telling the man she would have preferred to love unreservedly, "We must hold fast to our friendship and keep it free of stain. It shall hurt no one and it will help us" (*New Moon*, 91).

Now, in her room at the Swiss hotel, Monroe seems to violate that trust when Dorothy wonders why he is guilt stricken by his wife's superstition. Just at the moment when she feels sure of her own passion, "caring as I never cared before" (188), and signals to him to come to her, he appears at her door pleading with her to introduce herself to his wife. They embrace, passionately, but now shame and dishonor tinge their relationship. Dorothy promises to do anything in the world for him and goes to his wife's bedside. Retribution for Monroe's transgression is then effected by forces that appear almost supernatural. Fire breaks out in the corridor. The doctor struggles to save both his invalid wife and his dearest companion, but the effort turns into desperation. "*I can save one*" (209), he tells himself when they are surrounded by smoke and flames and stumbling for the passageway.

"Let no man say I did not choose," he tells his readers. As Dorothy predicted in her remark to Monroe, he is "so disgustingly good" that he struggles out with his wife. Then his uncontrolled passion for Dorothy bursts out with heightened mania. "I will come back for you, I'm coming!" he screams out to her even as he is prevented from re-entering the building and collapses himself. Monroe counts himself blessed because he has not escaped suffering: "I thank the gods for this obscure and baffling mischief, that manifests itself in such paroxysms of recurrent pain as have made my pen drop from my hand a score of times while I have been setting down these fragments of the past" (*New Moon*, 211–12).

Some elements of *The New Moon* are sensationalized, some derivative; yet Robins used the tale to transform her own ambivalence about close friendship and loyalty. On one level, she takes up the persona of Geoffrey Monroe in order to eulogize a Dorothy Lance who is much like herself. Dorothy is a woman who is investigating all that has been written about inherited insanity. Her mother died insane and, like Elizabeth Robins, she has ruled out marriage for herself because it would perpetuate the disease. Monroe minimizes her worry by doubting that her illness will prevent her from being the "mother of sons," thus subtly exposing his sexual desire. It is his acting upon this desire that makes the final action of the fire and their deaths a retribution.

The standards of respectability shared by Elizabeth Robins and her heroine Dorothy Lance are not as much those of society as of their own making. Robins might well have formed a more intimate friendship with Archer than she did and, at later periods in her life, might have had one with other men. Robins had an overriding sense of obligation to original partnerships, to her own with George Parks, and obligations of the men she knew to their wives. She would treat the George Parks dilemma of her life in other ways. Here in *The New Moon*, Robins found an initial creative release through the series of transformations which allowed her to speak as male narrator, accept blame for the death of a loved one, and free her conscience through the pain, suffering, and the imminent death of that narrator. In this way she was able to depict both Monroe's and Dorothy's personalities as versions of her own. While Robins satirized Milly Monroe's superstitions, she most certainly counted *The New Moon* as a fortunate development in her own literary aspirations. The book's title became her good-luck symbol for the rest of her life. She adopted Florence Bell's habit of looking for the new moon on the horizon every month in order to wish upon it while she rubbed a coin; then she recorded the event in her diary. Robins thus gave private associations fictional veils and added a dimension to her creative power.

Robins began writing *The New Moon* in early September, when she returned from a holiday in Westmorland with a resolve to work at it steadily. Within three weeks she was ready to begin assembling her company for Manchester productions of *Hedda Gabler* and *The Master Builder*. Amid her business arrangements and hours spent restudying Hedda and Hilda, and instead of accepting an offer to return to the Garrick to play in Pinero's new play, she became involved in further revisions of *The New Moon* and neglected almost all other commitments. She admitted to Bell in mid-October that the novel had "absorbed me curiously, for I didn't begin to get into it really until two or three weeks or so ago" (ER to FB, October 19, 1894). Heinemann was clamoring to see and publish *The New Moon*, unlike her earlier work, but Robins was determined to assert artistic control over her story.

Plans for Staging *Little Eyolf*

Three weeks of rehearsals began on November 6 for the Manchester productions of her Ibsen plays. During this time, the Danish-Norwegian edition of Ibsen's next play, *Little Eyolf*, arrived; and on December 7, the week after she returned from Manchester, Robins participated in the copyright performance. This public reading in Norwegian secured Heinemann's control over English staging and publishing rights. In a sense, the questions surrounding the future production of this latest play overshadowed Robins's revivals of her two most successful Ibsen roles during the last week of November. Henry James read the new play in successive segments as he received them, and he wrote Robins and Heinemann of his reactions. He was almost exclusively concerned with the acting opportunities that the play allowed Robins. Archer viewed Robins more as a producer who, given the right ensemble, would welcome a supporting role. In fact, Robins immediately felt more drawn to the part of Asta, the supposed half sister of Alfred Allmers, than to the more demanding role as his wife, Rita, a volatile woman who is starved for passion. Eyolf, the child of Rita and Alfred, drowns when he is lured off to the fjord by the intriguing Ratwife; he is unable to swim because of an injury incurred as an infant when his mother and father neglected him while they made love. The child's death motivates self-examinations, and an incestuous taboo against Alfred's love for Asta is lifted; they grew up as brother and sister but in fact are not related. Robins's preference for the supporting role says much about her own character; Asta is the voice of moral propriety who accepts a marriage proposal from another admirer to strengthen her demand that Alfred and Rita confront their own relationship.

Who would play Rita? This became the question of the hour in Robins's correspondence with Archer, Heinemann, James, and Bell. Robins had recently received an unhappy letter from Marion Lea, who accused Robins of always underrating her. Accordingly, Robins suggested to Archer that Lea would gladly leave her "barnstorming" in America and would come to London "as soon as we are ready for her" (ER to FB, November 25, 1894). Archer recognized Lea's suitability for the role, so as a result his objections were all the more cogent. He wrote to Robins: "Believe me, your friendship blinds you in this. I have always thought that Miss Lea's marriage was a most fortunate thing for you. . . . I positively cannot, either as your friend or as Ibsen's, aid and abet you in such a debauch of generosity (WA to ER, November 26, 1894).

Archer's scolding, in part motivated because he found Lea "absolutely impervious to any suggestions of mine" at rehearsals, was only the first of many problems in efforts to produce *Little Eyolf*, efforts which Robins at one point completely abandoned. Her instinct told her to invite Janet Achurch, the most talented Ibsen performer she knew. Achurch had amazed the public with her creation of Nora Helmer. On the first day of January, Robins made an agreement with Janet Achurch. She reported excitedly to Bell, "She gives up a princely salary in Australia and all kinds of luxuries and glories for my bare statement that if I produce *Little Eyolf* she shall do Rita!" (ER to FB, January 1, 1895).

The actual production of the play proved a great deal harder to arrange. At different times, George Alexander and Charles Wyndham were interested in producing the play. Robins felt obliged to turn over the rights to the Independent Theatre, now co-managed by Dorothy Leighton and Charles Charrington, because Archer advised her not to interfere with Shaw's claim to Achurch's services for the Independent Theatre production of Shaw's *Candida* that he was promoting. Finally, when Shaw himself accused her of withholding the play, she proposed the founding of a new organization to sponsor an independent production. This would not be until November 1896; as an actress, Robins was to remain idle from the end of her Manchester Ibsen series of November 1894 until her première of *Little Eyolf* two years later. Her inactivity on the stage was hardly by design. Nor was Robins as committed to playing Ibsen exclusively as the record of her performances might indicate. Publicly, she may have projected the image of actress with too high a standard for regular dramatic roles to satisfy her, for she rejected as many opportunities as were denied her. In fact, because—in secret—she wrote two plays that featured women protagonists, she perceived herself as someone who needed to control the roles she played and how she performed.

Her circumstances at the time when she was being considered for the lead in Pinero's new play, *The Notorious Mrs. Ebbsmith*, illustrate her priorities, which she honored even at the risk of being criticized by her friends. When she was approached in October 1894 by Compton, Hare's business manager, about the possibility of her acting in the new Pinero play at the Garrick, she expressed her fear of being the object of negotiations. She wrote to Bell, "Pinero's next play will be a fiery ordeal and I, well—I'm not in a competitive mood. . . . I know nothing about the part but I dread its being offered to me. I could explain if we were together" (ER to FB, October 9, 1894). The hint that she might forfeit another role prompted Bell to object at length, and so four days later Robins was obliged to explain her position. "There is a side of me unfitted for public life," she wrote. She then indicated how the play might be promoted: "Such a man as Pinero has not written for the English stage for 50 years and more; such a play as *The Second Mrs. Tanqueray* has not appeared on the English speaking stage for longer still—his next venture is of the widest *importance* as well as interest." She explained: "There is a lot more at stake than an individual success and I think I must tell him if he asks me to do the part that my sense of the responsibility he would lay on me would make me a poor soldier in such a battle. Don't you see I want to *act*. I don't want to vindicate Pinero and the English Drama and Elizabeth Robins. It's too much" (ER to FB, October 13, 1894).

Robins's battle imagery proved accurate when Mrs. Patrick Campbell came to her in desperation. For Robins it was as if her attempt to paint a sympathetic portrait of the struggling artist in "The Coming Woman" had returned to haunt her. She wrote in a long account to Bell, "She is apparently (has been for about three years) nursing a sense of injury because I 'shut her out of my life, allowed her to tell me all her secrets and gave not one in return.'" When Robins spoke of her plans for *Little Eyolf*, Campbell begged for the chance to play Rita. Then, almost in order to deflect Campbell from insisting on being involved in her Ibsen plans, Robins encouraged her to pursue the possibility that Hare wanted her for the Pinero play. "I of course advised her to ask Pinero if it's true and if so, go for it" (ER to FB, January 15, 1895). Two days later Robins reported that Campbell had settled with Pinero, and Robins's sacrifice of this role proved a wiser move than she might have anticipated. The critics were less than favorable to the play.

Criticism of Robins for having declined such a professional opportunity lingered, however, even among Robins's friends. In early March she reported that James "rated me for refusing the Garrick offer—indeed seemed quite angry, almost rude." She admitted that she could not "harbor any ill will" toward him, for she was sure that James "simply doesn't know the situation" (ER to FB, March 7, 1895). There was a great deal more about Robins's inactive stage life that James had little knowledge of, in regard to both *Little Eyolf* and several other opportunities. On the day before she heard of the Pinero role, one of the Gatti brothers, co-manager of the Adelphi, called on her to propose that she play his new heroine. Later in the month, Robins wrote to Bell that Carr, in offering Robins the part of the adventuress in his new adaptation of a play by Sardou, had irritated her by his "precautions and diplomacy and secrecy" (ER to FB, March 24, 1895). Furthermore, the Viscountess Maidstone asked Robins to perform Clytemnestra in an amateur production of Aeschylus's Orestian trilogy. Robins told Bell how appalled she was at the naive assumptions the Viscountess made about the theater. She concluded, "There's a lot else about the matter but it isn't worth ink" (ER to FB, October 24, 1894).

In a matter dearer to her heart, the new Ibsen play, Robins continued to experience disappointment. On January 15, 1895, Alexander sent word, through William Archer, that he was too busy with Oscar Wilde's new play (*The Importance of Being Earnest*) to consider *Little Eyolf*. Charles Wyndham had been seriously considering *Little Eyolf* during January, but on the thirtieth he rejected the play. In early March 1895, Archer visited Robins to report that Richard Mansfield was planning to do *Candida* in New York and that Janet Achurch had the first refusal rights to the title part. Archer advised her to release Achurch from the agreement. Robins consented, and Achurch took advantage of the New York engagement to stage *A Doll's House*.

"'Gustus Frederick"

During this period, the winter of 1894–95, Elizabeth Robins took renewed interest in her writing. More boldly than before, she experimented with plots, techniques, and themes which had little to do with her own life. In early December, she asked Bell for permission to "use" an account Bell had told her about "the girl at Clarence who had her child so blithely without the formality of marriage" (ER to FB, December 5, 1894). Three days later, she recorded in her diary that she had finished " 'Gustus Frederick." The story appeared in the March 1895, *New Review*. Robins shaped the incident to expose the hypocritical attitudes of a woman who is devoted to charity work. Mrs. Constance Willoughby discovers that a young daughter of one of her regular charity women has chosen to have a child, 'Gustus Frederick, out of wedlock, and she lets her younger unmarried sister know how much she disapproves. Robins presents the poverty-stricken woman's single motherhood as a matter of choice, not necessity; and when Mrs. Willoughby ridicules her sister for remaining unmarried, thereby being a "disgrace to the family," Mary replies, "A disgrace to the family? . . . I knew there was a bond of some sort between 'Gustus Frederick and me."[22]

"Valentine Cobb"

Robins shared with Florence Bell her every literary project, and the Yorkshire writer did the same with her own work (Bell produced during these years a three-volume novel, *The Story of Ursula*, and a volume of children's plays). In addition, though, Robins got a great deal of literary advice from William Archer. Her next literary effort, "Valentine Cobb," demonstrates that in some cases Archer's thoroughgoing criticisms stifled her creative powers. The 196-

page typescript indicates that Robins stopped work on the story in 1895, and in explaining why she preserved the document, she noted forty years later that she saved the typescript in order to "keep me in mind of how W.A. steadied and guided my early steps in the direction of novel-writing." She added that Archer's early tutoring had made her capable of writing, shortly afterward, her first long novel without counsel from anyone.[23] Her tale suggests with clever irony that a young woman and a young poet, Valentine Cobb, have saved each other. She describes her treatment of the poet as a "satire on the 'school' of which [Richard] Le Gallienne was perhaps the head." Le Gallienne's effusive romanticism was conspicuous with his publication of several volumes of poetry and his critical column in the *Star*, signed "Logroller." Archer had his own reasons for satirizing Le Gallienne, for Le Gallienne had ridiculed Archer's essay on suicide.

Robins's Valentine Cobb is a self-possessed romantic poet. Maysie Loudan, the very young daughter of a musician, becomes his copyist. When Valentine first acknowledges that he has fallen in love with her, he allows her to "beguile him for a Saturday or two," as it "made the little thing so happy!" ("VC," 96). Robins's focus, though, is on the awakening of the woman's passions, and she credits Valentine with more genuine feeling as he grows beyond the way he first sees Maysie as his. Valentine comes to Maysie after the collapse of his "great and tragic passion of the year before" ("VC," 96). His pain, from the wound inflicted by an older woman, is healed by this younger genius, who restores him. Robins portrayed him as a man who cannot confess his past (a theme to which Robins would return, with more direct focus on the woman's point of view). Archer, in three pages of notes, proposed a complex continuation of the action in order to demonstrate that Valentine prides himself on his indiscretions after marriage. Archer also stereotypically described the jealousy of the forty-year-old woman who first corrupted Valentine.[24]

In contrast, the character of Robins's who interferes is not a vixen but an older man, the uncle of Valentine. This uncle asks Maysie's father for permission to marry Maysie and then discovers that she has pledged herself to Valentine. In Robins's typescript, the reformed Valentine Cobb is worthier for Maysie than the uncle with his improper advances. The focus on Valentine's true affections defuses the satire, however, and probably indicated to Robins that she could not simultaneously examine a woman's serious emotions and parody romanticized male attitudes.

Robins recorded her progress on "Valentine Cobb" and hinted, in her correspondence with Florence Bell, at her reasons for abandoning it. "It would have to be a longish thing I find" (ER to FB, January 28, 1895). She also confessed that the attraction of the piece had worn off because she had disclosed the plot to other friends. "I'm let down—in fact horribly bothered at having taken the Crackanthorpes into my confidence" (ER to FB, January 30, 1895). Robins was particularly sensitive to the fact that young Hubert Crackanthorpe, good friend of Richard Le Gallienne and himself a rising star among the literati, had learned, by piecing together information from his mother and from Sydney Pawling, Heinemann's partner, that C. E. Raimond was Elizabeth Robins.

Later in the spring, the exposure of Oscar Wilde's private life, in a series of trials concerned with libel that accused him of homosexual sodomy, would dampen the satiric spirit that had thrived since his first forays into the artistic world. In late 1896, Hubert Crackanthorpe would be embroiled in a bitter struggle to defend his own actions in taking the married sister of Richard Le Gallienne as his lover after his own wife left him. His mother, Blanche Crackanthorpe, arrived in Paris in November 1896. Hubert and his estranged wife lived there together as a foursome with their two lovers, and Blanche's appearance on the scene precipitated the events that led to Hubert's suicide. These two events, the public exposure of Wilde and the death of one of the rising young writers of the 1890s, soon made Robins's "Valentine Cobb" outdated. The real events in Robins's stage life had made "The Coming Woman" too prophetic; by the same token her closeness to the Crackanthorpes prevented her from completing "Valentine Cobb."

Robins had already withdrawn from any negotiations to produce *Little Eyolf* when she became seriously ill in March 1895 with the influenza that took many lives. The specter of illness figured importantly in Robins's split career, however. Repeated colds and flu prevented her from making a total commitment to theater. Independent productions often drained her to the point of collapse. In subsequent years, recurring illnesses led her to try "cures" at various health spas. There is little doubt that she saw writing as a less demanding alternative than performing. From her sickbed, she reflected upon her own behavior and her own personality in the mood of one not hopeful about recovering from her illness. It was in this private document where she confessed that "I sometimes suppress and I sometimes embroider" accounts to her nearest friends. She added, revealingly: "If I see anyone trying to ferret me out, my greatest delight is to baffle and elude my pursuer and leave him contentedly following a false scent. I don't try to defend this little eccentricity. At times I deplore it." She could only regret that her friends would "not find me or any explanation of me in any one's description or in any letter or diary of my own" (ER "Will").

Robins further admitted, "My 'optimism' (!) is wholesale and blandly unprincipled. I will insist all is well, till all is over. It is my infirmity—my friends must bear with it" (ER "Will"). Robins's letters to Bell, characterized both by true intimacy and the projection of a playfully deceiving self-image, must be read in this context. In later years, she used her private writing more and more as a search for the truth of her character,[25] but she recognized that she was fatally possessed with the power of invention. While her fictions spun from her mind and through her creative metamorphosis into the imagined stories authored by C. E. Raimond, she continued to keep private the most intimate aspects of her life.

"The Mirkwater"

Her theatrical discussions, especially those with Archer, James, Fletcher, and Bell, no doubt prompted her to write for the stage. It was as natural a move for Robins as it was to take on the role of producer when she was determined that she would do *Hedda Gabler*. Acting was not enough. Playwriting was one means by which she could control her choices. In June 1895, barely two months after the publication of *The New Moon*, Robins reported to Bell, "I've just finished the first draft of the last act of my beautiful play, and I'm aweary. Oh but it's been fun!" (ER to FB, June 3, 1895). As with "Valentine Cobb," she credited Archer with help on the project, and her diary contains many references to meetings with him.

"The Mirkwater," Robins's first completed full-length play, is a suspenseful mystery about the disappearance, in the autumn before the action takes place, of Felicia Vincent's older sister, Mary. The young doctor, James Theobold, is in love with Felicia. His mother opposes the match and suspects Felicia's complicity in her sister's disappearance. Mrs. Theobold plots to haunt Felicia with vague insinuations of the young woman's guilt because she, Mrs. Theobold, has read in "Spiritualism Unveiled" that a murderer confessed his crime after being terrorized into believing that witnesses knew more than they did. Robins treats Mrs. Theobold's pressure upon the girl as an illegitimate maneuver. Still, the evidence that the sister has drowned is enough to prompt officials to order the dredging of the river Mirkwater. In a highly charged defense of her character, Felicia discloses to James the real story behind her sister's disappearance: Mary Vincent committed suicide when she knew that she was dying of breast cancer. Robins indicates that complicity in suicide is as abhorrent as murder, then absolves Felicia by having her reveal that her older sister had been more traumatically—psychologically—scarred when she discovered her father's unfaithfulness.

By making the effect of Mary's discovery of the father's licentiousness into something physical, Robins implicitly takes a feminist stance which becomes explicit in her later fiction and plays. Here, women are victims, one through her illness, the other through her complicity in the suicide. Robins would almost certainly have known that Alice James, sister of the novelist, lived out her struggle with cancer to the end. This first play suffers, however, because Robins mixed her parody of spiritualists with patterns of nineteenth-century melodrama and relied too much upon sudden reversals and contrived intrigue.

About a month after she completed "The Mirkwater," Robins showed it to George Alexander. She reported to Bell that she had had a pleasant talk with Alexander and had told him that he was not likely to see the play in printed form, thus giving him total rights should he decide to stage it (ER to FB, July 9, 1895). A few days later, she wrote that Campbell had taken another part from her. This time it was *Tess of the D'Urbervilles*, a stage adaptation of Hardy's novel, and Robins was not as willing to let it go as she had been to forfeit Pinero's heroines, partly because she learned that Hardy himself preferred her for Tess (ER to FB, July 12, 1895).

During the summer, Heinemann offered to put in a good word for the work of C. E. Raimond with the editor of the *Century Magazine* if she thought she would like to pursue the chance to publish in America. Immediately, Robins sketched for Bell an idea for an Anglo-American love story.

Less than a week later, on August 8, Robins began an essay, "An American Actress at Balmoral Castle," describing in some detail her experiences playing before the Queen two years previously. Most of the essay's color comes in her description of her anxiety about being presented to the Queen. The rest of the company had a formal audience on the previous night, when amateurs at court presented *A Scrap of Paper* to the actors, but Robins had spent her extra day sightseeing in Edinburgh and had to hope that her Countess Zicka merited some recognition. After she performed, she rushed to her dressing room to change from costume to a borrowed gown, and was standing in her combinations lathering her face when a knock came at the door to "Come as you are." She told the dresser lacing her up to "skip every other hole" as she prepared to go before the Queen. In contrast to others who later remembered only the look of their own hands as the Queen received them, Robins recalled "the dumpy figure, the stretched shiny red skin, the dull worn-down teeth, set like wooden pegs apart in the good-humored mouth." Earlier in the evening, she had caught sight of the Queen being wheeled and lifted into her place, and during the performance asked what foreign bird made the curious cackling noise she heard. (It was the Queen "appreciating the comic points.")[26]

"Miss de Maupassant"

In September 1895, the *New Review* published another C. E. Raimond story, a satire on publishers who were desperate to secure the fiction of a pseudonymous writer. "Miss de Maupassant" parodies the raging taste for sensationalism in fiction, a rage spearheaded by Hubert Crackanthorpe, who by then had the reputation of being an English Maupassant. More particularly, however, "Miss de Maupassant" ridicules publishers' inability to accept the fact that a woman can write what the publishers are hungry for. Robins cleverly turns the issue back against the woman writer by exposing her work as a derivative exercise. Thus she replicates the literary house of mirrors so characteristic of late Victorian London. Just as the parodies of Ibsen plays in *Punch* brought more and more attention to the Norwegian dramatist, Robins used her pseudonym to make legitimate, by means of satire, the New Woman writer. What had seemed at first to be "the biggest thing since Madame Bovary"[27] is finally shown to be derivative. The editor is spared his task of declining the manuscript when he receives a telegram from his partner at the office: "All the striking part sheer plagiarism—Merrimam" (246). Robins's notes indicate that her story spoofs publisher John Lane, whose first *Yellow Book* had appeared early in 1894, with Le Gallienne, Crackanthorpe, George Moore, and Arthur Symons the principal contributors.

There are hints, too, that Robins intended to satirize Heinemann himself, who had published Crackanthorpe's *Wreckage* in 1893. In placing the story, she took extra precautions to conceal the identity of C. E. Raimond. She enlisted the help of others to write corrections into the typescript so her handwriting would not be recognized. She also took delight in further confounding editors who might want to know who C. E. Raimond was. Just before "Miss de Maupassant" appeared, she arranged for Bell to type and post from any small town through which Bell was traveling a note from C. E. Raimond to Oswald Crawfurd, an editor who had rejected the story. Crawfurd had been spreading the rumor that C. E. Raimond was Mrs. Crackanthorpe (mother of Hubert), Robins's literary friend, herself a promoter and satirizer of new morals. Crawfurd must have been further confounded when he received the message from the phantom C. E. Raimond. The note thanked him politely for his refusal; then it offered him the next C. E. Raimond story: "When I settle down again in a few weeks' time I mean to exorcise a ghost that haunts me— by making it into a gruesome Xmas story. Shall you care to see it I wonder?" (quoted from ER to FB, August 21, 1895).

This ghost story became "The Threlkeld Ear," in which Robins imitated Edgar Allan Poe's style. Continuing her psychological investigation of the supernatural, Robins wrote "The Father of Lies" and published it in *Chapman's Magazine*. In this story, the young male narrator who is about to marry well learns from his fiancée that his father falsified his military records in India. The son has rejected his father's high moral principles, only to discover that his own decadence is inherited. Documents implicating his father are mysteriously destroyed as soon as he reads them. This piece, along with an unpublished story, "Stall B.25," illustrate the age's fascination with the supernatural and with strange twists of plot. In all of these stories, Robins was exploring her range, was successfully adopting a male persona, and was responding to popular themes. Almost as often as she dashed off a playful story, William Archer sent her studied criticism, often advising revisions along more complex and philosophical lines when Robins's instinct was to be whimsical and to write clever satire. Robins labeled Archer's proposed revision to "Stall B.25": "Condensed by W.A.," but in fact his criticisms also suggested a whole new beginning. He closed his note with a more telling reference to his need for her than many other documents which survive: "Dear one, I hold you to my heart and bless you and kiss you sweetest one—I kiss your eyes and lips" (WA to ER, n.d., from "Stall B.25" MS, ER Papers, Fales). Robins had heard such protestations of love before and perhaps had more affection for Archer than for other men, but she had already sublimated her energies into her artistic expression.[28]

"The Silver Lotus"

Between late fall 1895 and the following February, Robins wrote one of her most hauntingly somber plays. "The Silver Lotus" is the story of a woman's alcoholism treated with sophistication and complexity. The drama shifts alliances so that our reactions shift, from horror at the way that Eleanor, the twenty-nine-year-old wife of a prominent lawyer, behaves in public to empathy for her as we see how much her husband Philip Gervais is at fault. His protection of her—his unwillingness to confront the problem directly—has driven her to further despair. Yet Robins gives sympathetic attention even to the manipulating husband.

Although the central character is clearly Philip—evidence that Robins was consciously creating a vehicle for an actor-manager—the four women characters and their relationships with each other offer some of the play's more interesting dramatic encounters. Structurally, "The Silver Lotus" illustrates Ibsen's dramatic skill at its best; present events reveal past actions in ways that expose the lies that the main characters have been living. Only at the end do we fully appreciate that Eleanor was driven to drink because Philip blamed her for the death of their children. The play is well crafted; Robins's symbolic use of the necklace of the play's title is especially effective. Philip describes to his mother the events of their last night of entertaining in London; and at this early point, we sympathize with a husband, who, like Mr. Rochester, locks his wife away. Fearing her drinking would be an embarrassment, he sends a note asking her not to appear downstairs for dinner with invited friends. He promises to come to see her afterward and sends her, as a gift, a small silver lotus. From this point onward, the play recalls Tennyson's "The Lotus Eaters." Eleanor asks Philip's mother, "Did you ever think that the person who discovered how to make people forget would be more of a benefactor than any genius or Saviour [the] world has ever known?"[29]

Philip may have meant the gift to signify reconciliation. Eleanor sees it as his further penance, a way of blaming her for her inability to forget. The silver lotus acquires a double meaning for everyone as the play progresses. Camilla, whom Eleanor has earlier accused of wanting to form a liaison with Philip, returns in act 3 in order to collect the lotus as a memento of Eleanor. Philip accuses Camilla of wanting it because "you were afraid you might forget her!" ("SL," III, 16). They argue bitterly, and Camilla implores him to believe that a relationship between them, even if unthinkable now, might be possible in the future. She leaves the lotus behind, and he is staring at it as the final curtain falls.

Symbolism contributes to the play's effectiveness in probing the pain in a relationship in which the central memory is the death of children. Stylistically "The Silver Lotus" has much in common with Ibsen's *Little Eyolf*. Robins, however, made more explicit the delusions and betrayals between husband and wife. Ibsen was often attacked for his vague symbolic references. His critics thought that Solness and Hilda's private allusions to "castles in the air" and the Allmers' preoccupation with the eyes that return to haunt them were ridiculous devices overused to the point of absurdity. In "The Silver Lotus," Robins's use of symbolism is more engaging than that found in Ibsen's late plays.

Robins's correspondence with Bell indicates that further plans for acting and producing began to compete with her contemplated revision of her own play. First, there was a renewed plan to stage D. G. Rossetti's poem "Sister Helen" with musical accompaniment. In addition, a more concrete production opportunity arose when Bell, while traveling through Germany the previous August, had alerted Robins to the possibilities of an English version of *Mariana*, the work of Spanish playwright José Echegaray. Robins had begun negotiations with the English translator of Echegaray's plays, James Graham, to secure the acting rights. "*I shall have this play after all,*" she promised with double underlining in her letter to Bell (ER to FB, August 8, 1895). The following February, Robins worried that George Alexander or some other manager might offer Graham a very large fee for the chance to do the play. She knew she had no real claim to the part, nor did her own version of the play stand any chance of being staged unless she settled first with Graham. At first, Graham insisted on a payment of fifty pounds. She convinced him that her promise of production was better than outright purchase of the play, like Augustin Daly's purchase of American rights. Graham subsequently granted Robins the stage rights to *Mariana* on the condition that she produce it before March 1, 1897. "I'm to have a solid year in which to do something with *Mariana*," she reported to Bell in February, with a hint of victory (ER to FB, February 14, 1896).

Inevitably, plans for *Mariana* demanded Robins's full attention. She began her preparations with high hopes; Henry James had offered his assistance. In *Theatre and Friendship*, Robins credited James with close collaboration. Yet the revised typescripts (culminating in Robins's heavily annotated "side" to her role) plainly show that Robins herself strove for a speakable and actable text. The characters in the Graham version speak a stilted, formal prose. The acting version, a product of the collaboration that Robins oversaw, attests to her ear for crisp dialogue.

As with the Ibsen projects, Robins first approached the most respected commercial managers. During the spring of 1896 she offered *Mariana* to at least four commercial managers, Alexander, Carr, Tree, and Wyndham. Most often she read the play to them in meetings that lasted over several days.[30] Their rejections may have indicated that it was growing late in the season to plan a new production, but more than one actor-manager probably also thought the play served Robins better than it did the actor who would play opposite her.

Little did Robins realize in February 1896 that it would take her the entire year to mount the production. Nor did she realize that her first mention to Bell of "The Silver Lotus" by title would also be her last. She wrote on February 22, 1896, of having set the play aside to work on *Mariana*. Even though she considered it complete, she commented that she would need to give it another six weeks' work before it would be ready for Bell's reaction. Robins later wrote of publishing the play, but she never revised it to her satisfaction. The existing typescript nevertheless shows her command of dramatic form. She had warned Bell after seeing her first story in print that "so long as any theatrical scheme" was "to the fore," she had no desire to write (ER to FB, February 2, 1894). Now, after producing two novels, several short stories, a long autobiographical sketch, two full-length plays and a few shorter ones, she could hardly deny that writing was a second occupation and a serious one at that. Still, in spite of her literary accomplishments, when the conditions were hers and the role a worthwhile one, she preferred the life of an actress.

The public saw Elizabeth Robins exclusively as an interpreter of Ibsen heroines, but her own self-image was broader. As playwright and novelist, she sought fuller command of her own destiny.

4 | Toward the New Century
Further Ambitions, Wider Horizons, 1896–1900

> We have only to go on steadily and doggedly from this beginning to a kind of little theatre for the Minority which will year by year (for a few weeks or a few months) give a series of performances of plays not to be expected at the regular theatres.
>
> —Elizabeth Robins to Florence Bell, expressing for the first time her plans for the New Century Theatre, September 1, 1896

> I *have* got a market for the moment and if I had gumption I'd profit by it. But then why should I suddenly develop gumption any more than two heads?
>
> —Elizabeth Robins to Florence Bell, upon the success of *The Open Question*, August 22, 1899

T*HE SCENE*: The fast-darkening London art studio of the renowned painter Sir Edward Burne-Jones on a cold December afternoon in 1895. The artist asks his visitor, Elizabeth Robins, whether he should light a lamp. She says no, preferring, with Burne-Jones's acquiescence, the dim glow of the fireplace. Shadows deepen. The visitor's mission is to ask Burne-Jones's approval of her project to stage a dramatic adaptation of "Sister Helen," the short narrative poem by the painter's pre-Raphaelite "brother," Dante Gabriel Rossetti.

Burne-Jones catches the enthusiasm of the actress-producer. He inquires about the opening stanzas and retrieves the book to help her recall the lines she knows almost by heart. Again he asks if she wants more light. Again her answer is no. She kneels to make the best use of the light from the fireplace. In so doing she assumes the position of Rossetti's Helen when she burns the effigy of her lover, thereby inducing her lover's father to drive her to her doom.

Notes on the Scene: On December 12, Robins teased Florence Bell with a hint of her newly inspired plans. "Burne-Jones made me a thrilling and glorious proposition—no time to tell you of it."[1] In a subsequent letter Robins explained that the proposal was not, as Bell had guessed, Burne-Jones's offer to paint her, but "something much better." To Bell she described the meeting with the renowned artist:

We fell to talking about Rossetti and B.J. left off maundering and became sane and delightful and told me heavenly things about the work and enthusiasm and fun of those young days. Then he spoke of Rossetti personally— his wife—her suicide—Rossetti's burying his poems in her coffin, etc., etc., and by that road we came to speak of "Sister Helen" and my old dream of doing it—acting it with a musical setting. B.J. took fire and we talked like mad. He threw back his head after I described how I "Saw" the picture and the effect and he said: "I tell you what, Miss Robins! There's no one in England knows so well as I just what pictures Rossetti had in mind when he wrote those marvelous lines. If you do this thing come to me or let me come to you and for love of my old friend I'll design the scene and dresses and 'We'll do it beautifully.'" And before we parted we shook hands over the compact. [ER to FB, n.d. (December 1895)]

Looking back over Burne-Jones's sketches and the documents which trace the lengthy but ultimately unsuccessful effort to see "Sister Helen" staged, Robins attached a note: "This brings to life a whole chapter." Indeed, the fragment of the chapter she completed typifies what she claimed elsewhere was the theme of her autobiography, that her high ambitions could themselves be the substance of her stage life. There was thrill in the planning, hoping, and projection of a dream and a goal.

Burne-Jones's promise to provide scenic designs excited Robins and fired her with hope for the music that she knew was essential to the play's atmosphere. She discussed with several people the idea that the Norwegian composer Edvard Grieg might compose music. This possibility seemed so desirable that Robins arranged for several letters of endorsement to be sent to Grieg in a packet with her appeal. She facetiously speculated about his reaction to the "overwhelming batch" of letters: "I see Grieg *tottering* at the impact! And then reeling deliriously to the piano he will pick the new masterpiece off the keyboard and send it to us by the next post!" (ER to FB, January 22, 1896). Robins's energy for the project was prodigious. She met Burne-Jones for several lengthy sessions and enlisted the support of a great number of acquaintances.

Given the nature of the Rossetti poem "Sister Helen," it is remarkable yet fitting that Robins's idea for a dramatization captured the enthusiasm of so many of her friends and associates. Sister Helen and her young brother address each other as she burns her wax effigy of the lover who wronged her; she refuses to retract her curse despite the pleas of the lover's father. Each repetition of the refrain, with the slightest of alterations, heightens the mood of the moment. Sister Helen refuses to forgive her lover and so meets death herself. For Robins, the attraction of the character lay not in Sister Helen's one-line remark in each stanza but in the captivating mood set by the rigid verse scheme, the intensity of emotion, which she conveys in the short speeches, and the chance to work with a team of artists to bring to life on the stage a pre-Raphaelite vision. Sister Helen defies the social order and is doomed to hell but turns the torture of her sacrifice into an elegant penance. She is the evil woman sanctified by the justice of her act.

Florence Bell responded to Robins's original letter with a mild warning about Burne-Jones's reputation with young women. At this point in her life, such worries never stopped Robins from recruiting collaborators among artists, writers, and performers. Burne-Jones's decision to participate inspired others to support the actress's project. After Edvard Grieg declined her invitation to compose the music, Robins approached William Wallace, who composed his "Sister Helen Suite" with the dramatization in mind. Finally, the project was kept from production only by the failure to find the right companion piece for dramatization. Different projects engaged Robins as she looked for a play to complete the double bill.

Elizabeth Robins's acting opportunities during this period were all ones that she herself had chosen. She had not deliberately withdrawn from the theater. However, she believed too strongly in the ensemble and in the collaborative work of the theater to turn the New Century into a vehicle for her own talent. Many planned productions never materialized; the projected "theatre of the minority," for example, which aimed to set a higher standard for drama, never saw the dawn of the twentieth century.

Whenever circumstances discouraged her production efforts, her fiction engaged her attention. Indeed, during the last years of the decade, writing became her primary pursuit. For years, she had hopes of returning to America to present a repertory of Ibsen plays; in light of this ambition, her 1898 performance of *Hedda Gabler* in New York was a disappointment. The American trip served her better by connecting her to her American roots, the source and the setting of her long novel, *The Open Question*, which she was in the midst of writing. Just as *The Open Question* deserves reevaluation as a fin-de-siècle novel, other aspects of her literary career are underrecognized. Her published memoirs and historical accounts of the theater give William Archer much of the credit for the New Century Theatre. In fact, the project reflected *her* vision as much as his. She used her artistic directorship of the New Century Theatre to promote her goals for the idealistic theater by which she sought to counter the profession's crass commercialism and its subordination of women. If she failed as a theater organizer, it was because she had too much faith in artists' ability to work as a team and too few associates who could discharge responsibility. Perhaps, too, she failed because, once she began writing, she could devote only part of her time to profitless theatrical ventures.

"Below the Salt" and Other Stories, 1896

In the midst of her translation sessions with James, her meetings to plan "Sister Helen," and her appointments with various managers, Robins found time in the early part of 1896 to continue work on a series of short stories. Several of the C. E. Raimond stories had appeared in periodicals, and now Heinemann offered to collect them in one volume.[2] She barely considered the stories a serious effort. Between May and September she was distracted from her own writing because she devoted a great deal of time—most certainly because it provided her with surer income—to translating the writing of Norwegian explorer of the Arctic Fridtjof Nansen.[3] She did not otherwise identify the project, but it may have been a translation of *Farthest North* from the Norwegian. This two-volume work appeared in a number of editions in 1897. Robins many times recorded her progress on the translation in her diary and on September 21 received her proofs. Archer may have secured the work for her; in 1893, Longmans, Green, and Company had issued his translation of Nansen's *Eskimo Life.* Robins later used her knowledge of Nansen's journeys to the Arctic in her second Alaska novel, *Come and Find Me.*

By the time *"Below the Salt" and Other Stories* had been published on October 1, Robins was fully engaged in plans for her next dramatic production. These collected short stories, originally appearing in 1895 and 1896 in *Chapman's Magazine* and the *New Review*, presented a broader range of character studies than she had previously attempted. "Below the Salt" serves as the title for one story and the theme of the collection: servant life below the stairs. By using dialect and focusing on lower-class characters, Robins was capitalizing on the current popularity of realism in literature. In the story "Vroni" especially, Robins's dialogue in many places follows the format of a play. In these sections, quotation marks are eliminated; each speaker is listed at the head of a paragraph; gestures, movement, and private thoughts appear in parenthetical stage directions. As with Robins's other methods of eliminating the narrator, she moves her readers closer to the subjects and in that way treats each woman with greater sympathy by allowing her to speak directly. The stories in her volume *Below the Salt* might be seen as exercises for the developing writer and for the novice playwright as well. Taken together, the stories attest to Robins's compassionate interest in the underside of life in the London she now considered home.

Little Eyolf, Mariana, and the New Century Theatre, 1896–1897

Although Robins published often, her interest in her fictional craft was still a diversion from her principal occupation in the theater. Toward the end of 1896 Robins again found herself in a position to take charge of another Ibsen première. *Little Eyolf* had been in print almost two years without receiving the glamorous commercial production that William Archer was sure it merited, without even the Independent Theatre's production of the play. Robins had ceded to the Independent Theatre her stage rights to the play, but she became upset when Bernard Shaw spread rumors that it was her fault that *Little Eyolf* had not been produced. She considered the long controversy over the play and on September 1 decided to take steps. She thought her forfeit of production rights to the play had been clear, but her repeated clashes with Shaw awakened in her a new resolve.

From the time of his attempt to interview her during preparations for *The Master Builder*, Robins knew that Shaw was at least one part scoundrel. Others, too, found him self-serving in this period when he wrote criticism for the *Saturday Review* and was trying to establish himself as playwright. Toward Robins, however, Shaw was particularly antagonistic. The clever insults he circulated privately and in print did not assist her career at the time and did not improve her professional reputation in years to come. Just after Robins heard that Shaw wanted Janet Achurch for *Candida*, she followed Archer's warning and wrote to William Heinemann, "Do what you like with *Little Eyolf*" (quoted in EBook, March 12, 1895). She made clear, in a letter on October 25 to Dorothy Leighton, the new co-director of the Independent Theatre, that she had no personal claim on the play. Robins hoped Leighton would consider Achurch for the part of Rita, wished her luck, and added that every part was worthy of a highly talented performer.

In mid-December 1895, Leighton brought to Robins an Independent Theatre circular which, Robins reported to Bell, acknowledged that she, Robins, had given over to the newly organized Independent Theatre her rights to *Little Eyolf* (ER to FB, December 12, 1895). Robins was perfectly content to relinquish all claim to *Little Eyolf*, probably because she knew that Charles Charrington, as co-director of the Independent Theatre (nominated for that position by Shaw), would want to use the Independent for a production of the play featuring his wife, Janet Achurch, as Rita. Although Robins had previously made an agreement with Achurch, she knew she could not work with Charrington as manager. Shaw believed that no one could play Asta as well as Elizabeth Robins, but he also knew he could not himself suggest that she do so. When fall came and Shaw met her in the street, he claimed Robins was "sitting on the copyright of *Little Eyolf*" (ER to FB, September 1, 1896). Robins also reported that he said to her, "every human soul *he* knew" took that "view of my attitude: that I didn't care about doing it myself and wouldn't let anyone else do it." Perhaps Robins's response was just what Shaw wanted; she resolved to "show the few who cared that the case was otherwise." Even as she wrote to Bell, she formulated plans to raise a subscription fund for the purposes of presenting independent productions of *Little Eyolf* and *Mariana*. If this effort succeeded, she wrote, "We have only to go on steadily and doggedly from this beginning to a kind of little theatre for the Minority."

Before Robins finished the letter, several interruptions occurred: Gerald Duckworth visited and offered to help serve on her committee; he calculated that at least two hundred pounds was pledged or anticipated, and Robins decided to publish a circular in order to solicit other subscriptions. In a sense, Robins effected her own collective to promote Ibsen, whereas Shaw, working through Leighton and Charrington and their attempts to revitalize the Independent Theatre, had not succeeded. Janet Achurch agreed to play Rita in *Little Eyolf*. The Independent Theatre subscribers guaranteed the *Eyolf-Mariana* fund that they would purchase a block of tickets. Even the previously self-serving Mrs. Patrick Campbell agreed to take the smallest role in the cast, the bewitching part of the Ratwife.

The matinée performances of *Little Eyolf* in the third week of November 1896 were so well received that a commercial syndicate, the Morocco Bound, offered to finance an extended evening run of the play. At this point the experience of *Little Eyolf* turned nightmarish for Robins. "Janet Achurch throws over her agreement with me," she wrote in her engagement book on Monday, November 30. The next afternoon she posted a letter to Florence Bell explaining the rupture. Achurch, apparently prompted by Charrington, also pregnant and, as Robins made clear later, "drugging heavily," terminated the agreement to perform under Robins's management in order to arrange her own salary with the syndicate's managers. Achurch complained that Robins sought to cheat her by negotiating on her (Achurch's) behalf. Robins was stunned by Achurch's "act of suicidal grasping and unfaith." As manager, Robins had understood their agreement would hold for all subsequent performances. Now Achurch was declaring Robins's directorship of the company dissolved. Robins declared, "O but it's a lesson! I've been long learning it—but by the Gods I've got it by heart *this* time. These people are not to be *touched*." She enumerated the distasteful tactics of Charrington, who spent the previous evening "crawling about outside" and complaining, "'My wife' was not properly featured on the bill" (ER to FB, December 1, 1896).

Then, later in the week, Robins received another blow. Achurch was asking for a sizably increased salary, 25 pounds plus 3 percent of the profits over 500 pounds, when Mrs. Campbell made a proposal, directly to the new management, to play Rita herself. Campbell deliberately underbid Achurch; the new management accepted Campbell's proposal; and as a result Achurch was left out of the cast. When Achurch heard this on Saturday, December 5, she still had two performances to get through. Shaw himself knew that, in her state of morphine addiction, she was not likely to take her release from the part calmly. Backstage after the last curtain, Achurch poured out to Robins a story of grief: she had bills to pay and a daughter to care for. Later that night Robins wrote her and proposed to send Achurch one-half of her own salary, asking her to accept it for the sake of her daughter, Nora: "I haven't got any little girl as you know, but if I had and if another woman to whom I had done some service wanted to make this acknowledgement to my child I'd let her." She concluded, "It's just between you and me and I'd rather you didn't write or speak to me about it—only don't say I mustn't—that's all" (ER to JA, December 5–6, 1896). Elizabeth Robins's gesture contradicts Shaw's assumption that Robins was assisting Campbell,[4] and later developments indicated that she and Achurch were soon reconciled.

Achurch declined the offer with a bitter reply, "Conscience money! No, thanks." She must have learned later that Robins had actually had nothing to do with her dismissal, and she sent a beneficent letter in praise of Robins's acting after watching her rival recreate her own role.[5] Even after Robins learned from William Archer the "inside history of Janet Achurch's error" (EBook, December 7), the experience left Robins unsettled. The theater had to close on Monday for rehearsals. When Campbell took up the part of Rita on Tuesday, she practically read the part, with the script strung to her waist. Shaw reviewed the production again with the new cast and slighted Robins for her Asta, now greatly out of harmony with Campbell's Rita. Mrs. Pat, he wryly remarked, "succeeded wonderfully in eliminating all unpleasantness from the play."[6]

"The houses drop, drop, drop," Robins reported to Bell at the end of Campbell's first week in the part. She accepted Bell's offer to retreat to Redcar at the end of the run, which she was sure would be only a week away. Never had she wanted so much to "come and be quiet with you and 'my family'" (ER to FB, December 12, 1896). Before her departure, however, she was at work on her next theater projects. On Monday, December 14, she participated in the copyright performance of Ibsen's *John Gabriel Borkman*. On December 20 she read *Mariana* to H. B. Irving, eldest son of the Shakespearean actor Henry Irving.

Robins began the year 1897 determined to fulfill her promise to her subscribers and to produce *Mariana* before her rights to the play expired. She undertook the enterprise with great dedication. She began to take Spanish lessons, engaged a competent stage manager, gathered around her the people on whom she knew she could rely for support, and rehearsed thoroughly. When Bell realized that she would not be able to be in town for the performances, she sent a portable tea basket for Robins to use during rehearsals at the theater. Robins was delighted with the present and appreciated the tea-making set for years afterward. At the same time, she lamented Bell's absence: "Take oh take your tea basket away and come and pat Mariana on the shoulder before each act. That's the really important thing" (ER to FB, January 9, 1897).

The role presented the challenge Robins had been hoping for, the chance to prove that she could play both passionate emotion and intellectual complexity. Mariana is deeply in love with Daniel de Montoya, but when she discovers that Daniel's father has dishonored her mother, she gives him up and marries an older suitor. On her wedding night, Daniel attempts to persuade her to flee with him, but Mariana calls in her husband, who shoots Mariana when Mariana invites him to assume she will be unfaithful. The two men duel offstage, and two shots bring the final curtain down. Although the plot in its basic outline appears melodramatic, the fine subtleties of Mariana's tragic dilemma were convincingly written and more accessible to critics and the public than were the motivations of Ibsen's heroines.

The play ran for its five scheduled matinées during the third week of February, and its favorable reception led to the next phase of Robins's scheme for a "Theatre of the Minority." She measured the success of the performances not by what the critics thought but by the overwhelmingly positive private responses. William Archer, for one, gave her a superlative review. Even Shaw paid her a kind of tribute; he found fault more with the flaws of the play than with her carefully studied tragic romance. She did resent the fact that critics applied the same standards that they used for John Hare and Charles Wyndham to the young H. B. Irving, whom Robins called the only young romantic actor on the English stage with certain potential. Generally, however, Robins felt that the production had well served her higher aims of making the subscription theater a regular enterprise. She had promised in her *Eyolf-Mariana* circular to follow these productions with others and to apply any profits to a fund for future productions. As soon as *Mariana* closed, she reported to Florence Bell how the play had helped her cause: "Many who stood aloof because of Ibsen have been won over; it has established the catholicity of our sympathies and we have quite a budget of new subscribers" (ER to FB, February 27 [or 28], 1897).

A month later, the circular for the New Century Theatre, drawn up by William Archer with Robins's encouragement and assistance, formalized Robins's long-standing dreams for a theater organized with attention more to artistic considerations than to commercial ones. In reviewing the prospectus the critic A. B. Walkley noted that the New Century Theatre announced itself not as "an end but as a means" and commended the directors for hoping that a permanently endowed theater might come of their efforts. Walkley praised the NCT for insisting on an alternative to the expensive West End theaters, where economic conditions left "'no borderland between sensational success and disastrous failure.'"[7]

The first production of the New Century Theatre was *John Gabriel Borkman*, produced for five matinées during the week of May 3. When Shaw reviewed the performance, he mocked the modesty of the stage setting and implied that the organization, with its noncommercial guidelines, was not doing Ibsen the justice his plays deserved.[8] Other reviewers found the play too gloomy to be worth more than superficial comment; Ibsen's power to arouse controversy on social issues was lost in his focus on a triangle of aging characters—Borkman, his wife, and her twin sister, Ella Reintheim, whose love Borkman has sacrificed in order to spare her fortune when he realized he was going to be ruined. Robins's Ella Reintheim changes from a woman who seeks retribution for the lost passion in her life to a woman who pleads for reconciliation. Robins confessed afterward that she had been too diplomatic in choosing to act opposite Genevieve Ward, one of her earliest employers but an actress too thoroughly schooled in the older declamatory style to be effective with Ibsen's psychologically intense drama.

After she played Ella Reintheim in *John Gabriel Borkman*, Robins took no further roles under the auspices of the New Century Theatre. Far from planning a deliberate retirement, however, she used the occasion of *John Gabriel Borkman* to begin a campaign of appeal to American managers. In so doing she made clear that the New Century Theatre existed not to serve her acting talent but to promote generally higher standards of drama. She revived the idea of staging Rossetti's poem "Sister Helen" for production. She also considered for production the plays of Congreve, Massinger, and many respected playwrights of earlier dramatic times. Henry James submitted for consideration "Summersoft," the short play he had written at Ellen Terry's request. With the advisory committee's assistance, the New Century chose *Admiral Guinea* by Robert Louis Stevenson and William E. Henley for fall performances, and Robins began work on all aspects of managing the production.

The week following *John Gabriel Borkman*, Florence Bell attempted, in Robins's phrase, to "rouse" the actress into taking better advantage of her position as the leading performer of Ibsen. Robins had for a long time considered arranging a tour to America, and now she wrote to her friend on New Century Theatre stationery: "I have written those American letters and now we'll see! I am very conscious of the effort you made last night. It was a true instinct of friendship and don't doubt but I am grateful." Robins admitted, too, that it was her nature to "shrink unspeakably" from going out to face the world until driven forth (ER to FB, May 12, 1897). A few weeks later she was introduced to Charles Frohman, an American-born theatrical manager who had several theater companies in New York and was beginning to establish theater companies in London. Robins sent to Bell her report of the evening dinner party with apologies that she had not taken full advantage of the chance to promote herself. Robins's knee was in pain from a carriage accident the night before, so she had to excuse herself early. She felt "unable to revenge myself on Frohman's amiability by attacking him on a business matter the first time in my life I'd ever met him," and so she explained: "I've just written him a little note—if he wants to talk business with me I shall probably hear from him" (ER to FB, June 9, 1897).

The summer, as usual, proved more conducive to her writing career than to theatrical enterprises. She made a note in her diary after several days' stay at Redcar that she had completed four chapters of *The Open Question* and a dedication "to J.H.R.," or Jane Hussey Robins, Elizabeth's grandmother, who would serve as model for the fictional Sara Gano in Robins's first long novel (EBook, July 8). After this spurt of energy, Robins stopped work on the book. The cause of the longest interruption in her work on *The Open Question* was her lack of funds to support herself. She was invited to spend August with her friend Constance Maud on her first vacation tour of Europe and looked forward to the time as an opportunity to write. During her entire stay in Germany, however, taking in the Wagner festival at Bayreuth and the water baths at Wildbad, Robins interspersed her reports to Bell on the progress of her novel with worries about her finances.

"Scenes Behind the Scenes"

On August 25, Robins decided, very abruptly, to leave Wildbad; she returned to Edward and Dorothy Grey's fishing cottage at Itchen Abbas and worked steadily at her novel for a month. Just after she had set aside all her fiction in order to write business letters and begin work on *Admiral Guinea*, however, she made a note in her engagement book, "Begin Maria McMurdo at 10 A.M." (September 29, 1897). Sometime before rehearsals began for *Admiral Guinea* she sent the nearly completed set of Maria McMurdo stories to Florence Bell with a special plea for help. Robins was tempted by the chance to earn money because she knew it would take a long time to finish her novel. The letter asked Bell to help her by sending the pieces to a prospective editor. Robins was interrupted three times as she wrote the letter. After she received a notice that her rent was due, she renewed the plea with greater urgency. "My affairs cry haste," she declared and added that William Archer had advised her to "go ahead" with her scheme. It was particularly important that these stories of stage life not be in any way associated with the writing of

C. E. Raimond. Robins listed the real-life counterparts to her fictional characters and theaters, thereby revealing that the experiences of Maria McMurdo
were based on her own early days in London. The model for Ruben
Waverleigh, the actor-manager who flatters the young aspiring actress, was
Herbert Beerbohm Tree (ER to FB, undated [November 1897]).

The collection "Scenes Behind the Scenes" contains not only the Maria
McMurdo stories but also several other short pieces dealing with life in the
theater world. In them Robins displays some of her cleverest writing about the
stage. Her intimate knowledge of the actress's life behind the scenes is evident
in her portraits of men and women caught up in stage life. Although only one
was published, they show the writer at her best, spoofing a profession she
knew well.

"La Bellerieuse," published in *Pall Mall Magazine*, describes the triumph,
on her deathbed, of a famous opéra-bouffe actress. The priest who called for
the last rites proves to be a former lover, for whom she had been willing to
forgo her career; the man's mother forbade the match. As he holds out his
crucifix and asks her to pray, she clutches it defiantly and declares, "I thank
Thee, O God! that I have lived *much*," before collapsing in death with a smile
on her face.[9]

One interesting story is "The Highly Respectable Heroine." In it a playwright reads his modern play to an actress so vain that her portraits adorn
her boudoir and make him feel as if he were in a hall of mirrors. The playwright thinks the actress captivated by the spirit of his nontraditional heroine
until she scolds him for thinking that she would stoop to play so immoral a
role. The playwright goes away defeated; even his observation that she has a
real-life liaison with her married manager becomes a source of embarrassment
for him.

Perhaps the most brilliant of Robins's stage stories is "A Manager's Mistake," the first-person account of actress Estelle La Tour's attempt to find
work after a long period of unemployment. With colorful language, she condemns all actor-managers as "dolts, brutes, idiots," and accuses them of refusing to recognize that an actress who made a name for herself two decades
ago cannot feed herself on reputation alone. Two of Robins's stage stories employ male narrators. Other stories, especially her sequence on "Miss Mc-
Murdo," and "How to Succeed on the Stage," examine the problems of
women in a profession where one needs a patron to survive and where patron-
age often entails sexual favors.[10] Robins left the sequence unfinished and commented in a letter that referred to the project that it was "abandoned or
overborne by a 1,000 other things."[11]

One source of interference with her writing was her direction of the New
Century Theatre's production of *Admiral Guinea* in late November. Robins

did not take a role in the production, though she did speak the prologue William Henley wrote especially for the performances. At about the same time, William Heinemann, informing Robins of his plans to go to America, offered to take her book to New York in order to submit it to *Century Magazine*, which he could do "if I could finish it or a good part of it by mid-December." For Robins, publication by *Century Magazine* would mean that she would be placed, "once and for all, in the American market and that I'd get big prices for my work from other firms on the strength of being 'a Century writer.'" The problem, of course, was her theater life. "For weeks now I've been crippled and finally stopped dead by . . . *Admiral Guinea.* . . . I live in the theater and reach home at night too tired to hold a pencil let alone write new stuff" (ER to FB, undated fragment [?November 1897]). For the moment, her directorship of the New Century Theatre came first. Whether or not she performed a role, she invested much time in directing the productions and reviewing prospective plays.

Immediately after the week of matinées of *Admiral Guinea*, Robins departed for a stay of several weeks at "Red Barns." She left no detailed record of her activities there, but there is little doubt that she finally resumed work on her American novel, *The Open Question*. Upon returning to London, and in the midst of meetings for discussion of the next New Century Theatre project, she undertook a rigorous three weeks of writing, reporting her progress and her new priorities to Bell as she worked: "I eat, drink, and dream nothing but *The Open Question*." Even as she listed all the recent distractions—committee business for the New Century, further plans to stage "Sister Helen," and Miss Tadema's hopes that Robins would want to stage her play—she made clear they came in the way of her chief occupation: "And as for me I write all day and half the night and let the world go hang!" (ER to FB, January 8, 11, 1898).

America, 1898

Her chief distraction was her plan to go to America to present *Hedda Gabler*. She had no funds of her own, but she had William Heinemann's willing pledge to assist. There were sound reasons why even a loan from Heinemann would seem to threaten her freedom; Heinemann was still hoping to marry Robins. She reported to Florence Bell that his latest offer came when he accompanied her home after a dinner party:

> Oh dear, oh dear! On the way home he said to me without any of that old excitement: "I am going to ask you once more and I'm never going to ask you again," &c &c—and he went on in an odd cool way to restate his whole seven years business to say, "The time has come when I cannot and

should not wait any longer. I must have a home. I must *found* my life. . . . If you say No this time I must find the next best who will say 'yes'" &c &c all quite dispassionately—how he had waited, what he had shown me of his loyalty, how he would devote his life to making me happy—not heeding any interruptions of mine any more than the rolling of the carriage wheels. And in the end refusing to take the answer that was ready for him until there had been time for reflection for this was the "last time." This obscures and complicates his American outlook horribly. Oh that he were married and settled and this question not coming up. [ER to FB, January 15, 1898]

On January 21, Robins made her own decision to leave for America. A week later, Heinemann offered to advance her five hundred pounds for a New York production of *Hedda Gabler* if she could not find an American manager willing to support her. On February 2, Robins departed for Liverpool, boarded the White Star Line's *Britannic*, and was on her way back, after an absence of almost ten years, to her homeland. Heinemann followed on a later boat, bearing, as a dutiful friend, Robins's newly made ivory cloth gown.

Once she arrived in New York, she was invited on a "whirl of dinners, teas, luncheons." She kept busy with appointments, both social and professional, looking up old acquaintances and settling with new business agents. She met with Paul Reynolds, who would remain her literary agent for decades. Elisabeth Marbury and Elsie de Wolfe managed terms for *Hedda Gabler* and would later market her plays in America. She was surprised, she wrote to Bell, that there was "a very real interest in the New Drama here." As for her hopes of stirring up interest in Ibsen she wrote, "*I* felt quite a tame and mild adherent among the Professors and men of letters at the Authors Club who had read him in his native tongue and hobnobbed with him in Christiania." After almost ten days of everybody "giving things for me—'dinners,' 'at homes,' 'evenings,' and so on," she was still not sure a production of *Hedda Gabler* would materialize. "It's all quite changed here. I have to learn it all over again and walk warily," she wrote. She asked for the "terms" of several business propositions before she decided on a particular plan of production (ER to FB, February 20–21, 1898). Most likely, if she accepted any money from Heinemann, she borrowed a small amount and only provisionally. The production of *Hedda Gabler* that Robins secured was a modest single matinée at the Fifth Avenue Theatre on March 30. Robins had, upon her arrival, talked of doing other productions—possibly *Little Eyolf* and *The Master Builder*. She wrote to Bell that she had even received various invitations to appear across the country. Press accounts were generally favorable toward her acting and harshly critical of Ibsen's philosophy. Whether she was daunted by these notices, by lack of funds, by difficult rehearsal conditions, or by a combination of these factors, the single performance made it appear that Robins was fulfilling an obligation to herself and to the city which had launched her acting career rather than promoting her future on the American stage. She did record in a notebook "things learnt in New York," and from the list of warnings to herself, it is evident that her experience had taught her to contract for the terms of the rehearsals. She also noted that props, scenery, and promotional circulars had not been forthcoming as promised.[12]

Five days after her Ibsen matinée, she left New York on the sleeper car to Louisville to fulfill commitments that were even more private. She spent the week before Easter in the city of her birth, visiting her brother, Vernon, and her cousins and attending the christening of a new daughter of one cousin in the same church in which she herself had been christened. On the day after Easter, she visited her mother at Oak Lawn, in Jacksonville, Illinois. The next day she arrived in Zanesville, Ohio, to stay with other relatives in the town of her girlhood. Barely another week passed before she sailed for England.

After a brief visit to her institutionalized mother, Robins began negotiations with her family which eventually secured Hannah Robins's release from Oak Lawn and her return to Louisville, where she was cared for in a home run by her church. All the details of Hannah's behavior—she heard voices and imagined that people were persecuting her—suggest delusional behavior, perhaps schizophrenia, but Dr. James M. Bodine, Elizabeth's uncle, neither gave her condition a name nor suggested that it was treatable. He refused Elizabeth's request to move Hannah, assuring her only that "your mother ought to remain where she is until some decided mental improvement is manifest or death ensues" (Bodine to ER, September 7, 1898, ER Papers, Fales).

Before she received her uncle's response, Robins wrote to her youngest brother, Raymond, that she found their mother "immensely better." She had talked with her for two hours "without finding in her the slightest abnormal thing." Afterward, Robins discovered that their mother had harmless delusions about the dead returning, "but *that* she shares with the spiritualists and many excellent folk abroad in this world." The only thing that was keeping her at Oak Lawn, Robins declared, was the family's poverty. After seeing first-hand the conditions at the institution, Robins determined that "there is no kindness or even *common fairness*" in keeping her there "*if* we can make a home for her" (ER to RR, June 4, 1898).

Robins set down perhaps the best accounts of her weeks in America in long letters, twenty-three in all, to William Archer. Although the letters do not survive, her coded accounts keep track of when she began, finished, or posted most of them, numbering each and also recording his numbered letters to her. It is difficult to speculate about the nature of this intense literary friendship or about the tenor of Robins's first appointment upon her arrival "home"—in London—on April 30, with " ⴹ ," her engagement book's sym-

Elizabeth Robins as Hedda Gabler, for the New York City production, 1898.
(*Courtesy of the Fales Library. Reproduced with the permission of Mabel Smith, for the Backsettown Trustees.*)

bol for William Archer. Robins later expressed regret that Archer had destroyed the letters she gave him. The fraction of the Archer letters to Robins which do survive show him to have been a severe, if helpful, critic of her work. Frequently he adds a line about his affection for her, which apparently remained more intense than hers for him.

Robins's later fiction hints that she found a collaborative literary friendship more important than, and incompatible with, a sexual intimacy. That she turned to America for themes suggests the end of her apprenticeship; she found her close sharing with Archer of literary projects less and less productive. On a subsequent trip to America in 1900, she would write one of her more revealing stories about the nature of artistic inspiration. In the story "A Masterpiece the World Never Saw; or, Aphrodite of the West," the fulfillment of sexual passion demands a sacrifice of the artist's best work.

The Open Question, 1898

More immediately, Robins used her trip to the American Midwest and to her childhood homes to come to terms with her own past. In an unprinted preface to *The Open Question,* she speaks of Jane Hussey Robins's character and her influence over Robins's life. Robins's grandmother would, she acknowledged, disapprove of the moral sentiment of the book as much as the fictional Sara C. Gano disapproved of her grandchildren's union. Still, Robins found it noteworthy that hardly a trying event in her own life passed without her speculating upon how her grandmother might have reacted. In *The Open Question,* Robins validates her own defiance of traditional moral standards and creates a heroine fiercely independent, passionate, artistic, and determined to marry her own cousin. The two acknowledge to each other that they are committing a sin in the eyes of society, and they commit another to justify the first. Their marriage includes a solemn agreement not to have children. They believe that if they live together happily even for a year, they will have had enough joy for a lifetime. They promise each other that, if despair or grief overtakes them, they will help each other put an end to their lives.

Subtitled "A Tale of Two Temperaments," the novel functions as what Charlotte Goodman defines as the male-female double bildungsroman.[13] Goodman stresses, in the five novels she discusses, that the male and female grow up together, drift apart, display the limitations of a patriarchal society when androgynous wholeness is no longer possible, and are reunited in the end, usually in death. Robins was consciously writing an American novel but was working clearly in the tradition of British women writers also. Her first description of her heroine Val Gano shows her with a copy of *Aurora Leigh* in her hands. Like George Eliot's *The Mill on the Floss,* the book ends in a double drowning. In a departure from the regular form of the double bild-ungsroman, Ethan Gano grows up outside the world of his younger cousin, Val, but Robins shows how their temperamental development propels them toward each other.

Many elements of *The Open Question* were familiar to Robins. Like her hero and heroine, Robins's father and mother were first cousins. The key events in Val Gano's domestic life echo the youth of Elizabeth Robins. As with Val, the breaking up of the Robins home sent Elizabeth to live with her grand-mother in the Midwest. Like Val, Elizabeth was precocious at school and something of a heathen in comparison to her devout younger sister, who was Emmie in the novel and Eunice or Una in real life. Both Val and Bessie, as everyone called Elizabeth then, discovered their artistic leanings through a namesake aunt who wanted to be a poet and artist and who died young. Eliza-beth Robins the novelist borrowed from her own antics at Putnam Female Seminary the anecdote of Val terrorizing her gymnasium instructor by plant-ing matches on the floor where she jumps. Val and Bessie, despite many re-strictions, both determined that they would break out of their confined home existence. Moreover, the two families, the fictional Ganos and the real-life Robinses, are haunted by the same weakness of constitution.

Less obvious a parallel between Val and Elizabeth Robins is the way in which each validates suicide. Robins researched the ethical debate on this question in order to use it as a centerpiece in her book. She went to the British Museum to read Schopenhauer; she discussed with William Stead as early as 1890 the morality of suicide. Her experiences with Ibsen heroines Hedda Gabler and Rebecca West made suicide a familiar subject for artistic expres-sion. Robins, though, had a more personal reason for writing *The Open Question*. She had been haunted for a decade by the suicide of her actor-hus-band George Parks. By constructing the novel as a sensational "double sui-cide," Robins could create, in an artistic tribute to Parks, a union which she was incapable of rediscovering in real life. Less soul-baring reconciliations had not appeased her.

Critics did not see the novel's connection to her past, and one complained that it was twice as long as it should have been to be properly effective.[14] However, the willful suicides of Val and Ethan Gano are a single weave of a more complex fabric which shows how the two opposite temperaments come, first, to depend upon each other thoroughly and then, after their marriage, to exchange traits. Val, the ever-confident optimist, takes on the personality of the decadent Ethan. Val starts to dread the evidence that their happiness is vanishing. Ethan hopes that Val will agree to abandon their promise. The story, in the tradition of the multigenerational novel, has abundant details of the family's Confederate origins, of young orphan Ethan's upbringing in abolitionist Boston after his mother's family claims him, of repeated encounters between Northern and Southern attitudes towards freed slaves and the beliefs of the different cultures.

Robins carefully describes formative incidents in the young lives of the cousins. Ethan is certain that the wind which blows through his grand-mother's house during thunderstorms is a supernatural spirit and names it "Yaffti." When Val is sent away from her parents' home, she prays hard for the recovery of her sick mother. When she returns to attend her mother's funeral, she feels abandoned by God. At her grandmother's, she follows uncon-sciously in the footsteps of Valeria, her father's sister, whom she never met and who died without having had the chance to use her artistic talent. Ethan pur-sues studies abroad, and lengthy episodes treat his life among the Paris deca-dents as he develops an ethic of suicide and keeps vigil during his best friend's last days.

The novel is deliberately, calculatingly long because Ethan and Val, at-tracted to each other from their first meeting when Val is sixteen, give them-selves and each other necessary chances to deny that attraction. Their union, upon which their family frowns, is regretted by Ethan because he is fearful of communicating to Val his dread of life. Val, however, defines this union dif-ferently. She proposes a "compact. We Ganos are honest people; we'll play fair" (*OQ,* 424). She explains, "we will go out together before—before we've opened the door to another. . . . Can't you see I'd rather be sad with you, than glad with any other?" (*OQ,* 425). That night they fling the rings they pledge to each other into the river as a sacrifice. From respect for their grandmother's principles, they delay their wedding until after the death of Sara Gano. With marriage, they achieve complete happiness. They travel the world, anticipating more and more complete fulfillment of their joy. Ethan's doubts recur. Val finds him happiest when she is not in his company; he fears that Val's sadness is his doing and worries that "in sharing my life you have come a little—a little under the shadow" (*OQ,* 466). As Ethan asks why Val is so gloomy, he realizes that she is expecting a child. He understands instantly that, in the words of the compact, they must now face their pledge. The sudden change in his face shows her that her secret is no longer her own, and Val cries out, "What is it like to have hoped and longed all these months, instead of dreaded?" Val describes the pride she took in hearing it reported that she was the symbol of her parents' "single year of perfect happiness, the inheritor of the best moments life had brought them." Now the one thought that "clutches" her is: "That for a child of fear and shrinking there isn't much place in this world" (*OQ,* 500, 501).

The last, tension-filled chapter plays out a frightening dance of wills. Ethan rejoices when Val is happy but longs to escape from her when her mood turns dark. They are in Oakland, living on the bay, and Ethan longs for a few hours when he can take his sailboat, the *Yaffti*, out on the water. Val suspects that their last day has come, looks for signs of an impending storm, and finally finds her resolve when she reads from Ethan's journal his last entry, of several months previous, when she assumed that nothing intruded on their happiness. Ethan had written, "Forgetfulness! That is all my prayer. . . . I crave—forgetfulness!" She understands that, especially in their most congenial moments, their recent life together has been for him a life of suffering. Even the happiest moments of his waiting have been torture; he longs for the epitaph, "And they were dead together forever after" (*OQ*, 519).

Yet even in his written meditation, he suspects that they have a chance to escape their troth. Reading it, Val knows otherwise and subtly directs their journey together, to the boat, through the bay, and into the ocean. The novel ends, "That night the Pacific coast was strewn with wreck. But of the *Yaffti* no spar was ever found" (*OQ*, 523).

Robins risked a sensational ending; she was dealing with—and was seeming to endorse—a complexity of sensational issues, joint suicide, incest, the disappearance of God. For the first time in her life, her novel sold so widely that she could begin to think of writing as a lucrative career. The success eventually cost her her pseudonym.

Immediately after the first edition was published in November, just as Heinemann hurriedly prepared a second printing for December, the *Daily Chronicle* broke the story that C. E. Raimond was Elizabeth Robins. Her name, misspelled "Elisabeth," was added to the title page; selections from highly favorable reviews crammed another page; and Heinemann's prediction that the book would sell better when its author had been identified began to prove true. Early in 1899, Robins wrote to Bell that the book was in its third edition and that Heinemann predicted sales of fifty thousand in England and twenty thousand in America. She had the opportunity to make her first sizable investment and purchased one thousand pounds of stock in iron companies managed by Sir Hugh Bell. More tellingly, perhaps, Robins received scores of letters to congratulate her. The two she most valued came from Samuel Clemens, who was amazed she could have written as if from direct experience, and Bernard Shaw, who called Robins the American George Eliot. At about this time she published a brief essay, "Among My Books," and wrote a review sketch of Lady Mary Wortley Montagu, printed in the *Anglo-Saxon Review*. She also revived the idea of her first contemplated novel, "The Peruvian," and asked Bell whether she thought it would make a good serial.

At the start of her newfound financial independence, she received another invitation to perform. In March 1899, she accepted a call to replace Mrs.

Genevieve Ward in F. R. Benson's Edinburgh production of *Coriolanus*. She sent Florence Bell lively accounts of her brief return to the stage and highly favorable notices of herself as Volumnia. The critics gave as much and more attention to her in the role as they did Benson himself, and Robins gleefully wrote to Bell that he had ordered her to add years to her makeup so that the mother of Coriolanus would not look so young.

In July and August 1899, Robins accompanied Lady Lewis, wife of the famous solicitor, on a rest cure to the Alps. While traveling, she enjoyed the near celebrity status derived from the popularity of *The Open Question*. Wherever she went, everybody had asked her what she was writing and when her next book was to be ready. She debated with herself the possibility of getting back to London and concluded if she had "gumption," she would capitalize on her name: "But then why should I suddenly develop gumption anymore than two heads?" (ER to FB, August 22, 1899). It was in the Alps that she got the idea for a novella. Less than a month after returning to England, she wrote to Florence Bell from Lady Dorothy Grey's English fishing cottage that she was nearly done with the story (called at first "The Glacier Mills" and then *The Mills of the Gods*), described it as a work with a "slightly bogey theme," based upon something she saw in the Engadine, and asked Bell to read it. "When it's off my mind, then hey for Benvenuto and there you have *my* programme" (ER to FB, September 20, 1899). "Benvenuto" was a play project that Robins had planned earlier.

The Mills of the Gods, 1899

The several years' hiatus between C. E. Raimond's last novel *The Open Question* (1898) and Elizabeth Robins's first, *The Magnetic North*, in 1904, was not a time when her pen was inactive. *The Mills of the Gods* and "Benvenuto Cellini," composed in the fall and early winter of 1899–1900, are proof of her power to dramatize a thrilling story. In tone *The Mills of the Gods*, which would not be published until 1908, anticipates the feminist fiction of a decade later. Its central character is also reminiscent of the willfully mute Jean Creyke of *Alan's Wife*. Alicia, the twenty-six-year-old daughter of Bellucci's mortal enemy, is, except for a few brief, well-modulated responses and a mumble of phrases in her sleep, persistently silent. Bellucci wins her, a feat consistent with his conquest of other women, but as soon as he is married, Alicia's seemingly passive silence begins to haunt him.

When Bellucci asks why his new wife acts strangely, her stepmother, herself a victim of Bellucci's past exploits, explains, "She was the very woman for you—the only woman who with impunity could be trusted to your keeping. . . . Alicia is the one woman in the world whose heart you cannot break."[15] Bellucci's first obsession to know "what is behind the veil" (*Mills*, 94) turns to contempt because nothing looked out from the "windows of her soul" (*Mills*, 106); her eyes were "wells of darkness" (*Mills*, 107).

Bellucci settles with his young bride at the unfinished castle built by his father, which rises out of the rock of a mountain that towers hundreds of feet above the Val Bregaglia. The only other resident besides the servants is an Austrian friend of Bellucci's father, a poet-gardener-geologist interested in studying the rock formations in the surrounding terrain. Bellucci becomes irritated because Alicia spends all her time embroidering a long tapestry with silk thread. He forbids the work in his presence, but he finds Alicia fearlessly dangling the golden-hearted pendant he had had made for her wedding present over the edge of the steep cliff or hanging her tapestry against the window. He becomes obsessed with understanding her, repeatedly breaks his vow to himself to sleep in the chamber farthest from her, and finds himself creeping in to stand beside her and bend above her, listening to the legend of "the wells." He follows her at night to the spot where she has brought her heart pendant and her trains of silk. He sees her crouching intently over a deep crevice, dangling her pendant, and mumbles "Damned witchcraft" so loudly that she becomes aware of his presence. Succumbing to an "impulse of blind fury against the incarnate enigma" (*Mills*, 140), he throws her into the water of the deep pool.

Robins's sudden denouement makes plain her condemnation of his brutality and justifies Alicia's strangeness. The resident geologist is shouting for her, afraid she has been too excited by his discovery of the glacial whirlpool in the rock formations to wait for daylight before they plumb its depths. When his excitement runs on, "We will sound it first, and then we will empty it," Bellucci cries out with a frenzy that almost gives him away, "*I forbid you!* . . . The Glacier Mills are mine." The geologist replies, "They are the Mills of the Gods, Monsieur" (153–54). He continues his explanation, which mostly reflects scientific reasoning, with: "Ah, . . . *you* do not understand, but Madame la Comtesse could tell you" (*Mills*, 155).

Bellucci's insistence that she was strange, probably mad, elicits the geologist's correction, "Strangely beautiful and strangely sad" (155). Moments later, in search of clearer air, Bellucci steps to the edge of his courtyard, looks up for the moon, and finds it obscured by a giddy moving pattern of clouds and shadows: "Had he sent Alicia hence only that she might hang her tapestries along the walls of heaven?" (156). He grows desperate, fearing that Alicia's patterned stitching had "wrought the pattern of Bewilderment upon the tissue of his brain" (157). A comet flickers into the depths. He looks straight down the hundreds of feet into the Val Bregaglia, thinking, "'*There*, down there light is conquered, light is quenched. . . . That is my pathway, too.' And he stepped out of the wind-swept court into mid-air" (*Mills,* 158).

As with many fantastic tales, every element of mystery, suspenseful touch, and clever twist is imbued with significance. Bellucci is rightly persecuted for his conqueror attitude toward women. Furthermore, Robins makes her story of a woman's silence reverberate with women's centuries-long experience of disenfranchisement, as old as the use of language itself. Robins continued to use women's silence in her fiction to explore the differences between men and women.

Robins's own true voice had hardly begun to emerge in 1899. She antici- pated the forthcoming Ibsen play with the hope that she would once again have a strong stage role. But *When We Dead Awaken* greatly disappointed her. She wrote to Bell of her dismay just after she completed reading the play: "The interest of 10 years is ended and as I think of the nightmare the play really is, with its jumble of Hilda, Hedda, Borkman, Peer Gynt, etc.; it's as tho' in the loosening of that mind from its moorings one kept seeing swept by on the flood marred pieces of mighty work done in days of vigor—wreckage on a giant scale" (ER to FB, December 12, 1899).

The end of her decade of interest in Ibsen did not immobilize her or sug- gest that she had less of a place in the theater world. In 1902 she created two supporting roles, so the reluctance to attach herself to *When We Dead Awaken* did not signal the end of her acting career. Still, Ibsen's flawed dra- maturgy, which Robins saw as "wreckage on a giant scale," narrowed her options enough to make writing an essential occupation.

"Benvenuto Cellini," 1899–1900

Because she was energetically working on her own drama, the Ibsen dis- appointment affected her less than it might otherwise have. In many ways, "Benvenuto Cellini," the first of her original plays to attract genuine interest among actor-managers, was the polar opposite of Ibsen's drama. "Benvenuto Cellini" was nothing less than an actor-manager's play. In style and content, the play recalls the kind of drama that Robins had spent a decade repudiating. It was melodrama on the grand scale of *The Count of Monte Cristo,* the James O'Neill vehicle in which Robins had been featured at the very beginning of her acting career. She offered the script to Alexander and, when he remained uncommitted, read the play to Herbert Beerbohm Tree. Ironically, the last time she had approached Tree, it was with the offer to create Master Builder

Solness. Tree had refused to have anything to do with the architect unless the play and his part were rewritten and Solness was made a sculptor.

In a sense, Robins gave Tree his sculptor when she offered him "Benvenuto Cellini." Tree was predictably eager to secure exclusive rights to the play; indeed, the part seems written for his talents, and the play's spectacle calls for effects that would show off to advantage the gifts his scenery of wizards at the newly opened Her Majesty's Theatre. Robins's Cellini has all the flair and Renaissance splendor of a great artist among nobility. Gone from her portrait is the swaggering in Cellini's autobiography about how he kept his models as mistresses and brutalized them when they would not accept his advances. Robins's other source for her story is the French novel about Cellini's apprentice, Ascanio. The events of the play extend from the time when Cellini is first acknowledged by Francis I, king of France, to when the king honors him at Fontainebleau, and Cellini presents his bronze of Hebe at the Feast of St. Francis. Cellini thwarts the evil Duchess's cleverest maneuver when he discovers that the molten metal of his foundry has been allowed to cool before the metal has reached the critical temperature for pouring. In a spectacularly staged climax, Cellini takes the jewel among his creations, the famous silver ewer the king has admired, and thrusts it into the foundry. The triumphant sculptor is then driven from the furnace by the heat caused when the lighter metal melts, and he shouts a prayer of thanks as it streams into the ladle. Robins's hero emerges as valorous, noble of purpose, even willing to sacrifice romance when he realizes that his own passion is unfair to the young lovers. In scene after scene, Robins exploits the role to display a full range of talent.

Unfortunately, the play required a huge financial commitment because the scenes called for lavish sets. Robins certainly knew that the melodramatic spectacle she was writing would be commercially viable, and she specifically hoped that it would be seen as something far removed from Ibsen and the new drama. When she signed the contract granting Tree exclusive rights to the play for one year, she protected her identity by stipulating that she had the right to withdraw permission for production if her authorship was revealed. Late in the summer of 1900, the press publicized her authorship of the play, giving Tree an excuse to cancel the contract.

Regardless of this setback, Robins felt that anti-Ibsen sentiment had constrained her career so much that she needed to establish her abilities on a wider stage. She had great hopes for the play, but she dared not remain deaf to another calling. Just after receiving Tree's offer of first production rights, in late March 1900, she left London for the longest journey of her life. She went to Alaska to find her youngest brother, Raymond, who she feared was about to become a Jesuit.

"Aphrodite of the West"

In early April, while she waited in Boston to begin her trip to Alaska, Robins wrote "A Masterpiece the World Never Saw; or, Aphrodite of the West."[16] Chronologically this story belongs at the beginning of the twentieth century; thematically, it is unmistakably her response to Ibsen's *When We Dead Awaken*. On one level, it describes her own emergence from apprenticeship and evolution toward a fuller expression of the central struggle in her own life of the late 1890s, the sacrifice of passion in the pursuit of artistic goals. Robins's story is vitally relevant for an understanding of her writer's self; the idea that the artist/creator has spiritually raped his model/subject and, to atone for the misdeed, has compromised his career applies to Robins's own struggle with herself as artist. She may have borrowed Ibsen's device of model and artist, but she inverted Ibsen's treatment of it. A painter who has religiously kept his promise to a beautiful young woman that he is not to show his painting of her to the world renounces a greater career. Then, after years of longing in solitude, his desire appears belatedly to be rewarded.

The memory of desire figures in the hidden life of John Denio, the established American painter in London. In the midst of a fashionable party in London he finds himself defending the only return that he has made to his homeland since he became an artist.

The next section of the story takes place in Denio's Felton Castle in northern England and triggers action which leads to his flashback. After dinner in solitude on the evening of his arrival, he gathers up the narcissus from the great bronze bowl and retreats to his locked studio in the upper level of the castle. There he communes with the object of his desire: "the picture of a girl lying naked by a pool in a hollow of the hills—her knotted yellow hair half falling from under the confining hand on which her head was pillowed" ("M/AW," 9). He stares at the picture in order to "leech out of him" ("M/AW," 10) the travel grime and to relive the experience of his one visit to his southern homeland.

Elizabeth Robins knew James McNeill Whistler, the American painter in London, very well; he called her his "southern cousin." Whistler's late paintings evoke the erotic quality of his nude models.[17] Through her friendship with Henry James, Robins knew of James's friend, John Singer Sargent. Perhaps James had related to Robins Sargent's account of his first visit to his homeland, in the midst of his studio apprenticeship in Paris at the age of twenty. Furthermore, Robins's vivid memory of Oscar Wilde's recitation of his Poem in Prose, "The Artist," and the stark impression made upon her by

Ibsen's artist and model in *When We Dead Awaken* suggest even closer analogues.

In her story, the model for John Denio's painting that the world can never see is a young, very real "Summer Girl" who comes upon him while he worked in the wilderness at his easel. She is barefoot, unselfconscious, and inquisitive. She enjoys the same pools he swam in as a child. Her beauty compels him to discuss his ambitions. He tells her that he seeks a "High Priestess, leading troops of acolytes through the ages, till her world was purged and made as fair as she" ("M/AW," 17). In other words, if he has his perfect model, his career is made. In silent compliance, Denio's Summer Girl reappears to fulfill his vision. She emerges from the water to pose until voices in the distance scare the girl away. Although the young painter returns day after day, hoping to recreate the experience, the girl reappears just briefly to command him to destroy the picture: "You make me hate myself and all the world —and most of all the light" ("M/AW," 22). When he begs her to consider his point of view, the girl flees, and Denio shouts into space, "Wait—wait. . . . I'll do anything you ask. . . . I love you" ("M/AW," 23). Shortly afterward, the news that a girl's body has been found in the pond sends Denio numbed and grieving back to the pool at midnight. His vision of her appears and makes another demand, that he must keep the picture, never showing it to anyone "till I come again" ("M/AW," 25).

Back in his castle studio, the morning brings the white figure of a woman to him from out of the shadows. She addresses him: "I have come to say: You must destroy the picture." He pleads, "Ah be gentle. Think how, having the picture I have had you." But she insists, "Destroy the picture and you shall come to me." Robins explores the eerie intertwining of death and desire through her last paragraph: "And before the day had come into the room, he had done her bidding. 'The End' that she had prophesied found him staring sightless at an empty frame—but who shall say if, following her into the dark, he did not find her as she promised him—in some land whence the Summer comes and where youth goes" ("M/AW," 27).

The story has a universal ring in its portrayal of the conflict between art and the consummation of passion. The painter sacrifices his chance of a better reputation in order to be spiritually faithful to his model. Whereas in *The New Moon* passion was sacrificed and punished, here sexual fulfillment acquires an elevated and even holy purpose. Oscar Wilde's artist in his "Poem in Prose" refashions his only cherished masterpiece, a tombstone for the one person he has loved in life, in order to create a bronze image of momentary pleasure.[18] Ibsen's sculptor renounces work on his masterpiece in order to reconcile himself with the model he has ravished and abandoned. In like manner, Robins gives her female model command of the artist's life and art. Ibsen's Irene is a deranged, vengeful creature who threatens to murder the man who has ruined her life. In contrast, Robins's model returns to her painter in a vision: the painter's spiritual preservation of the young girl he "used" echoes the mood in a pre-Raphaelite painting, and passion, beauty, and artistic perfection are fused in a glorification of erotic desire. In revisioning Ibsen's last play and in probing her American past, Robins was not so much clinging to an earlier, romanticized sense of self as she was expressing, perhaps in a form Burne-Jones would have endorsed, a fusion of passion and art not previously found in her fiction. In doing so, she continued to reexamine the forms traditionally taken by female power. The muse does not simply inspire but also commands, just as Val Gano's power over Ethan has doublecrossed their original compact: Ethan becomes infected by Val's optimism, and her discovery of his fear that he has corrupted her frees her to direct their death voyage.

Upon Robins's completion of "Aphrodite of the West," she left for Alaska. Her main quest was personal, and her journalism offered the chief promise of support for the trip. In the end, the fiction generated by her contact with Alaska surpassed anything she had produced previously. Had she not departed for Alaska as a woman influenced by a feminist outlook, moreover, she certainly returned conscious of better opportunities for women and searching for ways to voice her awareness in her writing.

5 | The Magnetic North

Raymond, Alaska, Chinsegut, and "My Own Life," 1900–1906

For too long you have drifted and looked at the world thro' others' eyes. Time now to take hold again and direct the course!

—Elizabeth Robins to herself, sailing along the Yukon River a week after leaving Raymond at Nome, Alaska Diary, August 1, 1900

I am filled with dread lest I be found unequal to the part you would have me play in the world's drama and that the atmosphere of those high places where you swore so commandingly may prove too rarefied for my low habited lungs.

—Raymond to Elizabeth Robins, October 19, 1900

T*HE SCENE*: Childhood, Zanesville, Ohio. In the midst of a raging thunderstorm, jumbled together in the big four-poster bed in their grandmother's stately home, the little boy Raymond Robins listens to his sister Bessie, eleven years his senior, telling enraptured tales of the gods who made the thunder and lightning.[1] His theatrically minded sister invents for him a story of the mystery of the crashing clouds. For the youngster, his sister's invention is inextricably mixed with her other tales—stories of Achilles, Robinson Crusoe, the burning of Troy, and the River Styx. Raymond creeps closer to the young girl, puts his small arm around her neck, and with his free hand tightly grips the bedclothes. As the storm rages, Raymond is swept away by his older sister's seemingly transcendent courage and her all-embracing wisdom. Her love seems to him a sure protection against all the evil forces of earth and sky. The stars break through the clearing sky, and Bessie turns the puddled driveway into a beautiful lake and creates for Raymond a fairy story to make him imagine, "I will conquer—we will have a castle in the woods and a lake and swans. You a queen and I your knight."

The stories with which she reassures him become his "deep abiding purpose." Bessie Robins promises to love only Raymond forever and ever. She makes her brother kneel and kiss her hand and swear an oath—just as the books Bessie read had repeated it—his promise to kiss the hand of no other woman in all the earth. As little Raymond contemplates the consequences lest he should break the solemn troth, his sister kisses him to sleep.

Fade to New Scene: Reunion after fourteen years of separation. Deck of the *Tacoma*, June 14, 1900, two miles offshore from Nome, Alaska.[2] Elizabeth has planned the meeting in her head. She will be able to see his boat approach, then avoid the crowd on the deck and go below to wait for him to come to her in private. But no. As she is scanning the horizon from the crowded deck, he approaches from behind; she turns.

"Raymond."

"Sister." They hold hands fast, brother and sister who have known each other only through letters since family misfortune broke up their childhood. Raymond kisses her, the first woman he has embraced since leaving his cousins four years earlier. She takes him to the ship's parlor where they talk intimately.

Fade to New Scene: Seattle Hospital. October 17, 1900.[3] Elizabeth has been close to death for six weeks. Typhoid, contracted in Nome, or somewhere along the route from Nome to Seattle. She can only think of the last words she heard before she collapsed: Raymond has typhoid, too; he is on his way out of Alaska—but on a ship which has no supplies or fuel. She looks up to see familiar eyes in an unfamiliar face. He is gaunt, bearded, pale. He looks like Christ. Raymond. Without a word, he draws up a chair alongside her bed and lays his head down next to hers.

During their days in Nome, Raymond and Elizabeth evolve a plan to found a family home as the adult counterpart of Raymond's pledge and need for comfort. Elizabeth risks health and months of productivity to be with him in America. When she cannot be with him she sends money, to add to her trust fund. He travels to the Florida of his boyhood and arranges the purchase of a stately plantation home now in need of great repair. Later he said that during a visit here in his youth he was treated like one of the servants. Now, with Elizabeth's support, he would refurbish the place where his poverty had so humiliated him. Elizabeth arrives to share the first Christmas at the new family home. Instead of joy and peace, they have a grueling confessional conference. This, too, ends with their embrace.

Elizabeth is ill, and Raymond comes to her. The effects of typhoid linger. She travels Europe and America in search of cures. Her writing and her fatigue from overwork are blamed for her neuralgia and other circulatory stresses. She is another victim of the rest cure treatment that demands total physical inactivity. At times Elizabeth is psychically connected to him, sensing his illnesses and dangers. When Raymond is at the height of his political influence, he disappears without a trace en route to advise Herbert Hoover about his 1932 reelection campaign. Only Elizabeth knows the childhood history of Raymond's "Shadow" of debilitating mental stress, and she books passage from England announcing to reporters that she senses he is alive. While she is at sea, Raymond is discovered, suffering from amnesia, using an alias, but following the accounts of his disappearance in the newspapers. Hours before she reaches his hospital bed, his memory returns. This reunion is intense and all too brief. It is as if they have come to know each other so well that to remain in each other's presence becomes a burden.

Notes on the Scenes: The bedside scenes, replayed with variations, are a recurring motif in their relationship. In Alaska, they make a ritual of saying goodnight to each other with an embrace in Elizabeth's room. She falls very much under his spell during her six-week stay in Nome, and she senses a kind of tense triumph in Raymond's confession to her as he sees her off at her departure. Raymond tells Elizabeth that it is she who makes the difference in his life, and she records in her diary his confessed feeling for her: "I am the magnet" (Alaska diary, July 26, 1900).[4] She discovers, too, as the days put more and more distance between them, that she feels more strongly than before her need for his presence.

The adult intimacy between the youngest and oldest Robins siblings, begun during the six intense weeks in Nome, Alaska, and developed in their later meetings and correspondence, would affect each for the rest of their lives. To Elizabeth, Raymond would always be "My dear boy," and Raymond signed his letters to her "Little Brother." Most immediately, the close bond they established in Nome revived in Raymond the dream of their future life together that he had conceived during childhood. Alaska also came to mean much more for her: it awakened in her a new sense of herself as writer; and it assumed a negative presence as a consequence of the typhoid epidemic which nearly killed them both and may have contributed to the death of their oldest brother, Saxton. It would take months for Elizabeth to recover from typhoid and years before she turned her ideas for a story based on her brothers' experience in Alaska into *The Magnetic North*.

In her diaries, she took to noting her return to health with a phrase altered from Shakespeare (from Colley Cibber's acting version of *Richard III*), "Elizabeth's herself again." Finding her own psychological self, independent from Raymond, becomes the real quest of these years. Not *The Magnetic North*, but the novels that followed it represent Robins's greater achievement as a writer. This later fiction marks her growth toward a feminist stance because she not only transformed some of the legends and tales of Alaska into woman-centered texts but also used her own experience undergoing a rest cure to portray the symbolic battleground between a woman writer and the doctor who orders her cure.

Robins undertook the Alaska journey determined to prove that she could make money as a writer. Her intimacy with Raymond became the supreme test of her own independence. After she persuaded him to leave Alaska, Raymond became active in Chicago's Settlement Movement. His maverick and morality-based politics raised him to leadership in Illinois's Progressive Party. His work for the Red Cross in Russia enabled him to witness the Bolshevik revolution and lobby for recognition of Soviet Russia by the United States. Each made political issues integral to their mission in life and supported the other's commitments, yet they lived in widely different circles.

Raymond's personality was troubled even when he and Elizabeth were most in harmony. For all of his high moral principles and captivating affection, he suffered from self-deception and blind confidence. A quirk in his nature and in the complex circumstances of his life made him betray Elizabeth's trust at several crucial points in their relationship. Because those betrayals hinged upon Elizabeth's financial well-being, she found his behavior particularly difficult to accept.

Elizabeth had some reason to believe that the childhood scene had kept Raymond enthralled. During his growing up he experienced little womanly affection except when Elizabeth played the surrogate mother and took on her duty of teacher, at which she excelled. Shortly after she left the Zanesville home of their grandmother to pursue her stage ambitions, Raymond had a sudden and serious bout of illness, manifested by seizures and spells. His father took him to Louisville, where he could live with his mother and be under the care of his uncle, Dr. James M. Bodine. Thereafter his uncle and aunt were his closer caretakers. Charles E. Robins found it expedient to leave young Raymond with his in-laws while he looked for work in Ohio or traveled to southern Florida to try his hand at land development. Raymond had hardly known his father and would always wonder why he was so abandoned. Only after Charles became ill a short time before his death did Raymond spend much time with him, and the obligation of caring for a father who had not cared for him made Raymond all the more fiercely determined to rise above his circumstances. After their father's death, Raymond expressed his loyalty to Elizabeth and wrote her about his efforts at self-education. From Burnet, Texas, in 1894, Raymond confided to Elizabeth that he was devoted to the pursuit of the "Yellow God"; he measured his fortune by riches alone. His periodic reports to Elizabeth included what he had done to save Saxton, the black sheep of the family, from a life of misery. Raymond's concern for Saxton caused the younger brother to abandon his apprenticeship to a lawyer in San Francisco. It was Saxton who first caught the craze for Alaskan gold; and the two brothers, traveling as Raymond Robins and "Harry Earle" (because Raymond insisted on an alias for Saxton), boarded a ship promising the swiftest route to the Klondike. The "outside passage"—by water through the Gulf of

Alaska, Bering Sea, and Yukon River—was longest in miles; but, when all conditions were favorable, was proclaimed the most sensible and fastest approach to the Klondike goldfields. The sprawling Yukon River dissects Alaska like a giant, meandering artery. From its mouth on the southern edge of the Norton Sound, it is navigable the whole way to Dawson, as it heads almost straight south, then east and slightly north until it intersects with the Arctic Circle. From that northernmost point, Fort Yukon, it angles southeast for hundreds more miles, into the disputed boundary with Canada and the rich goldfields of Dawson. During the same winter that many men and hundreds of horses froze to death along the treacherous inland route—through the port of Skagway, straight over the infamous Chilkoot Pass, into Whitehorse, and on downstream into Dawson—ice left Saxton and Raymond stranded with three other men a mere four hundred miles up the Yukon River. After helping to build a chimneyed cabin—the first of its kind on the shores of the river— Raymond and another man, Albert F. Shulte, grew impatient with camp life and set out on foot to meet those who would travel by boat as soon as the ice retreated.

Gold Fever: Nome, 1900

Elizabeth Robins learned of Raymond's ordeal much later. At the outset she received from him only a brief message that he was about to depart. A full year after he had left for Dawson, he wrote her that seeking a fortune was immaterial; his life in the northern wilderness had converted him to Christianity. He spoke of three separate experiences which fed his belief: he witnessed the devout ministry of the Jesuits at Holy Cross; he had found in the wilderness the real-life manifestation of his vision of a cross, erected probably to mark a grave; then, in the library of a small Christian improvement society in Juneau, he read Drummond's *Natural Law in the Spiritual World*, which emphasized the appropriateness of Christian spirituality in a modern scientific world.

When Elizabeth received word that he would write her before the ice closed the North for another winter, she had time only to cable. Later, moved deeply by his account from his new post in Nome yet fearful that he might resign himself to the ministry in Alaska, she wrote to Raymond that if he were not yet ordained, he should, for her sake, wait.

Elizabeth Robins's determination to see and know her brother after the years of distant communication was matched by her efforts to understand his world. While still in London, she interviewed several people who had visited the Klondike in the gold rush of 1897–98, including Flora Shaw, special correspondent to the London *Times*. Before her departure, Robins secured from

William Stead the promise that he would attempt to place articles that she sent back to London as she traveled. Stead advanced her three hundred pounds. Before she left London, she began her series of reports with a description of what Cape Nome promised. Speculation and rumors of the gold-pebbled beach had prompted another frenzied exodus from ports along the west coast and from the Klondike itself. On March 19, the article appeared, declaring "*It is going to be a great race.*" A few days later Robins herself left London. Unfortunately, Stead would not carry through on his promise to print the subsequent articles, partly because he was uncertain of the state of Elizabeth Robins's health.

Beginning in New York on April 5, Robins kept a careful diary of the journey. She used this later as reference when writing her fiction and especially when she composed *Raymond and I*, her tribute to Raymond, conceived when he disappeared and was presumed dead in late 1932. By then Raymond was recognized as a progressive politician and spokesman for moral values. (Although the liquor Mafia would be suspected of his abduction, he was discovered weeks later, suffering from temporary amnesia.) The diary expresses no awareness of the impact Raymond Robins would have in the future on American politics. It tells a more intimate story of her relationship with Raymond, and it includes more detail of her own experiences before, during, and after Nome than does her later book. Elizabeth was shattered when, after she had worked on the memoir for more than a year, Raymond forbade its publication during his lifetime.

Robins had other reasons for traveling to Alaska besides her desire to see Raymond. She looked forward to a radical uprooting of her life: "A growing sense of restlessness, a desire to be out of England, even stronger than the desire that brought me here, was no stranger before that amazing letter had come from Raymond" (*Raymond and I*, 48). Far from fleeing reality, however, Robins set the circumstances of her voyage as a test for herself. She needed to know whether she was indeed a writer and whether the years of publishing under a pseudonym had been more than idle distraction.

While in Boston before her journey began, she interviewed the Reverend Loyal L. Wirt, who reported to her the details of Raymond's involvement, first with his library in Juneau, then with his Congregational church in Nome. At a special service in Newton, Elizabeth heard Wirt speak of the good work of his mission, giving as an example the salvation of her brother. Robins was eager for news of Raymond, but she felt curiously exposed as Wirt preached of her brother's good works. Only later did she learn how Wirt had deceived Raymond and others whom he lured to Nome.

In preparation for her trip Elizabeth took lessons in gold assaying at the Massachusetts Institute of Technology, which served as a review of the process by which precious metal was extracted and measured that her father had taught her in Colorado. Also in Boston, she met W. H. Rowe and his wife, who were planning to lead an expedition of twenty men and women to Nome. Rowe gave advice and insisted that she change her passage from the *Senator* to the ship on which he and his company had booked passage, the *Tacoma* (renamed the *Santa Teresa* in *Raymond and I*), scheduled to leave Seattle Harbor as soon as the danger of ice floes had passed.

Stead had given her an advance in exchange for articles that she promised to send back. She had other means of financial support as well. Upon her arrival in New York, she collected $720 from publisher Frederick A. Stokes for serial rights to *The Mills of the Gods* and *Under the Southern Cross* (Alaska diary, April 5, 1900). In addition, if she had chosen, Robins could have borrowed on the funds in a Zanesville, Ohio, bank, the proceeds from the sale of their childhood home, which Jane Hussey Robins had left to her oldest granddaughter. Instead, she announced to all she met that she was going as a newspaperwoman. This status earned her a pass from Montreal to British Columbia on the Great Northern Railroad. Along the route, she quoted Flora Shaw to Professor William Saunders, the government director of the Dominion's experimental farms. Saunders's speculation that Shaw knew "nothing of this part of the world except what she's been told" (Alaska diary, May 17, 1900) suggests that Robins had resolved to gather her information firsthand, from her talks with the people who lived and worked in the locations she visited. In Seattle, she made an agreement with the mining editor of the *Post Intelligencer* to send back articles for his paper.

Robins anticipated a crowd of passengers desperate for passage and arrived early at the Seattle wharf to secure her berth. This and other personal experiences—shopping in Seattle with the Rowes for their year-long supply of goods, falling prey to the inflated prices, mixing on board the *Tacoma* with a crowd determined to make it to Nome at any cost, and experiencing the stranding of the ship on a sandbar—became source material for her second Alaskan novel.

Although she had cultivated the image of herself as a journalist, she thought it somewhat amusing that "so far as I am known at all, I'm known as the lady who writes for the newspapers." She steeled herself to the fact that many men had customs and mealtime manners much cruder than any she had seen before. In her diary she commented, "I begin to distinguish, I see nice distinctions, and fine shades." One man asked for butter and "made as *if* to use his own knife (which is intended you should do, no butter knife being provided ever), but this particular man carefully and thoroughly *licked his knife* before he helped himself to butter" (Alaska diary, May 31).

Robins wrote down the stories of those who sought adventure in Nome.

She learned the story of Etta Cunningham, who had gone to work to pay the bills for her brother's illness and burial and was now supporting her sister-in-law. Robins wrote, "It is this little delicate-featured refined courageous stenographer who interests me most of all the ship's company" (Alaska diary, May 31). This young woman told Robins of her life in Colorado, one of the few states which had granted woman suffrage; and Robins learned from Cunningham many details of life in a frontier America. Robins took careful note of the woman's determination to make a better life for herself. Cunningham's dissatisfaction with her own position came from her subservience to men. On her way to the North, she expressed her determination to "put up with any and everything"; if she slaved for five years, she might be able to buy a little home, she told Robins, and "know a little Peace before I die" (Alaska diary, May 31).

A man on board discovered that she was the sister of the Raymond Robins he had seen doing so much good in Nome, and Elizabeth wrote in her diary, "I am curiously excited and stirred by the sense of Raymond's nearness and his life circles touching, beginning to blend with mine" (Alaska diary, June 13). After their poignant reunion, Raymond was alternately protective of his sister in a fierce way and oblivious to the occasions when he slighted her. Elizabeth expected to have to live in a tent, but Raymond had arranged for her to have a private room in his church's newly built hospital, the Hospice of St. Bernard. Bit by bit, Elizabeth learned how the facts of Raymond's affairs with Reverend Wirt conflicted with Wirt's confidence that had won her in Boston. Raymond explained how Wirt had squandered money and made false promises to attract people to his work.

It took Raymond two days to approach the subject most important in his thoughts, that he planned to marry Rosa Lamont, one of the missionary women whom he felt Wirt was pushing beyond her commitment. He confessed to Elizabeth that he was not in love with her. When Raymond described for Elizabeth his idea of a wife, it appalled the sister whose independence Raymond had admired. Until well past midnight, with Raymond lying across the foot of Elizabeth's bed, she heard his description of his plans, of Rosa's character, and the difficult political situation with Wirt which had prompted Raymond's plan. Then she got her chance to reply. "I speak of the impossibility in these days of keeping a wife wholly out of a public man's public life." For Elizabeth, the "notion of a wife buried in the country to be paid visits to by her husband at intervals" was absurd. As she wrote up the account of their intimate talk she marveled at Raymond's "beautiful frankness" and cautioned herself, "I must be careful I don't look on the selfish side." She proposed to take him abroad to give him time to reflect and said to him, "By waiting you may come to *assurance* that it's best—and that's worth something." When Raymond rejected this offer, she yielded willingly: "If it's for his good . . . , I'll help to bring them speedily together" (Alaska diary, June 16). She announced to Raymond that she must become acquainted with Miss Lamont. (Robins renamed her Clare McAlmont in *Raymond and I* and gave pseudonyms to a number of other people she met in Alaska.)

Raymond's principal service as a public figure involved much peacekeeping and civic leadership. Elizabeth learned from others that he had pulled the winter residents through a crisis as the town faced drainage and sanitation problems with the anticipated explosion of settlers. The influx of summertime gold seekers, many of them either derelict or one step away from economic ruin, led to sometimes violent disputes over property and land. Elizabeth by her presence began to command Raymond's devotion. Each night, she looked forward to his spending the final moments of the day with her. When she had given up expecting him one night at the end of June and had gone to bed, she heard a slight knock at the door. Though she made no move to answer it, she was warmed by Raymond's gesture. That night she formulated a plan that they discussed extensively. It became an adult version of the fairy tale she had created for him in the thunderstorm. She proposed to Raymond that the $6,600 she had saved in the bank in Zanesville, Ohio, be used to buy a place they could share together. It would be called the "Road House," its name derived from the Alaskan version of roadhouse inns, a "half-way place to the country seat of the old dream" where each could find "shelter and a sense of *Home*" (Alaska diary, June 30).

Two days later, in a self-reflective entry, she worried that she could become too close to her free-spirited brother. When he came to Elizabeth's room at the hospital and found her resting on her bed, he lay down beside her and either roused her with his stories or announced some great impulse and was off again. He always came to her for a goodnight talk, which ended with a goodnight kiss. On one particular night, Elizabeth noticed his deliberate motion of early withdrawal, held his face in her hands, and asked him if he were really going to bed. He said simply, "No," and was gone. She looked out the window at the disappearing figure, wondered if he were going to meet Miss Lamont, and wrote:

> I am looking into the future as I stand at the window—thinking how much trouble I might be laying up for myself if I linked my life closely to the existence of this dear free-lance. Other men I might hold fast—a brother was free at any moment to cut himself adrift and no mere sister might say him nay. Did I run a risk of laying up heart-ache for myself—hoping to hold that bright drop of human quick silver? [Alaska diary, July 2]

Curiously, Robins seems never to have come any closer than she did at this moment to analyzing the emotional void in her own life, which must surely have contributed to the bond she felt with Raymond. For the first time she learned that eleven-year-old Raymond had been devastated when he heard of her marriage to George Parks. Her sense of self as an independent creature had for so long held sway that when Raymond reminded her of her letter to him which told of the early days of her marriage, she remarked to him that she had not only forgotten the letter but had also forgotten the incidents described in it, specifically her trip to Maine, during which she grew more intimate with her husband. Now she was as torn by the prospect of losing Raymond as he had felt when Parks claimed her affections. The more she confided to her diary, however, the more altruistic became her concerns. She knew how deeply she and her brother felt each other's presence, but she determined that any influence she had over him would be wielded for his good, not for her own benefit.

Elizabeth's activities were by no means fully circumscribed by the marital preoccupations of her brother. As Raymond began to depend upon her more and more for advice and for respite from his involvement in town affairs, Elizabeth continued to pursue her journalist's observations.

Elizabeth received a hard blow when, at the first church service she attended, on what turned out to be her last Sunday in Nome, Raymond announced to his congregation that he was staying on with them. As she confessed after Raymond's decision, however, "I found a sense of relief mixed with the disappointment" (Alaska diary, July 22). Elizabeth was glad she was not responsible for determining the direction his life would take. Despite the dread of their parting, Elizabeth filled her last days in Nome with busy activities. On the Monday after his announcement, she sent Raymond away when he wanted to talk about himself; she needed to correct her typewritten manuscript so that it could be posted to Stead. On the next day, she went, again without Raymond, to the Powers camp. What she learned there she recorded in one of her longest entries, which ultimately became the nucleus of her second Alaskan novel. Even though Raymond objected to her plan to visit Saxton, Elizabeth was determined to look up her eldest brother on the trip up the Yukon River that she had planned in London. She learned quite suddenly, on July 26, that her boat was leaving that day; consequently, under pressure to hurry, the two felt strongly the poignancy of their farewell.

The Yukon

As she retraced the journey up the Yukon that her two brothers had taken together in 1897, she began to see herself again as a "creature apart from another life" (Alaska diary, August 1). She realized that Raymond's life had totally absorbed hers. She met travelers who pointed out to her the cabin that her brothers had stayed in and settlers who gave her in great detail the history of the Alaskan fur trade and white man's exploitation of the Eskimo. She insisted on being wakened in the middle of the night so that she could go ashore at Holy Cross and talk to the missionary people who had befriended Raymond, but as she grieved over her separation from Raymond, she admitted: "My individual life has been a thing subsidiary without present weight or future significance." She copied over in her diary a short meditation written nearly a week after saying goodbye to Raymond and admitted that "slowly and with pain" her "old life and old point of view had begun to swing back into place." Her old pursuits spoke to her. "We are not absorbing, they seemed to say (We are not *life*) (we are not human *love*) but we are a bulwark against many evil things." As she began to think of her own books and the art of writing, she summed up, "I am not a helpless person. I have a hundred resources—but what are they all against one heartache!—They are something—*something* my dear, get out your books and your writing and *organize* this fortnight's life." As she sat in her stateroom in the seemingly interminable daylight, she told herself, "For too long you have drifted and looked at the world thro' others' eyes. Time now to take hold again and direct the course!"

She had to renew this call to self-determination again and again over the next months and even years, for Alaska and Raymond so absorbed her thoughts and her literary ambitions that she careened—like a ship repeatedly obliged to correct its course—from work to sickness again, from performances in London to rest cures, from travels to America in search of both Raymond's presence and the home they could establish together, then back to England, where writing with a purpose and a public in mind once more became uppermost in her thoughts.

She wrote her meditation in a mood of depression, suffering from a cold and a worsening headache. Yet she took charge of herself by insisting on seeing and learning all she could. She let the captain of the steamer *Susie* know she wanted to be called whenever the scenery merited, and often from the observation deck she caught sight of the lush green riverbanks. She arrived in Anvik and awaited Saxton with her camera poised. She guessed that the unshaven man in the curious dress clothes might be her brother, but was not sure until he spoke. Saxton arranged to put his canoe on board the *Susie* and travel with Elizabeth to the next landing. He spent his brief hours with her relating the experiences Raymond had not thought worth telling, the details of the winter camp on the Yukon. He described building the stone chimney and spoke of sailing upriver on the first steamer of the spring. Things were so busy in Dawson, he explained, that he had never reached the goldfields. Elizabeth listened attentively but wrote privately, "I suddenly feel with a sinking of the heart I have no more to say to this poor brother of mine, whom fate has used so harshly—I am full of sorrow for him—but I feel helpless—at a deadlock" (Alaska diary, August 5). After Saxton's all too brief stay with her, she befriended a newly married couple on board who knew him from his life in Anvik, and she learned more conclusively the difference between her youngest brother, whose drive and commitment so captivated her, and Saxton, whose easy come, easy go attitudes made his simple life close to the natives satisfying to him.

Once in Dawson, she seized every opportunity for reportage, describing in detail the festivities for the celebration of Dominion Day, visiting the outlying mining districts, and recording the reminiscences of those who had been in the Klondike when it was booming. As she traveled from White Horse to Skagway on the newly completed railway, she observed, "People all about are telling their experiences." She thought of Raymond, "toiling through here with a pack," along the treacherous Miles Canyon where so many lost their lives on the way to the goldfields. Later, she turned her observations into a lively story, "The Alaska Boundary," published when the court settlement of the boundary dispute was in the press.

As Elizabeth completed the last segment of her journey, from Skagway to Seattle, on the steamer *City of Topeka*, she began to suffer the effects of what was later diagnosed as typhoid. The ship stopped to tour canning factories and a large stamp mill. While in Juneau, Elizabeth tried to find the Congregational Reading Room which had so influenced her brother but discovered that Reverend Wirt's debts and a fire had closed it down. She reflected: "So of all that work Mr. Wirt talked about so glibly at Eliot Church [in Newton, Massachusetts] no vestige remains that I can trace except the diversion of Raymond's life work. The irony of it" (Alaska diary, August 25, 1900).

The farther she journeyed away from Raymond, the stronger grew the feelings he had aroused in her. She composed a letter, telling him he should leave Alaska only when he wanted to, but she never got the chance to post it. When she arrived in Seattle at 7:00 A.M. on August 29, she had been suffering from what she thought were a fever and cold. After breakfast, she went to the bank and "was knocked down by the news from Nome: 'Find Miss Robins and wire her that her brother Raymond on the eve of leaving here to join her was taken with typhoid and is now very ill' " (ER to FB, September 26, 1900). Raymond had found a cleric to take over his duties and planned to join her in Seattle if she would wait. His ship, the *Senator*, originally due within hours of her own, had been reported lost. She had to call for a doctor, who found her temperature between 104 and 105 degrees, so she agreed to put off traveling anywhere "till the next day" (ER to FB, September 26, 1900).

Even after entering the hospital and discovering that she had typhoid, she did not realize how long she would be ill. Weeks later, it took her a full day to write to her friend Florence Bell from the hospital an account of her worries over the effects of typhoid and news of her reunion with Raymond, who had arrived at her bedside three days earlier (ER to FB, October 20, 1900).

A week later, Raymond accompanied Elizabeth on the five-day train ride to Louisville. Elizabeth delivered Raymond to the family and, after a brief stay, returned to England. The last entry in her Alaska journal, written on board the SS *Maniton* in the North Atlantic, describes her visit to her mother in the "narrow pitiful room" of the Church Home in Louisville. It was the first time Elizabeth had seen her mother since she visited her in the Oak Lawn sanitarium in 1898; and although Elizabeth's efforts were responsible for her mother's gentler surroundings, Hannah Robins still suffered from delusions. She was sure, she told Elizabeth, that Uncle Edward and Grandma Crow had just visited her. The two long dead relatives, Elizabeth sadly realized, were her mother's apparitions; Hannah spoke of having identified her mother by "the way she used her fan" (Alaska diary, November 18, 1900). For Elizabeth, her mother's phrase recalled with a hollowness "the faint far-travelled fragrance of ancient gentility"; those days of her grandmother and these, part of her mother's empty life, contrasted starkly. Elizabeth acknowledged having decided that Raymond would not be allowed to visit his mother. "For her sake I would not have her youngest born (who had not seen her in 18 years) have *this* memory of his mother. . . . He can do her no smallest earthly service now —let him be spared this vision of her" (Alaska diary, November 18, 1900).

In the final paragraph of her 262-page Alaska diary, she wrote, "So that's done! Louisville and Alaska! Raymond brought back. Saxton seen and 'understanded,' and now London and my own life for awhile" (November 18).

England and Italy, 1901

After she arrived in England, Elizabeth Robins's attempts to resume her own life were interspersed with bouts of illness. At Christmas, she traveled to a nursing home, Soquel, in Paignton, South Devon. There, in early January, she wrote "All Aboard for America," a brief tribute to the immigrants seeking better lives, which *Harper's Monthly Magazine* published as "Embryo Americans" in September.

When Raymond came to England for his long-hoped-for visit in mid-January, Elizabeth tried to give the appearance of having regained her strength.

Together they read the book that had inspired Raymond's religious conversion, Drummond's *Natural Law in the Spiritual World*, and Raymond's Yukon journal, the account kept by Shulte and Raymond in their days on the trail to Dawson. Raymond's visit helped him to decide his future course; by April he wrote that he had decided to take up social work in the settlements of Chicago.

Just after Raymond left, a relapse in March prompted the first of Elizabeth's six-week rest cures during which she was forbidden to read or write. As she completed the enforced retirement, her friend Caroline Grosvenor invited her to Florence for a vacation. She began the trip still weak from the rest cure but determined to enjoy the rich treasure spots of Italy. She took with her Pater's *Studies in the Renaissance* and began a meditation on her days in Italy by stating that she had always thought that a visit to Italy divided one's existence into a "before" and "after" and that she counted on "some great personal Renaissance"[5] to mark a new phase in her life. Instead, after a fortnight in Florence, she remained so weak she felt only half alive. She had struggled to some of the legendary sights that were to have wrought a miracle.

Even so, Robins was able to record detailed impressions of her journey. Traveling to Italy as she had was not like visiting a foreign country. Many English and American artists and intellectuals lived there permanently. Robins was stirred by encounters with English people whom she met while sightseeing and also by the splendor of the ages, preserved so respectfully. She viewed Benvenuto Cellini's bronze of Perseus and wrote that she felt as if, after the ordeal of the last year, she had finally "come home." Yet she saw the Italian treasures while battling physical weakness that made her uncertain whether she would ever again write productively.

In mid-June, as the English party began to swelter with the oncoming summer heat, Robins learned that her mother had died in Louisville more than two weeks earlier. Her brother Vernon had written her a detailed letter describing her last days. He described the death, the funeral, and the burial.[6] Elizabeth, in turn, wrote to her closest friend, Florence Bell, "The end was tranquil and conscious. She recognized the different members of the family and they were gathered about her when she breathed her last" (ER to FB, June 17, 1901). Vernon himself administered a lethal dose of morphine. Robins tried to keep her loss to herself, and only when Caroline Grosvenor found her crying did Robins tell her companion the cause of her sadness. Despite the heat, she set about ordering her mourning habit. She also shared with Bell Vernon's comment that Elizabeth's visit to their mother in 1898 had enabled Hannah Robins to be released from Oak Lawn so that she could live the last few years of her life in greater comfort.

On July 5, she recorded having learned of Saxton's death in Alaska the previous winter. The fortunes of this brother who had lived so contentedly in primitive surroundings were to shape the course of her writing plans.

Struggle to Complete *The Magnetic North*

Amid recurring pain and exhausting heat, Robins decided to go to Aix, where the cooler air might relieve her. After a few weeks there, she sent for her huge wooden box of Alaskan sources—notes, bundles of photographs, a great deal of literature, and Raymond's Yukon journal. As she outlined her plans for Alaska stories to Bell, she proposed a modest scheme, a way to write a few short pieces, in lieu of a novel, in order to "feel 'tidy' intellectually that all these odds and ends are incorporated into something and done away with so far as I am concerned" (ER to FB, August 29, 1901). She did not know that she would still be "concerned" with Alaskan material intermittently for another ten years. Her hope was to offer to the American publisher, Frederick A. Stokes, a series of Alaska tales which, together with *Under the Southern Cross* and *The Mills of the Gods*, would make a full-length book. Robins had deposited the two stories of 1899 with Stokes, with the understanding that her delivery of a third story could complete her part of a publishing agreement.[7] The main source for the Alaska tales was to be the journal Raymond and his partner Shulte kept in camp and on the trail during the winter of 1897–98. She predicted that the proposed set of Arctic stories would be "more truth than fiction, but which may go as 'a story,' aided by a memory so full of marvels as I heard and I saw there" (ER to FB, August 29, 1901).

Robins conceived her story as the experiences of two men who decide to leave camp in midwinter and travel across the Yukon ice and snow to reach Dawson. Morris Burnet, mentioned once by name and thereafter called The Boy, is modeled upon Raymond. The Boy's hope is to make enough money from prospecting to return to Florida and buy back the Orange Grove that had belonged to his family. "Colonel" George Warren from Kentucky, a man twice the age of Burnet, is his unlikely partner. Much of Robins's focus in telling their tale is upon the way hardship affects their relationship. Each feels tempted to abandon the other at various points along the trail, but in the end the bond they form becomes more important than the pursuit of riches. In grounding her story on the reality of relationships, Robins captured the fundamental themes of man's search for meaning and a sense of self.

Although she did not yet regard the stories as a consecutive sequence, she wrote a preface, as she often did to sustain her drive on a project once it was begun. The Eskimo word "Kaiomi" became Robins's watchword for her tale. In this never-published preface, she described the "settled Agnosticism"— Kaiomi—as the Spirit of the North. Nothing there is predictable, not the early freezing, not the drought when rain is expected, not even the tides, the compass, or the daylight. "Aurora plays her fantastic tricks before her high heaven." Sometimes a man sees more suns than one. Often there is a lunar rainbow. In such a land, every beseeching question is answered with a shrugging "I don't know." Nature's broken rules affect the human spirit. Something more ominous than predictability shapes life ("Kaiomi" notes, ER Papers, Fales).

After returning to London on September 20, Robins continued to write while looking for permanent rooms in London. The ambitious task of moving again caused another physical setback. Little did she realize at the time that she would spend the ensuing two years in temporary quarters, visiting with friends, or staying at health spas. More than she realized in her agreement with Raymond, perhaps, she needed to secure a home of her own. First, of course, she had to be able to afford such a dream. Early in December, she agreed with Florence Bell's earlier concern, that she needed "a good fetching and frozen name for the sketches . . . , something if possible with Snow and gold in it." In her engagement book the next day, she began to refer to "the Yukon" as a book with chapters, and had made a new beginning that set the story of the trail within the larger framework of the great stampede to the Klondike (ER to FB, December 6; EBook, December 7, 1901).

Despite her poor health, she remained torn between life on the stage and her career as a writer. In the midst of expanding her Yukon sketches into a full-length novel, two separate theatrical opportunities came her way. Lewis Waller, who had performed opposite Robins in three major Ibsen roles in her Repertory Series of 1893, was interested in "Benvenuto Cellini." Furthermore, the actor-manager with whom she had worked a decade earlier, George Alexander, was anxious to cast her as Lucrezia in Stephen Phillips's recent verse play, *Paolo and Francesca*. On December 12, Robins dashed to Brighton to sign the contract with Alexander, then returned to London in order to read "Benvenuto Cellini" to Waller at 9:30 P.M. Nothing definite came of Waller's interest in Robins's play, but the engagement with Alexander became both a major distraction from her writing and one of the more lucrative engagements of her performance career.

Before rehearsals began for *Paolo and Francesca* on January 8, Robins spent the holidays in Redcar, on the North Yorkshire coast, with the Bells. There she completed the essay "Placer Mining."[8] When she was beginning to see her material for the long novel clearly, however, she was obliged to lay it all aside in order to play a minor role in George Alexander's company; just as the compass loses its sense of direction when closest to the pole, Robins was again thrown off course. She had written to Bell on September 2, 1901, that she "found it difficult to imagine sitting down under a severe bodily affliction and not moving Heaven and Earth and spending whatever one has in trying to get rid of it." Now, when her financial outlook was not favorable, she was moved to accept the twenty pounds a week which Alexander offered to her.

In addition to the expenses incurred in conjunction with her illness, Robins was determined to pay back all of the three hundred pounds that William Stead had lent her. The twenty-five dollars she collected from one story published in the Seattle *Post Intelligencer* she turned over to Stead. She also gave him other small payments. After her rehearsals had begun, she received a letter from Raymond, saying that he had read her first Alaskan sketches and dispatched them to *McClures*. Although he thought that two of them, "The Esquimaux Horse" and "Monica's Village," were "gems," he confessed that he lacked sympathy with her work. He had come to see his journal and the experiences it recorded as too painful a reminder of life before his Christian conversion (RR to ER, January 27, 1902).

Robins's position in Alexander's company was particularly taxing and not simply because her health suffered and the performances prevented her from continuing to work on her novel. As Lucrezia, Robins was a moral and emotional center for the play's action. Robins performed most of her scenes opposite Alexander, who played Giovanni and whose instructions to her to exaggerate her emotional responses ran counter to her sense of Lucrezia's character. In desperation, Robins appealed to playwright Stephen Phillips on the eve of the première. She wrote to Phillips that the character whom Alexander was forcing her to play was not the character she saw in Phillips's script and had agreed to perform. Disparate accounts of her performances suggest that Phillips encouraged her to modify her character after the first night. At the first performance, William Archer sent her an encouraging note and observed that she was one of the few performers who could actually be heard. Max Beerbohm's published review, however, deplored her melodramatic raving on the first night. He attributed it to Robins's concern to show that she was not just an Ibsen actress. The *Times*, in contrast, thought that Robins's tragic intensity was "the proper female complement" to Alexander's Giovanni.[9] One of Robins's personal friends, Lady Dorothy Grey, saw her performance a second time and encouraged her with praise that anticipated Robins's later speaking career: "I understand better than I did why you love acting," she began, adding that she had no interest in the play. "But Lord! How well you do that part! All the same, I feel sure that you ought rather to be an orator. There would be physical play for you, and a real cause, and the working of your brain, and no Alexander. When this play stops you really must consider about sublimated politics and try making speeches. Do now."[10]

Only to Florence Bell did Robins hint of the difficulty of fulfilling her contract to perform. In letters dated March 10 and March 15, 1902, she placed her current exhaustion within the context of the long history of her struggle with ill health. The contract with Alexander lasted until the play closed at the end of the season in late May, further impeding progress on her novel. Just as she began to write again, illness interrupted her work. Recuperation, this time at Harrogate, was in turn abbreviated by the promise of another engagement.

As far back as the previous November, the novelist Mrs. Humphrey Ward, friend of Henry James and Florence Bell, had been planning a production of her own adaptation of her popular novel, *Eleanor*. Ward asked Robins to play Alice, the mad and haunting sister, a minor but influential role which attracted Robins as much for its convenience as for its quiet fascination. She could leave the theater after the second act when her scene was over and could thereby reduce the strain of the work on her. Robins accepted the role and almost immediately regretted having done so. Rehearsals were trying because of Mrs. Ward's supervision and the extended revisions of her scene. Physically, she was able to keep her strength only by staying on her back for the time not spent at the theater.

Reviews of *Eleanor*, though not very favorable to the play, complimented Robins. However much the critics saw in Robins's performance, she used the experience to confirm that her acting days were over. Except for a short role she took in a benefit performance of Florence Bell's *The Heart of Yorkshire* in the early 1920s, Robins did not perform again.

Within days of the final performance of *Eleanor*, Robins was on the move again, her urge to be in America prompted by Raymond's having the month of December free from his position in Chicago. They spent several weeks at the Boston home of Robins's friend Mrs. Clement Waters and further deepened their relationship. Although Raymond took little real interest in her *Magnetic North*, Elizabeth read much of the novel to him and got his response and suggestions for changes. They began to talk of the home he dreamed they would have together as if it were a reality. They gave it an Eskimo name, Chinsegut, the "recovery of things lost," and exchanged suggestions for sites. Elizabeth's recurring illness, her anxieties about finishing her book, and her brother's commitment to his work in Chicago, prevented their meeting again until just before Elizabeth returned to England, eight months later. They had little opportunity to do more than hope for a future home together. At the settlement Raymond lobbied for the Child Labor Bill and worked with Jane Addams. He later became a leader in the fight against graft and corruption in Chicago, but the Raymond Robins whom the public saw as a forceful positivist longed for the sense of home his sister gave him. He wrote to her, "My life is more barren and empty on the home side than ever before. . . . I love you utterly and wish I might hug you close" (RR to ER, January 28, 1903).

In June, Raymond accepted the directorship of the Northwestern University Settlement, a position he had wanted to refuse in March. He spoke of the demands of his new work and suggested that Elizabeth come to Chicago to write a book based on the movement for social reform. When it became possible for Raymond to spend a few days with her in August in Winchester, Virginia, outside Washington, D.C., she had completed and was able to share with him all that she had written. Raymond arranged to meet her on the eve of her birthday. They spent much of each day taking long rides together. After spending a week in each other's company, Elizabeth began to read later chapters of *The Magnetic North* sitting in the woods. Their rides and discussion of her work continued for several days. Raymond heard all but the last chapter, which had not yet been written. Very suddenly, Raymond himself became ill and hastily departed for Chicago. On September 2, Robins took passage to England. On her first day at sea she wrote, "An unexpected peace comes. I begin to hope again" (EBook, September 3, 1903).

Upon returning to England, Elizabeth traveled immediately to Redcar and just as immediately drafted, read to Bell, and revised her final chapter of *The Magnetic North*. Dawson is troubled by typhoid and filled with derelicts hoping to strike it rich. The Colonel leaves each of his four companions a stipend to use only for passage home. A humorous final scene shows the Boy headed downriver in the direction all his friends assume to be the wrong one. His retreat is inexplicable unless he plans to return to Holy Cross or he has heard of a new "strike." Robins's carefully planted hints that either would be possible leave the ending open, thereby signaling Raymond's own next moves, his religious conversion and his departure for Nome.

While she was still in America, she had written to Bell that she had instructed William Heinemann to begin setting up the proof of the chapters she had completed. Robins insisted that Bell was to have a set of galley proofs identical to hers and asked her for help in deciding what one or two chapters she could cut "for space sake. The book has been under my hand so long I myself am numb to it. Raymond doesn't really care a penny about it. . . . If I am told that the last half of the book is 'sick' I may refuse to let it appear. Please correct *any*thing. . . . Mark any possible cuts—and all the stagnant places in the mild current of my story" (ER to FB, July 11, 1903). She also solicited Archer's advice on revisions and sent to Lady Grey chapters of the book to read in proof.

One result of Robins's decision to cut the book was that she removed one of its original parts. She was cheered to learn later that the excerpt had been accepted for separate publication. "Monica's Village," which appeared in the May 1905, *Century Magazine*, describes the two prospectors' introduction to a white woman living among the Eskimos. Monica is educated, has abundant gray hair, and has enjoyed all the amenities of civilized life, yet she has assimilated Eskimo traditions and customs. The men are amazed to learn how her healing and benevolence have led the Eskimos to treat her like a goddess. In contrast, the prospectors cannot even persuade the Eskimos to bargain for some fish to feed their dogs. Whereas the novel presents an exclusively male world of adventure and comradeship, "Monica's Village" stresses that the dominant values in civilization as we know it are male and that, when confronted with female power or influence, men respond by mystifying it. Later, during her suffrage years, Robins read "Monica's Village" at gatherings to raise money for the suffrage cause.

During this period Robins socialized and continued with new writing. She saw Tree and Wyndham in their latest offerings, heard William Archer read to her his scheme for a National Theatre, and shared with him her article on "The Alaska Boundary."[11] No hint of her worsening physical condition appears until she noted in her engagement book that while accompanying Bell to see Eleanora Duse in *Francesca da Rimini* on October 13, she said nothing to her friend about Dr. Vaughn Harley's prescription, delivered earlier that day: "I must go and be cured" (EBook). Five days later, she finished packing, delivered the last of the corrected galley proofs of *The Magnetic North*, and began a rest cure under Harley's care at 7 Queen Ann Street.

In Search of a Cure

In the early 1870s, the American nerve doctor S. Weir Mitchell had pioneered an "enlightened" treatment based on rest and confinement in order to counter nervous complaints. He prescribed absolute rest and large quantities of food to rebuild red blood cells. Later, massage was added to the treatment to effect the benefits of exercise without exertion. Mitchell refused to pamper his patients. He believed that the stern rule of a doctor was better than the overindulgence of relatives or friends. He insisted on total control in the sick room. Mitchell himself was a minor novelist, and his fictional female invalids embodied his own view of the female psyche. He began his innovative treatment upon soldiers suffering from war fatigue, but his clientele soon included the upper and middle classes and women writers and intellectuals whose mental fatigue was extreme.[12] Charlotte Perkins Gilman turned the experience of her treatment by Mitchell into a short story, "The Yellow Wallpaper," which was intended as an exposé of Mitchell and was printed in *New England Magazine* in 1891. Forbidden to write and tormented by the mental boredom, Gilman's narrator-patient identifies with the women she imagines trapped behind the wallpaper in her room of seclusion.

Robins, too, experienced psychological trauma when her doctor, Vaughn Harley, ordering the now-fashionable rest cure that had originated with

Mitchell, removed almost every means by which she might communicate. Ten days after beginning the regimen of rest and massage, she informed Florence Bell that she had agreed to "stay the six weeks out and make a good job of the business" (October 28, 1903). Except for that note, the tiny book in which she kept her engagements served as her only written record until her release in early December.

The Harley rest cure was a failure in all respects but one. The total seclusion to which she was subjected—"Even the cards that come with the flowers do not reach me," she wrote to Bell (October 28)—and the brusque, unannounced visits by Harley gave her the subject for her next novel. In her engagement book, she records, day by day, the sensation of succumbing to the spell of his presence. The novel she wrote based on these experiences revealed, as did Gilman's story, the psychological cruelty of imposed total rest. Robins's tale, unlike Gilman's, however, explored a female patient's growing dependency on her doctor and explored the sexual politics of the encounters between a man who denies emotions and a woman writer whose emotions are heightened.

At one point, Robins noted in her engagement book that Harley had told her there was "absolutely nothing in my condition (physical) to account for the state I'm in." Puzzled, Harley asked, "What are you worrying about?" Robins insisted, "I'm not worrying" (EBook, November 13, 1903). Yet on a later occasion she cried out, "Oh help me." Harley replied, "Don't I try?" (November 21). Indeed, Harley tried everything. He tested her blood and called it "wretchedly poor stuff." He ordered a milk diet (against which she went on strike) and insisted that she continue with her massage (sometimes two sessions a day) which Robins felt "nearly knocks me to pieces." When Robins early in her stay confronted Harley with the remark, "We've used all your horrible inventions, taken all the filthy medicines, shaken all the bones according to directions—don't know *what* we can do now unless we shake the doctor," Harley on the next day "uses stomach pump!!" (EBook, November 9, 10). More and more, she began to depend upon his visits, recording and numbering each of them and finding herself "better when he was here as usual" (December 8). Harley told her when he saw her on this day that she could leave at the end of the week. Within two days of her release she had lost almost six pounds (slightly more than she had gained under his care) and was suffering from overwhelming pain.

As she struggled to put her life back together, she continued to meet Harley. On January 1, Robins looked over notes she had made for the projected book which she would base on her experience with Harley. She proposed to publish it anonymously and at the time planned to submit it to him for approval. If he thought her novel likely to affect his reputation, she would not publish it in his lifetime, even though she suspected that it might bring a price in the market and might create a sensation. She made notes on the project as if she herself did not expect to live. In her diary she predicted it would be a "wild love story I must write *if* I have enough days left that are not wholly swamped in pain." She knew that she would propose not only to publish anonymously, but "for caution's sake," not publish with William Heinemann —"for fear that people should imagine it to be autobiographical and recounting Harley was my doctor at the last, fit the cap on his innocent head" (Diary volume, 1903–1908).

Robins attended to the final pages of the corrected proof of *The Magnetic North* in late December. She began January still very ill, but after several further consultations with Harley (it is unclear whether she did, in fact, discuss with him the subject of her proposed book), and after exploring the possibility of selling some of her shares of Bell Brothers ironworks stock, she was on her way to Dresden, where she would submit again to the *Kur*, this time at Dr. Lahman's. She was desperate again to "move Heaven and Earth" to get rid of the "severe bodily affliction." Amid the rounds of massage, baths, rests, and health-restoring exercise (the last of which directly contradicted the confinement of the rest cure treatment), she noted on February 11, "Begin to work again, 1 hr. a.m. and 1 hr. p.m."

Five days after *The Magnetic North* was published in London, Robins sent Bell her reaction to its reception. She had received clippings of the reviews and William Heinemann's news that a big subscription had warranted the "speedy need of a new edition." She was pleased most of all with the private letters of congratulation (which, in addition to praise from friends such as Lucy Clifford, also included a note from Samuel Clemens). However, to this work of hers, unlike *The Open Question*, which Clemens had also praised, she said, "I feel curiously cold to it myself."

Her current project engaged her in a much different way. In the same letter, she warned Bell not to "breathe a word" and confided that she was "at work on a novel—a flaming love story and am hoping to publish it under another name." Again, she expressed her worry that publishing with Heinemann would reveal that her own life had been the novel's source. She did not want this pseudonymous work to be published as *The Open Question* had been, "which too many people knew about." "It would be great fun" to have yet another pen name. "I'm spinning with it! . . . But bury the knowledge in your deepest brain cranny" (ER to FB, March 15, 1904).

By the time she left Dresden for England three weeks later, Elizabeth was nearly halfway through a draft of the novel that at first she entitled "The Black Magic Man." A year after she made her first notes, it was published as *A Dark Lantern*. Both titles refer to the compelling presence of a mysterious,

Heathcliffian doctor in a woman's life. Contrary to her prediction, Heine-mann brought it out and her own name graced the title page.

A Dark Lantern, 1905

Robins's newfound reputation upon her return to England after the pub-lication of *The Magnetic North* manifested itself in part by her acceptance into the Women Writers' Club. She attended meetings in May and June and on July 13 was elected to the chair. In the midst of these activities, she had qualms about "The Black Magic Man" and wrote to William Archer for some —any—suggestion as to what she should do next. She wanted, she said, a good plot that she could dramatize. Archer replied, "As for plays I have none 'in stock.'" He disparaged his own creative powers and advised Robins not to write a play. "To tell you the truth I don't think you have the power of concentration required for playwriting. Certainly you could find a novel far easier than a play." Archer suggested that she turn to a short story instead "just to occupy you while your big work is at a loose end. . . . What you really need," he strongly hinted, "is to find a big, elemental, typical theme" (WA to ER, July 9, 1904).

Robins ignored Archer's warning that she was not capable of writing a play. To her other friend, Florence Bell, she proposed a dramatic collaboration on matters they had begun to discuss. They often called Archer "Wet Blan-kets" for his lack of encouragement. As the summer progressed, the collabo-ration became a serious enterprise. Then, prompted by her social weekend at the Danish Pavilion, home of George Lewis, Robins sent another long letter with her new ideas for a plot based on the craze for gambling at the game of bridge that was popular in high society.

The embryo plot that Robins sent to Bell became *Angela*, and for a long while Robins and Bell both worked on it. As they corresponded, Robins saw Alfred Sutro's play, *The Walls of Jericho*, and worried that his play impinged on their own theme. Eventually, Robins turned over her interest in the project. Only Lady Bell's name was associated with the play when it was published in 1926 and was performed in 1927.[13]

Other relationships engaged her autumn months, as her letters to Bell and from Raymond indicate. To know Elizabeth Robins counted for something in London. She undertook to persuade the staunch moralist William Stead to go to the theater for the first time; they saw Beerbohm Tree's performance of *The Tempest*. Stead wrote an opinion of the production, brought it to Robins for emendation, and talked for more than two hours with her about his article, the theater, and life. Beerbohm Tree, she had learned, was "all on end about what Stead was going to say" (ER to FB, September 29, 1904). Robins proceeded to make the novice theatrical critic and the actor-manager good friends by inviting them to lunch. Her assistance with Stead's criticism gave him the idea of putting his theatrical adventures into a volume. She accompanied Stead on many of his theatrical adventures throughout the fall. Finally, he interviewed Robins and brought this manuscript to her to work over again. She spent hours "doctoring, cutting out, writing in" (ER to FB, October [?29], 1904). Tree, in his way, sent an appreciation also. Robins passed on to Bell the actor-manager's report: "Stead's account did a great deal of good. They turn away money every performance."[14]

Amid these and other social engagements, Robins made plans to meet her brother in America. Robins marked in her date book for September 30 "Sail *Cedric*," but she crossed that out and inserted, "Instead of sailing sit in Chilsworth St. and write B. M. M. [Black Magic Man]." In addition to Robins's editing Stead's "Theatre Adventures" for the *Review of Reviews* and her work on shorter projects of her own ("Caribou Stand" was completed on October 1), Robins by the end of the year took up with new seriousness her "flaming love story." As she worked on the last chapter "outlined of course ages ago," she commented, "But oh it needs to be steered so carefully and pruned and condensed and held by the scruff of its neck" (ER to FB, December 28, 1904). Within a month, she had completed these difficult revisions, this time cutting and editing without outside advice.

Like much of Robins's writing, the ending of *A Dark Lantern* grips the reader. Her ability to present compelling emotional encounters is masterful. In this book, however, the first of four sections is entitled "Prologue," and Robins somewhat diminishes the coherence of the whole by treating her introductory material as a detached story. Nevertheless, the themes of the prologue resonate throughout the main action of the book in a manner that shows Robins's growing artistic mastery of her material. Certainly, its sexual politics make it far more original than a traditional romance. In "The Prologue" Katharine Dereham is a woman who suffers the pain of the worst insult her sex can imagine. She falls in love with a German Prince who courts her elegantly, even though he is affianced to another aristocrat. After he has married royally and produced a son, he promises Katharine that his wife will divorce him. Katharine is led to believe that he is prepared to be faithful to her. Instead, she finds out that the Prince has been living with a notorious singer. In a tense encounter, he confesses that his wife, a Catholic, will not grant a divorce, but he has arranged their meeting to make it appear that she has no escape from his attempt to seduce her. Katharine does narrowly evade him, but the pain of her discovery of Prince Waldenstein's two-faced behavior seems to mark her for life. She remarks ruefully afterward, "Even through all the disillusionment of this last meeting [with the Prince], the old wound throbbed and ached. If the old love stood for nothing but pain, it *did* stand for that."[15]

Robins returned time and again to the theme that women never recover from their first love. It found some support in her own life. While Robins gave the appearance of being fiercely independent, she was in fact haunted by her husband. Her strength as a novelist comes from her readiness to transform the personal experience into meaningful investigations of the difference between men's and women's natures.

In the main part of Robins's story, Katharine is virtually isolated from any human contact by Dr. Garth Vincent's ordered rest cure. As a result of her confinement, Katharine falls under the doctor's control, hating yet longing for the emotions he arouses in her. One conversation might have been taken from the pages of Robins's own accounts. The doctor returns and asks,

> "Any better?"
> "No."
> "What are you worrying about?"
> "Nothing."
> "Yes, you are. There's nothing in your analysis to account for the state you're in. What are you worrying about?"
> "Only at being so ill."
> "You are beginning to fret at confinement."
> "No . . . "[DL, 206]

Katharine *is* worrying, however, and her nervousness intensifies because she senses Garth Vincent's gross misreading of her situation. His looks reproach her for being too preoccupied with the Prince whose picture hangs over the mantelpiece. Katharine considered it "a matter of honor to disavow concern with all that life where he—Garth Vincent—was not" (*DL*, 206).

Her first submission develops into an increasingly romantic dependency on Katharine's side. Garth shows no sign of reciprocating, and part of Katharine's response to this man with the dark-lantern face is that she recognizes that it is he who needs to be cured. She learns that some injurious incident in his past led him to mistrust all women and prevents him from loving her. The story focuses on Katharine's need to know everything. At first, she becomes unconsciously dependent on her healer-imprisoner. Under the influence of the emotionally wounded doctor, she devotes herself to him, first as patient, then as mistress, and finally as wife. Her determination to know the story of his life is not appeased until a final confrontation makes her see that Garth's cure depends upon her unquestioning acceptance of his past. Through a final angry misunderstanding, Katharine comes to a realization that Garth finds it as difficult as she does to dwell on a past that once brought pain and regret. Because we know of Katharine's own pain, graphically described in the "Prologue," her acceptance of his silence can be read as reconciliation and not her submission without question. Katharine realizes that her assumption that "other husbands close to their wives in sympathy and devotion, told them their past," is misleading. Men, too, suffer pain. "Her good fortune it was, that Garth would never make those old days live again, by any word of his. They seemed the more securely dead. They were as if they had never been" (*DL*, 400).

One contemporary review argued that such an ending drove forcefully home the fact that a double standard prevailed. Katharine concludes that it is best for her to know nothing about Garth's unknown years and appears to support a man's right to a different code of behavior. Her acceptance suggests another reading, however: that a man's pain can be equal to a woman's and that mutual forgiveness and willingness to silence past agonies is the beginning of equality. Katharine recognizes that Garth is inarticulate, incapable of expressing the things he has needed to forget and has consequently forgotten as he begins to love her.

In a variation upon Robins's tendency to show the effects of silence, she makes her heroine a writer of verses who belittles her own expressiveness because her poems become hollow as soon as they become public. Very early in the book, Katharine's inclination to write is shown as "too great a peculiarity to be pleasant" (*DL*, 11). Her doctor is among those who blame her nervous collapse on her writing, and he forbids any writing or reading as dangerously fatiguing during her rest cure. By the time that a collection of her verses expressing her passion for Garth has been published, Katharine has persuaded herself of the futility of her writing, using the imagery of birth and death:

What rot he must be thinking it! And not he alone. Little books of verse were always dropping, still born, from the London press. Hers just another, like the rest. Those sonnets she had written out of such an eager heart. How dull, belated, lacking in significance they had looked forth from the proof. Ah, they had not stood the proof, those frail little things of her making! [*DL*, 301]

Privately, Katharine continues to write, even as the silence between Garth and Katharine grows to jealousy and suspicion. Finally, Katharine's locked diary, which contains verses dedicated to her newborn child, symbolizes the distance between them. Garth's wrenching open of the diary foreshadows his forced entrance into her locked bedroom, but each apparent abuse of power turns to powerlessness. He falls weeping into her lap pleading, "*Don't lock me out*" (*DL*, 398). His love for her makes it impossible for him to bear the distance between them. Katharine's true articulateness comes in her unspoken understanding of his emotions.

Years later, Robins would learn that Olive Schreiner was mesmerized by the book, especially by Robins's true-to-life characterization of Garth. As she worked on revisions, Robins sought her friend Lady Dorothy Grey's reaction to a prepublication copy. Grey was also struck by Robins's ability to depict the male psyche. She took note of the way that Garth's own inarticulateness prompted the final confrontation, and she complimented Robins's final action by writing, "I was almost afraid he might 'burst into song' at the end. But you know too much."[16] Not only had Robins translated into fiction the silencing of her voice that occurred when Harley forbade all writing and reading; in the novel, she had also demonstrated that communication between man and woman transcended the restrictions of language. Whereas Gilman exposed the psychological terror in shrilly nightmarish terms, Robins exposed gender differences in realistic terms. She captured one aspect of the innate difference between men's and women's communication styles that Deborah Tannen studies in *You Just Don't Understand: Women and Men in Conversation.*[17]

As publishing negotiations proceeded, Heinemann managed to secure an American edition that would be published at almost the same time as the English. He also succeeded in persuading Robins to use her own name. She expressed her anxiety to Florence Bell: "I am seized with a desire to cut and run when I think of the Lantern ceasing to be Dark and throwing out its beams upon an unprepared and innocent public. Oh dear, what *will* happen!" (ER to FB, April 29, 1905). One review, written by the young Virginia Stephen, commented that Robins was "one of the few novelists who can live in their characters. . . . Miss Robins has the gift of charging her air with electricity."[18]

Just after completing *A Dark Lantern* in early January, she began another Alaskan story. She was to work on this, the "Fairy Tales" or "Go to Sleep Stories," on and off for over a year. In addition, she renewed her plans to collaborate with Bell on a play.

Chinsegut

Affairs of more consequential nature than her own day-to-day writing arose in the late spring of 1905. Robins experienced the loss of one place she considered home and obtained both a replacement for it and a home of her own. The Hugh Bells were leaving their Redcar townhouse in order to move into Rounton Grange near Northallerton. Robins wrote a farewell note to her beloved "Red Barns," the "Dear House of Happy Memories" she had known as home for almost thirteen years (ER to FB, April 12, 1905). During the week before Easter she visited the Bells at Rounton Grange, and on Easter Saturday Hugh Bell took her over the grounds of nearby Mt. Grace Priory, the ruin of a medieval religious center which had also been acquired by the

Lady Florence Bell, perhaps Robins's closest friend, with her daughter Mollie Trevelyan and Mollie's eldest daughter Pauline, circa 1906. Bell stipulated that the many letters she had received from Elizabeth should be returned to aid her in writing her autobiography, which Robins never completed. Florence Bell was often the first reader of Robins's fiction. (*Courtesy of the Fales Library. Reproduced with the permission of Mabel Smith, for the Backsettown Trustees.*)

Bells. Robins found a keen sense of place in the remains of the original church and the seventeenth-century manor house built from the stone of the demolished priory. She came often to visit Mt. Grace. Later it was the home of Gertrude Bell, and Robins was able to write in rooms that loomed over the skeletons of holy archways now open to the sky and the lush green countryside. Elizabeth posted a letter to Raymond about her first visit to Mt. Grace on Easter. On the same day, Raymond began a letter to her from "Chinsegut," the property he had purchased with her money in Hernando County, Florida, not far from his aunt and uncle's former property and his boyhood home. "My beloved," he began his letter to Elizabeth on "Resurrection A.M." He went on to describe the elevation he had rechristened "Chinsegut Hill," and the rundown estate house that boasted windowsills handhewn from twelve-by-twelve-inch cyprus. "You own 214 acres," he wrote her, and described the vistas afforded by the hilltop site in a region that was predominantly flat. He estimated the current values of the timbered acres, the cleared land, and the timber value of the house at more than $3,200. He had purchased it for her through "forced sales and the process of the court" for $1,800 (RR to ER, April 23–28, 1905).

Raymond had begun negotiations to acquire the property earlier in the year but had wavered inexplicably between nearly abnormal longing for her and almost complete detachment. The letter he began to her on Easter at Chinsegut Hill was continued over the next several days. He mentioned that he had become ill and had decided to stay in Florida. On April 27 Raymond received her letter of the tenth and begged to know the meaning of her statement, "Things are not easy with me." In his next day's installment, he returned to a subject he had mentioned earlier, the fact that he had dined at the home of Margaret Dreier in Brooklyn, in order to announce to Elizabeth that he had had a sudden vision. He described Dreier, the leader of the Women's Trade Union League, as "a woman of some 33 years, attractive not beautiful, of the first social position, splendidly educated and reputed quite wealthy." What affected Raymond more than these attributes was that "she has caught the enthusiasm for social and industrial justice, helping the working women of New York, and next to Jane Addams is the best incarnation of the social conscience I have yet seen." Dreier had called him up before he left town to report that, thanks to the efforts of her League, a manufacturer had increased the wage scale of every girl in his factory by the sum of one dollar per week. Because Raymond knew nothing of her marital status or inclinations, he was quite struck by his vision, "I am under a profound conviction that I shall marry her within a year of this date" (RR to ER, April 23–28, 1905).

Most certainly with Elizabeth's encouragement, the marriage became a definite prospect even more quickly than his prediction. On May 27 his telegram informed Elizabeth, "Margaret accepts. Both send love." A shorter wire on June 7 spoke with greater certainty: "June 20th. Come." Elizabeth immediately dropped her work and, within three days, had left for America. She spent several days before the wedding at the Dreiers' Brooklyn residence, 6 Montague Terrace, and stayed in America for only two weeks afterward, at the home of Margaret's three sisters in Stonington, Connecticut.

From Brooklyn, two days before the wedding, Robins wrote Florence Bell of the new happiness that was in Raymond's life. She thought it "wonderful that these two people have found each other." Without the slightest regret, Raymond broke his pact that for his sister's sake he would not marry. As Elizabeth described the Dreier family of three younger sisters and a married brother—their life of wealth, good society, and even luxury—she marveled that Margaret was so willing to give up her life in order to join Raymond in Chicago. Dreier had an independent income and, as leader of the Women's Trade Union League, was more than a political organizer. Elizabeth reported that "she kept some starving people going last winter—7000 or more on strike, she supplying their needs at the rate of $5000 a week till her brother went mad—if the strike hadn't opportunely ended Margaret would have had to be rescued in some way not clearly discernible" (ER to FB, June 19, 1905).

Elizabeth's recognition of the importance Margaret would assume in Raymond's life made her want to give him half the home he had purchased with her money. Raymond refused to accept the gift, "No I am never going to have anything of my own," and suggested instead that Elizabeth give the half share to Margaret. "So that's what I'll do," Elizabeth wrote to her friend in England, adding: "It will seem rather like coaling Newcastle except for the fact that in her eyes the material consideration will be so infinitesimal." Sharing her American home with Raymond's wife, she confirmed, seemed like "the wedding of the old dreams to the new, and my complete and thorough-going identification of Margaret with my own life so far as America goes." The two newlyweds went so far as to invite Elizabeth to accompany them to Florida on their honeymoon journey to Chinsegut. She declined, jesting to Bell, "but of course I'm not such a silly" (ER to FB, June 19, 1905).

Elizabeth soon found that her investment entailed more of an obligation than she had envisioned with her little roadhouse conception. Raymond wrote his sister on June 27 from the still unrepaired Chinsegut that he and Margaret had agreed to spend five thousand dollars during the next twelve months on improvements. In September, from North Yorkshire, Elizabeth composed a meditation on what she hoped to achieve with Chinsegut. She wanted to learn botany, to "learn that hilltop by heart . . . , come to know the name of every flower and shrub and tree . . . , of every bird that nests there." She wanted to build a "Sun Tower" of cyprus, or coral, or adobe, set off from the main dwelling. In October, Raymond elaborated on what he and Margaret hoped to spend per year. He detailed Margaret's assets as if he were reassuring Elizabeth that his wife's money would cover their plans to renovate and expand Chinsegut. In November, Raymond invited Elizabeth to spend Christmas with them in Florida. Elizabeth did, taking with her the half-completed manuscript on which she had been working since May. The sensations she experienced on her train ride south, to a "homeland" she had last visited in 1886 when she was summoned to her father's orange grove at the death of her sister, emerged in a later novel, *Camilla*, in which a remembered landscape evokes the woman's youth in the South. Chinsegut made possible for Robins a reconnection with her American roots and a commitment to native themes in her writing.

Soon after her arrival at the Brooksville, Florida, property, she experienced a number of emotional shocks. All of the furniture that had belonged to her grandmother in Zanesville and had been in storage for so long was damaged—most of it beyond repair—when it was crushed by the heavy machinery being shipped with it. Gradually, it became clear to Elizabeth that Raymond had not been candid with Margaret regarding his finances. Elizabeth was appalled when she understood what Raymond had promised Margaret for the repair of Chinsegut. When she confronted Raymond privately to ask what had become of the remainder of her trust fund—less than a third had been spent on the acquisition of the property—Raymond confessed to having spent it all, apparently to help his associates through a political campaign. Meanwhile, Raymond and Margaret announced plans for the rebuilding of Chinsegut and assumed that they could spend more of Elizabeth's money, money that she simply did not have. One particular point of irritation for Elizabeth was that Margaret insisted on two bathrooms, upstairs and down, furnished with heated running water. This luxury meant building a water tower and acquiring a wood-burning engine. Elizabeth had little power even to veto the cutting of the precious forest to supply the firewood; Margaret considered a gas-burning heater too expensive. Robins was shattered not by Margaret's demands but by Raymond's duplicity and presumption. Yet somehow she continued to feel obligated and authorized Raymond to borrow money to pay for the rebuilding.

During the family financial crisis that marked the days of Margaret's and Raymond's stay, Robins transformed her modest Chinsegut diary from a record of day-to-day facts and events of a new experience into a chronicle of her disillusionment with Raymond. "I had one person in the world who stood close to me," she wrote when she heard that Raymond had spent her "poor little savings." Now she had lost him: "He does not even come to see how I fare when I am ill."[19] When she discovered that Raymond and Margaret had

Chinsegut, in Hernando County, near Brooksville, Florida. Elizabeth attempted to keep the translation of the Eskimo word, which means "the recovery of lost things," a secret between her and her brother Raymond. The house was purchased with Elizabeth's legacy from the sale of the Stone House in Zanesville. (*Photograph by the author.*)

gone off for a walk together without her, she wrote that the intensity of her anguish would be connected forever to the spot in the hall where she stood "with dim eyes and clenched hands wondering which way I'm to turn, where go, how win back what seems lost or how accept its going" (CD, 33). She told herself, "Work, Work," but could not rest comfortably until she put down the details of the family disagreement. In the midst of her worries, she wondered, "Am I so hard to live with? Shall I have to do without love?" (CD, 36). Her compassion and her need to reconcile matters evolved after she first recorded the depth of her heartbreak. For Elizabeth, Chinsegut would mean the demolished dream, the extravagant property not worth the "lost things" that seemed now never to be recovered—Raymond's trust, a haven for their family's papers, her need of a home where she could rest and write without care.

After Raymond and Margaret had returned to Chicago in early January, Elizabeth Robins stayed on to oversee the construction. She was alone except for black servants and, as a result, did not have Raymond's wholehearted approval. She gained perspective on her situation when white intruders demanded entrance to the house on the ground that Raymond's reputed wealth obligated him to provide for the poor. They warned her that Raymond's earlier poverty, in his youth in the same locality, meant that his present claim to superior status would be resented (CD, 90).

These white neighbors did not seem to grasp Robins's meaning when she introduced herself as the owner, who had to earn a living by writing. Robins's visits with the black servants taught her that they, too, regarded Raymond as a rich benefactor. She furnished them with basic provisions that they were too afraid to request from Raymond. In her solitude and despair, Elizabeth began to treat Chinsegut as a home that she might occupy at least a few months of every year. She ventured out on long rides to explore the wilderness and returned to record anecdotes in the diary that would, in turn, become a source for later fiction.

Come and Find Me, 1905–1906

For the present, she was preoccupied with finishing the Alaskan novel she had begun in May. It was entitled at first "The Great Legacy" or "The Mother Lode" and was published in 1908 as *Come and Find Me*. Because she credited Bell with giving her the inspiration to see the story clearly, she wrote often to Bell, of "your" book and "our book," even though the writing of it was more her own than anything she had previously shared with Bell. In a remarkable letter of May 31, 1905, she first outlined the plot on an impulse, having begun a little note to say to Bell, "Thanks for the light." From the germ she presented then, Robins rewrote the story of male quest that had been *The Magnetic North* and redefined the Alaskan adventure as one of female faith, perseverance, and women's bonding. Grafted onto the legend she had heard when visiting the Powers camp, of a man knowing about the Mother Lode as early as thirty years prior to the Nome rush of 1899–1900, she created a heroine—the prospector's daughter, Hildegarde—who encourages her father to return to his claim and who, when he does not come home for two years, "raises funds and goes there to bring the old man home." She continued her outline to Bell: "She goes there as I did in 1900, in just such a crazy ship among some such amazing crew as were my companions on that really very wonderful and perilous cruise in a rotten old boat forcing her way thro' the ice-floes to be first in the field." She brings her father home and discovers that she is truly in love with the man who had looked after her father for her sake.

Raymond Robins, 1901. (*Reproduced with the permission of Mabel Smith, for the Backsettown Trustees.*)

In addition, she witnesses the last moments alive of the man she had known in stories first as a protégé of her father when he was young and later as the bridegroom-to-be of her girlfriend Bella Wayne. This explorer, Jack Galbraith, had married, then inexplicably abandoned Bella when he learned that the great explorer Fridtjof Nansen had returned from a two-year excursion to the top of the world. Galbraith, hallucinating now in a small tent in the tundra, induces Hildegarde to help him destroy his charts and maps verifying his successful solo conquest of the Pole.

Robins's greatest achievement lies in demonstrating how the friendship of two women supersedes all misfortune and any reward. The reunion between Hildegarde and the man she loves comes as a clever afterthought in the last chapter, which takes as its larger theme the women's reconciliation and pledge to each other. In this way Robins subtly subverts a traditional form at the same time that she capitalizes on it for the sake of her heroine's more complete happiness. When the book version of *Come and Find Me* came to be published in 1908, its feminist implications did not escape Katherine Mansfield, who reacted in her journal, "Really, a clever, splendid book; it creates in me such a sense of power. I feel that I do now realise, dimly, what women in the future will be capable of. They truly as yet have never had their chance." In realizing the independence of Robins's female characters and the mutual support they gave each other, Mansfield sensed that although women in New Zealand had had voting rights for over a decade, she and her countrywomen were "firmly held with the self-fashioned chains of slavery."[20] Robins, in short, was able to incorporate the free spirit of American women and give her heroine a scope beyond the traditional romantic plot. The perspective would continue to color Robins's writing and feminist politics.

All during the summer of 1905, Robins had worked at "The Great Legacy," mostly at Rounton Grange. When she left for Florida in December, she took the manuscript with her and began to read it to Raymond and Margaret in January as they sat around the fireplace at Chinsegut. After they had left, Robins had the "biggest house in the county" to herself. As she struggled to immerse herself in her work once more, she composed a "dedicatory letter" to Florence Bell describing the distractions she faced and how much she needed Bell's moral support to carry through her work. In a sense, Robins's fiction transformed what in her own life had been a collaborative and devoted relationship with a fellow writer and critic of her work into the story of two girls who, because they believe in each other's dreams, can lend support and be understanding even when doing so seems to mean relinquishing personal happiness.

Robins increasingly felt the fascination of the woods and included in her writing plans a woods tale. She often rode alone and, in order to appease Raymond's fears, adopted the local custom of carrying a loaded pistol. She kept it beside her as she slept and wrote. She explained: "The great fear is the Negro. A lady rides out from Brooksville to pay you a visit[;] she brings her pistol as a matter of course. If a white woman is alone in a carriage you may be sure there's a pistol beside her." Already formulating the social aspect for a later novel she added, "And the effect of all this on both races is full of evil" (ER to FB, February 8, 1906). Their black servant "Fielder"—Fielding Harris, who was proud to admit that he had raised Raymond—arrived after Raymond sent word to find him and was installed as principal caretaker of the estate. His position was not regarded with favor by the local populace, who had stricter rules about the segregation of blacks, and the Robinses later paid dearly for their devotion to Fielder. When Elizabeth chose to have company, Fielder escorted her on her rides.

As she dispelled any fear for her own safety, Robins received word that Raymond had narrowly escaped an attack upon his life by mobsters in Chicago. The news had been kept from her for six days, and by that time Raymond had returned to his daily routine of campaigning for social justice. Elizabeth traveled from Chinsegut to Brooklyn and there kept in touch with Margaret by telegraph. Although she continued to feel distressed with Raymond for disappointing her, she wrote, "my heart misgives me. I am not sure that I can go so far from him." Robins resolved to visit Raymond overnight in Chicago because she knew "what a peril he is in of his life between now and the Election of April 10" (ER to FB, March 1, 1906). She extended her stay in Chicago to six days. While she was there, she visited Hull House and witnessed at first-hand Raymond's impact upon politics. Raymond had encouraged Elizabeth to write a book about the struggle between reform and corruption in Chicago. Her visit stimulated her to begin collecting information on one of the city's leading social issues, organized prostitution, a theme that would become the core of a London-centered novel.

Elizabeth was more immediately concerned with the completion of her latest Alaska novel, "The Great Legacy." As soon as she returned to England, she prepared the final version and posted it to her agent Paul Reynolds in mid-April. Her engagement book was filled with dinners, theatergoing, and another serious effort to place "Benvenuto Cellini" in production. In addition, she completed another Alaskan tale, a set of interconnected short stories which transformed traditional Eskimo legends by the way in which the tribal storyteller's, or shaman's, daughter takes over the routine of narrating the "Go to Sleep Stories," tales so familiar to the Eskimos that they help people fall asleep during the long winter nights. Princess Muckluck manipulates the well-known stories and arouses ire among the normally complacent men who listen. Robins further contextualizes the fables by chronologically placing them in the midst of the action of *The Magnetic North*. Princess Muckluck's auditor from the outside world is "The Boy," hero of that book. As if Robins could not rest easy with the published form of *The Magnetic North*, she inverts a typically male narrative and has the Princess rewrite a traditional courtship story so that her telling of it affects the way she herself is courted. On the surface, the stories are troublesome as portraits of an ethnic minority, for Robins depended for her characterizations upon the broken English of the Eskimos' speech. In fact, Robins did not demean her Princess storyteller but embodied in her an independence that was a bold corrective to what she, Robins, had observed of the suppression of women in the Eskimo culture.

As she saw to their completion the two Alaskan-centered writing projects which had engaged her for months, Robins was attracted by another enterprise from an almost improbable source. She wrote to Bell with a plea for advice about an offer that was put to her: "Now I wonder what you think I ought to do. For several weeks, months rather, I have been at intervals pelted with notes by Gertrude Kingston asking me to luncheon, to dine, to do all manner of things. I have never done any of them until last night when I went to dine with her." Kingston, who, like Robins, had begun to act in London during the season of 1888 but who had established a strong reputation with her full-time playing, was thinking of forming her own company. Kingston proposed that Robins write a play for her. Robins asked her friend whether such a commission was a "reasonably sensible investment of time." She asked Bell to meet with her so that Bell could help her "mature it or cast it out." Robins worried that she could not think of a promising plot: "That woman is very clever, you know. I can't think of anyone of my sex on the English stage that I would rather do something for, but of course it has got to be, or should hope to be, a quite special kind of part" (ER to FB, June 23, 1906).

With Bell's full encouragement, Robins undertook the commission. For most of July, she worked on "Judith," a play that was set in nineteenth-century France at the time of the great dramatic actress Rachel. On August 1, she signed a contract to deliver a play to Kingston. Then, quite suddenly, her plans to write a historical drama changed. In late August, she became fired with a new idea and started making notes for "A Friend of Woman." Eventually the new work had a more specific title—*Votes for Women!*—and proved to William Archer and the London public that Robins could write a successful play. In the English campaign for woman suffrage, Robins found a vital sense of direction. Little did she realize it at the time, but the interest she took in the debate over women's suffrage would come to be for her the "big, elemental theme" that Archer had urged her to seize upon.

6 Votes for Women

The Suffrage Campaign in England, 1906–1909

I would not have you think me unwilling to do what I can. I am just embarked upon the task of turning a play (which I've written at white heat in the last two months) into a novel, as the indications are that the play is held to be too partisan to be ventured upon by the regular managers. . . . Instead of wearing out my soul by battering at their doors, I shall set to and turn the thing into a book as fast as ever I can. . . . It will be the first thing I shall have written under the pressure of a strong moral conviction.

—Robins to Millicent Fawcett, November 1, 1906, on the prospects of her play, *Votes for Women!*

"I know what she's like! The girl in Ibsen's *Master Builder*!"
"I don't think I know the young lady."
"Oh, there was a knock at the door that set the Master Builder's nerves quivering. He felt in his bones it was the Younger Generation coming to upset things. He *thought* it was a young man—"
. . . .
"You are right," she said to Jean. "This is Hilda, harnessed to a purpose. A portent to shake middle-aged nerves."

—Lady John to Jean during the Trafalgar Square Suffrage Meeting, in *The Convert*

THE SCENE: Savoy Hotel Banquet Room. London. December 11, 1906.[1] A gala suffrage gathering, to celebrate the release from Holloway Prison of some of the earliest Votes for Women protesters who welcomed jail sentences in their defiance of governmental authority. The guests of honor are dressed in white. Flowers and plants decorate the hall. Applause of the previous speech dies down. A wide shot of the room zooms in on the women seated at the dais, many elegantly dressed in suffrage colors, deep or pastel shades of green and purple tinged with white. Elizabeth Robins rises to stand at the podium.

ELIZABETH ROBINS: Mrs. Fawcett, Ladies and Gentlemen: I am called upon to propose a toast that needs little commending here. I think we all realize that the publicly expressed sympathy of a representative gathering, such as this, is a fact of no small significance.

[The actress/speaker hesitates, momentarily unsure of herself, then continues.]

ELIZABETH ROBINS: But an even more wonderful thing is true. There is now a large company outside these walls who say when the question of Woman Suffrage is broached: "I am in favor." We have it on the authority of the late Prime Minister that four hundred and twenty Members of Parliament stand committed to this Cause. We are told that the gracious-sounding phrase "I am in favor" is on the lips even of Cabinet Ministers. The strange thing is that so much favor should be so ineffectual. I hope some fair-minded men will remember that, when they criticize "methods." They are not to forget that their "favor" left the question where it was.

The women who did the talking in the lobby of the House of Commons on October 23rd made it their method to announce the end of the world—the end of the world as it *had* been. You all know how they paid the price in that grim place, His Majesty's Prison at Holloway. When we think of what they went through there, when we think of what they have suffered from the tongues and pens of people safe outside . . . , when we think of these things to-night, we are proud of the type of woman the suffrage cause has forced to the front. . . .

To the honor of our sex, the fact that 82 percent of the women of this country are wage-earning women, the fact that the average wage for a working woman is barely half that of a working man, these facts have only had to be known to the better-off women in order to inspire many of them with a sense of responsibility towards their less fortunate sisters. Women are at last learning to look to women for help.

Nothing less than a sense of duty and a resolute self-mastery could bring women of the character of those who have done most for this cause to face the misunderstanding, the hideous discomforts, and the lasting hurt to health that they have been called to bear. Every fair-minded person must realize it is very hard for women to face these things. It was George Eliot, I believe, who spoke with envy of those who could lead what she called "the sheltered life." When woman as a sex considers her own dignity and satisfaction alone, it is the shelter that she chooses. I am reminded of that happy tribe in the inclement North called the Achéto-Tinneh, which being interpreted out of the Esquimau tongue is: *The People Who Live Out of the Wind.*

Enviable folk these, for in the Arctic it is not still cold, but the wind that kills. The vast majority of women would belong to the Achéto-Tinneh if they could with honor. For this generation, the fighting and the sacrifice. Your great-granddaughters, brought up in the exercise of public duty, may find it not duty alone, but pleasure as well.

I have the honor to propose the toast: "Success to the Cause of Women's Suffrage."

Notes on the Scene: When the militancy of the Women's Social and Political Union (WSPU) brought the thirty-year-old lobby for women's suffrage into the streets and into the homes of Edwardian Britain in 1906, the pro-suffrage forces gathered momentum because their tactics struck at woman's position in a male-controlled world. Previously, the societies advocating suffrage had stressed cooperation, education, the active lobbying of politicians, and work on behalf of a parliamentary change. With the WSPU's move from Manchester, where it originated, to London, in early 1906, a new element was added. "Deeds not Words" served as the motto for a strategy that entailed attracting sensational attention to the protracted debate. The women defined their militancy as "moral violence,"[2] and while their first actions—parades, disruptive actions provoking arrests, and hunger strikes in prison—had the same sense of purpose as the illegal but passive resistance of later radical movements, their autocratic leadership led to increasingly violent and destructive policies. Later, the level of WSPU violence—window smashing and the burning of pillar-boxes, golf courses, and stately homes—seriously threatened both public support and legislative proposals. In 1906, though, the voices raised in protest and the women who went to jail as a result fueled even the expansion of the organization that opposed the WSPU's tactics, the National Union of Women's Suffrage Societies (NUWSS).[3] For this reason, Millicent Fawcett, leader of the NUWSS, presided over a banquet for the WSPU prisoners; and Elizabeth Robins, both in writing to Fawcett in 1906 and in speaking at the prisoners' banquet, endorsed the concerted effort of the two organizations.

The NUWSS had begun to affect parliamentary and party politics with their broad grass-roots campaigns. However, the infusion of WSPU tactics added a revolutionary element to the very way women viewed themselves. The exuberant freedom with which the WSPU women speakers faced outdoor crowds of mostly antagonistic working men showed other women that their previous responses—all their behavior and their false sense of having influence—had been conditioned by a now internalized role playing, initiated in order to please men. The newfound release from this bondage occurred not simply because women spoke out, or braved abuse, or aligned themselves with women of different classes, "shoulder to shoulder"; it happened because each collective response, whether scrappy and confrontational, ceremonial, or rhetorically impassioned, dramatized the possibilities of women's political strength.

The most defiant saw their potential most clearly. Mrs. Pankhurst, with her daughters the founder of the Women's Social and Political Union, which openly avowed confrontation with government, was stunned by the banquet held to honor her and Christabel's release from prison. She addressed a break-fast at the Inns of Court Hotel on December 22, 1908, to say that, though she was here "standing on this chair," looking out at a lushly decorated ban-quet hall, hearing cheers and a rousing chorus of "Rule Britannia," she also still felt as if she were in solitary confinement. "We women who have been to prison have acquired a dual personality which we shall never lose," she de-clared. "We are the women out in the open, at the meetings, speaking with fire and enthusiasm, . . . and then we are the women who spend so much of our time in that awful solitude."[4]

As the militant campaign became more widespread, so, too, did the indi-vidual acts of defiance aimed at challenging the roles to which women had been confined. Jessie Kenney dressed as a telegraph boy in order to infiltrate the House of Commons. Many of the WSPU leaders who were under a stand-ing order for arrest made their way secretly to meetings by taking up disguises. Mrs. Pankhurst avoided arrest when someone dressed to look like her served as a decoy for the police. The Actresses' Franchise League often came to the assistance of Grace Roe as she effectively led the WSPU while Christabel Pankhurst was exiled in France. Roe was secretly conveyed from event to event in London, sometimes in the costume of an old lady, sometimes as a chorus girl. Lady Constance Lytton, in the most dramatic example of a dis-guise used as a political tool, prevented her family's status from being cited as grounds for treating her preferentially in prison. She carefully dressed herself as a common seamstress, took the name of Jane Warton, and under that alias, was subjected to force feeding. The prison doctor never checked to determine whether she had a weak heart. She wrote of the physical trauma of the forced feeding tube:

> At first it seemed such an utterly contemptible thing to have done [for the doctor to slap her, assuming her distress was feigned] that I could only laugh in my mind. Then suddenly I saw Jane Warton lying before me, and it seemed as if I were outside of her. She was the most despised, ignorant and helpless prisoner that I had seen. When she had served her time and was out of the prison, no one would believe anything she said, and the doctor when he had fed her by force and tortured her body, struck her on the cheek to show how he despised her! That was Jane Warton and I had come to help her.[5]

Women lived with a double consciousness that existed long before they went to prison and openly flouted police handling and surveillance with dis-guises. Those who had not previously recognized that their seemingly privi-leged and secure existence in fact helped to deny them basic freedoms began to realize what else the voting privilege represented. Even though the demand for women's suffrage was itself an appeal for a single parliamentary statute, and the WSPU often seemed blind to any cause besides securing the "vote this session," the issues raised by the activist women were more far-reaching. The fact that women could not vote meant also that inheritance laws favored male heirs. The government proposed eliminating all women from the labor force. Plural voting—by which some men could have more than one vote—could be proposed, in all sincerity, as a condition of Parliament's consideration of female suffrage.

The failure to grant the franchise to women, argued Elizabeth Robins, in a political drama called *Votes for Women!*, had brought about a society in which a man destined to inherit his father's fortune can insist that the woman he loved get an abortion because the man's father will never condone his son's marriage. The woman, Vida Levering, agrees to the demand of her lover Geoffrey Stoner but later realizes that the sacrificed child creates an impassable barrier between her and her lover. "Happy mothers teach their children. Mine had to teach me . . . , teach me that a woman may do for love's sake [what] shall kill love," Vida tells him in their confrontation near the end of Robins's story, years after she has refused his appeals for reconciliation.[6] By this point in the drama, Vida is a spokeswoman for a cause with ramifications that extend well beyond her own personal pain. Her speech at Trafalgar Square and her lobbying of other women, especially of Stoner's new fiancée, makes Stoner, now a prominent Member of Parliament, aware that she is in a position to affect his political future directly. His fiancée discovers that he mistreated Vida earlier and insists upon reparations; Vida accepts his public endorsement of the suffrage plank as a substitute for private emotional debts he cannot repay. By combining the personal story with the political message, Robins was able to explore their interconnectedness.

Robins's own experience had taught her that women were conditioned to behave in a way that won men's approval. The growth that she had experienced in previous years of self-defined freedom was insignificant compared to the change she underwent as she began to investigate the suffragists' issues with the idea of writing a play. Initially, Robins became interested in the Votes for Women campaign as a solution to a commissioned project that she hoped would establish her credentials as a playwright. Her sense of the importance of the cause prompted her to make a lifelong commitment to women's issues.

The evolution of Robins's own political conscience and the expression it found, both in her overtly political service to the WSPU and in her plays, novels, and stories, provide important insights into the militant suffrage movement. Robins was able, from her first contact with the WSPU cause, to integrate her new feminist self with her artistic self. As is especially evident in *Votes for Women!* and in *The Convert*, the novel which retold the story, these two sides of her work and her writing were in harmony. At other times, however, Robins the creative writer clashed with Robins the political spokeswoman. Often the conflict related to time commitments. When she agreed to political work, she was often forced to forgo work on a novel, which required a concentrated effort. In this period Robins examined her own mission as a writer, argued that women's writing needed to address women's lives in more direct ways, and herself endeavored to respond directly to a tradition of women's fiction that she saw beginning with Charlotte Brontë. Although Robins herself neither went to prison nor assumed a disguise in order to make her sponsorship of suffrage known, she lived the dual persona of the women whose protest against the secondary position of women was so strongly voiced.

Votes for Women!, 1906–1907

In late August 1906, with the desire to make good on her promise to deliver a play to actress Gertrude Kingston her only goal, Robins began to attend the mass outdoor suffrage meetings organized by the WSPU and to interview Emmeline and Christabel Pankhurst. It was inevitable that Robins, herself an actress and novelist, would find the flamboyant tactics and the captivating personalities of the WSPU leaders attractive. Soon Christabel was supplying her with suggestions, and Robins began to draft what she called, in a letter to Millicent Fawcett, the leader of the National Union of Women's Suffrage Societies (NUWSS), the "first thing I shall have written under the pressure of a strong moral conviction."[7] She had deep reservations about her own full participation in militant activities. She accepted the presidency of the Women Writers' Suffrage League, for instance, a society that had an affiliation with the NUWSS. While she supported the WSPU's most defiant activities, she never herself considered going to jail. She was repeatedly taxed by requests from WSPU leaders to mount the platform. When she refused, it was partly because she found it difficult to speak extemporaneously (in fact, public appearances severely tested her fitness) and partly because she needed to give fuller attention to writing fiction. She eventually acknowledged to herself that the WSPU's demands of total allegiance were incompatible with her needs as an artist.

Writing to her sister-in-law Margaret Dreier Robins in America in early November 1906, she filled in the background to remarks she had made at a Tunbridge Wells Labour Conference which were later reported widely in the press:

I have been brought to realize the gross unfairness of the press in its attitude towards the recent agitation in favor of woman's suffrage. The way that these women have been vilified, and the way that even at a great convention of the National Union of Women Workers the false reports about the women of the forward party made the women at the conference—even their friends—afraid so much as to speak of them in a morning entirely devoted to papers and discussion upon the political status of women:

It was this fact which brought me to my feet for the first time in my life to make a public speech without any written paper or even notes to fall back upon.[8]

In January, Robins reported to Margaret Robins that she had "refused scores of invitations to harangue the public since my quite unprecedented little speech at the conference at Tunbridge Wells." Instead of platform speaking, she stressed that "one must do the thing one does most naturally." It was because she saw that "there are heaps of admirable speakers, few or no concerned writers (that is of fiction, etc., who can reach the masses)," that she had completed a play "which is to deal with the Suffrage Question for the first time in a serious fashion."[9]

Before the play could be produced, Robins experienced a difficult severing of her contract with Gertrude Kingston. Having opened in a highly successful and profitable comedy, Kingston wanted to produce Robins's play by staging it as a limited series of pre-Christmas matinées. While Robins arranged for more time to revise the script, it became clear to her that Kingston could not follow through on her promise to employ a strong supporting cast. By this time Elizabeth Robins had interested the manager of the Court Theatre, Harley Granville-Barker, in producing the play. It was he who encouraged her to rename the play "Votes for Women!"

No doubt what prompted Granville-Barker's interest in the play was Bernard Shaw's great enthusiasm for the piece. The encouragement of Shaw, his wife Charlotte Payne-Townshend, and other long-standing theater associates made up for Robins's falling out with Kingston. She talked over the play with the Shaws on January 1, 1907. Later that week she had tea with James M. Barrie and wrote to her confidante Florence Bell of her new burst of energy. Shaw, she reported, was "*very* encouraging and will be a great help for I think he'll come to the rehearsals and help with the stage-management of the act of the meeting—which he declares to be original and amusing. The theme he says is very good and oh 20 things beside that lifted me up and sent me spinning." With Barrie, she "talked play making and Suffrage and every thing in Heaven. I came away walking on clouds" (ER to FB, January 4, 1907). The previous month, Henry James had met with her as she was formulating her plot and had contributed his suggestions. Shaw, James, and Barrie's remarks were the kind of advice upon which Robins thrived. From the comments she received she saw more and more that the play, which she had at first feared would lose its topicality if it were not produced within a period of a few weeks, might be shaped instead, over a somewhat longer period of time, into a highly effective artistic and rhetorical drama. She added to her descriptions of meetings with Shaw and Barrie, "Certainly all the men I've showed this thing to have been immensely good about it and— the *trouble* they take!! (Barrie'll come to rehearsal too.)" Charlotte Shaw wrote to assure her that the women's suffrage question would continue to be a lively one, even after the large demonstration planned by the WSPU in early February.

Robins's heroine Vida Levering invites censure. As an outspoken advocate of suffrage, she speaks her mind about the plight of homeless women and irritates her hostess's other weekend guests. While she is offstage, one of the party tells of her earlier acquaintance with Vida in the manner of hinting at the younger woman's disreputable past. She had found Vida deathly sick in an old Welsh farmhouse after a visit from a crank doctor. It is strongly implied that Vida has had an abortion, yet no more is said, perhaps for the sake of propriety; a young girl in the gathering is about to announce her engagement. The young woman, instead of heeding warnings to avoid Vida, follows her to the outdoor suffrage rally at Trafalgar Square, the setting of act 2. At the rally, in the presence of the man she is about to marry, Conservative Member of Parliament Geoffrey Stoner, the young girl learns, merely from the look on Vida's face when she sees Stoner, that Stoner is the man in Vida's past. The confrontation between Vida Levering and Stoner in act 3 secures for Vida the politician's endorsement of women's suffrage as partial "payment" for what he has done to Vida. Robins skillfully heightens the dramatic tension by using politics to focus the personal crises for all concerned.

The *Times* account of the first performance of the play indicated that there had been rumors of a "suffragette demonstration" planned at the theater, but that in fact the audience was "very orderly," followed the play with "rapt attention," and applauded enthusiastically "but was never boisterous." In keeping with her long-held conviction that any work of hers must stand on its own merits, Robins did not come forward to take public credit for her drama. She intrigued the largely partisan audience with one of her disappearing acts; the *Times* reported, "Persistent calls at the fall of the curtain did not induce the author to appear."[10]

One of her friends accurately observed, "You fled away from your ovation too quickly this afternoon," and complimented Robins more boldly than the establishment press, for the "vivid and wonderful exposition of the problem of the hour." The letter continued: "Nobody could mistake its force or fail to grasp its importance. You have torn the very heart out of the matter and held it up quivering. You seem to have missed nothing—not one of the telling things. One by one they roll mercilessly home." Whereas the *Times* had felt that the suffrage argument was too greatly diluted with issues of women's basic economic and sexual liberties, this woman understood the interconnectedness of these issues. The friend especially appreciated the way in which Vida broke every tradition in the last act. "It will make a difference," she concluded, "this play with its hope and its courage and its passionate appeal. It is a public event—the very wine of the hour is in it."[11]

The Convert, 1907

Public acclaim may be measured not only in the widespread critical reaction but also in Robins's reports to Bell. Robins delighted in the fact that the boards in front of the theater announced sold out houses for almost every performance. The play's success allowed Robins to pursue a plan she had earlier formulated when negotiations with Gertrude Kingston were at a standstill and Robins had grown impatient with production difficulties in the theatrical world. Following up on her vow to Mrs. Fawcett, on April 12, after the second performance of *Votes for Women!*, Robins began the novel version of the play. The success of the play had enabled Robins to secure an advance of one thousand pounds from Methuen, on condition that she deliver the completed novel by September 1. As Robins rushed to meet her deadline, she did much more than turn her political tract into a novel. By extending the action backward from the time at which the dramatic section is set (the last five chapters correspond to the three acts of the play), she transformed propaganda into art. Like Robins's earlier novels, especially *A Dark Lantern* with its "Prologue" section, the beginning action of *The Convert* is carefully grounded in events which lead up to Vida's conversion and which justify the novel's different title. What makes the play a political tract and the novel a more complex artistic and rhetorical structure is Robins's preparation of the reader for the confrontations that make up the action of the play. Themes, images, and recurring scenes acquire increased meaning retroactively in the novel.

Vida is presented in the play as the already converted suffrage speaker, upsetting weekend visitors at Lady John's with her talk about shelters for homeless women and reminders to people that the suffragette antics must now be taken seriously. In the novel, however, Vida's first social function is to provide the men on either side of her with frothy conversation at a dinner party. She uses her sense of humor to rescue an embarrassed Member of Parliament from another woman's insistent talk about "The Bill." The only indication that Vida does not play at the game of feminine conversation with complete sincerity is a whispered remark in which she confesses to loathing this method of entertaining.[12] Thus, long before Vida allows herself to listen to political arguments, the reader suspects that she is critical of woman's artificial function.

Vida continues to flatter men with her conversation, often at the expense of the suffrage platform, about which she knows very little. By presenting Vida as the ironic humorist in the first part of the book, Robins makes her verbal acuity more credible for political purposes in the last two chapters. In these chapters—corresponding to the third act of the play—the reader perceives a much more complex web of doubts and motivating causes than that which is evident to the theatergoer. Vida Levering is seen in the play as bent on only one purpose, but the more gradual development of the heroine's character in *The Convert* illuminates Vida's memories of being a social accessory now that she is an organizer for meaningful reform. Robins admitted to her sister-in-law that she was unsuited to public speaking, and Vida in the novel has the same hesitancy. It may seem inconsistent that Robins, an experienced actress, should have been uncomfortable on the platform, but the two modes of public performance were vastly different. The platform speaking that Robins observed at suffrage rallies and described in her novel was a mode of confrontation; the best speakers were those who provoked negative comments from the crowds and then turned them into jests. When she acted, Robins always needed ample rehearsal time to perform at her best. She knew that she would be at her most effective as a suffrage speaker when she had a prepared and rehearsed text.

Despite Robins's own unwillingness to enter platform politics directly, the next years of her life were marked by repeated appearances. Robins confessed in an essay printed in *Collier's Weekly* for June 20 that her head (like Vida's) was full of "masculine criticism as to woman's limitations" until one "memorable afternoon" when she first heard women "talking politics in public" in Trafalgar Square. Since then, she stressed, she had been "prosecuting my education almost daily," both in the direction of what men had to learn about women, and, significantly, of what women had to learn about themselves.[13] Robins drew on her own experiences to give her fictional Vida Levering a true self-awakening.

In accordance with the novel's background dimension, Robins shows not just one Trafalgar Square outdoor suffrage meeting, but three earlier ones preceding the climactic demonstration in which Vida addresses the crowd from the platform (act 2 of *Votes for Women!*, chapter 16 of *The Convert*). In the play, the audience is given only two weak clues that Vida is new at speaking publicly for the cause. In the novel, however, Robins does not use her plot simply to provide her readers with official WSPU arguments. Only gradually, in the course of four demonstrations, does Vida become committed to the cause. On her first trip to a Sunday afternoon demonstration, Vida and her half sister have disguised themselves in thick veils and tattered gowns so that they will not be recognized. With the consciousness of a former actress, Robins highlights the deliberate use of the dual persona. Vida persuades herself that she needs a second trip—this would be her last—but cannot revisit the suffrage meetings without another elaborate pretext. This time she tricks her newly hired maid into accompanying her, ostensibly for a walk to some other destination. They happen upon the meeting; Vida pretends that her curiosity is spontaneous, and persuades her servant to hear the speakers.

The first two encounters with the suffrage debate stimulate Vida to invite a Union leader to her home, not so that she will be converted, she carefully explains, but because she is at the "inquiry stage" (*Convert*, 154). The suffragette leader reports that the responses to her evidence of sexual brutality vary widely. Many women whose class and culture prevented them from contemplating such an offense disbelieved her. Vida learns that the dog whips that the suffragette women are ridiculed for carrying have more than symbolic meaning; they deter police misconduct. In fact, as Elaine Showalter observes in *A Literature of Their Own*, the brutality by men that Robins described in this scene was suppressed in all other contemporary accounts.[14]

The private conversation makes Vida's support wholehearted, and the account of her third foray into open-air politics shows Vida on the platform. She is distinctly an associate, not an organizer, and refuses to speak to the unruly mob even though the suffrage chairman encourages her and other women to try out their capabilities. Vida sits "nursing the handbills" (*Convert*, 187), confident enough to argue her newfound beliefs only one-to-one, in conversation with the male companion at her side. By the time Vida is introduced as a new speaker in the final public meeting of the novel, Robins has prepared the reader to accept her viewpoint.

The novel provides more background for Vida's feelings both when she makes her argument from the platform that "every woman who has borne a child is a Labour woman. No man among you can judge what she goes through in her hour of darkness" (*Convert*, 269) and when she confronts Stoner privately with the pain that he caused her with his insistence on an abortion. Vida in the novel manifests an attitude different from the bitter polemic which is the strength of the play. In the novel, the entire first chapter shows Vida among her hostess's children before she puts on her social mask and descends to attend the dinner party. With the children she is genuine and intimate, and the time they spend together is mutually nourishing. When she appears at the dinner party, her demeanor is equally charming but pointedly artificial.

The novel is also significant for its detailed focus on the working-class roots of early support for the WSPU. Biographers of the leaders of the movement and suffrage historians point out that the WSPU's break with the women of the Independent Labour party reflected the Pankhursts' autocratic tactics. Because Robins completed her novel before the split became manifest, she captured the spirit of the early WSPU. Indeed, the value of the book for today's historians is that it documents a very early phase of campaign tactics and the responses to them. Robins clearly predated almost every other literary figure's endorsement of the cause. H. G. Wells, Bernard Shaw, May Sinclair, Cicely Hamilton, Evelyn Sharp, and Laurence Housman would only later come to write on behalf of suffrage. Henry James's earlier novel, *The Bostonians*, which centered on the issue of women's suffrage in New England in the 1870s, merits comparison to Robins's work. Each novel depicts a young woman torn in her allegiance between the man she could marry and an older woman whose feminist campaign she can assist. Vida knows she has power to win the young Jean to the cause of suffrage but forgoes that personal victory of luring her away from Stoner. Unlike Olive Chancellor, Vida will not capitulate to the tactics of sworn alliances; she sees her present life only in terms of the moral purpose at hand. She contrasts especially with Robins's previous heroine, Katharine Dereham, who, in *A Dark Lantern*, clung for a long time to the idea that men's and women's past affections marked them for life. Vida's once deeply felt bond with Stoner and her dead child are presumed by others to have determined her present commitments, but she makes it clear in her final remarks that the significance of her own "secret pain" is that it "joins on" to other women's suffering—and that only collectively, "if *many* help," can the wider wrongs be remedied. Robins's own sensibilities underlay Vida's last statement to Stoner: "Since men have tried, and failed to make a decent world for the little children to live in, it's as well some of us are childless. Yes, . . . *we* are the ones who have no excuse for standing aloof from the fight! (*Convert*, 303–304).

The run of the play coincided with the first spring marked by Women's Parliamentary Conventions, by the first mass marches, and by the first widespread brutality of the police during suffrage protests. The support for and the activities of the WSPU grew so extensively during 1907 that Robins's account of the struggle for a single politician's pledge of support was dated by the fall of that year. Robins in *The Convert* preceded *Votes for Women!* with a historically accurate account grounded in events of the earliest phases of the suffrage struggle.

In the play, the possibilities of Stoner's promotion to a cabinet post upon the victory of the Conservative party is entirely hypothetical. Liberals held power throughout the first decade of the century and had achieved an astounding victory and return to power in the general election of 1906. For the novel, Robins of course had no need to retract or alter her fictional possibility of Conservative rule. It is nonetheless noteworthy that Robins makes a connection between Vida's awakening and the real events of an earlier period of ground-breaking suffrage activity. Mrs. Chisholm in the novel is clearly a fictionalized Emmeline Pankhurst; Lothian Scot is the Labour leader Keir Hardie. Robins's Ernestine Blunt is modeled upon Mary Gawthorpe, a superb political speaker who retreats from active WSPU politics after the split with Labour. As Jane Marcus notes in her 1980 introduction to the novel, Robins drew on transcripts of actual speeches, capturing not only the speakers' words but also the atmosphere of the open questioning and heckling of the suffrage speakers at Trafalgar Square. Later, Robins admitted that she, like her heroine, had resorted to secrecy and disguise when she first investigated the outdoor suffrage gatherings. In these ways, the novel survives as an important document of the political history of an era.

As Robins completed her novel in late August, she felt some qualms as to its possible effect on her literary reputation. She threw into the hands of Florence Bell the decision of whether or not to withdraw the book from publication. She wrote to her friend after she had sent her the final chapters, "I knew the thing was disjointed. I knew it wasn't remotely a piece of Art—but just pleading, pleading, pleading." She acknowledged that it was pleading for a cause that left Bell cold; yet she told her, "And do you know what I had decided? That if you hated it mortal much I wouldn't publish it." Robins offered simply to give up her thousand-pound contract and consider her year's work a sacrifice: "If the book troubles and hurts you—for all your air of calm acceptance—let me hear" (ER to FB, August 28, 1907).

Bell's reply was an enthusiastic approval. The suffrage agitation of the WSPU which Robins endorsed would stand as an area of difference between Bell and Robins, yet their political disagreement seemed to strengthen their friendship. After Bell had commented on the manuscript of the novel, Robins asked her to read the proof for "Woman's Secret," a pamphlet hurriedly composed for publication the day before *The Convert*. The essay had been conceived as a preface to the book, but, she explained, "in the printer's mad haste to get the MS out of my hands," she had to arrange to have it printed separately (ER to FB, October 10, 1907).

"Woman's Secret"

Robins's decision to publish the pamphlet came despite various setbacks. She had taken a spill when the brakes failed on her bicycle. She cut her ankle, lacerated her thigh, and had to spend a lengthy time in bed because the dye in her stockings had poisoned her wound. On the day of the accident, September 3, she began to keep her diary in a longer book. The first entry, made in a 1907 diary, left much more room for each day's record than had her previous tiny engagement books. She continued to use these larger diaries for the rest of her life. In a measurable way, the change in format marks a new sense of self, one that is equally evident in the essay that she had conceived as preface to her novel.

There can be no doubt that the essay marks a political watershed for Robins. "Woman's Secret" originated from Robins's own initiative and outlined a new literary agenda. As such, it expanded Robins's view of the vote itself, which she came to see as more than an essential political step. Robins, it must be remembered, had no personal stake in the parliamentary decisions because she remained an American citizen. Consequently, her endorsement of the Englishwomen's appeal for enfranchisement could be seen as an argument unclouded by the technicalities of specific political, party, or suffrage society arguments.

Looking at the essay from the perspective of other women writers' manifestos, it is possible to compare "Woman's Secret" with Virginia Woolf's *A Room of One's Own* and Adrienne Rich's essay "When We Dead Awaken." All three examine a patriarchal society's insistence on a masculine norm in literature and its personal effect on the woman writing. "The silent woman was the paragon,"[15] Robins reminds us as she develops her theme by showing that before 1907 men dictated women's behavior and their attitudes as writers. Rather than invoke exceptions (as she would in later essays, where she noted, for example, that writers like Mary Wollstonecraft had formulated early feminist theory), Robins observes that most women who took up the pen did so constrained by a male consciousness. "There were cogent reasons for concealing her knowledge," she declared. A woman writer did not automatically convey women's thoughts and feelings because, "With that wariness of ages, which has come to be instinct, she contented herself with echoing the old fables, presenting to a male-governed world puppets as nearly as possible like those that had from the beginning found such favor in men's sight" (*WS*, 5–6). Because her publisher, her critics, and her advertisers had been and still were male, the real nature of women's lives was often withheld even by women who established their own independence with novels sympathetic to a female readership. Now, Robins saw woman's adoption of a male pseudonym—something she parodied in *George Mandeville's Husband*—as the ultimate self-effacement. When the woman writer is prompted to "borrow his name to set upon her title page," she is "conscious it is *his* game she is trying her hand at." She was doing it "not only that she may get courage from it to talk deep and go a-swashbuckling now and then, but for the purpose of reassuring the man. Here is something in your line, she implies, for lo! my name is 'George'" (*WS*, 7). Robins must have been conscious that her own writing met with a different reception after the publication of *The Open Question*, when her authorship was disclosed. Her countryman Samuel L. Clemens had written her then, in a letter full of praise: "At your age you cannot have lived half of the things that are in the book nor personally penetrated to the deeps it deals in, nor covered its wide horizons with your very own vision and so what is your secret? How have you written this miracle?"[16] It was second nature, Robins was answering in her essay, for woman to adopt the values of the dominant gender. Her real secret was that she had heretofore suppressed her own.

Not without some reserve, Robins agreed that the suffragists were justified in their disillusionment with man. She stressed that any bitterness women were now expressing deserved great tolerance. Man, after all, had been allowed to "proclaim his poor opinion of women, lumping them all together in a general condemnation (after the fashion of certain so-called philosophers), saying the worst he can of all because he had bad luck with one or two" (*WS*, 16). Robins also spoke, as would Rich and Woolf, of the time it could take for a long-silenced woman to make her own case with artistic skill. She mentioned woman's lack of practice in expressing herself and the lack of a women's literary aesthetic as reasons to nurture women's writing.

Florida and "Suffrage Camp Revisited"

Robins articulated her feminist philosophy even more forcefully in an address delivered shortly following her return to England after a three-month stay in America. She had sailed for America in late December, there made final arrangements for the book publication of *Come and Find Me* (her 1906 Alaska novel, serialized in *Century Magazine* in 1907), and spent most of her time in her own country at Chinsegut in Florida, reading and arranging old family documents, burning some of her husband's letters to her, and organizing an open house for the neighbors. Part of her stay must have been intended to ease the strain of relationships with Florida neighbors. The previous summer, arsonists had destroyed the Chinsegut barn, the buggies, and Robins's beloved riding horse, Dixie. Raymond wrote to her that he was sure of the cause: local whites objected to the position he gave to the black man Fielding Harris. "Fielder," who had known Raymond as a boy, always slept in the main house when the owners were away. Elizabeth hoped to explore the racial problem in a novel but knew, too, that she would need to spend more time in the South.

When she addressed her London audience, she used a childhood memory of the connection between the slavery of blacks and the disenfranchisement of women in order to demonstrate the scant value accorded women's lives: "I have been reminded of the impression made upon me as a child by my mother's telling me of the trouble she had in persuading her trustee to allow her to manumit her slaves." Robins went on to point out how male relatives—both her mother's and those close to British suffragists—saw no reason for the conviction, saw "only a romantic young woman whose foolishness must be kept down with a firm hand." Robins went on to describe how her mother decided to save enough out of her personal allowance to purchase the freedom of one of her slaves each year. What amazed the young Elizabeth more than her mother's conviction was the high sum required to free her favorite maid: "All concern in the transaction was merged for me in sheer envy of that black woman who, in the open market, was worth such a lot of money. Should I ever be worth a thousand dollars to anybody? It was unthinkable."[17]

The story of her childhood sensations effectively illustrated one of Robins's main points in the essay. All young children, she pointed out, think of themselves as the most important people in the world. Everyone and everything exists for them. The girl child outgrows this very natural first conception; it is "'put away' along with other 'childish things'" (*WS*, 53). Robins concluded with the suggestion, "This is the sort of soul-searching that no little male-child in a comfortable home ever knows at its highest poignancy" (*WS*, 65).

Delivered at the Portman Rooms, March 31, 1908, "Suffrage Camp Revisited" takes a larger look at the agitation for the vote than the immediate political rhetoric. In addition to linking the abolitionist issue—one that had initiated the women's suffrage movement in America—with women's freedoms, Robins called for a rejection of the attitude of the "exceptional woman," developed at length in Mrs. Ellis's books, *The Wives of England*, *The Daughters of England*, *The Women of England*. Robins observed that even the great intellectual stars George Eliot, Margaret Fuller, and Lady Mary Wortley Montagu made the freedoms they had won individually "maimed and makeshift," examples of the options open to the "exceptional woman," for as they insisted on freedoms for themselves, they presumed that "Liberty probably *would* be bad for other women" (*WS*, 72).

Robins concluded her argument by demonstrating that any exceptionalism which individual women claimed, or which men accorded them with flattery, was a delusion; because when those women assumed or "insisted on Freedom *only for themselves*, they lost it even for themselves." It was working together, "shoulder to shoulder," that would "lay the foundations of a power which is to change the course of history" (*WS*, 74).

A Sense of Place: Backsettown

The lecture put Robins in the front ranks of speakers for the cause, but again, very much like her slowly awakening heroine, Robins hesitated to make the commitment. She had two concerns. First, she wanted to begin creative work again. Second, she was eager to relocate in a country atmosphere more conducive to writing. Robins had found, since the fall of 1906, when she began regularly to retreat to Woldingham in Surrey, that she could write better outside London. In fall 1907, she had been ready to purchase a home near Blythe in Woldingham, where she had spent much pleasant time with her housekeeper, the translator and art critic Flora Simmonds, and with Simmonds's ward, the youngster David Scott. Suddenly the plan backfired. When Robins obtained a valuation for the property, she discovered that it was not worth half of what had been asked. She began casting around for a suitable country place and a topic for a play that might follow *Votes for Women!* and found both, with the help of two good friends, during the same week in April 1908.

Mrs. Sidney Buxton of Newtimber Place, north of Brighton in Sussex, whom Robins had met through Sir Edward and Lady Grey, encouraged Robins to look at the Becket farm in the quiet village of Henfield, just west of Newtimber. Robins was delighted with the old farmhouse. (Later she learned from a tombstone at Woodmancote Church that the earlier Beckets had been Backsets. She incorporated the earlier version of the family name for the name of her house, Backsettown.) Yet as Robins recognized, acquisition of the property had disadvantages as well as advantages. It was too far from London, which more and more Robins saw as the center of her political and literary life. The railroad passed through Henfield, but the two-hour train ride and the journey from Henfield station to the farm on the other side of town made day trips to London long and tiring. Moreover, the old and unrepaired farmhouse needed much work to make it livable. Robins took a week to decide; then she went ahead and made the offer to lease the house for fifteen years with an option to buy. As she undertook renovations, she discovered that her acquisition was archaeologically noteworthy for its slate roof. Parts of the main structure dated back to the fourteenth century.

On one of her excursions with Mrs. Buxton, the two women crawled around in the attic. Afterward Robins decided to have her bedroom ceiling raised so as to expose the massive oak-beamed structure that supported the weighty roof. This alteration gave her bedroom (the largest room in the house) even more airiness. Here, she knew, was a place where she could work. The installation of bathrooms and electricity and various repairs would take months. Robins gave up her London apartment in Iverna Gardens, West Kensington, retreated again to Blythe, and from there traveled occasionally to Henfield to plant bulbs and transfer flowers. As she applied the earnings from *The Convert* to her new residence, for the first time in her life she had spatial

Backsettown, in Henfield, Sussex. Shortly after the success of her novel *The Convert*, Robins signed a lease on the farmhouse, parts of which date to the fourteenth century. It is the setting for her prosuffrage story "Under His Roof." Dr. Octavia Wilberforce persuaded Robins to establish a shelter for women at Backsettown, and it served as a shelter from 1927 to the late 1980s. (*Photograph by the author.*)

control over her living situation. Backsettown became her haven and a temporary retreat for many who knew her. The gardens she cultivated became, as the years passed, an added solace and source of pride.

The Florentine Frame, 1908–1909

In the midst of Robins's decision to relocate, she wanted to start work on a new play. On April 22, 1908, while visiting Florence Bell at Rounton Grange for a few days, she and Bell discussed literary schemes. She wrote steadily at a scenario for a play she called "The Florentine Frame" until May

2, when a letter came from her agent, Paul Reynolds. She recorded the effect in her diary. "Such news of momentary success of *Come and Find Me* that I feel the risk too great of going for the play *first*. The novel is for me the surer thing. Play after. Do rough draft Chapter 1."

She was still torn between the form of *The Florentine Frame* as play and novel, however, and before she continued with her work, she consulted Henry James. Her idea was to show an American widow's influence on New York dramatic literature by describing a collaborative relationship between Isabella Roscoe, wealthy and still in her thirties, and a young academic who has stashed away his first manuscript and lost all hope for the commercial theater. The ivory and silver hand-carved Italian frame which sits empty on Isabella's writing desk is the symbolic center of the story, for it allows the young playwright to explore the woman's notions of art and human relationships on a higher plane. The story of the creative collaboration between the playwright and the widow permitted an exposition of woman's intellectual powers and political attitudes.

James pronounced *The Florentine Frame* not a play but a novel. Robins registered "my feeling too" when she recorded the meeting with James in her diary (June 3) and then abandoned the play version. *The Florentine Frame*, completed in January 1909 and published later that year, was problematic for Robins to finish. The conspicuous flaw of the book is that the bluestocking widow sacrifices her own relationship with the playwright so that her daughter can find marital happiness with him.

Especially with *The Florentine Frame*, Robins many times lost the thread and had to pick up her "dropped stitches" as a result of the political work and other commitments that interrupted her writing. Robins's politics of this period indicate why she considered *The Florentine Frame* a failure. Certainly she tried in this work to strike a less didactic tone than she had in *The Convert*; she had written to Bell as she awaited *The Convert*'s publication, "You need not be afraid that I shall go on hammering at that same nail. The inevitable reaction with me has set in and I don't want to hear any more about women for a blue moon" (ER to FB, October 14, 1907).

Perhaps the single most disappointing feature of Robins's suffrage years is that she did not continue to break new ground in fiction. After *The Convert*, and after the pamphlet meant to be its preface, "Woman's Secret," too much of her fiction reiterates old truths about women's being denied a full range of experience. Robins's "divine rage to be didactic," as Jane Marcus terms it,[18] did not diminish; rather, Robins too effectively divided her political contributions from her artistic goals. Although she hinted to Florence Bell that her Portman Rooms speech would likely be her last political address and often gave evidence that she had little stamina for public speaking, her suffrage activities during 1908 and 1909 were in fact a much more significant aspect of her productivity than her fiction.

"The Meaning of It," 1908

On June 19, 1908, in between bouts of ill health, she proudly reported to Bell that she had accepted an offer to record her impressions of the Hyde Park suffrage demonstration on the following Sunday for the *Daily Mail*. Robins herself was scheduled to be part of the procession which she would join at Euston, accompanying Mrs. Pankhurst and others to the Park. She anticipated her plan of work when she wrote to Bell. Between 5:30 and 7:30 P.M. she would work at the Ladies' Athenaeum Club, where she had arranged with Miss Marshall's typing service to have a secretary. Expecting no more fortification than a cup of tea and sandwich en route, she planned to set down in an essay what she experienced. After hours spent in the crush of bodies, she had very little time to put her observations on paper. She completed her article "The Meaning of It" and delivered it to the paper by 8:00 P.M. The article provides exacting descriptions of the size and exuberance of the event and explanations of the logistics of the Conning Tower speeches. On a designated cue, speakers addressed the masses below them from towers. At another signal, the speeches ended and simultaneous cries went up: "Votes for Women." Cheers, banner waving, cap tossing, and a surge of crowd noise from 300,000 enthusiastic supporters answered back until everyone was hoarse from shouting. Even a newspaper as skeptical of the cause as the *Daily Mail* allowed her to editorialize. Robins asked of this great display of women's political purpose, "What does it mean?" She pointed out that even women opposed to such publicity had united to show support and declared that unless the government responded with legislation, the question was moot. Continue this political pressure, Robins's essay seemed to say, for it is too easy to be a sunshine protester, march among a mass of sympathizers, and then fail to follow through on a commitment to work for change.

In her many-sided personal life, Robins herself could not rest content with one vital commitment. Possibly because she was ensconced in Florence Bell's antisuffrage household for part of the summer, where Gertrude Bell, organizing the antisuffragettes, was making her feel miserable, Robins worked at her nonpolitical commitments. She had been invited to lecture on Ibsen at the Philosophical Institute in October, and she reread many plays in preparation. William Archer's warning that her suffrage work was interfering with her writing prompted her to resume work on *The Florentine Frame*. Within a week, however, she had received two appeals from the Pankhursts—to speak on behalf of suffrage at Newcastle during the by-election campaign and to address the prisoners' banquet. Robins answered "yes" to both. At Newcastle, after her own lecture to a women's group, she accompanied Mrs. Pankhurst to meetings where Pankhurst addressed working-class men, some of them angry because women had worked as scabs during their union's strike, and learned how Pankhurst linked labor and women's issues. More significantly, Mrs. Pankhurst's invitation to Robins was for the express purpose of having Robins write in support of the cause: "So come and get material for your next political book," she urged her.[19] Robins's own address at a special meeting in the town hall reminded women that two previous institutions once regarded as illegal had become part of English life. One was the Bank of England. The other was the lending library. Her analogies asked why woman's suffrage should be so reviled, just because for a time it was still illegal.

Robins's perceptions of Mrs. Pankhurst's public meetings during the Newcastle campaign, documented in Robins's essay "Why" and in her commentary to *Way Stations*,[20] provide insights into Mrs. Pankhurst's persuasive power that few other descriptions match. Robins described Mrs. Pankhurst's attendance at the Amalgamated Society of Engineers Labour Union Meeting with particularly vivid detail. Mrs. Pankhurst dealt with the men's refusal to admit women to their union point by point. Woman's suffrage was only belatedly addressed, after long explanations of why women were underbidding men and why men needed to include women in their own labor struggles. With her declaration, "You will never be safe, you will never yourselves be free till women are free" (*WS*, 172), Mrs. Pankhurst won the last of the doubtful to her cause. Robins added that at this particular meeting, and invariably, the effect was of "the initial hostility giving way to interest and in the end to championship" (*WS*, 172–73). Gruff men who had seemed ready to brutalize Mrs. Pankhurst offered to serve as stewards, and other branches of the union invited her to speak.

In the midst of Robins's very careful preparation for her Ibsen lecture, she was called upon to refute Mrs. Humphrey Ward and the antisuffragettes at Queens Hall on October 5. Her diary suggests that she reconsidered this appeal to deliver a formal reply; "I merely say a few words." She also responded to Mrs. Pethick-Lawrence's request on October 13, the night of the spectacular rush on the House of Commons, to "help stir people up against the 2nd Division Status for Mrs. P. and Christabel" (Diary, October 13, 1908). The words "2nd Division" referred to the fact that women who were kept overnight because no courts were in session were given the harsher treatment reserved for the confinement of violent criminals rather than the First Division status associated with political prisoners. On this occasion, as so often, she went to Sir Edward Grey and left a strong letter of appeal. Grey, whom Robins had known closely when his wife, Lady Dorothy Grey, was still alive, was the first politician whom Christabel Pankhurst and Annie Kenney interrupted in public. It had been during Grey's public appearance at the Free Trade Hall in Manchester on the night of October 13, 1905, that the militant tactics had begun, with a voice raised from the back of the hall, "Will the Liberal Government give women the vote?" Christabel would come to Robins for assistance whenever approaching Lord Grey.

Because the trial for the arrested leaders kept Mrs. Pankhurst from fulfilling her Scottish engagements, Robins agreed to speak in her place. All of Robins's appearances during that third week in October were extemporaneous. The schedule was so exhausting that she had to cancel one day in Edinburgh because of illness. Three weeks after she had returned from the trip, she reported to Margaret Dreier Robins that she was still suffering from the exhaustion of public speaking and had to do all her writing in bed in between short rests.[21]

Partly because Christabel handled the main defense, the trial of the women arrested at the House of Commons created unusual publicity. Robins and other women were further incensed upon hearing that the defendants had been sentenced to three months' imprisonment. In response, she personally lobbied Grey again and attended the large Queens Hall meeting on November 2.

In the midst of this suffrage leadership crisis, with the Pethick-Lawrences and the Pankhursts in jail, Robins grew determined to finish *The Florentine Frame*, even if she should decide (she resolved in her diary several times) not to publish it. As soon as she had discussed the novel with Bell and sent it off, she started work on a lecture. Political essays, in the years ahead, often afforded her relief after a long stint on a creative project.

"Shall Women Work?" 1908

Nevertheless, her speech at the St. James Hall on March 23 was still an ordeal. She then began to divide her time between revising and correcting proof for *Votes for Women!* and her next essay, "Signs of the Times."

Taken together, Robins's two lectures composed in the early spring of 1909, "Signs of the Times" and "Shall Women Work?," demonstrate that, after the official split of Labour party suffragists from the WSPU, Robins continued to make strong connections between the militant suffragists and the women of working classes. Historians of the suffrage movement have pointed out that the WSPU's split with the Labour party crippled the effectiveness of the suffrage campaign in promoting appeal across class lines. The Pankhursts' militant organization risked loss in sympathy because of their confrontational tactics. The "radical suffragists"—the name given to the Women's Labour party activists by Jill Liddington and Jill Norris in *One Hand Tied Behind Us*[22]—less and less frequently used tactics of the Women's Social and Political Union. The prevailing understanding of Emmeline Pankhurst's reorganization of the WSPU board of directors is that she replaced the Labour party representatives with officers who had no function but to disguise the Pankhursts' control. Elizabeth Robins, one of those new members, was very much an active participant. Her diaries contain frequent references to her attendance at WSPU board meetings. Given her background, Robins herself would not have been seen to stand for a working class constituency. Her words proved otherwise. Robins's two 1909 essays present solid evidence that workers and women who wanted the vote made a strong alliance.

"Shall Women Work?" is a far-ranging analysis of opinions fostering a dual standard for women. Robins points out that the claim that women are inferior—and would not hold up under pressure of labor—conflicts with another strongly felt presumption, that women's presence in the workforce is a threat because women would replace men and would thereby disrupt the "home" environment supposedly necessary to enable men to engage in productive work. Robins recalled the fear that bicycles would make women unable to bear children. More seriously, she asked about the agenda awaiting voting women. If working men in England could, by virtue of the ballot, bring about workers' compensation laws, what could voting women do? Robins in this essay sought to persuade working-class men that their movement would be better off if they supported women's enfranchisement.

"Signs of the Times," 1908

"Signs of the Times" further extended the connection between labor and woman suffrage. In this lecture essay, moreover, Robins took a courageous stance. She announced: "I shall disobey the unwritten Suffragette law and say a few words about this same prison ordeal which I have not gone through myself, and which I yet know something about" (*WS*, 103). This attitude, common in civil disobedience actions, particularly suited Robins's experience. Robins could convincingly describe prison from the point of view of an outsider whose incarceration consists in the fact of her being a disenfranchised woman. She argued that, by serving time to assert the importance of the vote, workers could identify themselves with the imprisoned suffragettes. In contrast to those who sat around at dinner parties joking that prison cannot be so bad if the Holloway suffragettes looked so happy when they came out of it, Robins insisted, "To the toiling millions, prison is real" (*WS*, 106). The workers' awareness of the conditions of prison made the witness of the suffragettes a powerfully effective political tool. Enormously great numbers of people were converted to the suffrage cause by the women who voluntarily entered Holloway. "Anyone who doubts this," Robins wrote, "has only to watch the electric effect of the coming of a relay of newly released prisoners into the field during a by-election" (*WS*, 107). Robins sought not to gather recruits but to broaden sympathies, and her stance directly refuted analyses which concluded that the suffragette demonstrations and resulting prisoners alienated potential supporters.

The suffragette in her prison experience proves two things—"signs of the times"— which Robins challenged her audience to identify: "She has proved her faith to those who know the harsher side of life; and she has brought herself into more direct relation with the masses than she could have done by all the academic eloquence in the world" (*WS*, 108). Witness is greater than eloquence, Robins argued, because in that witness, women have experienced the enforced silencing, "the strain on the nerves and the courage, the unconquerable sickness at sight of the food, the windows that cannot admit air" (*WS*, 108).

This defiance and resistance, then, emerged from centuries of women's silence. Robins's eloquence drew on her literary knowledge. She quoted Sir Walter Scott on the crippling effects of a woman's confinement and observed that the French prisoner Verlaine, guilty of manslaughter, had been allowed to read Shakespeare in prison. (Suffrage prisoners, in contrast, were deprived of everything.) She enumerated the conditions of women working for freedoms in four other countries, and took her text and title from Christ's words from Matthew: "Ye know how to discern the face of the heaven: but ye cannot discern the signs of the times."[23]

Although Robins's title may have alluded to the kind of philosophical argument used by Emerson in an essay, Robins's feminist strategies may more appropriately be compared to those of Florence Nightingale. Ray Strachey, in her history of the suffrage movement, *The Cause*, printed for the first time Nightingale's "Cassandra" fragment (written in 1852 and, as a result of J. S. Mill's advice, withheld from any wider circulation than private publication in 1859). Strachey's connection between Nightingale's indictment of the secondary position of women and the "sufferers" of the militant Votes for Women campaign demonstrates the receptivity of Robins's stance, certainly.[24] The forthrightness of Robins's argument, however, sharply contrasts with Nightingale's disjointed accusations and spiritual metaphors.

"White Violets"

During these same months of her suffrage activity, quite a different kind of eloquence was emerging in Elizabeth Robins's writing. Her voice entered into dialogue with women writers who had gone before her, a response to her own tradition of the sort that Virginia Woolf encouraged with the advice, "For we must think back through our mothers if we are women."[25] For Robins, the instinct to do so was not wholly new. She had earlier encountered and honored her literary foremothers; she had, in *The Open Question*, given to her heroine Val Gano in her first scene a copy of Elizabeth Barrett Browning's *Aurora Leigh*, a copy of which Robins herself had inherited from her aunt, Sarah Elizabeth Robins, a poet who published under the name of Sidney Russell. In 1899, Robins had written a long review of Lady Mary Wortley Montagu's *Life and Letters*.[26] In her suffrage essays Robins invoked her predecessors, Mary Wollstonecraft and Margaret Fuller, and her contemporaries, Charlotte Perkins Gilman and Beatrice Webb. She explained in "Woman's Secret" that women's disguises were prompted by centuries of female silence and female imitation of men. Now, however, with the new sense of place Robins had from Backsettown and from her new engagement with feminist issues through her suffrage work, Robins found a new perspective on herself as artist. She began a novel that forthrightly paid a tribute to Charlotte Brontë and, in doing so, placed herself in a tradition of women's fiction. Robins used her novel as an occasion to analyze—and attack—male critics' views of women novelists. One character singles out Leslie Stephen's patronizing treatment of George Eliot for special condemnation. Moreover, like so many women writers after her—including May Sinclair and Jean Rhys—Robins saw in Brontë's life and works a response to a circumscribed existence which she herself must not only take up and reclaim but also complete and advance.

"White Violets," begun in April 1909, the month that Robins moved to Backsettown, seeks, in its focus on women's connection to their locale, to do for Sussex what Brontë did for Yorkshire. Unfortunately, the story shows some of the same weaknesses that were evident in Robins's previous novel. This time she creates a successful writer of formula fiction, Selina Patching, who, in her further exploration of Charlotte Brontë's life, determines to advance a more feminist interpretation of the novelist and pledges not to marry until she completes her task. She welcomes the collaboration of a young assistant, but discovers that the young Barbara, in her freedom to express passion, becomes the more productive writer.

Several times Robins submitted "White Violets" to publishers or agents, only to have it rejected. Finally, she recalled the typescript from her New York agent, Paul Reynolds, with the intention of reworking it, and noted on its cover that she thought it "not strong enough."[27] Part of Robins's discomfort no doubt arose from the mixed tone of the piece. Many segments are parody of the sort that worked well in *George Mandeville's Husband* and her other C. E. Raimond fiction. One conspicuous difficulty for the modern reader is that Selina invokes the spirit of Charlotte in séances and presumes that Charlotte Brontë returns from the dead to help her write her book. At the conclusion, Selina discovers that Barbara is her automatic writer. This was not the first or last time that Robins made use of—and satirized—the spiritualism which was part of her American cultural experience. In many ways, the overt feminist consciousness in the book seems in conflict with plot devices and fictional conventions chosen to test the limits of the novel form.

Both "White Violets" and her previous novel, *The Florentine Frame*, touch upon factors that were prevalent in Robins's life, the nature of collaboration and the relinquishment of passion for the sake of art. Robins had long before come to an understanding with William Archer about their working relationship. Still, the difference between the way she worked with Archer and with Florence Bell is apparent in her different treatment of the collaboration between a man and woman in *The Florentine Frame* and that between the two women of "White Violets." In each novel, Robins quite consciously created an older woman whose need, or capacity, for collaboration made the cross-generational link between women an important dimension. In doing so, however, she exposed her own fears that sexual fulfillment deadened any artistic creativity. In a special twist, she shows that at least the older woman's pain or sacrifice has allowed a younger woman, a daughter or a literary daughter, to blossom and to experience double fulfillment, in a loving relationship with a man and in literary achievement.

"Bowarra"

The prospect of actual collaboration enticed Robins away from her fiction. She was distracted from her work on "White Violets" when a visit to Florence Bell in the fall of 1909 revived their hopes of collaborating on a play. During Robins's stay at Rounton Grange, Robins drafted and Bell oversaw and commented upon the scenario for a children's play that was based on the Eskimo child who appears briefly in Robins's 1904 novel, *The Magnetic*

North. As soon as Robins returned to Sussex, Bell realized that the collaboration could not be sustained long distance, and she encouraged Robins to proceed alone with the play. Bell wrote to her that she felt that "Bowarra" was so much Robins's by this time that her withdrawal would, in fact, stimulate Robins's efforts.

There was considerable incentive for Robins to complete the script promptly. The Christmas pantomimes that were popular in the London theaters of the nineteenth century had grown even more original and colorful with the première of James Barrie's *Peter Pan* in December 1904. If she could not complete a children's play in time for it to be considered for this season's Boxer Day, the traditional start of the children's theater season on December 26, she would have to wait a year. Robins created for her little Eskimo orphan two worlds as alive and filled with fantasy as those in *Peter Pan*. One was the world of the Big Chimney Cabin, where five miners rescued Kaviak from the cold; the other was the animal-dominated world to which Kaviak is transported in his exploits to recover the all-powerful bow and arrow without which he cannot claim his chiefdom. Kaviak's pronunciation of "bow and arrow" forms the title of the play, "Bowarra." The crow, Robins had learned from her Alaskan visit, was sacred to the Eskimo. Her theatrical crow had the power to appear and disappear at will and can be heard and understood by Kaviak alone. She invented an especially rich world of animal spirits, some of them evil and thwarting the exploits of Kaviak, some of them benevolent and capable of magic. One exploit takes Kaviak into a cave where Polar Bears help him retrieve his bow from a great mastodon skeleton. The finale for each act takes place under the ice of the Yukon, the domain of "King Salmon."

Robins's sudden preoccupation with a children's play and her renewed interest in the plot of *The Magnetic North* appeared irrelevant to her suffrage activity. However, the presence of young David Scott in Robins's Backsettown household reawakened Robins's enjoyment of storytelling and Alaska. Robins also entertained Scott with readings from *Huckleberry Finn* and *Uncle Tom's Cabin*. Her tales included Joel Chandler Harris's legendary "Br'er Rabbit" and African folktales derived from Floridian blacks. These prompted Scott to nickname her "Florida," and " 'Bar."

Harley Granville-Barker, who had directed *Votes for Women!*, stepped in to become a helpful adviser, and with him Robins worked out a new beginning to the overlong play. Robins and Bell had conceived the play for Herbert Beerbohm Tree's theater. Bell had remarked to Robins that Tree's ability to create spectacular scenery would cause him to be interested in the play. After long delays, Tree told Robins that he was in fact not interested. His reasons were that the play had no "feminine element"—no roles for the female members of his company—and that her action was too "intimate" for his vast theater.[28] Her disappointment at Tree's rejection of the piece did not daunt Robins for very long. During the ensuing year, she and Granville-Barker approached several managers in the hope of arranging for a New York or London production.

During the late fall of 1909, Robins was so busy with multiple projects that she taxed her own capabilities. *The Florentine Frame* had received unfavorable reviews, and it would be 1913 before Robins published her next full-length work. Her earlier works were appearing in print at this time, however, and were further establishing her reputation. Robins prepared an outline for *The Magnetic North* and a dedication to Raymond for a new edition of the book that was published by Harmonsworth Educational Publications. Mills and Boon published *Votes for Women!* Her 1899 novella *The Mills of the Gods* was finally published by Frederick A. Stokes. When she wrote an introduction to Harriet Beecher Stowe's *Uncle Tom's Cabin* for the Bath Classics, it was appropriate to her new perception of her own priorities to recall that "Mrs. Stowe was not a novelist using reform as a theme, but a reformer using the novel as a weapon."[29] Her longest suffrage essay, "Why?" appeared as a pamphlet in America; she prepared her speech "Shall Women Work?" for publication in the *Fortnightly Review*; and Paul Reynolds encouraged her to collect all her suffrage essays for a possible volume. She completed the children's play "Bowarra" in a few short weeks.

In addition, Robins lobbied and wrote letters concerning the treatment of the Hunger Strikers, warning the government in a letter printed in the *Westminster Gazette* that if any woman suffragist succumbed in Holloway Gaol, her death could not be declared "death by misadventure"; the government would be responsible for murder (*WS*, 129). Robins had addressed the organizational meeting of the Women Writers' Suffrage League as its president in May 1909; now in the fall, she went over her Alaskan story "Monica's Village" to make a shorter version to read at a Suffrage League event. In early October, she spoke from the platform at the meeting which raised two thousand pounds on the occasion of Mrs. Pankhurst's departure for America, and Mrs. Pankhurst carried with her personal letters of introduction from Robins to her sister-in-law, Margaret Dreier Robins. Her major creative project during this period was her novel, "White Violets," inspired by Charlotte Brontë.

In late November, Robins had the occasion to revive an idea for a story for which she had been collecting notes for two years. It was a novel based on the true story of a young girl abducted by traffickers in white slavery. The young poet John Masefield, the man who accepted Robins's suggestion that he collaborate with her on this project, fell in love with her, and their relationship revealed to Robins more strongly than anything else in her experience that men saw women primarily in relation to themselves. Indirectly, the liaison with Masefield allowed Robins to examine her own nature and, after years of casting about for the right story lines, to use her own life in more creative and artistic ways.

7 | Political Crises and a Pilgrimage into the Past, 1909–1916

Telephone call, Christabel Pankhurst's voice: "You said you'd speak if a crisis came. It's *here*." So I have to.

—Elizabeth Robins Diary, November 22, 1911

There, a light breaks. I may be closer to you at last than I ever was, if I can be honest. Shall I try? Would you *dare* be my Father Confessor as well as my lover? I wonder if that could be—even now.

—Elizabeth Robins, "To G.R.P.," a "Letter from Your Wife," begun January 1912

T*HE SCENE*: Graveyard of the Church of St. Andrew, Richmond, Staten Island. A cold February day in 1913. Elizabeth Robins stands looking over the pit of a newly reopened grave at St. Andrew's. Two workmen are below ground. The only others present are the St. Andrew's rector, Reverend Robert Kimber, and Mrs. Hedley, a Staten Island resident who knew the Robins family when they lived at Bayside and who provided a temporary home for Robins when she first began to act in New York. Robins is now fifty, a successful writer anticipating the publication of her next novel, a feminist indictment of white slave traffic. On this very brief sojourn away from England, art and politics are suspended; the search for the relics of her past is foremost in her mind. She braves the winter weather for this day-long vigil in hopes that the gravediggers can find evidence that the coffin they exhume is that of her husband, George Richmond Parks, whose suicide note to her in 1887 rambled incoherently from accusation to apology but which devastated Robins with its claim, "Your love for me is dead."

Her only clue to the location of the coffin is that it is buried above that of her sister, Amy Robins, who died in infancy in 1871. Robins has received word from the Reverend Robert Kimber that a first attempt to locate the coffins was unsuccessful, but Mrs. Hedley, Robins hopes, will remember better the details of the family burial plot. Mrs. Hedley looks briefly at the first "great hole" the men have dug, goes to a different spot, says, "Here," and the sexton and day laborer are called over to dig anew. Robins persuades Mrs.

Hedley to accompany Reverend Kimber to the rectory and stays on alone. She keeps the rest of her vigil in silence.

"A strange hour," Robins writes that night in her diary: "We find his coffin. They break the outer shell and the one[?] within. There is the coffin. We cannot find the plate and I am troubled." Reverend Kimber returns and tries to reassure Robins that, with Mrs. Hedley's assistance, they have located the right grave, but Robins, struggling with painful memories, urges them to continue. "Oh the thoughts, the thoughts! I feel in my heart it is his grave but I bid them go on, leaving instructions for them not to disturb the larger coffin but to dig under it and get at the baby Amy's. If there is a plate on that! Or even if there is a baby's coffin there I shall feel I have proved the case" (Diary, February 23, 1913).

Robins leaves money for the cost of the digging and later copies out the phrases for the memorial stone that she wants to mark the site: "To the memory of my husband, George Richmond Parks and to my brother Edward and sister Amy Robins, this stone is placed." Quoting from Lady Margaret Sackville's poem, "The Ghost," she adds the inscription, "Oh many's the time day out, day in, I called in vain to you, / Now you may knock at my closed door: I shall not let you through."[1]

Notes on the Scene: It had been more than twenty-five years since Parks's death and more than forty since she stood over this precise spot and watched the sexton trample the earth over Amy's grave: "The picture of that great rough man standing over where she lay and planting his heavy feet just above her lovely head will never leave me" (ER to Una Robins, October 15, 1881). These graveside scenes at St. Andrew's attest to the depth of Robins's private grief. Her memories of Parks, once suppressed for years, stood at the center of a broader compulsion to deal with her past. In late 1909 the past with which Robins had not fully dealt was reawakened by an unexpected episode. The young poet John Masefield met Robins and almost immediately fell in love with her. His frequent letters expressed both passion and a desire to be regarded as her grownup son who absolved her of her sins of the past.

Robins felt more deeply Masefield's admiration than she had that of George Parks, William Heinemann, William Archer, or even her brother Raymond. More recently, Robins had been alternately burdened and sustained by friendships with women who shared her house and her daily life. Flora Simmonds, her housekeeper from Blythe, had begged to stay on with Robins when she purchased Backsettown. Robins quite willingly agreed. By prearrangement, Simmonds's ward, David Scott, became part of the household during his school holidays. Robins knew that some people believed that Scott was her own child and told only those closest to her that he was not. Simmonds's former friend, Zoë Hadwen, also visited frequently. Hadwen's London apartment became a convenient stopping place for Robins when her affairs took her to London. The young Octavia Wilberforce, introduced to Robins at Newtimber Place by mutual friends, the Sydney Buxtons, thrust herself upon Robins with a devotion that was at once reverential and selfish. Wilberforce was twenty-one, searching for something to do with her life, and troubled by her family's expectations when she met Robins in 1909. Her friendship with Robins, though repeatedly strained, deepened for both women until each regarded the other as a primary companion.

Each of Elizabeth Robins's relationships cast her in the role of mother, provider, and confider, yet each pulled Robins away from simultaneous dedication to anyone else or, in Masefield's case, remained exclusive and secret. Simmonds was upset that Wilberforce appeared able to take up Robins's time at will. Wilberforce, for her part, was bothered when Robins chose to spend her free time with David Scott rather than with her. Zoë Hadwen hinted that it would be nice for Robins to use her earnings from her best-selling novel, *My Little Sister*, to provide young David with a real "little sister," by which she meant that Robins might take in another adopted child. The artistically inclined Katherine Dreier, sister of Margaret Dreier Robins, often appealed to Robins for sanctuary and at one point declared that she wanted to live with Robins. Unlike Katherine Dreier, Robins sought retreat from personal ties but felt more and more torn by the obligation not to hurt others who depended on her.

Just as the web of Robins's intimate friendships was complex, her private pilgrimage into a past charted by previous diaries, letters, and date books manifested itself in her fiction in many intricate ways. She began by studying her beginnings as an actress. Most important, perhaps, Robins made several false starts and finally persevered—helped by the encouragement of a commission from *Cosmopolitan*—to write *Camilla*, the story of a divorced woman who rejects the offer of a second marriage.

Although in many ways *Camilla* was a personal statement that was evolving as her relationship with Masefield came to an end, her life and artistic development in these years had grown more complex. As her fiction began to explore her past, Robins took up the issues of the militant suffragists, then became involved with moral reformers protesting the white slavery traffic, and finally spoke in support of women's contribution to the war effort. Despite the fact that she increasingly saw her life divided into two realms, even Robins's personal novels had a political mission: a feminist critique of society. In the 1910s, fiction was her retreat from her direct attacks on society's restrictions against women. Her political commitments were nonetheless vital to her expression of her self. She thought first of her needs to create, and although she was often swayed by political appeals to speak, write, and lobby, she knew that unless she protected her physical strength and her privacy, she could not sustain her artistic endeavors.

Certainly the effort involved in balancing the two commitments some-times made her feel unsuccessful at either. Once, when she returned to her historical fiction after an intense period of political activity, she called her creative work "my miserable misstitched writing" (Diary, November 13, 1914). Yet when she resumed her work on her political novel after a similar period of suffrage writing, she confided to herself: "I fly back to my novel with a sense of speaking my own language after stumbling in a foreign tongue" (ER Diary, June 9, 1912). The "foreign tongue" of political address was in fact Robins's eloquent second tongue, but when she spoke from the platform she often prepared by spending long hours reviewing notes and press accounts, revising many times, and practically memorizing her speeches. For-tunately, her feminist position may readily be assessed, because many of her speeches were collected and published, with her commentary of 1913, as *Way Stations*. The years 1909–16 reveal Robins as a middle-aged woman who continued to defy the bounds of one or another role with new exploits and a deepened sense of her earlier self.

John Masefield: "*Docet Umbra*," 1909–1910

For almost as long as she had been a committed suffrage speaker, Robins wanted to write a story exposing the forced enslavement of young girls into prostitution. Her friend William Stead had aroused an earlier generation of moralists with his investigative reporting in his series, *The Maiden Tribute of Modern Babylon* (1885), which brought him a prison sentence when he ad-mitted to posing as a customer in order to obtain evidence. She had heard the true story, told so many times in London that it had grown into a legend, of the two sisters who had been abducted by a woman posing as an aunt. In 1907, she wrote to the woman from whom she had heard the story and re-ceived encouragement to use the account in her fiction. The incident had be-come everybody's story, the woman wrote, and Robins need not hesitate to use it.

She continued to collect information for her story or play—she was not sure which, for the last two of her published novels had been conceived as plays and transformed into novels—but two years went by before she had a chance to work on the idea. In November 1909, unable to sleep after a visit to the dentist, she stayed awake reading John Masefield's novel *Multitude and Solitude*. His novel transforms into positive social action the despair that a young writer feels when his fiancée is drowned. The narrative is an obsessive paean to the woman of beauty that the young writer still worships. On the same day, John Masefield read her play *Votes for Women!* and was deeply

Elizabeth Robins during the suffrage years. (*Courtesy of the Fales Library. Reproduced with the permission of Mabel Smith, for the Backsettown Trustees.*)

affected by Robins's power to convey her political message in artistic form. He wrote asking if he might come to interview her. Robins, resting at her secluded farmhouse in Sussex, was moved that she had first been introduced to Masefield's work at the moment he had learned of hers. She wrote to suggest a day and a train he could take from London to Henfield.

As soon as Masefield met Robins in her rural retreat, he put her on a pedestal. He was married, and his wife was expecting their second child. Nevertheless, his letters to Robins soon began to convey his desires in explicitly sexual terms—even as he maintained a son-to-mother relationship and spoke of their relationship as holy. One presumes she showed the house to him as she would to any first-time guest. But she wrote in a private memo to him later that he was the first man she had taken alone to her large, second story bedroom. It was an open-raftered, cathedral-like space, her oval bed prominent, and the room, painted in white and gentian blue, mostly spare of decoration. Windows on three sides looked out to rose gardens, to the quiet shade of a magnificent oak, and to the secluded front walk a long way distant from the next nearest dwelling.

Masefield claimed after he knew her more intimately that she had shown him upstairs in order to make him miss his train—he had come for lunch and had insisted on catching the 2:23 back to London. Robins told him as he left her house that, if he did not get to the station on time, he was to return to her home to wait for a later train. As Robins and her housemate, Flora Simmonds, were setting in place the new sundial with its Latin legend, *Docet umbra* ("the shadow teaches"), he returned across the field. Robins took him for a walk, and in the graveyard at St. Peter's Church, sitting on a tombstone of one of the previous owners of her house, she told "my story of the two girls and the unknown address." She wrote in her diary, "He is good to tell a thing to" (Diary, November 26, 1909).

Over tea, Masefield proposed to write an article on her. Robins was careful to dissuade him. The next day, Robins received two letters of his thanks and praise. He suggested that *Docet umbra* would be a title for her book.[2]

Robins then proposed that they collaborate. It was not unusual for Robins to do so; she had frequently proposed collaboration to Florence Bell. Masefield agreed, reluctantly at first, sensing that his great admiration for Robins needed sustenance. He admitted that he was appalled at the horrors of organized prostitution but also felt compelled to confess his guilt by association with the baser members of his sex. Robins confessed to him that she had lost a husband in America, and that, in the words of Masefield, "the miracle of life had begun within" her.[3] He told her that his own mother died when he was six years old as she gave birth, prematurely after a carriage accident, to her sixth child. As he demonstrated in the subtext of his letters to Robins and the poem he composed as a tribute to his mother (but dedicated privately to Robins), the young Masefield transferred his mother's pain before her death to the pain she felt at his own birth.

In early February, Masefield wrote to Robins that he had failed her, that his "hands and soul" were "not quite clean": "When I was a boy in New

York, I stayed for two days with a French singer." He had met her on the boat from Liverpool. The woman went on to San Francisco to fulfill her contract, and he never heard from her again. "But the stain is there," he told Robins. "I can't say, as I would give the world to say, 'I've been scrupulous to women.'"[4] At the same time that he sought to prove his ideas of the purity of a spiritual relationship between them, with Masefield playing the role of grownup son, his letters to Robins spoke of more erotic sensations. He wrote to her that he felt as if he were in Paradise, and that "son-like" he was eating her joy from her, "drawing the ecstasy from your life, as once before when you were my food."[5] It became his custom to enclose a small note inside his daily letter, meant for Robins's "Good-night sacrament. . . . Let us kneel together. Your son holds you for one white instant," he wrote her typically in one of the three notes that he composed for her on February 6.[6]

It is quite probable that Robins had been pregnant by George Parks before his suicide and it is just as likely that Masefield imagined her bearing a child so that he could sanctify his sublimated sexual desire. He made it clear in some letters that he thought continually of Parks and that he, Masefield, might be not her unborn child but her lost love restored. She allowed him to perpetuate their relationship as mother and son as "poetic license," but she insisted that she was a shelter for him, with whom he could think lighthearted thoughts as compensation for his motherless childhood (ER to JM, January 27, 1910, Berg Collection).

Their affair tells us much about Masefield's psychology; even more perhaps, it suggests a pattern in Robins's own relationships. In her private life she was constantly defending her choice to remain celibate after the death of her husband. Though she was not raised a Roman Catholic, she kept her marriage vows as faithfully as a Catholic wife whose husband had not died. In one exchange, Robins insisted, in a reply to an assumption Masefield made about a recurrent theme in her earlier fiction, that she did not "intentionally cultivate mystery," that two of her characters he had singled out expressed mystery only in so far as it was an "echo of the man-made ideal of woman which women have made shift to accept or to seem to humour" (ER to JM, January 25, 1910, 9:30 A.M., Berg Collection). In another reply to Masefield's persistent efforts to break down her private being, she wrote him, "If I am a solitary person, it is because I came to have a passion for solitude beyond any other passion" (ER to JM, January 25, 1910, 10:30 P.M., Berg Collection).

Constance Babington-Smith has asserted that Robins's initiative in terminating the affair devastated Masefield and blocked his writing for a year.[7] She fails to deal with one dimension of the confessional relationship, Masefield's obsession to be forgiven for his promiscuity; and she ignores information in

Masefield's letters to Robins that he feels pressured to churn out work to fulfill publishing contracts. It is clear from Robins's diary that she traveled to meet Masefield when she sensed he was most troubled by her reserve. After mid-May 1910, they wrote only brief formal notes to each other on several occasions, and their paths crossed equally infrequently. In the fall, when his two historical novels were published, Masefield assured her that he had burned the novel she had inspired, but in 1912, in his story *The Street of Today*, he created a widow who influences a young writer and who can be seen as a portrait of Robins.[8]

Throughout their months of correspondence and meetings, Robins had alternately worked at her novel, "White Violets," and continued with her suffrage work, but she was troubled by recurring illness and eyestrain. By mid-May 1910, she had decided that she would take herself to a German sanitarium for the cure, on which she had come to rely as the best treatment for overwork. She quickly drafted a short story to help pay for the trip. Before the summer was over, *McClure's* of New York offered her seventy pounds for "Miss Cal," in which a male narrator recalls a young girl in Nome, Alaska, after ten years have elapsed and she has become a professional singer.

In Robins's life, Masefield's presence lingered. In early February, Masefield had enclosed in his morning greeting a copy of the poem he wrote as a tribute to his mother when she was suffering, connecting her pain to that which women continued to suffer in their political inequality. At the end of March, Robins took out her mother's diary of 1862 and reread the entry that Hannah Robins recorded when she was carrying her first child. Robins remarked in her own diary: "Curious experience to be given the key to some of the influences that shaped one" (ER Diary, March 31, 1910). To Florence Bell she marveled that her mother went about visiting, that she sang songs, ate a "vast amount of fruit," and read devotional literature (ER to FB, April 2, 1910). But in private notes to her mother's diary, Robins recorded other impressions. She was relieved to find that Hannah Robins was very much in love; she also detected that her mother was not pleased that her first child was a girl.

"Theodora: A Pilgrimage," 1910–1911

Brief notes in her own diaries mark the genesis and development of Robins's novel founded on her earliest experiences as an actress. Robins read *Wilhelm Meister* at the time she was preparing to go to Germany. "I think about my Wilhelmina book," she wrote within days of her arrival at the sanitarium outside Schrieberham (Diary, June 7, 1910). While taking baths and exercises, she began keeping a special notebook for her own bildungsroman, in which the growth of the heroine would reflect Elizabeth Robins's new perspective on her past. After the interruption, when she had returned to England, she resumed the project in late summer. She keyed her fiction to events in her old diaries and went to the British Museum to look up the lives of the stage personalities who had inspired her—Charlotte Cushman and Anna Cora Mowatt. She read the *New York Herald* to capture the spirit of New York City in the early 1880s. By mid-October she had plans for a trilogy; her heroine was named Theodora Lancing, and her title was "Theodora: A Pilgrimage." The first volume, subtitled "A Study in Egoism," was Robins's chief enterprise for the next year. She returned to other sequences in the story intermittently throughout the rest of her life.

The 1910–11 composition period was not without major distractions. She complained to herself alternately of "my late writing very pedestrian" and "my rickety technique"; then she saw "new hope tonight" (ER Diary, February 13, 1911) or made a note, "I feel I 'see' it all very clearly—now for strength and eyesight to get it down on paper!" (Diary, December 20, 1910).

By April 1911 she had nearly completed her first volume, treating Theodora's determination to leave her home in "Sparta" (Zanesville) and take up life in New York. Later volumes, never completed, were to treat her professional life and the complexities of romance with a character loosely modeled on George Parks. Her "letter dedicatory" outlining her purpose to Florence Bell—who she knew was prejudiced against the historical novel—gave her reasons for undertaking the project; she sought to produce a "composite portrait" and wanted to show "the significance of the Theatre in the scheme of Civilization."[9] Because she had experienced the vast changes in woman's position, she saw the relevance of her own history because it taught something about the present.

Robins's perspective as a recently reborn feminist contributed to her portrayal of Theodora. She treated her earlier self as a fiercely independent creature who had scoffed at marriage, defied a family that had relied on her at home, and firmly determined that to attain the highest form of artistic expression she must communicate the emotions which reached beyond her own circumscribed existence. Robins grasped the comedy of her character's fervor as she looked back over her creation and applied her own skills as writer to remake young Bessie Robins into Theo Lancing. As Robins had done, Theo also borrows money from her invalid mother, adopts a stage name (Dorothea, or Theodora with the syllables transposed), has few qualms about her great aunt's fears that the family name will be ruined if she becomes a professional, and struggles with the difficulties of being alone in an unfamiliar city.

In many ways, "Theodora" invites comparison with the struggles with self depicted in Dreiser's *Sister Carrie* and Willa Cather's *The Song of the*

Lark, two other American novels about midwestern young women who work their way toward self-fulfillment and recognition on the New York stage. Dreiser is mainly interested in the forces of man against the environment, and in his use of the theater he only hints at Carrie's possible salvation; Cather's study of the artist's development has more in common with "Theodora." The professional career of opera singer Olive Fremsted is Cather's model for the woman her heroine becomes, but Cather's young Thea, like Robins's Theo, transforms the author's personal experience of the developing artistic imagination in moments of epiphany.

Robins detailed Theo's early visions amid the commonplace reality of her heroine's home life but then saw that this form required her to give too much attention to girlhood sensibilities. She put aside "Theo at Home" and began afresh, this time locating Theo's struggle in the events just after she flees home to look up family friends on Staten Island and persuade someone, anyone, with influence in New York, the great city of the theater, that she had talent and determination. This section of the book culminates in her first appearance on the professional stage, but the more significant personal breakthrough comes earlier, when Theo returns to her bare room in a cheap boardinghouse, after her interview with a potentially influential actress has made her despair of ever performing. The actress had asked her to recite. Theo had declaimed her best speeches, only to be told that the expensive, old-fashioned elocution lessons were hopelessly out of date. Theo's mother had pawned her diamond wedding tiara to support her daughter's start in New York, and Theo reaches home, thinking, "Poor mother. She has gone and wasted her diamond comb on a no good daughter" ("Theo," chapter 16, p. 32). As she weeps inside her room she "begins whispering the Ophelia." She keeps on, standing in front of the cheap mirror that sends back a horribly distorted image, experimenting with her voice. She tries to ask herself how the esteemed actress would feel the speeches as she recites the lines, "O woe is me. / To have seen what I have seen, see what I see!" Her voice seems to ring "to the accompaniment of a phantom overtone." She listens, tries again, and the "faint singing overtone" recurs, "—like the vibration of some fine thread of pain." Finally she traces the sound to its source, "the metal bar that carried the flowered curtain." It was "an answer out of brass! She laughed: I have moved the heart of the curtain rod!" But since she knows that she had stood for weeks in this very spot, rehearsing, and "always till tonight the bar was dumb," she has to exclaim, "Oh miracle of the human voice!" This is what misery has taught her, and the discovery of her powers gives her fresh determination ("Theo," chapter 17, pp. 3–7).

Robins's notes for her autobiography recall her real experience with the brass rod and make clear how that moment of epiphany inspired her for the rest of her life. In Cather's novel, Thea's salute to the eagle as the culmination of her Panther Canyon experience as a "persistent affirmation" likewise represents the author's own discovery, a fusing of "endeavor, achievement, desire, glorious striving of human art."[10] In her chapters on Cather in *Felicitous Space*, Judith Fryer sees, in Cather's expressions throughout her fiction of the "flowering of desire," the primordial connections between women artists, the real spaces they occupy, and creative possibility.[11] Virginia Woolf recorded her own vivid personal discoveries as "Moments of Being" and connected the objects in the world of her childhood to emotional and aesthetic discoveries. Like other women writers, Robins transformed her own life into fiction by using as touchstones experiences that are deeply rooted in childhood bedrooms and everyday surroundings.

Although parts of Robins's unpublished "Theodora" prefigured Cather's *The Song of the Lark*, published in 1915, Robins's model was her own. For all its "rickety technique," "Theodora: A Pilgrimage" was more in tune with new currents in the novel than she might have suspected. Dorothy Richardson began her own *Pilgrimage* in 1913 and, in a foreword to the 1938 republication of her first three books, exactly defines the impulses Robins felt in her focus on her own life and in seeing her heroine through her own consciousness. Richardson stressed the subjectivity of works by other authors whom she considered masters. Proust had broken ground with his "opulent reconstruction of an experience focused from within the mind of a single individual." She credited Henry James with a prose style that demanded a reader's concentration and gave much the same delight as a "spiritual exercise." It was, however, with a "sense of relief" that Richardson had "recently discovered in *Wilhelm Meister*" what she claimed for her "manifesto." She drew on Goethe to assert: "'In the novel, reflections and incidents should be featured; in drama, character and action. The novel must proceed slowly, and the thought processes of the principal figure must by one device or another, hold up the development of the whole.'"[12]

Robins, too, made the same claims. In a later memo appended to the preface of her first beginning of "Theodora" she wrote: "Henry James's preface to *Tragic Muse* Vol. I speaks of the indispensable *centre* of the story. My centre is the *Bildung* of a girl through the theatre. I have for many a year spoken with innocent arrogance of the philosophic core of any story of mine—the something at the heart of fiction which would perhaps be clear to nobody else but where being there made it worth *my* while to write it."[13] James declared in his preface to the New York edition of *The Tragic Muse* that his center was a wholly objective Miriam Rooth, seen from the subjective perspective of the many men who are fascinated by her but never from her own consciousness. In response to this, Robins might have continued that "Theodora" and her own decision, characterized by James's phrase, to "*do* the actress," came from instincts closer to Richardson's than to James's. Robins's center was a very subjective treatment of a fictional being close to her own consciousness.

Robins's notes for her project show how much further she wanted to take Theodora. Like fellow American novelist Mary Austin, whose autobiographical *A Woman of Genius* was published in 1912, Robins's ultimate goal was to represent the woman artist's dilemma between forfeiting her career and fulfilling her passions. After she had completed her initial work on the early volumes, Thomas Wells, an editor at Harper's, declined to publish them. She did not return to her autobiographical series with the same intensity for almost twenty years. Between 1927 and 1930 she wrote a detailed separate volume focused on Theodora's—and her own—summer spent with her father in a gold mining camp in Colorado. Charles Robins hoped that his daughter's experience with nature would cure her of her theatrical ambitions; in fact the experience helped her decide to pursue her dream of a life on the stage. Chronologically, "Rocky Mountain Journal" belongs between "Theo at Home" and her first volume, "Theo on Stage." Developmentally, it was the retelling, with different outer circumstances but with the same psychological center, of a young woman's self-discovery.[14]

Politics and Essays, 1910

"Theodora" was never a project on which Robins could work uninterruptedly. From her first involvement with the suffragists, Robins's personal writing necessarily accommodated the demands of her work to give women the vote. In the midst of her involvement with Masefield, as she planned her book on prostitution and completed "White Violets," she managed to bar H. G. Wells's scheduled speech for the Women Writers' Suffrage League on the grounds that Wells in *Ann Veronica* had exploited his extramarital affair with Amber Reeves and had used her connection with the suffrage movement to promote his own sexual freedom.[15]

In 1910, immediately after Robins had conceived her idea for "Theodora" and had returned from Germany, Christabel Pankhurst appealed to her to respond to the publicity the Anti-Suffragist Societies had generated by their announcements that they had raised a £100,000 fund. Robins's essay, "Mr. Partington's Mop," published in *Votes for Women* on August 12, 1910, cleverly converts the appeals of the antisuffragists into effective prosuffrage logic by observing that women previously complacent about their own franchise would be moved to contribute money to secure it: "Many a ten-pound note that would have gone into clothes, or holidays, or what not, will find its way to Clements Inn, to be transmitted into strength for the Suffrage Cause" (*WS,*

225). Throughout the essay, Robins corrected impressions regarding the relative strengths of the two movements, the anti- and the prosuffragist, and reminded her English readers that, if the "Antis" did not have paid leaders, they would hardly have an organization (*WS*, 238). Ironically, Robins had the opportunity to review Gertrude Bell's two latest travel books. Gertrude, the stepdaughter of Florence Bell, was active as an antisuffragist, but the review of her Arabian desert travels caused Robins most concern not because of her conflicting politics but because the work distracted her from other matters. The article proved much too long, and Robins spent considerable time cutting it. It was returned by the *English Review* and was eventually published in *Fortnightly Review*.[16]

Crisis: Black Friday, November 18, 1910

On the day she sent her Gertrude Bell review to the United States, Robins noted in her diary, "The political crisis acute" (November 16, 1910). Two days later, she was on the 10:16 train to London, ready to participate in the largest militant suffrage action that year. A truce against militancy had been in effect since early in the year when the forced feeding of Lady Constance Lytton had embarrassed the government into promising to facilitate a Conciliation Bill. Now, as a result of a crisis which prompted the dissolution of Parliament and new elections, the future of the bill was in jeopardy. The WSPU quickly organized demonstrations to urge Prime Minister Asquith to promise publicly, before the dissolution of Parliament, that the bill would be favored in the next session. Friday, November 18, was the first day after the start of the crisis when Parliament was scheduled to meet. Robins attended the great Caxton Hall meeting, at which Mrs. Pankhurst addressed the gathered suffragists to tell them that they had every legal right to demand an answer from Asquith. Hundreds followed Mrs. Pankhurst into the street. Home Secretary Winston Churchill, nervous that negative treatment of suffragists would hurt his party at the polls, had made it known that no women would be arrested. Police took their own measures, however, and proceeded to treat the women brutally. Women under twenty-one, and women considered too old or not strong enough, were not allowed to march in the deputation. Women who volunteered for "danger duty" wore white satin badges printed with the words "Deputation, 1910."[17]

Others, and Robins among them, rode in taxis on the outskirts of the crowd in order to give relief to the women who pushed persistently into the cordons of police. The unprecedented brutality of the police—and of the many officers dressed in street clothes, disguised as young roughs, and at liberty to assault the women physically—caused the day to be remembered as

"Black Friday." The only remark that Robins entered in her diary on this day was that she had spent an hour and a half circling the demonstration in a taxi. Later, when preparing *Way Stations* for publication, Robins recalled the vivid impact of being so close to the skirmish and remembered that the 115 women who had been arrested were summarily dismissed without a hearing in court.

"I did not myself see the worst," Robins wrote, "but I saw enough to send me away sick and shuddering" (WS, 257). Upon further reflection, Robins commented on the impact that this attempt to terrorize women had made. In the short moment during which a suffrage skirmisher sprang out of the "little haven of the cab," the witness felt the commitment of the activist: "Only perhaps through some such conflict could the sheltered learn the need of the shelterless, learn the contempt felt by Authority for women as a sex, the disrespect of the man in the street for the women in the street" (WS, 259).

Robins was torn by the urge to be in London for the next demonstration and by the desire to return to her novel after the interruption represented by her short story and book review. She returned the next day to Backsettown and wrote, "I longed to stay in London yesterday, today I rejoice to be here" (Diary, November 19, 1910). On November 23, another 153 women were arrested, and Robins felt torn again. "It isn't easy to stay here in safety." This time, however, the drive to organize her novel swayed her, and by late January she could boast, "I sketch out final chapters of Theodora—having long had it all in my head" (Diary, January 25, 1911).

January also found Robins amid household cares and other contemplations. Although she had been a widow for twenty-four years, she recorded on the twelfth: "My wedding anniversary." Florence Simmonds troubled her with household accounts. David Scott distracted her from writing. Zoë Hadwen read her new novel to Robins, and Octavia Wilberforce was too insistent a visitor to be received without reservation. Robins, nevertheless, wanted to purchase the place she had made home during the three years of her lease and now made an offer to annex neighboring land at thirty pounds an acre.

Pressed to continue writing, she left in early February for a German water cure. As soon as she had adjusted to the routines of baths, exercise, and rest, she worked on "Theodora" steadily and on the first day of her return five weeks later attended a suffrage meeting. Although the truce pledging no militancy was again in effect, in hopes that the new government would take action on a suffrage bill, another sort of mass demonstration enlisted the support of women who had never engaged in civil disobedience before. On census night, April 2, thousands of women defied official policy and spent the night away from their homes. Many slept on floors in temporary shelters; others attended all-night entertainments in theaters and skating rinks. Those who did not relocate for the night simply refused to be counted. Robins noted, "I wrote across the census paper: the occupier of this house will be ready to give the desired information as soon as the Government recognizes women as responsible citizens. Elizabeth Robins (Mrs. George Richmond Parks)" (Diary, April 3, 1911).

We Write Best What We Know Best: Addressing the Women Writers' Suffrage League, 1911

Florence Bell arrived later in the week to discuss literary projects. In mid-April, Christabel Pankhurst stayed at Backsettown overnight. During May, Robins's work on her major project was again interrupted when a Women Writers' Suffrage League meeting made it necessary for her to deliver an address. This time her speech was more in concert with her creative work. She reflected on the lack of recognition accorded to great women of the past and urged women writers to write women's biographies: "When I first began to be interested in the Stage," she told her audience, "I scoured the libraries for lives of actresses. But the biographies seemed to be nearly all about actors, and very poor when they weren't!" With not so much as a hint of the theme of her "Theodora" novel, she added that it was not until women of the stage took to writing their own lives that the more illuminating stories were told. She listed Fanny Kemble's *Records*, Clara Morris's *Life of a Star*, and Ellen Terry's *Memoirs* and commented, "These and books like them, are a foretaste of the library that waits to be written." She called upon the writers to claim women's history from the "literary scavengers who search women's lives in the spirit of Peeping Tom," who "have a distaste for recording the domestic life of woman," and the worse distaste "for contemplating her in any other relation" (*WS*, 246–47).[18]

While most of Robins's references to men who attempted to write women's lives forgave the men for not being able to celebrate the variety and achievement of women's lives—"We all write best what we know best"—she singled out, without naming him, Leslie Stephen, that "man whom every lover of literature must honor on other grounds." She attacked his biography of George Eliot as the "reward of his secret contempt for greatness when it appeared in the guise of a woman" (*WS*, 247).

"Would that George Eliot had found a Mrs. Gaskell, too!" she asserted, as she stressed that the "fine example of literary friendship" between Gaskell and Brontë had produced a "fine example of art." She inspired her audience to take up this newest of biographical forms: "Fellow members of the League, you have such a field as never writers had before," she concluded. "You are in that position for which Chaucer has been so envied by his brother poets, when they say he found the English language with the dew upon it. You find woman at the dawn. . . . The Great Adventure is before her. *Your* great adventure is to report her faithfully" (WS, 246, 250–51).

The Coronation Suffrage Pageant, June 1911

Robins's next literary response to the next political crisis might, except for the hurried circumstances of its composition, have fit neatly into some plan to stress the importance of women's lives, for her *Westminster Gazette* article of June 16 previewed the women of history who were to be personified in the Women's Coronation Pageant. This most ambitious of suffrage parades was scheduled to march through the streets of London the next day, just a week before the authentic coronation of the new king. Robins's essay detailed the work that had gone into the preparation of the women's pageant and explained why it should be seen: "There are other arms, protective not destructive; arms which have helped to build this Greatness. In the Royal Pageant they will be given little space and scant remembering." Yet they were "half the Empire" (WS, 263).

The prose of her preview of the Women's Coronation Pageant is not remarkable, nor is its argument profound. Robins outlined both the historical women featured in the pageant and the descriptions of the individual contingents of women—suffrage prisoners, historical queens, college and university graduates, the Franchise Leagues, the musicians, the representatives of regional suffrage societies, the international contingents: "Four miles of women marching toward one goal" (WS, 268). Robins's brief invitation printed in Saturday's *Westminster* was not remarkable *except* for the circumstances of its appearing at all: Robins had been contacted just four days earlier by both Christabel and Mrs. Pankhurst "complaining of press boycott of Pageant" (Diary, June 12, 1911). Robins wrote to Spender, the editor of the *Westminster Gazette*, and asked him to take an article. On the next day she noted his answer, "He wires he will," and that day she traveled to London, visited the WSPU offices at Clements Inn, lunched at the International Suffrage Club, toured the preparations for the pageant, and got information about the marching order. She returned home the same day "dead beat" and spent all the next day in bed but working on her article. She finished it at midnight, packed for the return trip the next morning, copied the article on the train, delivered it to the *Westminster Gazette*, and spent several anxious hours worrying because she had not seen the proof.

The day after the article appeared, she marched with the Writers' League carrying a bouquet of irises and lilies in the league colors. Robins's section formed at the Embankment end of Northumberland Avenue and waited there for three hours before starting. She was "dizzy with fatigue" when they reached Albert Hall, but after refreshment at a neighboring hotel, she returned to the hall to hear the speakers.

In Support of W. E. B. DuBois, July 1911

The threat of a more complicated boycott than a press blackout prompted Robins to involve herself in quite a different political controversy. For the week of the Coronation, the black American W. E. B. DuBois had been invited to be a guest at the Lyceum Club. However, the invitation had come from the committee "in the absence of the American member." The American woman, identified in Robins's diary as "Mme. Thayer" (Diary, February 4, 1911), had, Robins wrote to Florence Bell, "not been content to stay away herself. She makes a shindy: insists the club shall insult the black reformer by canceling the invitation." The Lyceum had appealed to Robins to save them from embarrassment. Robins's effective lobbying involved her more than she wanted to be: "Then the return of the boomerang! Will *I* dine with (in company with others) this black man." Robins, at first reluctant, agreed and was faced with a further appeal: she was asked to introduce DuBois when he addressed the Club. "This finishes me in the South," she wrote privately to her friend (ER to FB, April 10, 1911), but she surged forward with her new commitment. She read DuBois's collection, *The Souls of Black Folk*, and drafted her address.

No copy of Robins's speech survives, but from what she told Bell of it later, both her speech and DuBois were a "great success. He took the shine out of an English Bishop and Maurice Hewlett I tell you" (ER to FB, July 14, 1911). Even though Robins had earlier expressed interest in DuBois's work at Atlanta University, the contrast between the obligation Robins felt toward the speaking commitment before she met and heard DuBois and her enthusiasm for him afterward shows how the occasion had for her some of the qualities of a conversion. In his speech,[19] DuBois compared the struggle faced by women in England and the struggle for racial equality; Robins had done likewise in an earlier suffrage speech and had stressed, in her preface to *Uncle Tom's Cabin*, that the work of real Reconstruction had yet to begin. Robins met DuBois again on the day following the Lyceum dinner, invited him to Backsettown for a day, and hoped to introduce him to Octavia, great granddaughter of the abolitionist William Wilberforce (ER to FB, July 14, 1911). DuBois was forced to cancel his visit to Henfield when his ship sailed earlier than expected, but Robins remained interested in his work, and her determination to write a novel about racial relations in the American South increased.

Suffering again from illness that was aggravated by summer heat and pressures to complete "Theodora," Robins spent most of July in Harrogate. Upon her arrival in the Yorkshire bathing resort, she saw a doctor, who prescribed a treatment. The pressure to complete her first volume of "Theodora" was particularly intense, for she had recently made the acquaintance of Thomas Wells, editor at Harper's, and had "foolishly promise[d] to let him have what's done to take back to U.S.A." (Diary, June 10, 1911). Wells in the meantime had repeatedly requested the remainder of her novel. At the time, she saw her entertainment of the Harper's editor, married to the leading American suffragist, "Pippa" Wells, as a diplomatic necessity. She described him to Florence Bell as the "kind gentleman who doesn't mind paying £100 for a short story and who is angling for my next book" (ER to FB, June 11, 1911). This meeting was the modest beginning of Wells's admiration of her, which expressed itself in ways that Robins found uncomfortably intimate. With a few notable exceptions, Wells proved to be ineffectual in giving her fiction an American outlet. He rejected "Theodora" in August. Over the next twenty years he made professional promises he could not keep and apologized for his behavior with the excuse that he was tragically in love with Robins.

Even as she let the completed part of "Theodora" out of her hands, Robins was thinking about other aspects of her early life. She read, in preparation for more autobiographical fiction, all of her old letters to her father and grandmother. On her forty-ninth birthday, her connection to her past was even more intense. She had by this time returned to Backsettown and acknowledged, "I think of G. R. P. and have a sense of longing to be alone with thoughts of him." She took a small cache of her late husband's effects to the "great fir tree on the margin of the pond," where she dug a little hole, placed in it "fragments of his letters, some too dear to fall in other hands, & photographs of him and of me & I set fire to them & when they blaze I scatter incense over the flame & the sweet smoke blows in my face & the poor little records still sweet to me & still most sacred were turned to dust." As if making a deliberate invocation she added, "Something of him forever after will haunt this garden. How he would have loved it. And yet more how he would have loved Florida!" (Diary, August 6).

"Under His Roof," 1911

Two weeks later she wrote her landlord of her renewed interest in buying Backset, once more expressing the hope that along with the house and garden she could buy additional surrounding land. Meanwhile, Robins put Backsettown to other uses. She had again offered shelter to Christabel Pankhurst, and now, in early September, she imagined a story of militant suffrage which would use the structural features of her old farmhouse—its massive stone roof and the oak beams which supported it—as a backdrop. The story concerned a widow who inherits Hugh Kenyon's house and a younger woman who at one time loved him deeply but who was driven away by the conniving older woman. The widow tries one last time to manipulate her husband's lover. Although years have passed since his death, she invites the young woman to her house, hoping to persuade her to sleep there so that she will not attend a suffrage rally the next day. The younger woman's commitment to politics never falters; in fact, her thwarted love for Kenyon seems to give passion to her suffrage politics. The masterfully executed plot includes superb parallels between the psychological warfare of the two women and the gnawing rats that cause the house to collapse. The widow, living under the roof of the man whose property she usurped, has tolerated the rats for years, it seems, but denies their presence. The young suffragist finds beams that the rats have gnawed hollow. Shadows scurry through the dark corners of the rooms as the silence between the two women reveals unspoken motives and conjures up their past antagonism. While the women lunch in the dining room, the huge stone chimney collapses and exposes the outside wall. As the rats' presence becomes pervasive, the widow's hatred of the younger woman's freedom becomes clear. The young woman's immunity from the evil powers associated with the older woman and with the house results directly from her suffrage commitment. The suffrage worker leaves without spending the night, and the massive slate roof collapses onto the widow and crushes her to death. This was Robins's fictional punishment for a woman suspicious of the WSPU's goals.

The widow's bedroom is a duplicate of Robins's own; from her pillow she looked up at its exposed oaken beams, once the structural framework of seafaring ships and now supporting the heavy roof. Periodically, the local rat catcher visited Backsettown. Just before she began to compose the story, the coal shed had collapsed with a thunderous roar. Although she set her tale in her house, the only parallel between the story and Robins's life is that she is both the widow and the suffragist, dramatizing the split in her own life.

"Under His Roof" was more soundly rejected than anything Robins had sent out for publication. *Cornhill* returned it; other magazines declined it. "Nobody will have it," Robins observed after two other refusals (Diary, January 11, 1912). Determined that censorship should not affect the fate of this story, Robins paid for its private publication and then sold copies as a fund raiser for the Suffrage League. In 1913, it was published in *Good Housekeeping.* Two other stories that she wrote at this time also centered on sexual politics, "Discretion" and "Sixes and Sevens."

It was not always what and how much Robins wrote that defined her as a writer during her suffrage years but how she took charge of circulating her work and the attention she paid to other women writers and politicians. She knew a good many writers in the Women Writers' Suffrage League; she judged the Women Writers' Suffrage League's one-act play contest and offered *Votes for Women!* to them for a benefit matinée.[20]

Another Crisis

Even progress on the short political fiction which took Robins away from longer projects was often thwarted by interruptions. On October 2, 1911, a packed meeting at the London Pavilion heard Mrs. Pankhurst's farewell before leaving for America. Robins went backstage to see her personally and promised Christabel that if the Conciliation Bill did not pass, she would speak. In November, Lord Asquith, wavering on his commitment to Parliament's Woman Suffrage Bill, introduced a countermeasure proposing to extend the franchise universally to men. Every woman suffrage society—moderates, militants, and representatives of the Franchise Leagues—organized a deputation to Asquith and Lloyd George. Christabel Pankhurst appealed to Robins to be part of the deputation, and Robins agreed but named two conditions: "I make her understand that I won't speak and that I reserve my independence as to further 'steps'" (Diary, November 15). Asquith took the occasion to listen quietly to the women's speeches and then admitted that he still did not favor suffrage for women. He told them they were free to "Get rid of me by all means if you can, but at the moment I am head of the Government and I am not convinced."[21] Robins took note of his reactions with the observation, "Asquith very conciliatory but no good." Something worse offended her: "Mrs. A. flatters me and runs down the other women—ugh!" (Diary, November 17). Robins spent the next few days composing a letter to the *Times*, negotiating with Edward Grey, and participating in the November 21 protest demonstration. Many windows were broken. Two hundred and twenty-three women were arrested. The following day Christabel telephoned Robins, "You said you'd speak if a crisis came. It's *here*" (quoted in ER Diary, November 22, 1911).

"So I have to," Robins added when she recorded the appeal in her diary (November 22). She was not comfortable with the assignment, but Robins followed this commitment with others. She gave teas, wrote letters, authorized "Under His Roof" to be sold to raise funds; yet she longed to get back on track with her writing. On December 20, she took her leave of London by giving a farewell dinner party.

She left for Henfield relieved to discover, as she told Florence Bell, that "to try to write about current affairs *and* make speeches *and* live in the London hurly burly is simply a thing I must not try again. . . . A great Peace comes of finding one can't stand a given thing which has put on a false air of being a duty" (ER to FB, December 21, 1911).

Again writing to Bell, sure that she would gain possession of Backset, she spoke of "three years of scant productiveness"; yet she needed "a spot where precisely I *can* rest and be content as I am here. I have worked, and worked hard up to 1908 since I was in my teens. Not to have some such background to one's life as Backset, would be a great loss—an impoverishment in fifty ways." As soon as she professed her claim to the spot, she contemplated moving, if necessary, in order to make the most of her powers to write. She knew that "London in these next months (during the next session) will be a Pandemonium. If I were physically stronger I should be in the thick of it. I have proved that things being as they are I am no good in that fray. But nobody believes me—nobody, that is, among those who want me there" (ER to FB, December 31, 1911).

She did resume writing, but her sense of a double duty and split commitment intensified as a result of the events of early March. After reading with great disappointment Masefield's recent poem "The Widow in the Bye Street," with its caustic portrait of an overprotective mother, Robins had taken out her packet labeled *Docet umbra* and looked over her notes for a story about a young girl abducted into prostitution. Her initial beginning, entitled "Whatever Happened to Betty Martindale?," was partially influenced by Masefield's suggestions and his stories with a seafaring setting. Then, on February 29, "A great revulsion" came over her "in respect of the present form of *Docet umbra*. I 'see it' suddenly quite differently. And tho' I lose all that I've done on the old lines I feel a great lightness and relief." The new form, interestingly, was closer to the original story as she had envisioned it before she began to confer with Masefield. She could, she realized, write a first-person account from the point of view of the older sister who herself escapes being abducted but who is tortured by the shock of discovery of what has happened and who lacks the power to change social attitudes or to persuade the authorities to search for her sister.

The following day Robins began her new version of the book about "Bettina" which would become *My Little Sister*, but on that day, March 1, an expertly planned, totally unannounced, and unsuspected suffrage demonstration took place in the retail business district in central London during the busiest half hour of the day. Dusk had fallen, and the streets were brilliantly lit and crowded with shoppers—and with an abnormal number of women carrying the latest fashionable accessory, very large muffs. On this particular evening the muffs were heavily laden with concealed hammers and stones. At about 5:30, Mrs. Pankhurst and two companions succeeded in approaching 10 Downing Street by taxi and broke four panes of glass by throwing stones.

They were promptly arrested—their goal—and almost immediately after-ward, the storefronts in Piccadilly turned into a mass of splintering glass. The next wave of the attack hit shops in Regent Street and the Strand. Then, barely fifteen minutes later, Oxford Street was also in shambles. A few women es-caped arrest by hiding. Many others waited for their arrest as the crowd sur-rounded individual perpetrators and held them until the police came.

The reaction to the destruction was negative in the extreme. Newspaper editorials and many letters to editors blamed the militants for having lost all chance of seeing any bill through Parliament. Part of the suffragists' point was that too many compromises had made the Conciliation Bill too weak a fran-chise. "The defeat of the Conciliation Bill of 1910 had been sincerely mourned. The defeat of the Conciliation Bill of 1912 was a foregone conclu-sion," Robins wrote in retrospect (*WS*, 316). The WSPU had originally an-nounced a demonstration for March 4, and on that day Robins wrote, "I waver about going to town after reading of arrests of W.S.P.U. members etc., etc. The House of Commons Raid for tonight determines me." Robins spent two hours among the vast crowd, heard word of "arrests which we do not very clearly see," and the next day opened the *Times*, expecting to read an objective report of the event. She was disappointed.

Immediately she began a "Letter to the *Times*," taking issue with "your leader of yesterday," which stated, "'when enthusiasm brings about a tragedy, there is some error latent in it, however fine its cause may be'" (*WS*, 288). Robins sought to remind the *Times* and its readers just how vast and right the enthusiasm for suffrage was among women. Though exhausted, she felt obli-gated to read some of the "masses of papers" which covered the event. Then, in the wake of a police raid on the WSPU headquarters at Clements Inn, Rob-ins went there on March 6. In the storming of the office the day before, the police had arrested Frederick and Emmeline Pethick-Lawrence on the charge of conspiracy. Every record and file that the WSPU kept had been confiscated and carried off in two taxi cabs. Robins found Evelyn Sharp in charge of *Votes for Women*. Christabel had gone into hiding. A friend of Mrs. Pankhurst's gave Robins a box, "Mrs. Pankhurst's valuables to keep for her." Robins sat at Christabel's now barren desk and finished her letter. The *Times* printed it the following day under the heading: "The Militant Suffragists—Miss Rob-ins's Apologia."[22]

Robins argued, "The truth is that the ideal for which Woman Suffrage stands has come, through suffering, to be a religion." The sooner this truth was recognized, she went on, the shorter the time of bitterness. "Yet we are told that because some glass has been broken, any show of understanding, or consideration, towards Militant Suffragists would involve a menace to the foundations of civilization." In a one-sentence paragraph characteristic of her political voice she continued: "The woman's answer to that is they are fighting against the real, not a fancied menace, and fighting for a less imperfect civilization" (*WS*, 289).

The tragedy, she implied, was not the destruction of property but the escalation of repression: "Does anyone seriously think that the hundreds of imprisonments, the forcible-feeding torture, the death and insanity already to the credit (?) of the policy of repression have had the intended effect?" Any further repression, Robins warned, would on the contrary, "blow the flame to conflagration" (*WS*, 290). Pressed by WSPU leaders to defend, even to encourage further acts of militancy, Robins was evolving her own more studied position. She had made it known that she could not directly participate in militant acts. Acutely conscious of the suffering that women had endured, she addressed the editor, "You were shocked and astonished at the broken glass. I assure you that many of us have come to read of broken glass with an intensity of relief" (*WS*, 291).

Further tensions arose. Evelyn Sharp and the other temporary officers told Robins she was needed on the platform on the Royal Opera House on the night her letter had appeared. "Trouble expected," she explained in her diary. Hostile crowds had gathered in the street outside. Robins had difficulty getting through the door. Once inside there was a huge audience, with many hecklers, but there was "great enthusiasm also for Lady Constance Lytton." Because the police feared the angry street crowd, Robins and other speakers were smuggled out (Diary, March 7, 1912).

The following day Annie Kenney summoned Robins to Clements Inn to show her Christabel's twelve-page letter leaving Kenney in charge of militant operations. Robins noted, "They want me. I say if I'm to write I *must* get away. . . . We talk policy. I show where I am" (Diary, March 8). Once again, Robins made clear she would support militancy only to the degree that her writing sympathized with the broader aims of the suffragettes.

In Defense of Militancy, 1912

Robins returned to Henfield after leaving requests with various writers to lend support to the militant position. She was relieved to think that Christabel was still at large but arrived in her quiet town to find "rumors rife in village that I have her concealed here" (Diary, March 9, 1912). On that day, the *Contemporary Review* requested an article from her, and Ford Madox Hueffer agreed to write for the WSPU. A few days later, playwright and author Laurence Housman (brother of the poet A. E. Housman), active in the Men's Suffrage League, sent Robins word that he would contribute an article to *Votes for Women,* and Robins forwarded to the WSPU both Housman's offer and her "2nd refusal to sign office instructions since I can't be at office to direct or oversee" (Diary, March 12, 1912). Even as the leadership of the WSPU grew more and more autocratic, Robins retained her freedom to contribute to the organization on her own terms. Evelyn Sharp's editorship of *Votes for Women* during this period solicited the contributions of a large number of distinguished writers, and it is clear from Robins's personal records that she herself recruited a number of them.

Robins drafted "The Perfidy of Sympathizers" for *Votes for Women* and "Sermons in Stones" for *Contemporary Review*, and during the rest of the month traveled back and forth on business to London. The local postmaster reported to her that the police were watching her correspondence. On threat of being deported, she went to the consulate to see about being naturalized. She rode in the car that went from Clements Inn to Holloway to take books to Mrs. Pethick-Lawrence and while there was also granted an interview with Mrs. Pankhurst. Robins found the already frail woman ready to begin a hunger strike if she did not get "facilities"—the officials' term for legal materials—to enable her to prepare her defense. When Robins tried to appeal to Edward Grey, he refused to see her, so she promised WSPU leaders that she would make a reference to Mrs. Pankhurst's harsh treatment in her upcoming speech.

Robins spoke on the night of March 28, when a crowded meeting at Albert Hall raised ten thousand pounds for the WSPU and the Pethick-Lawrences, just released on bail, sat on the platform. Her theme was the free and unfettered spirit of Christabel. She enjoined the officials to look for her in China where the National Assembly had ratified votes for women, to look for her in Persia where women were the active force in struggles for freedom, and to recognize her effect in America. Christabel's liberty, she assured her audience in an argument she referred to as her "diatribe against fear" (Diary, March 24, 1912), signified a far greater thing, that women had discovered for themselves that "*they cannot ever more be afraid . . .* , that, however they decide to conduct their campaign, they are delivered from the old tyranny of dreading pains and penalties" (WS, 311).

Robins used one voice in her platform stance when she was speaking to the already converted and another when she wrote in the public prints for a wider audience whom she knew to be mostly critical of the militant action. Perhaps the best example of the latter is "Sermons in Stones," an article in *Contemporary Review* in which she stresses that the majority of all suffragists love peace and abhor physical force as a means to political change. However, because "women are quite as human as men," they are "liable to be pleased and won by fair promises; women are liable to be angered and antagonized by betrayal" (WS, 317).

"Why not?" she asked, invoking the rhetoric of Shakespeare's Shylock: "Hath not a woman eyes? Hath not a woman hands, organs, dimensions, sinews, affections, passions? Fed with the same food, hurt with the same weapons, subject to the same diseases, treated by the same means, warmed and cooled by the same winter and summer as her brother is?" (WS, 317). Robins placed the actions of the stone throwers in a perspective that reminded her readers that "in comparison with the measures adopted by men under less provocation, women are still pursuing a policy of pin-pricks, hoping still that a prick, after all, may rouse the men of the nation" (WS, 327–28). Militant destruction of property, she reasoned, was less than the price being paid by the "uncounted thousands" who "yearly suffer and die. They die for lack of proper housing; for lack of uncontaminated milk; for lack of segregation of contagious diseases; through the absence of State-trained midwives; through the dangerous trades" (WS, 328). The leadership of the WSPU was veering away from its labor-identified roots (Christabel declared Tory sympathies and the former mill girl Annie Kenney unflinchingly paid allegiance to Christabel). Nonetheless, Robins appealed to the wider common bond she felt united the working classes and the women who had found a drastic way to speak out against their condition. The Labour party suffragists in fact deplored the violence of the WSPU, but Robins saw beyond the factionalism and emphasized the importance of a broadly based woman's movement united across class lines.

At the end of March, Robins returned to Henfield hopeful that she could now withdraw from active participation. It was the first time that she had stepped on the land that was now legally hers. Her very first act was to carry to a favorite spot the "last memorials" of her husband, "those I should not be willing any hands should touch but mine, those possessions which went down with him into the sea & the daguerreotype of him as a baby in his mother's arms." Again beneath her fir tree she dug a hole, started a fire, and watched the incense-sweetened smoke filter through the flowers she had planted. "So that is done," she wrote. "I have not let the first 24 hours of my ownership go by without consecrating the ground here to Memory" (Diary, March 30, 1912).

In mid-April the news of the sinking of the *Titanic* with "My dear W. T. Stead on board" (Diary, April 16) sent her back with renewed commitment to the white slavery fiction. Stead had died "as he lived," helping the women and children into lifeboats. The example of his advocacy of the regulation of prostitution prompted politicians to draft a new measure in token of his death. Publicly, Robins would call attention to the irony that one man's death and the attempt to honor him with a memorial had produced the legislation which many hundreds of women—without the vote and without political power—

had been unable to effect. Privately, the impact of Stead's death upon Robins made her feel "dreamlike and full of strangeness . . . , as though I were very near something new and transforming" (Diary, April 20, 1912). The sense of something new and transforming also carried Robins into her new novel with a conviction that made the writing of it uplifting.

The philosophy Robins had developed of regarding the suffering of others as effecting conversion was most forcefully expressed in the article that she wrote to conclude her collected essays on suffrage. It was accepted by *Mc-Clure's* for separate publication. She stressed that stone throwing had to be seen in a broad perspective. "The evil of bad relationship between the sexes is not the new thing. The attack upon it is the new thing" (*WS*, 366). Robins stressed that militancy's failure, up to this time, to win the vote was not the point; the ballot was a symbol, but the sense of freedom that women had already found in their need to speak out was itself a victory.

Before she devoted herself wholly to her book on prostitution, Elizabeth Robins attended the last day of the conspiracy trial indicting Mrs. Pankhurst and the Pethick-Lawrences. During the first break in the trial, she went to Clements Inn to draft a "letter to go to 100 big wigs to press for first division treatment of suffrage prisoners." After the charge to the jury, the court recessed until 3:00 P.M. "Mrs. P. takes my arm as we go out, asks me to come and lunch with her." At lunch, Robins sat with those who, in the Pankhursts' absence, would come to take up positions of leadership: the composer Ethel Smyth, Lady de la Warr, and Lady Sybil Smith (who had confided to Robins that *The Convert* had persuaded her to become active). Robins also observed: "Mr. and Mrs. Lawrence alone 'for the last time' perhaps." The jury verdict was "Guilty 'with pure motive.'" The accused made their speeches: "Mrs. Pankhurst breaks down" (Diary, May 22, 1912). The sentence—nine months in prison—outraged even those unsympathetic to the militants.

Robins went back to Clements Inn, signed 103 letters, returned to Henfield, and there received replies "chiefly *against* militant tactics. A curious and unexpected window opened upon Opinion" (Diary, May 26, 1912). Three days later she telegraphed her resignation to the WSPU leaders, but their reply was to ask her to reconsider—and to speak again at Albert Hall. "I am distracted. Don't know how to refuse second time" (Diary, May 29, 1912). She experienced the usual anxieties in the course of preparation. On the night of her speech at Albert Hall she found herself "half dead" until she stood up to speak, but she hardly had to look at her manuscript. "It goes! A blessed relief when it's over" (Diary, June 15). The printed version of her speech shows how Robins made advantageous use of the mostly negative replies to her letters that had elicited support from the "big wigs." One actor-manager had written to her that he was "'dead against the inartistic methods of the Militant Suffragists.'" Robins ridiculed him for thinking that what had happened—to the plate glass, to the women's lives—was a play. She ridiculed the reply of one author who suggested the women ought to constrain themselves to pageants, processions, and singing and alluded to several plays—*Hedda Gabler, The Master Builder, Richard II*—in order to show how unacceptable was his position (*WS*, 342–43).

My Little Sister

Relieved to have the speech making behind her, Robins put the latter half of June to productive use. Most of the first draft of Robins's novel indicting white slavery was drafted by early July. She had discussed the project with William Heinemann in February. Now she found him both eager to secure its publication and extremely nervous about how it would be received. He told her, as she was completing the book, that he was adamantly opposed to publishing it anonymously and was sure that booksellers would boycott it. "I am disappointed, but fear [I] cannot risk anonymity," Robins noted in her diary (June 26, 1912). In early September, *McClure's* accepted the novel for publication in two parts, beginning in December, on the condition that the English edition would be held up. Heinemann, with his proof for the novel completed and awaiting the presses, agreed to this arrangement. The novel, entitled *My Little Sister* both in *McClure's* and in the American book edition, was published by Heinemann as *Where Are You Going To?*[23]

Robins, in giving the story its final form, erased the notes and files she had been keeping for five years. Instead of following Masefield's suggestions or using facts and cases showing how young women were forced into prostitution, she described a young woman discovering society's acceptance of prostitution in its most horrific dimension. The unnamed narrator and her younger sister, Bettina, are abducted into "one of the most infamous houses in Europe" (*MLS*, 286) when the procuress poses as their aunt. As Bettina sings "Where are you going to, my pretty maid?" at the piano, her sister learns where she is when a man who is supposed to be her seducer instead risks helping her escape.

In many ways the two sisters' initiation to the adult world is a realistic "Goblin Market" that turns dark and sinister rather than redemptive. Without Christina Rossetti's fruit imagery, Robins carefully hints at dangers in the adult world as the sister narrates Bettina's childhood. Their mother is fiercely protective of the children, especially as regards contact with strangers. Perhaps the closest equivalent to the way Robins reveals her information about an unmentionable vice is Bernard Shaw's play *Mrs. Warren's Profession*, which, though it did not refer to prostitution by name, had been banned from production by the censor in England and stopped by police in New York. Similarly, Robins crafted her indictment with the veiled euphemisms cultured society used when it accepted the institution by dismissing it. The narrator's discovery that the world allows such injustices is more shocking to her than the work of the villains themselves. When Bettina's sister is struggling to absorb the horror, she hears her male host explain the predicament she is in with the phrases, "Human nature . . . Take India— . . . They're called 'Government Women.' The women are needed by the army" (*MLS*, 295).

In despair because she never learned the address and yet must track down Bettina before it is too late, the sister discovers that "the police have a list of 'these houses,'" that they are "expected to have an eye on such places" (*MLS*, 317), and that they will nevertheless not search every house on the list. Even the commonplace excuse that little can be done—"But usually it's poor girls" (*MLS*, 326)—makes a simple, searing revelation.

Robins explained in retrospect why she told her story, not of a legion of poor girls forced into the same fate, sometimes by economic desperation, sometimes by abduction, but of girls from a privileged class. In her essay praising Christabel Pankhurst's later campaign against male vice, Robins would write that there would have been no audience for *My Little Sister* had she written about the common girl. Robins had sent Christabel a preliminary copy of *My Little Sister* before Christabel's articles on the "Great Scourge" began to appear in *Votes for Women*, and Christabel admitted to being very moved by the tale.[24]

Robins's motive was to reach an influential audience. In America, Emma Goldman and other working-class advocates spoke out for the poor girl, and Robins evidently got much of her information on conditions of prostitution from working-class reformers who were associates of her brother Raymond. Katharine Houghton Hepburn, influential as the president of the Connecticut Woman Suffrage Association, had more than local impact with her attack on organized prostitution in Hartford.[25]

As she revised her novel to lengthen it as Heinemann had asked, Robins donned the uniform of a Salvation Army officer; by this means she hoped to become more involved in rescuing young girls from the fate of the streets. Her extended diary entry of July 25, 1912, shows how the costume and the role failed to accomplish their purpose. The young woman with whom Robins succeeded in talking was angry at all Christian charities, and in order to persuade the street girl of her sincerity, Robins revealed that she was not really a Salvation Army volunteer. Robins told her, "I am not used to this and I shan't be here again. I live in the country. Just once out of all my life I am here and able to speak to you." Robins made the girl promise to come to Robins's London address the next day, but she never came. The disappointment and her vivid impressions lingered. Days later she wrote she was "haunted still, . . . *bruised mentally*" by the scene: "I practically knew it all before so I don't know why at my age the scene should eat into my consciousness like an acid" (Diary, July 28, 1912).

The real-life harshness of the experience must have seemed to Robins in sharp contrast to Shaw's portrait of the messianic—and ultimately capricious —Major Barbara. If the sales of her book measured its impact, her novel had a more pronounced effect than her one foray into the streets in her uncomfortable disguise. In the United States, the book sold more than eighteen thousand copies in the first six months.[26] In England, she noted in her diary, the twenty-five thousandth copy had been ordered within weeks of publication (March 24, 1913).

Robins's commitment to the issue of white slavery sent her in two directions. First, it propelled her toward further direct political involvement. She attended meetings, made speeches, gave interviews, and continued to lobby for further legislation against prostitution. Second, it prompted her to use her story for a more direct audience. Soon after publication, the opportunity for a dramatization of the novel began to materialize. As she received cables from agent Paul Reynolds and dramatic agent Elisabeth Marbury suggesting that an American stage adaptation might be possible, she determined that, if her presence in America would facilitate a theater contract, she would sail immediately.

She had several other reasons for wanting to revisit America. Robins had been one of four witnesses in the WSPU committee meeting on October 14 which resulted in a split between Mrs. Pankhurst and the Pethick-Lawrences. The Pankhursts had forced the resignation of the Pethick-Lawrences and the dissolution of the advisory board and had thereby brought bitter criticism of the WSPU. During the meeting, Robins tried to call for reconciliation and afterward regretted the breakup of the board. In her memoir, Emmeline Pethick-Lawrence blamed Mrs. Pankhurst more than Christabel. Robins noted that Mrs. Pankhurst sat "sphinxlike" in defiance. Robins was saddened by the mass meeting three days later, at which Mrs. Pankhurst delivered her challenge, "I incite this meeting to rebellion," but at which Robins noted there was applause at any mention of the Pethick-Lawrences. Robins felt, "I cannot feel that she [Mrs. Pankhurst] has realised the situation. . . . very different evening from those in the past when all the leaders were there" (Diary, October 14, 17, 1912). In mid-November, while fires set by radical militants broke out in pillar boxes and at historic sites, Christabel Pankhurst, exiled in Paris, sent several long letters to Robins. Robins's diaries show that she took Flora Simmonds's advice and criticized the Pankhursts' policy. Simmonds told Robins that if she did not "say more" in her letter, "no one else will." Robins agreed and redrafted her letter (Diary, November 24, 1912). Although Robins would again support the movement with articles, letters, and petitions, it is clear that after the Pankhurst/Pethick-Lawrence split she withdrew from direct participation in WSPU work and no longer condoned militancy.

American Travels, American Themes

Robins arrived in New York on December 21, hopeful of winning a theater contract for *My Little Sister*. Elisabeth Marbury advised her to wait until the book was released. On January 26, Charles Frohman offered her a contract for sole rights to the dramatization for a year.

More personal reasons compelled Robins to visit the sites of her earlier existence. On Christmas Day, 1912, after attending the Pontifical Mass at St. Patrick's Cathedral, she traveled to Staten Island to look at the house of Mrs. Andariese, the home where she had stayed during the first months she had spent looking for work as an actress. The place had also been the setting for the first chapters of "Theodora." Through the snow, she could see the melancholy house and the neglected garden, the ruined fences and fallen trees; and she felt the past come back: "Many thoughts of Mrs. A. and of George. We were young there together and there I got the news" (Diary, December 25, 1912), a reference to the day, twenty-five years earlier, when Robins had heard of the discovery of Parks's body. On January 1, she traveled again to Staten Island to be shown the St. Andrew's Graveyard in Richmond and to learn that there were no records of unmarked graves. She visited Louisville for the first time since her mother's death and laid flowers on her mother's grave. She reached Florida with all her thoughts in England, thinking of Sussex with a "passion of homesickness" (Diary, January 10, 1913). Two days later she noted, "My wedding anniversary." Upon her return to New York, she revisited St. Andrew's in hopes of locating Parks's grave. She had confided to Masefield her grief that Parks believed she had "ceased to care" for him. Apparently it was not enough for Masefield to have reassured her that Parks knew otherwise (JM to ER, February 11, 1910, noon, Berg Collection). Robins supervised the digging on the spot where Parks was believed to be buried. On her return trip in October, she ordered a headstone to be placed there.

Robins's next published novel was not completed until 1916 and was not published until 1918. Between 1913 and 1916 she made four other visits to America; on three of them she spent time at Chinsegut and on each visit established ties and a connection with her past self that she was to write about clearly. The months she spent in England during the middle of 1913 she divided between a dramatization, with the help of Cicely Hamilton, of *My Little*

Sister, the continuation of her Theodora series, and a story she first identified as "Camilla" in her diary entry of May 6.

Her trip to Florida, later in 1913, revived Robins's productivity, even though her commitments were still divided. Elisabeth Marbury wanted a revised last act of *My Little Sister*. Paul Reynolds placed with *Harper's Weekly* her first article on Christabel Pankhurst.[27] Still hopeful of proving her strengths as a playwright, she worked for several weeks on "Evangeline," a drama set in New York which takes its qualities of social conscience and moral justice from the title character's attitudes toward forgiveness and economic reforms in the South. Robins learned that her subjective portrait of a heroine who rejects marriage and her own motherhood in order to aid black mill workers was not material for the commercial stage. Shortly after Elisabeth Marbury sent Robins her reaction "practically saying Evangeline is no good" (Diary, March 14, 1914), Robins introduced Henry James to the material from her father's records that she had retrieved from moldy storage at Chinsegut. James, having just completed *Notes of a Son and Brother*, exclaimed to her, "You are committed to this." James described his own family heritage as "meager scraps" in comparison to Charles E. Robins's legacy and remarked, "What a rich storehouse" (ER Diary, April 6, 1916). "The Pleiades," centered on her father's experiences in Colorado during the late 1870s, occupied her for the remainder of 1914; but this piece too was rejected by Thomas Wells. In the wake of a series of rejections of "Theodora," "Evangeline," and "The Pleiades," Robins began to tap her own roots in order to get at the "something at the heart of fiction" which "being there made it worth my while to write" (Preface, "Theodora").

Camilla

Camilla enabled Robins to work through her marriage and the death of George Parks creatively and also to explore her reluctance, despite repeated appeals from admirers, to yield to other romantic attachments. In its broadest outline, *Camilla* tells the story of a divorced woman's rejection of a second offer of marriage. It shows the painful effects of divorce and the equally difficult and soul-searching decision to reject a second opportunity. Robins's effectively plotted novel begins in the middle of the story, with the divorced American falling in love with a man she had met six years ago when he was traveling with the woman trying to steal Camilla's husband from her. The Englishman Michael Nancarrow is sensitive and caring. Camilla falls in love with him and his centuries-old family home, but just as their marriage is announced and Camilla has come to depend on his safety, she realizes that she can no longer hold her memory at bay. She flees England in order to revisit her girlhood home in Florida. In the long second part of the novel, Camilla recalls her past as she crosses the Atlantic. She uses the voyage to review—in the way that "Maeterlinck tells of [what] goes on in the soul" (*Camilla*, 339)—the years of her schooling, her romance with Leroy Trenholme, and their bitter separation. In a complex and fast-paced conclusion that exemplifies Robins's best fiction, Camilla arrives in New York and attempts to depart for Florida. As would-be suitors press their rival claims upon her, she maintains her need to be free from all romantic attachments.

In its critique of American attitudes toward marriage and divorce, the novel responds to Edith Wharton's fiction and her provocative treatment of the same topics. In the midst of unpacking and rearranging her family's documents in Florida, Robins had read Wharton's *The Custom of the Country* (Diary, November 25, 1913). *Camilla* is in many senses Elizabeth Robins's reply to Wharton's characterization of Undine Sprague, the American woman whose business is marriage first with one man who can satisfy her craving for money and status and then with another. Robins's novel has a conniving husband snatcher, Linda, in a world where sex is used almost as vindictively as in Wharton's; but Robins's focus on Camilla makes the book's critique of Undine's world distinctive. Robins presents a woman whose position as a divorcée has cost her society's respect but who is nevertheless pursued and won for the sake of sexual possession and who, when she realizes that she must forfeit passion to find herself, is not taken seriously.

Camilla is Robins's unique vision, and this is best exemplified in the way that remnants from her own experience—her reconnection with Florida, the hint of the loss of love in her own marriage, her later devotional attitude toward the memory of Parks, the pull to accept English life and an English husband, and her cultivation of solitude as a passion "beyond any other passion" —merge with the way Camilla's character is the culmination of Robins's career-long focus on women and silence.

Recent feminist literary criticism helps us appreciate Robins's exploration of silence as it represents woman's otherness. Especially in a social world where speech is a game that makes woman the object of man's display of power and possessiveness, or when speech means accepting a subservient position, silence is not simply an alternative; woman's silence has, in Jane Gallop's words, a "subversive effect."[28] Camilla is so thoroughly a silenced character (partly because she is the youngest and frailest daughter, partly because she uses silence to protect herself from the crasser world), and is so acutely conscious that her silence is taken as evidence of her inferiority, that she has difficulty using language to articulate her opinions. Others in the book are easily frustrated with her lack of response, her "dullness," her inability even to show emotion. However, the moments where Camilla falters at response are matched by her feeling of strength in silence—and feeling a closer connection to her body—and thus confirm Robins's use of woman's silence as a feminist critique. Although Camilla is not a "shrewd observer," she "took in . . . states of feeling through the pores of her skin" (*Camilla*, 23). She "bathed" in the "inanimate beauty" of the Nancarrow estate, but when she might express her rapture, she "slipped back into the sea of inarticulate sensation" (*Camilla*, 63). Others come to admire her for her silence. Michael tells her she makes him "wonder . . . whether other people could say so much without words if they gave themselves a chance. Is it lack of faith that throws them back on chatter?" (*Camilla*, 107). Leroy, when he most admires Camilla, is converted to her impression that words are chains, yet he manipulates her: "He celebrated 'the eloquence of softly shut lips,' and next moment, characteristically, he set traps for speech" (*Camilla*, 329). When Leroy berates her, as when he criticizes her for never making friends, silence is Camilla's protective armor: "She could easily have answered: 'You used not to let me.' In the face of sudden pleasure, or sudden pain, silence was the instinctive shelter of her soul. She was silent now" (*Camilla*, 371).

Susan Gubar and other feminist critics have suggested that a woman's silenced voice affects her attitudes toward her physical being.[29] Robins used Camilla's sensations to trace Camilla's changing attitudes toward her female body. At the beginning of the novel, she repeatedly recoils at Michael's physical advances, but her frigidity protects her from experiencing deeper passions. When she breaks free of her memory to express what she feels toward Michael, she moves toward him to kiss him on the mouth (*Camilla*, 112). When she thinks of her first romance, she recalls feeling the closeness of Leroy's body in bed. Her disillusionment with their union provokes images of terror. Trapped in an underground cave in Florida with Linda, Michael, and Leroy, at the moment when Camilla realizes how much power Linda has over Leroy, Camilla is terrified to see Leroy take up Linda's challenge and venture farther into the cave. He disappears with a lighted stick. In the dark and alone now, Camilla sees at the bottom of a cave "the apparition of a stark naked giant with immense moustachios on fire" (*Camilla*, 412). It is Leroy, who has swum to safety with a lighted stick in his mouth. Later, Leroy and Linda use a nighttime hunt for a rattlesnake as a pretext to consummate their affair. Camilla wanders through the woods calling for Leroy, thinking he is lost. She recalls the horror of a childhood experience during another such hunt, when she came upon their black servant flailing a snake to death with a fencepost and cried out for him to stop. To calm her, the black man told her that the snake deserved its fate, for he had caught it coiled around the body of a heifer, crushing it to death. "That picture was replaced tonight by one of Roy and

Linda. Drawn close together, squeezed to death, in a scaly embrace" (*Camilla*, 433). Thus, Camilla's earlier responses to physical love as sensuously pleasurable take on connotations of betrayal and violence.

Robins's earlier drafts and correspondence with her editor indicate that he asked her to deliver a story that ended in a marriage. Robins dared to do something else. Camilla is torn between a promised happy second marriage and the strong urge to comfort—and capitulate to—the renewed claims of her first husband. In her rejection of both men, however, Camilla finds herself. She claims a life of solitariness which she cannot even define; it is "too new . . . but something I haven't been . . . , something worth being" (*Camilla*, 466). While Camilla's future is vaguer in the published version than in earlier drafts, Robins achieves tension by setting the uncertainty of Camilla's next life against the surety of her discovery: "She met it with the deep bell-note: Renunciation" (*Camilla*, 501).

Robins clearly took a stand on renunciation in dealing with Masefield. In a letter which seems to reply to an affirmation of her own principles, he expressed the hope that they could continue to "be great lovers in that like the lovers in a great poem." If she wished it, he told her, he would accede to her position, but he grieved: "Renunciation is a sharp agony and love like ours a holy beauty."[30] In her own life, Robins felt painful obligations to memory, but in settling for these, she accepted both her own "capacity for passion" and the strength she finds in living wholly for herself. If her view toward her own sexuality was guardedly Victorian, she nevertheless shared with Emily Dickinson, Willa Cather, Bernard Shaw, and Leo Tolstoy, the conviction that an artist's obligations were first to his or her own art.

In the circumstances of her writing, Robins faced the kind of silencing that Tillie Olsen mentions when she considers how women's writing has been suppressed. Although Elizabeth Robins did not face traditional family obligations, she was confronted not only with distracting influences but also with pressure from a publisher who wanted to dictate what she could write. The world war and Robins's participation in relief efforts were more than a distraction, of course. At the same time that she pursued her fiction, she involved herself in political efforts. Her experiences negotiating a contract with *Cosmopolitan* illustrate publishers' censorship of women's voices. In October 1915, Edgar Sisson, *Cosmopolitan*'s editor, made her the best offer of her life, proposing to take her fiction for the next three years. The next week she found the notes for *Camilla* that she had begun making in 1913 and delved into her long-formulated plans with new encouragement. Because the magazine wanted a particular kind of story, however, she faced difficulties. Thomas Wells at *Harper's* responded to her appeal for advice about the offer with a detailed commentary. He described *Cosmopolitan* as a publication owned by

Elizabeth Robins at her writing desk. (*Courtesy of the Fales Library. Reproduced with the permission of Mabel Smith, for the Backsettown Trustees.*)

the Hearst Corporation, which offered high prices to authors who dared to write scandalous, almost unprintable, fiction. Sisson was hoping to bribe Robins into writing more sensational novels about white slavery.[31]

Robins became more fully aware of Sisson's preference for formula fiction after inviting him to Florida in 1916 to discuss her progress and to show him the nearby underground cave, a setting for one of her most highly charged memory scenes. She tried to hold out for an early advance but signed a contract without it. Since serial publication was planned, Sisson at first objected to Robins's proposal to tell her story in a nonchronological sequence. She began, but then abandoned, a version of the story, which began with Camilla's infancy. He also disliked her plan to end her book with Camilla's renunciation. She noted in her diary: "Sisson dead against Camilla not re-marrying. Magazine would suffer for months. Circulation fall off at once." Then she added her own response: "Confidence disturbed!! (Oh the great child of a public)" (Diary, March 29, 1916). Robins found, too, that her brother Raymond disapproved of her alliance with the Hearst syndicate. He wrote in anger about her receiving Sisson at Chinsegut, and she regretted that he had not telegraphed a response to her cable, which would have prevented her from signing her contract. Then she thought beyond Raymond's censure: "Yet Sisson will give me ease and independence and I shall not write 'down' either" (Diary, April 1, 1916).

She did not "write down," and, after completing her novel despite much interference, she received Sisson's cable on December 28, 1916: "Congratu-lations on fine novel." Her advance for *Camilla* enabled Robins to purchase more land surrounding Backsettown. Together with Octavia Wilberforce, who had come to admire Robins more passionately through Robins's portrait of Camilla and to speak of herself as the "Sister of Camilla," or "S.C.," she named her new property "Camilla's Field."

The novel also gave Robins the freedom to move beyond the ghosts that haunted her own past. Assuredly, she drew on her own experience in writing *Camilla*, but to regard Camilla as Robins would be to misinterpret the novel. Fiction consists of the parts of former selves that we have killed, Kenneth Burke has commented; otherwise we would not be able to use them so boldly.[32] Somewhere, during one of her ritual observances of Parks's memory, Robins buried that part of herself which had clung to him—and so freed her-self to write *Camilla*. In completing this novel, moreover, Robins availed her-self of a different power, for the next phase of her fiction more thoroughly incorporated her political outlook; her next two heroines were not silenced characters but women acting upon the voice they found when they acquired an awakened sense of themselves as women.

8 "My Share in Graver Business"
Fiction and Feminism, 1915–1924

I make clear my passion for Peace and how it must govern the degree of interest I take in *Time and Tide*.
—Diary, November 28, 1920

I have a queer feeling of this being "a join" in life. Or rather as if after long wandering in a valley I have got up on a height whence I can "look before and after."
—Diary, April 11, 1921

T*HE SCENE*: British Museum Reading Room, March 19, 1923.[1] Elizabeth Robins hands a slip of paper to library clerk and takes a seat. A stack of books is brought to her. She puts on her glasses and starts through them. The clerk returns and speaks quietly to her.

CLERK: Professor Budge will see you now, Madam.

ROBINS [mild surprise]: But I only just this minute opened his books—

CLERK: He is a very busy man. Can you follow me please?

[ROBINS takes off her glasses, rises, collects her bag and follows the clerk. They pass through the Egyptian Mummy Rooms, and Robins glances furtively at them, trying to keep her mind on what she is going to say to the eminent Egyptologist Ernest Budge, who has characterized the dead Priestesses of the Temple of Amen-Ra as "Ladies of the College" in a recent article.]

[The clerk ushers her into a side room, Budge's office. Even more precious artifacts adorn his walls, and Robins glances at expertly crafted jewelry in a glass case.]

BUDGE. Miss Robins, I believe you had some questions. I am Professor Ernest Budge.

ROBINS [taking a seat in the proffered chair]. I only asked to be referred to any study, any book, that could explain in more detail the findings recently outlined in this article. [She shows him the article from a newspaper.] I am interested, you see, in a clarification of the status of the "Ladies of the College."

BUDGE [after a quick glance at the article, sternly]. Why are you asking me this?

ROBINS [flustered]. I did not mean to interrupt your work. If you could tell me where I might read—

BUDGE. Nowhere. There is nothing. The ladies' positions were immaterial. They were chief supplicants at the early morning rituals. It is the high priest of Amen-Ra you should be asking about. He controlled all the access to knowledge.

ROBINS. But the women?

BUDGE. You have some motive, don't you? *Why* are you so interested?

ROBINS [again caught off guard, trying to remain cautiously tactful]. It would interest other women. I might pass it on.

BUDGE. Exactly! And that will make me extremely careful in what I say. You are not the first inquirer; there are whole schools of you—college degree women bringing their chattering students. You people presume to think [he begins to tap out his Authority as his fingers dance rhythmically on the desk top]—you seem to think I have nothing better to do than answer women's questions—

ROBINS. Excuse me, but *I* have never been here before. [She gathers her cloak as if to go.]

BUDGE [stops her with a commanding reply]. But I dare say you, too, have got the idea in your head that these priestesses were "ladies" in the sense of women at Girton and Newnham. [He waits for Robins's full attention, then proceeds with self-satisfaction.] Nothing of the sort! There were no learned women in Egypt! No woman—with one exception [with belittlement], a copyist of the Book of the Dead—*no woman could read*!

ROBINS. But women were allowed into the temple?

BUDGE. Yes, if you call the lowest type of household service a form of entrée. These priests, like any others in a religious hermitage, needed people to cook for them, to wash for them. It would be a curious innovation in any age—in any climate—were not the main part of this work done by women.

ROBINS. But you call them priestesses!—ladies of the college—?

BUDGE. Their only function with respect to "learning," Miss Robins, was in learning how to please the priests. [A sly, clever confession; he communicates in as tactful a way as possible, his enjoyment of the dirty joke:] They brought their offerings. Some were "ladies of the house." They saw to that side. If they had money they gave their money. If they had beauty—they gave their beauty.

ROBINS [images of richly adorned youthful women pass through her head as she whispers]: Concubines!

BUDGE [suppressing a soft chuckle]. Even the Queen of Egypt authorized the "plurality of wives." The daughters of a chancellor, you recall, were given royal burial—?

[The scene dissolves to Robins, now walking away from Budge's office, back through the halls of mummies. Focus on her face as the background fades to animated street scenes. Painted modern women linger and strike coy poses. Men, many dressed in soldiers' uniforms, form casual groups and taunt each other with a dare or a shove toward the women.]

Notes on the Scene: The British Museum encounter that Robins recorded in her diary became the basis for a central chapter in *Ancilla's Share*. Jane Marcus has commented on its similarity to the scene "immortalized forever" in the British Museum chapter in Virginia Woolf's *A Room of One's Own*. It was a scene that repeated itself often for Robins; as she presented herself to some "Authority," or went in search of information that she could pass on to other women, she was confronted with trivialization, dismissal, and outright antagonism toward her sex. She wanted in *Ancilla's Share* to show that women could not afford to drop the struggle for women's rights, for world peace depended upon women's active part in government. After *Ancilla's Share: An Indictment of Sex Antagonism* had been published, when she was sixty-one, Robins continued to keep an "Ancilla" notebook, in preparation for a new edition, or an expansion of her "indictment" into a second volume.

In late December of 1924, Robins read Olive Schreiner's *Letters*. One passage of her notebook records the effect upon both Schreiner and Robins of their sight of "girls and women," in caps and gowns, "academically *equipped*." Robins recalls her own "emotion when the Cap and Gown contingent came marching in the Suffrage procession." She suggests an analogy between her feelings and those of a soldier going into war without a rifle who sees other soldiers going, even to sure death, but "*armed*." And then she rejects this simile to reflect: "Yet no . . . , no; all that is pale and useless to convey the vastness of difference between the power of the new woman and the defenselessness of the old-time woman." Given her years and her lack of formal education, Robins was an old-time woman in the early decades of the twentieth century. Educated by experience, however—by the experiences of the stage and the suffrage campaign, by the experience of war that led to her passion for peace—she spoke out in bolder ways than her contemporaries.

Overview, 1915–1924

After she had lived her first half century, Robins often contemplated her state in life. Her health was never certain. She wondered how long she might continue to write, and reminded herself that Ibsen had completed most of his literary achievements after turning fifty. In diary entries on her birthdays, she set new resolutions, reflected on the accumulating years, and worried that the most productive time of her life had passed. Except during several long illnesses, Robins hardly slowed her pace before she reached her mid-sixties.

At the beginning of the war, she made speeches and wrote articles on the effectiveness of the Women's Emergency Corps and other aspects of women's participation. Her feminist philosophy matured into a powerfully reasoned treatise on feminism and pacifism. As the war progressed and she volunteered for various war-related duties, she formulated her own antiwar philosophy and used the arguments of the British and American pacifists as a backdrop for her war novel, *The Messenger*. However, in contrast to other women who condemned the war (including Jane Addams, Olive Schreiner, Emma Goldman, and Rosa Luxemburg), she was not actively pacifist. At first she endorsed the position of the Christabel Pankhurst-inspired Suffrage Union, which declared a truce in the campaign to win the vote. Like fellow American expatriates Henry James and Edith Wharton, she spoke out against the United States' policy of neutrality.

Early in 1917, she began to challenge in print the truce's failure to win the vote for women. When the fighting stopped and she followed the disappointments of the Treaty of Versailles, several events marked her move toward a more pacifist political stance. She saw women asked to give up their jobs, observed the continuing emphasis on militarism, and specifically noted the popularity, after publication in 1920, of Colonel Repington's two-volume personal diary, *The First World War*.

The sense of urgency with which she moved into new areas of feminist politics after the war did not mean that she abandoned other commitments. All her life she had lived a split existence. During this period, on her fifty-seventh birthday, she resolved to "continue yet awhile" her "double duty—fiction and what I can't escape of my share in graver business." That business, she saw, consisted of writing in the press about women's affairs, in "trying all I know to make the better counsels prevail," in communicating her "passion for peace" with a feminist's conviction. Robins's pacifist philosophy evolved naturally from her life, which had encompassed many obligations. She was first of all a novelist, and her three novels of this period, while they relate to her political concerns, represent essentially a separate occupation and a different calling, one that required a concentration difficult to preserve in the midst of her efforts to initiate and urge public appeals. She often wrote in her diary of the "joins" in her creative work—the patches she wove to connect segments of a longer project, written months apart, because she had to attend to political concerns. Her many pursuits necessitated her patchwork method. The method, in turn, allowed her to see a clear turning point, for example the completion of her indictment of militarism in 1921, as a "join in life."

The valley in which she "wandered" between her mountaintop views of her purpose was not unproductive. She was instrumental in the founding of several important women-controlled organizations, most notably the women's weekly paper begun in early 1920, *Time and Tide*, and, as chair of its board of directors, the New Sussex Hospital for Women and Children. Her personal life during these years was defined by her continuing literary friendship with Florence Bell, by her acquaintance with Bell's new protégé, young Sybil Thorndike (whose friendship sustained Robins's interest in the theater), and by the growing dependency of Octavia Wilberforce upon her. Even as Wilberforce clung to Backsettown as her only haven from an unsupportive family and the rigors of medical education, Robins found out from her own doctor that the damp atmosphere at Backsettown contributed to her rheumatism and ill health. She was reluctant to tell Wilberforce of her need to spend long periods away from Backsettown and acceded to Wilberforce's pleas that she continue to maintain the large home despite financial difficulties.

This period, too, between her activity on behalf of Britain's war effort in 1915 and her publication of her pacifist tract in 1924, was framed at the beginning by the death of Henry James, and at the end, in the last week of 1924, by the death of William Archer. Their deaths and the death in 1920 of William Heinemann, another very close friend, affected her deeply. She incorporated feelings of loss in *Time Is Whispering*, her novel about postwar issues. This book was conceived in 1919, was written in fits and starts because politics demanded more of her attention, and was published to popular acclaim in 1923. It centers on the mature relationship of a man and woman who collaborate and grow to depend upon each other. At the same time, the book addresses many complex issues: the effects of war on the men who fought, independence for India, and the promise of an independent, younger generation of women.

War Service for Women: Endell Street Hospital, 1915

Robins was conspicuously out of place when she arrived at the War Office to interview the director-general of medical services, Sir Alfred Keough, in July 1915. She noted afterward that the office "swarms with khaki." She was a volunteer worker who visited soldiers daily, but her mission on this day was a singular one. For two months she had volunteered her time and energy to the Endell Street Hospital for Soldiers, a medical unit organized by Dr. Flora Murray and staffed entirely by women. Her duties ranged from organizing and cataloging the large donations of books to writing letters for soldiers and giving readings. As Robins and Beatrice Harraden, co-director of the library, created order out of chaos, she grew to understand the men who sacrificed their lives to save their country. During Robins's early weeks at the hospital, she approached Dr. Murray and her co-organizer, Dr. Louisa Garrett Anderson, with the argument that women might serve as stretcher bearers. The two medical women had spent the early months of the war with the Red Cross in France and understood the demands of battle duty. In the course of what Robins described as a "*most* interesting" interview, she gradually won the doctors over (Diary, July 21, 1915).

A day later in the War Office, Robins put the suggestion to Sir Alfred. Robins found him "dead against women in danger."[2] As she followed his reasoning, she saw the age-old division of labor by gender take on new dimensions. Sir Alfred indicated that women's anxiety would be dreadful.

"Isn't it anyway?" Robins asked. To Sir Alfred's claim that the women serving as stretcher bearers would "get blown to pieces," she answered, "Men do." He showed her a map of the Dardanelles, the precarious beaches off the coast of Turkey, with "little flags stuck in for markers."

"Here is a hospital *underground*," he stressed. His arguments on behalf of women's special nature failed to convince Robins. Sir Alfred explained that women stretcher bearers would also have to render first aid and that they were not strong enough to do so.

Robins replied that they were "strong enough to scrub floors." Sir Alfred reasoned that men had fine feelings and could not stand seeing women under fire. At this remark, Robins restrained herself from saying "You stand far worse." She added as she wrote the account of the interview, "No, I spare him that. But I did say at parting, 'Well, think it over. Don't let France again take the initiative and show the way to take English women into the public service.'" (The French Red Cross had welcomed English women's volunteer medical assistance in the early weeks of the war when the British government refused to send women to the continent.) After the interview she recalled the medical director's rejection of her suggestion and his hint that she was not alone. Robins recalled: "Then after telling [me] my idea was madness he veered round and said I needn't think I was the only person who entertained these notions." She wrote of her reaction during that moment: "Oho, thinks E.R., that's interesting!" (ER Diary, July 22, 1915).

When her article "Stretcher-Bearing for Women" appeared in the *Daily Mail* the following month,[3] the responses proved that there was widespread endorsement of her position. The many letters received by the paper included offers to volunteer—with stamped envelopes for return replies—from "all the would-be stretcher bearers" (Diary, September 2, 1915).

Robins's argument in the article sought to prove women fit and to show that women were already serving in countless capacities. She criticized the recruitment posters which showed women saying "Go." The recruitment slogans would produce better results, Robins argued, if they showed the women crying "Come!" Two short years later, Robins modified her position on women's appropriate service when she attacked the proposal for universal conscription for women. In 1915, however, after watching male authorities dampen the spirits of women to face equal dangers, she responded to the typical objection, "These horrors are not for women," with this reasoning: "No —nor for men—who not infrequently go to pieces under the strain. These horrors are our common burden. Why should the specially qualified woman, who knows herself capable of bearing a share, not be allowed to? 'Not women's work?' Shade of Florence Nightingale, hold a little higher the light of your lamp!" ("Stretcher-Bearing").

As Robins continued her volunteer work in the Endell Street Hospital, completion of *Camilla* was her principal occupation for all of 1916. Even though the novel is not directly concerned with the war, she explained in her dedication of the book version that work on it served, during the emergency conditions and air raids in London, as "a kind of air-raid shelter for the mind" (*Camilla*, vii). Other events besides air raids seriously delayed the completion of this book. When her brother Raymond offered to finance her stay in Florida, Robins traveled to America in March 1916. She could not know that the journey and illnesses would cause her to forfeit months of writing time.

Tribute to Henry James: Killed by the War

The passage to America laid the groundwork for the next phase of her reaction to the war. Robins was deeply concerned that America's position of neutrality might turn into an endorsement of Germany. She was encouraged by her longtime friend Sir Edward Grey, head of the British Foreign Office, to make the acquaintance of a fellow traveler, Col. Edward M. House, President Wilson's special envoy to Germany. The German press had reported House as having said, "Each time I visit Germany, I love it more."[4] When challenged by his own press to repudiate this statement, he refused. House spent much of the voyage avoiding any public comment upon his position. Robins counted it a fortunate breakthrough when she introduced herself as a fellow Southerner; thereafter House was receptive to Robins's companionship. As they walked the deck she saw her "usefulness as a buffer between my companion and a considerable portion of the passenger list" (*T&F*, 293–94). House explained to Robins not only that he would not disclose to her his political sympathies but also that he had very little influence with Wilson beyond reporting the facts as he saw them. As House set barriers to prevent others from getting information from him, Robins decided that "there was no reason to disguise where I stood" (*T&F*, 295). She made clear how she had come to take the same view of the English attitude in the war as Henry James, who months earlier had resigned his U.S. citizenship in protest of America's neutrality. Although Robins could not believe that signing a piece of paper and reciting a formula could really change a person's nationality, she was moved by the political protest embodied in James's act. She recalled what it was like to endure the "stigma Alien" (*T&F*, 288) which, in time of war, required her to submit to fingerprinting and to report to authorities each time she traveled from her country home to hospital work in London.

She told Colonel House that she had discovered, in her volunteer work at the hospital, what England really meant to men, primarily men of the "rougher sort." The lower classes, who formed the vast majority of any country, were men who were unable to read or write—"I knew, for I had read letters for them and written them" (*T&F*, 295). She stressed that any country that could put its mark of "civilization of the spirit" on the poorest, the most suppressed classes of its Empire "means something beyond Price." House was moved enough to encourage Robins to write of her experiences. She downplayed the suggestion; these yet-to-be-set-down "Hospital Sketches" were, in England, a "blessed commonplace," she explained. "Everybody knows them" (*T&F*, 297). Colonel House stressed to her Americans' ignorance of them; furthermore, if she would not write of her personal experience, she must write an article which told Americans that England had changed. The Colonel offered to bring her piece to the attention of the editor of the *New York Times*.

While Colonel House was encouraging Robins to write an article, she was acutely conscious of how she might tell Henry James of her opportunity to reach an American audience. On the crossing, she had met and had long talks with Henry James's nephew and namesake. They stood together on deck as the ship steamed into the harbor. Robins looked out at the Staten Island she had known in her childhood, the same neighborhoods James had frequented in his youth. She looked forward to sending word to him that America was listening to his position. Just as they docked, the first men up the gangplank took young James aside to tell him of his uncle's death four days earlier. "And so all that has gone out of the world!" she wrote in her diary (March 5, 1916). Fifteen years later she concluded her tribute to James, *Theatre and Friendship*, with an account of this crossing and her observation, "I knew the war had killed him as truly as though he had died in the trenches" (*T&F*, 298). She reprinted in this book the letter for the *New York Times* that would have gone to James, had he lived.

Two days after her landing, the *Times* set the letter—with a two-column headline—on its editorial page. The piece is one of her strongest prowar statements, but it also illustrates how she stressed a love for peace in the face of the threatened destruction of civilization. Because Robins feared that America would capitulate to the arguments to align with the more organized and advanced German military organization, she demonstrated how England's very lack of war preparations made it a civilization worth supporting. Like other Anglophiles, she saw Germany's threat to destroy England worth fighting against because Germany's victory would mean victory for militarism.

America, 1916

Robins's plan of writing at Chinsegut was interrupted in early May by severe illness; she rearranged her itinerary several times in her pursuit of proper dental care. She spent most of May and June with her friends Pippa and Tom Wells, then underwent painful tooth extractions in New York and tried to recuperate at their home in Greenwich, Connecticut. When she learned that the dentist who had begun work was reluctant to continue with the operations that she needed, she arranged to go to a sanitarium in Battle Creek, Michigan.

After she had spent days having her teeth painfully ground down to their crowns, she was told that her tonsils had to come out. By this time, she was determined not to spend a day more than necessary in America. All shipping had ceased for fear of German submarine attacks. She booked return passage for August 8, the day that shipping was scheduled to resume.

Her months in America were not wasted, for her firsthand observation of American attitudes and her brother's involvement in the national scene encouraged her to observe the political climate with some detail. Raymond Robins was the temporary chairman of the National Progressive party, and the Republican presidential candidate, Charles Evans Hughes, sought his endorsement. At one point, Robins grew angry with the *New York Times* for its assertion that all the national political parties had capitulated to empty arguments in their adoption of women's suffrage planks. The *Times* had claimed that the political parties were being blackmailed by suffrage leaders who asserted that women had a unified political voice. There was no such thing as a woman's vote, the *Times* had declared. Robins's reply began by scolding the paper for its editorial stance and ended with the prediction that American women were "within sight of their goal"—national suffrage. She observed that woman's natural tendency was to work with man; only "when man as a sex acts against woman as a sex" would women take it upon themselves to act collectively. But act together they would, as if they had a duty to do so. She also pledged that women, if given full citizenship, would "lay aside sex distinction to show that public work may be done on the broader human ground of our common need and our united inspiration." Robins's letter was printed with the signature "Elizabeth Tobin," and when she saw the misprint, she exclaimed in her diary, "So much for my writing!" (Diary, June 20, 1916). Yet she did not give up efforts to influence public opinion in the press for very long.

Women's Service Demands Women's Citizenship, 1917

After returning to England, recuperating from a tonsillectomy, and completing *Camilla* (which took the last four months of 1916), Robins plunged back into feminist politics with two essays that attacked the government for its reluctance to grant women's suffrage. "Conscription for Women"[5] listed the ways in which women in the labor force had become essential to virtually every industry and public service. Robins cataloged the injustices perpetrated upon women. They were denied union organization, were often paid less than rates offered men, and were expected to produce at greater capacities. Without the right to vote and with no chance to organize in labor unions, she claimed, "conscription of the unrepresented" was "indistinguishable from Slavery" (485).

Robins's second article, "Women at Home and Beyond the Seas: An Anomaly,"[6] took up the same argument: women were doing immeasurable service without the full status of citizenship. In this essay she charged that the government was taking advantage of the suffragists' truce and called for women to be given the franchise immediately. She predicted that reconstruction after the war could be effected with half the effort men anticipated because, unlike women in almost every other country, British women were ready to assist; they had taken active interest in political issues for many years.

The War Topic in Fiction

The first paragraphs of Robins's article opposing women's conscription clarify her position on the war vis-à-vis her creative writing. In the context of showing how the war left "vital questions of future welfare not only untouched but out of mind" ("Conscription," 478), she addressed the issue of "two sorts of censorship, the official and unofficial." The latter, she suggested, was most effective, because it operated "through a thousand editors and spokesmen, in the guise of a very natural conviction that on the serious side of affairs people are interested in nothing but the war."

Editors of fiction, she found, subjected their writers to "unofficial censorship," and Robins resented this policy. Mrs. Humphrey Ward visited the front several times and produced both appeals to the war effort as well as a spate of novels set (at least superficially) in wartime England. Edith Wharton organized relief work in Paris and wrote war literature and appeals in support of France, but she wrote essentially no long creative work during the war. Elizabeth Robins's fiction, in contrast, was more in keeping with her political stance. Her protagonist in the short story "The Tortoise-Shell Cat" is a woman who devotes all her time to raising money for Belgian refugees yet despises the general attitude generated by her discussion of the refugees' plight as "morbid hunger for excitement-dope."[7]

In reference to the paucity of Edith Wharton's literary output during the war, R. W. B. Lewis has written, "One of the fascinating themes in literary history is the impact of a great war upon the creative imagination."[8] The discrepancy between the war service to which women writers such as Gertrude Stein, Wharton, May Sinclair, Evelyn Sharp, Mrs. Ward, and Robins committed themselves and the amount of literature they produced might be explained as well by Robins's comments. All the editors wanted war stories. They would have nothing else. The women writers were staffing hospitals, organizing appeals, or giving lectures. It is little wonder that they disapproved of the tastes of the editors and the editors' readers. If, in fact, the war literature of women writers was not very good, it was because, like Ivy Spang, Wharton's poet and volunteer nurse's aid, in "Writing a War Story," the women attempted to describe something beyond their own experience of the war. Wharton in her war fiction wrote more frequently about a man's experience than about her own. Willa Cather's novel of a soldier's coming of age won the Pulitzer Prize, but this distinction represented more a retroactive longing to justify the loss of American lives than anything else; of the women writers who addressed the war, Cather had been furthest from the fighting.

Then again, some of the literature used the war as backdrop and did not really comment on the war. Wharton's "Writing a War Story," and Robins's more subtle parody, "The Tortoise-Shell Cat," say little of direct significance about the war, even though the war affords their backdrop. Each story focuses on the inability of women and men to understand each other. Wharton, by judging Ivy's effort to write a war story as hopelessly futile, not only exposes Ivy's ignorance but parodies the war story formula. Wharton's male novelist is an invalid soldier who further distances Ivy from the war when he jokes that women make inexhaustible subjects. Men can write about women, he suggests, but the reverse does not apply, especially in war.

Robins's heroine of "The Tortoise-Shell Cat" is also engaged in war relief work, and she is also perplexed to find that a man can regard her only as the subject for his art. Robins's story explores further the irony which is the real theme of both stories, hers and Wharton's. Robins sets the inability of men and women to understand each other constantly before the reader. When Aurea realizes that an admirer who is painting her portrait has misinterpreted her statement regarding her husband's unfaithfulness, she leaves him. She goes back to her husband, who long ago had stopped loving her, because if she is with him, she knows, she can help with his Belgian relief work.

The Messenger, 1917–1918

Robins confronted more directly the issues of official and unofficial censorship with her novel *The Messenger*, a novel that treated not only German espionage but also the official censorship of pacifist activity in Britain and America. Perhaps the two most widely recognized examples of such censorship were the deportation from America of Emma Goldman and other antiwar undesirables, and Britain's denial of passports to the entire delegation of British women to the Women's Peace Congress at the Hague in 1915. Robins made it known that censorship of groups opposed to the war was more "commonplace." It is not surprising, given entries in her diary, that Robins deplored the organized suppression of the end-the-war organizations. She read Clive Bell's *Peace at Once*, noting that it had been ordered "burnt by the Crown" (Diary, October 26, 1915), and responded positively to Rose Macaulay's pacifist, woman-centered novel of 1915, *Non-Combatants and Others*. She attended meetings called to discuss the end of the war and, while she was in New York in February 1915, heard Carrie Chapman Catt address the New York organizational meeting of the Women's Peace party at the McAlpern Hotel. Catt reported on the Washington meeting that had inaugurated the party, and several people invited Robins to speak (Diary, February 4, 1915). A few days after the sinking of the *Lusitania* in 1915, Robins traveled from her home in Henfield to London to hear the report from the peace conference at the Hague, but the meeting was canceled (Diary, May 12).

What is surprising is that Robins, in an atmosphere where most editors insisted upon material with the "excitement-dope" of a world at war, explored a pacifist theme by remaining true to actual events. Robins was hardly at the forefront of the sizable war resistance movement, and her novel does not rank with the antiwar literature written after hostilities ceased. In the midst of the fighting, however, Robins courageously took an unpopular stance. In *The Messenger*, Julian Grant becomes a tragic victim who repudiates his nonviolence when German submarine officers threaten to abduct his lover. The lover, Nan Ellis, a young American "girl messenger" who, in defiance of censorship, has carried British pacifist messages to American organizers and to the White House, gradually reaches the conclusion that Julian's antiwar efforts are actually playing into the hands of the Germans and in some cases are promoted by them. Nan, an American idealist, comes to realize that she opposes what Germany stands for, that she wants her country to be against it, and that effective opposition "isn't, not yet, the way of Peace."[9] Like Robins, Nan accepted the position that America had to enter the war for the war to end. While Nan worries that she has failed Julian politically, she knows she cannot fail him personally. Even though she thinks she loves another man, she stays with Julian on their eventful return voyage from America when their ship is torpedoed by a German submarine.

Despite the thrust of the novel—the gradual unfolding of America's need to enter the war—Robins at no point sought to simplify her study of passions and moral commitment. Julian's best friend, the young man Gavin Napier, whose sympathies for Nan and allegiance to England are also at war with each other, exposes Nan's best friend and German-born former governess as an espionage agent. Nan and Gavin have earlier confessed their passion for each other; yet their reunion in the last chapter—after Julian's death, after the German woman's suicide in prison, and after Gavin has been crippled by his wounds in France—makes the "happy" ending fraught with the losses brought by the war. At one point Robins tells us that the books scattered around Julian's deck chair as he struggles to save the allegorical "house on fire" are the "modern exemplars of that literature of peace which seems, like the old, to bring the sword" (344). Indeed, for a writer like Robins, who was to write her own peace manifesto yet would find herself lobbying for America's entry into World War II, the image is apt indeed.

Robins faced additional censorship when, after *Cosmopolitan* had reneged on its offer to buy the novel, *Century Magazine* accepted *The Messenger* on the condition that certain cuts be made—and not for length alone. Robins found herself obliged to rework her story and commented in a brief diary entry after the *Century*'s conditional acceptance: "all the Julian motif is to be sacrificed" (Diary, September 23, 1918). The Julian motif, of course, was Robins's pacifist theme.

Robins's model for Nan as the messenger linking the Old World and the New was the model that Henry James had established in his novels with the same theme. James analyzed his own focus on the American girl in *An American Notebook*. Robins echoed James in that she personified a concept of America by depicting its values embodied in a young American girl, but Nan is neither victimized by European experience, as is Milly Theale in *Wings of the Dove*, nor does she become complicit in an evil world in order to survive, as does Maggie Verver in *The Golden Bowl*.[10] Robins focuses on Nan's growth toward maturity and independence to show just how far she develops beyond the stereotype. In a telling moment at the end of the story, Nan tries to persuade Gavin that the death sentence of her German governess, who has been captured as a spy, must be commuted. She admits death might be better for the woman but "not for us. I mean, *we* couldn't do it, nor let it be done in vengeance. That isn't for us" (425). The statement shows that a sense of morality is still possible in a world ravaged by war; unlike James's heroines, Nan does not compromise or accept defeat.

The period in which Robins wrote the novel coincides almost precisely with America's participation in the war. Her novel was first read by Edgar Sisson, editor at *Cosmopolitan*, then rejected, then conditionally accepted by *Century Magazine* in July 1918, with Robins completing revisions so that it could begin with the November 1918 issue. During this time, Robins was more involved than ever in war-related work, in bringing before the public the concerns of women, and in defining the importance to society of women's continued participation in a postwar world. This period, together with the months immediately following, when Robins watched compromises being made in the name of peace, was for her a "join" in life; she wove a web of her participation in individual causes that gave her late middle age a necessary purpose. She was not less divided between commitments than she had been when fiction and theater competed for her attention or when suffrage politics interrupted her private, fictional, assertion of independence, *Camilla*. As in earlier periods, multiple projects defined her life in these years.

Lectures for the Ministry of Food

The most time-consuming commitment during 1917–18 was Robins's work with the Ministry of Food. She was one of a number of women trained to speak to schoolchildren about their role in the production and preparation of food. America's Victory Garden campaign was nothing compared to the reorganization of the English home in the absence of the traditional servants. Robins lectured, often twice a day, several times a week, from guidelines established by the ministry, in a program organized by the Fabian writer Maud Pember Reeves, a longtime personal acquaintance of Robins and author of the influential report on working-class family economics, *'Round about a Pound a Week*.

On May 11, 1917, when Sisson cabled, asking to see the rest of *The Messenger* immediately, Robins was obliged to keep her commitment to lecture on Food Control in Ireland. The highlight of her ten-day tour was a meeting where her comments on cooperation sent "sparks in the air." An Irishman boasted that "never again" would Ireland send food to England, for exports had caused the famine of 1847. Robins learned that Ireland counted on imports of essential food stuffs: "I play on that. Interdependence." She recorded that her challenge prompted "altogether the most interesting meeting" (Diary, May 18, 1917). The texts of Robins's Food Ministry speeches do not survive, but several things are clear: she got very specific directions for her lectures from the ministry office, she spoke so frequently that she did so without the painstaking preparation of earlier speeches, and her interest in seeing children take a responsible role toward food carried over into a children's story, *Prudence and Peter*, written in collaboration with Octavia Wilberforce.

Raymond Robins in Russia, 1917

Quite a different sort of food problem, the relief of the Russian population, did not engage Robins directly but nevertheless affected her personally: Raymond Robins was appointed head of an American Red Cross delegation to Russia in the summer of 1917. His relief party sailed by way of Seattle and the Pacific and arrived in Petrograd well ahead of the November revolution. Raymond Robins broke with the American Ambassador, David R. Francis, when the United States refused to recognize the Bolsheviks. Elizabeth Robins learned this news, but hardly much else, from official or personal channels, and the uncertainty of Raymond's safety caused her distress. Raymond was in close contact with Kerensky, then with Trotsky and Lenin, and perhaps influenced the revolutionary government not to seek an immediate and separate peace with Germany, which was crucial to the Allies' campaign on the Western front. He knew that there would never be a reclamation of Russia by Czarist forces, and felt convinced that, if America threw its economic support to the Soviets, their proposed socialist state would be forced to accept capitalist-oriented modifications. In May, Raymond was abruptly recalled, President Wilson denied Raymond Robins's requests for a meeting, and he was ordered to remain silent about his position, which was presumed to be supportive of Bolshevik recognition. Surveillance by the Secret Service enforced the censure. Wilson, meanwhile, ordered a blockade around Soviet Russia—a fatal, barbaric mistake, Raymond Robins was convinced. Although Raymond Robins never endorsed the principles of the communist system (in fact, he hoped an American influence could dilute Russia's state socialism), his commitment to the recognition of Soviet Russia defined his political position for fifteen years.

The blockade imposed by the United States and supported by other countries in the West caused massive famine in the Ukraine after sustained periods of crop failure, but still the factions in American party politics prevented the nation from taking action to bring relief. It was the beginning of a phobia, lasting until the late 1980s, that caused any socialist program to be viewed as an opportunity for Soviet expansionism.

Women's Institutes

Elizabeth Robins gave her support to collective production of a different nature. She became an active force in the Women's Institute movement, a campaign to organize women in local communities for purposes of cooperative home production. According to Robins's own account of the Institutes, published as "A New View of Country Life" in 1919, the movement was begun in Canada before the turn of the century and was introduced to England in 1913 by Mrs. Alfred Watt. Robins began her own participation in the fall of 1917 with her attendance at the Conference of Women's Institutes. Within a month, Henfield held its first meeting, an event in which Robins certainly had an organizational part, for the local postmaster approached her several days later with the rumor that he had heard: "there's to be a Ladies Socialist Club started!!" (Diary, October 5, 1917).

In her postwar article, Robins described the Women's Institute in some detail, asserting that the cooperation of women in rural communities was essential to postwar reconstruction and giving numerous examples of the benefits of country living and the importance of women's organizations there. She also asserted, "If Women's Institutes did not already exist, the Board of Agriculture would have to invent them."[11]

Women's Vote, a Woman's Parliament

One aspect of Robins's work in war-related women's issues related to her earlier involvement with prostitution and the white slavery issue and specifically to the spread of venereal disease among military units. Her response to the "morals question," as it was called, was to seek out official information and then to advocate reforms. At the committee called by the Women Writers' Suffrage League to discuss the issue, she noted, "Statement of 'Vice Facilities' for our soldiers in France read out. Authority chapter and verse." Robins pledged at this meeting to approach Lord Derby and the Archbishop of Canterbury on the question. The Archbishop promised action, and the editor and writer Massingham promised her that "he would get Pringle to ask question in House of Commons if I wished" (Diary, January 2, 27, 1918). Later, she interviewed a United States Major General about conditions among American troops. She participated in the Caxton Hall Conference of the Association of Social and Moral Hygiene in April 1918 and brought to a private meeting of the Association the U.S. government literature on its fight against the spread of venereal disease (Diary, February 1, 3, 1919).

Massingham invited her to write regularly for the *Chronicle*, and her first article, "The Main Peace Asset," charged that the general press had ignored the "peace sentiment and the peace purpose of women,"[12] and apparently aroused debate. She planned a second article on the League of Nations (Diary, February 6, 1919), but later she noted that the *Chronicle* was "no longer interested in controversial material" (Diary, April 3, 1919). Robins lobbied for a woman delegate to the Versailles Conference until she was told that if a woman were appointed, it would most certainly be Christabel Pankhurst. By this time, she differed too completely with Pankhurst to pursue the effort.

The same inclination to discontinue organizational work—after an initial commitment—arose with the issue of a women's parliament. Again, Robins found herself opposed to the lack of pacifist sympathies in the plan. She was invited to make the opening address at a council called to propose the Woman's Parliament. Her speech in favor of the resolution prompted "hot debate" at the Denison House meeting, but the resolution carried (Diary, June 2, 1918). When she discovered, at an executive meeting of the Council several days later, that no pacifists were welcome and no Labour women were represented (Diary, June 13), she was sadly disappointed.

Robins did not permit the idea of a Women's Council to evaporate. In 1920, she advocated the formation of a "Commons" as a clearinghouse for women's issues. She built her argument, laid out in a *Fortnightly* article, upon the experience she had had with the earlier proposal. She explained that during earlier discussions of the women's parliament, when woman after woman rose to say that she had organized a certain society for a certain purpose, each speaker discovered that her efforts were duplicated by another society she had not known existed. The title for Robins's article, "Bolt Seventeen," referred to her conviction that individual women had for a long time been engaged only in isolated efforts, efforts comparable to those of the motorworks employee, who boasted of his nine years' service by saying he had put in only Bolt 17 for his entire working life. A great many women, Robins pointed out, had been engaged in putting in "Bolt Seventeen," to the point where they had become "too absorbed, too hypnotized by bolt seventeen to see it and kindred important details in their true proportion as means to an end." She added that, although the metaphorical bolt was a necessary component of social good, or individual woman's economic advancement, "we need not, as we do, devote to it our best brains." Not only would a house for women's affairs (Robins called it the "Mother House," to distinguish it from the House of Commons and the House of Lords) serve as the clearinghouse for all women's societies, organizations, and common concerns; it would also be a training ground for "future members of Parliament." Robins's article was in the press, accepted by *Fortnightly*, and apparently typeset by the time that Lady Astor, the first woman to take her seat in the House of Commons, made her initial speech in Parliament. In a footnote, Robins commented on the importance of that "first voice raised" by a woman in the House of Commons.

Robins was to see more of Lady Astor, the former Nancy Witcher Langhorne of Virginia. Robins had written Lady Astor to congratulate her the day after her election to Parliament (Diary, November 29, 30, 1919). She noted in her diary after she read the account of the address: "Read Lady Astor's *admirable* rough diamond speech. Her wit and good feeling will smooth the way . . . , *shorten* it more effectually than qualities some would rate more highly" (Diary, February 24, 1920). Lady Astor later invited Robins to receptions, including the one given for the International Suffrage Congress (November 23, 1922), and Robins appealed to Lady Astor for support in the campaign to press for passage of women-related issues endorsed by the Six Point Group.

Indeed, it might be argued that Lady Astor and, to a degree less lavish, Elizabeth Robins herself, were hostesses who had the ability of Virginia Woolf's fictional Mrs. Dalloway. These two expatriates brought people together—at receptions, teas, dinners, in their London or country homes—yet were motivated by their *political*, their predominantly pacifist and feminist, concerns. Robins's own social affairs included dinners and teas to introduce Raymond and Margaret Dreier Robins to the London political world, garden parties for the local Women's Institute, and fundraising for women's health issues.

Women and Health

Robins's commitment to women's health care was far-ranging and many sided. Her letter to the *Times* of March 25, 1919, deploring the failure of the bill to create a Ministry of Health and identifying health as a woman's concern demonstrates that it was a political issue for her. Health was also a very personal issue, partly because her father had wanted Robins to have a medical education, partly because of the need she saw for women doctors, and partly because of her own poor health and her disappointments when undergoing treatment.

She had seen firsthand the expertise of women in medicine in the Endell Street Hospital and agreed to chair the Board of Directors of the New Sussex Hospital for Women and Children. Its gala fund-raising bazaar in November 1919 made use of some of the strategies that suffrage societies had used to raise money. Robins contributed to the bazaar by requesting donations of signed books from a large number of prominent authors. She also wrote a privately printed circular, the hospital's appeal for funds, and worked behind the scenes to secure some of the larger donations. Robins's participation on the board was as an active member, not an honorary one. She ran board meetings and called for decisions on governance, funding, and staff appointments.

Later, Robins wrote a tribute to Flora Murray in the *Observer* and, for *Time and Tide*, reviewed the autobiography of "The First Woman M.D. of

London," Dr. Scharlieb.[13] To the London *Sunday Times* in 1922, Robins vehemently protested the move to restrict the medical training of women.[14]

The most personal of Robins's commitments to women in medicine was her support of Octavia Wilberforce in Wilberforce's decision to become a doctor. The financial and personal commitment reflected close friendship as well as a feminist political purpose. Their companionship was punctuated by Wilberforce's stormy jealousies or gloomy sulking and demands for Robins's attention. Octavia, furthermore, did not show a proficiency in her years of studying for her qualification exams (she failed various exams, sometimes more than once). Wilberforce's demands upon Robins often delayed Robins's completion of her literary projects or discouraged her from involving herself in political causes. Despite these frictions, the friendship became a vital relationship for each. In her autobiography, "The Eighth Child," Wilberforce explained how she felt charmed by Elizabeth Robins's intelligence, wit, and facility at conversation. Wilberforce was less than half Robins's age when they met in 1909, when Robins was forty-six. Robins's diary shows that the young Octavia represented an intrusion on Robins's private life and yet shows also that Robins's attitude toward Wilberforce became deep affection.

Wilberforce worshiped Robins with all the anxieties of a lover, yet a passage of her autobiography describing an encounter with an unnamed acquaintance reveals that any overt suggestion of lesbianism repelled her. Until the encounter, she knew nothing of homosexuality and thought the "obsession on the part of XY, as I will call her . . . something ugly, alarming, unhinged."[15] Still, Wilberforce's relationship with Robins undeniably included many physical and emotional intimacies. Letters from Wilberforce to Robins are troubled and self-analytical in their descriptions of her feelings when Robins kissed her farewell or embraced her. Wilberforce was often distraught at their partings and at Robins's prolonged absences. Her dependency upon Robins meant that Robins often canceled engagements at Wilberforce's urging. Even while they shared the same quarters, Wilberforce wrote long and demanding letters to Robins and declared that she could not sleep at night unless Robins were home. Wilberforce became fiercely possessive of Backsettown and several times thwarted Robins's plans to rent the place. During the period while she was studying for her exams, she often read Robins to sleep with the literature she was studying. She was an overcaring and protective nurse when Robins was ill and arranged for specialists when they were needed.

Despite her possessiveness, Octavia Wilberforce's presence in Robins's life during the years 1917–20 was tremendously supportive and nurturing. Several times Wilberforce encouraged Robins's creative endeavors when Robins was not sure of their merit or had difficulty in giving them concentrated at-

Octavia Wilberforce (1888–1963) met Elizabeth Robins in 1909, shortly after Robins moved to Backsettown. Elizabeth encouraged Octavia to pursue her medical education, and Wilberforce was responsible for the eventual incorporation of Backsettown as a shelter for women. (*Courtesy of the Fales Library. Reproduced with the permission of Mabel Smith, for the Backsettown Trustees.*)

tention. For example, Wilberforce encouraged Robins to follow through on the idea of a short story—"The Frog Baby"—which dealt with a wealthy lady's desire to adopt a foundling child. This story and other fiction dealing with the adoption or mothering of unfortunate children were inspired less by Robins's own instincts than by experiences of her acquaintances.[16] In the case of "The Frog Baby," Robins drew on the experience of her friend, Lady Jean Hamilton, and the noted religious leader, Maude Royden. Each had adopted a foundling or baby born of servants they knew. Certainly Wilberforce herself assumed the role of a foundling whom Robins had saved, and Robins treated their shared life as an aspect of her own maternal caring. Leonard Woolf characterized Wilberforce's relationship to Robins as that of a devoted daughter, but Wilberforce understood in retrospect that this relationship was problematic for Robins. Wilberforce was not aware, she wrote in "The Eighth Child," when she asked Robins to look upon her as "my adopted Mother," that she "conscientiously shied from anything in the nature of a mother complex after her association with [John Masefield] the young poet" ("Eighth Child," 201).

Robins's own feelings toward Wilberforce combined a deep appreciation for the younger woman's caring with a sense of satisfaction that she, Robins, could provide for someone's education in the way her father had hoped to provide for hers; she had derived similar satisfaction from trying to provide for the education of her brother Vernon. It was Wilberforce whom Robins had foremost in her thoughts when she wrote a "little review" of her "situation" on her fifty-seventh birthday and concluded that, for "the money consideration," and especially for Wilberforce's sake, she could not give up fiction in order to write about women's issues (Diary, August 6, 1919). She considered whether, in view of her uncertain health and the pressing needs of political work, she ought "to turn aside from fiction as 25 years ago I turned my mind from acting." She added, "I could if I make up my mind to it, make a place and a center of New Time influence in the British press—ultimately in the American. Isn't that an aim more in keeping with the Years of Experience?" She listed the advantages and disadvantages of choosing fiction or choosing politics. Her decision was influenced most by the fact that "O.W. isn't yet launched & may be a year or two finding her feet—Even then she may need financing to make her start." Robins prefaced her entire reflection with the remark that her prevailing effort was the "great present reward and future hope bound up in Octavia." She concluded, thankful that she still had the "illusion of choosing": "It must yet awhile be a double duty, fiction and what I can't escape of my share in graver business" (Diary, August 6, 1919). It is interesting that Wilberforce's long quotation from this entry as summation of her own autobiography makes no reference to her part in Robins's sense of duties; Wilberforce simply admires Robins for transforming her worries about aging into an assertion that she still has the capacity to choose ("Eighth Child," 390). Wilberforce idealized Robins's freedom; she felt strongly drawn to Robins's woman-identified existence. Their companionship answered Wilberforce's need to break away from a family that expected her to marry and had disowned her because she wanted to pursue a profession in medicine. Elizabeth Robins's relationship with Wilberforce allowed the older woman to express, and to accept, devotion that was lacking or superficial in her relationships with men. The friendship between Robins and Wilberforce was surpassed only by Robins's closer friendship with Florence Bell.

Bell and Robins shared a keen interest in literary projects and grew to be faithful critics of each other's work. Wilberforce was not altogether successful in her attempt to act as Robins's literary assistant. They did collaborate on one book, the children's tale *Prudence and Peter*. This story, about twins whose backyard cooking experiments become important help in the kitchen when the cook resigns during the Great War, was written, Robins explained privately, almost entirely by herself, with Wilberforce supplying the inspiration, some of the ideas, and the appendix of recipes.[17] Wilberforce tried out her dishes on Robins, and Robins declared her to be an exceptional cook. They began the project to give Wilberforce some soothing and productive distraction from worry over her upcoming medical exams. The story was conceived just as Margaret Haig, Viscountess Rhondda, solicited Robins's support for a new woman's weekly paper that Rhondda, as she was known by her friends, planned to organize and finance. Their correspondence relating to Robins's earliest involvement in *Time and Tide* refers to Robins's offer to be responsible for the children's page.

Prudence and Peter appeared in ten installments, beginning May 21, 1920, in the second issue of *Time and Tide*. Wilberforce adopted a pseudonym for her first effort in fiction, Robins signed her own name, and the story was credited to "Elizabeth Robins and J. Wooley Paddock." In the book publication in 1928, Wilberforce used her own name, and the noted illustrator Lois Lenski supplied sketches.

Time and Tide, 1920

After the writer Maud Pember Reeves had read Elizabeth Robins's introduction to a series on the present conditions of women in early 1920, she wrote to Robins, "I like 'Paternalism' immensely: the word and the idea and the way you handled it. It is a delightful new coinage."[18] The article was the first of a six-part series, edited as well as introduced by Robins, which appeared in the prolabor paper the *Daily Herald*. In the same letter, Reeves asked Robins for help with her own piece, telling her it needed Robins's "best efforts at licking into shape."

The series was inspired by Viscountess Rhondda's concern that "the attitude of the Press towards women and women's work" was having a "detrimental effect upon their present condition." Viscountess Rhondda, a long time acquaintance of Robins's, active in the militant campaign for suffrage and a fellow fundraiser for women's projects, was building a network of women that would make its mark in the publishing world. She wrote to Robins about efforts in the press to make women revert to their prewar, second-class roles in the work force. Rhondda proposed that a number of representative women approach the press and invited Robins to be part of the delegation (Rhondda to ER, December 1, 1919). Although Robins was unable to attend either the organizational meeting or the meeting with representative journalists, her "Paternalism" essay, published as "Woman Comes of Age—Throwing Over the Traces of Paternalism," reflected her sympathy for the problem. Before articulating her gender-specific definition of paternalism, she enumerated the ways in which the press endorsed unequal expectations with regard to women's and men's work and roles in society. One reason that the *Daily Herald*'s treatment of women demanded attention, Robins explained, was that it was running a beauty contest for waitresses and working girls. Robins demonstrated that it was not "deliberate ill will" but ignorance that fostered attitudes that did a disservice to women. "We call the root cause Paternalism," she stated. Paternalism, that "Enemy with the benevolent face," emerged most commonly in the ways that men enjoyed their "pet hobby" of "arranging women's lives for them." Cannot men see, she asked, that women, like the nations of the world, deserve self-determination?[19]

Even as Robins edited the series for the *Daily Herald*, Rhondda approached Robins with a further request, that she serve on the board of directors of her newly organized woman's paper, tentatively to be called *Time and Tide*. In her acceptance letter, Robins declared her point of view: "I am for the people," she stressed, implying both that she agreed with Labour politics and that she saw a need for privileged women to speak for women less well off (ER to Rhondda, February 18, 1920).

The organizational effort on the paper came at a time when Robins was midway through writing her next novel (published as *Time Is Whispering* in 1923); commitment to the paper also led to other interruptions in her creative work that caused a two-year delay in the completion of the novel. Her other contributions to the paper included a short sketch on the American film actress Mary Pickford and her impressions of a conversation with Otto Kahn.

In fact, Robins's behind-the-headlines counsel helped to shape the enterprise as a political organ, one that eventually endorsed a program of parliamentary reforms. In addition to her initial advice on various matters, it was Robins who, in early 1923, would write the introduction to *Time and Tide*'s Six Point Group supplement—tracing the history of this feminist political action lobby and the paper's strategy of keeping a tally of Members of Parliament on both sides of the woman question in its Black and White Lists. Robins's essay, "The Six Points and Their Common Centre," reviews the equality principles behind the issues raised (equal pay, equal opportunity, and

equal guardianship) and stresses the widespread support for the points, first
from the endorsements of twenty-four societies interested in similar goals and
next through the Six Point Group's affiliation with the Consultative Committee, of which Lady Astor was chair.

"The Book of Revelations," 1920–1922

During the first few months of the paper's existence, Robins made a concerted effort to continue with her novel, called at this point "Autumn" or
"Judith," but the illness she suffered as a result of further work on her teeth
suspended most of her activity. In late September 1920, she first mentioned
"Repington" in her diary. She discussed the publication of Colonel Repington's personal diary of his experiences as recruiting officer and consul to the
military and political leaders with Lady Jean Hamilton, her friend, whose husband, Sir Ian Hamilton, had been implicated in the disaster of Gallipoli. She
learned from the Hamiltons how Repington was desperate to reclaim his reputation and financial standing with the book. Within two months she completed her article and named it "The Book of Revelations." By early December
she had made clear to Rhondda that her "passion for Peace . . . must govern
the degree of interest" she took in *Time and Tide* and had begun work on a
second piece on militarism. The kind of task these essays required was that of
a carefully documented refutation. She was not unused to this mode of dis-
course. She found this effort particularly demanding, however, commenting
upon it in one diary entry, "The interminable task of showing up Repington.
The mere verifying and copying of extracts . . . !" and later, "*What* this has
cost me" (ER Diary, November 11, 17, 1920).

Her hope of seeing the book through publication never materialized. Although much of the second essay forms the beginning of her introduction to
Ancilla's Share, the unpublished attack on Repington in the first essay stands
as an important link between her feminist politics and her pacifist argument.
Most of her correspondence with potential publishers of the essays insists
upon strict anonymity. She expected her voice to be taken as male, even as
that of a man of Repington's own social standing, who, Robins must have
reasoned, could more convincingly expose Repington's attitudes. Nevertheless, her analysis of Repington's perception of women's place in society forms
a central part of her quarrel with the military habit of mind which Repington
exemplified.

Robins never expected her refutation of Repington to absorb so much of
her time. Repington's war diary, according to the first page of her manuscript
(begun in the fall of 1920), was now in its sixth printing. Its popularity was
no doubt due to Repington's appearing to speak as an insider. Robins risked

being accused of making an ad hominem attack, yet from her indictment of one man's attitude about war, she formulated a wider critique of warfare mentality. Already appalled at the way that negotiations had set ally against ally in the division of spoils, Robins used the Repington diary to show that the war could indeed have ended much sooner except that the "greatest enemy" of the "professional soldier" is "peace" ("Book of Revelations," II, 24).

Robins later refined her feminist-pacifist argument. Here, she showed how Repington discussed women of honorable standing "with impudent references to women's physical 'points'" ("Book of Revelations," I, 9). Repington was a man so "crazed by self conceit" that he was "sucking up flattery like a vacuum cleaner" and setting down "among cabinet conclusions and lists of the dead" the compliments rendered him (I, 40). She told her audience that they had to worry about such a man because he had so much influence in the government. He was "Our Great Authority," advising on almost every aspect of the war. "And always the counsel is the same: Give the war lords more men. If the older men jib and talk revolution give us boys. More and more and more. And give us, who do the recruiting—one in particular—give [him] expensive food and pretty subservient women and 'good bridge' and gossip." While the "carnage raged abroad," Robins continued, Repington had bragged of his "'pleasant parties' in London and in the great houses of the English country side." After the "transcendental horror, the unnameable agony" of the battlefields, Robins asked the question so often asked, "Did we save anything worth saving?" Then, more pointedly, she asked, "Were those boys sent from us by the Repingtons of the world to make the world safe for Repingtons?" (I, 40–41).

Robins's second essay starts with a continuation of her indictment of the Repington diary and proceeds to examine the current policy of preparedness and to warn that this policy always brings war. One of the most important aspects of her argument is the example she gives of the white man bringing warfare to native Africans and Asians. When most lovers of a free England were still grateful that native colonials had enlisted on the European front, Robins attacked imperialism because it imposed a system of warfare on a previously primitive and relatively peaceful society. An analogue to Robins's thinking as she revised this section for later publication was undoubtedly Waldo Frank's *Our America* (Diary, October 18, 1922). One can see why Frank's discussion of these indigenous Americans affected Robins, for he shows how white conquerors brought their warfare to the Indian civilization and caused its destruction.[20] Robins carried this reasoning further. She enumerated the ways in which the European nations had exploited their colonies and had depended on them for much of their fighting, not only during the previous war, but throughout their domination. She drew an analogy between the subjugation of woman as the handmaiden of man and the use of Eastern and African peoples by white men to carry on their system of warfare.

Time Is Whispering, 1923

If Robins had not concerned herself with her novel, *Time Is Whispering,* from its conception in 1919 until 1922, she might be remembered, as a feminist writer, only for *Ancilla's Share,* which Jane Marcus has described as shrill and angry.[21] From a modern feminist perspective, certainly, the bitterness of the polemic seems warranted by her documentation of man's suppression of woman. Robins warns against the centuries of antagonism between the sexes, it is true, but at the same time demands an end to the division. Robins had repudiated the kind of hatred of men that Christabel Pankhurst came to espouse, and a central part of *Ancilla's Share* was devoted to an analysis of the ways in which the militancy and autocratic structure of the WSPU were counterproductive.

Time Is Whispering proves what *Ancilla's Share* and much of Robins's political writing advocated—that friendship between man and woman can be a harmonious partnership and that a mutually shared life does not always mean loss of independence for the woman. The role of women need not be ancillary for all time. The working title for the novel at one point was "A Study in Antagonism," and Robins was pleased with the way that the words fit the novel's opening. The book's real theme, however, is the conversion of her hero and heroine to loving interdependence.

"Autumn," as Robins also called *Time Is Whispering* in its initial months of composition, tells the story of a widow and mother of a young soldier who tries to reclaim a neglected apple orchard. The orchard stands on the property of her landlord Henry Ellerton, who immediately resents her presence on his estate. Early in her work on the novel, Robins stated with directness and over-simplicity her plan for the book: "His Story. Hers. Theirs" (Diary, August 6, 1919). As the two grow interested in each other, they identify each as a potential confessor to the other. They had known of each other, when they were both in India, mainly because of the scandalous behavior of their respective spouses; Ellerton's wife ran away with a younger officer; Judith's husband was openly flirtatious.

Like so much of Robins's full-length fiction, the book is notable for its final few chapters of well-handled climax and resolution. The final scene—in which Judith watches over Ellerton as he lies on his deathbed—shows how much they have grown to depend upon each other. Like *The Convert,* but more subtly, the book addresses the political questions of the day. Robins's ability to use a fictional relationship to express her political convictions continued to be her special achievement.

Interpersonal differences between the older man and woman suggest again and again the general state of gender politics. Judith comments to Henry at an early point, "You don't hate women. . . . You think of them—as foreigners."[22] As Henry grows toward new receptivity, we see that his political treatise on the treatment of India is increasingly reflecting his concern for all peoples. With Judith's help, he moves beyond colonialism, beyond the paternalism of nationalism. Robins was acutely conscious of the political position of women in the world and approved of Gandhi's movement in India. Her fictional achievement consists partly in her ability to explore gender issues in a single couple's unorthodox romance.

Robins's politicizing of the love story is further evident in passages that describe Henry's relationship to his daughters. When Judith learns that his wife has left him for another man, she declares that it was nice of him to give his wife the children. His reply is, "They were girls" (*TIW*, 165). Later, when Judith is thinking of questions about the girls, her acceptance of his views keeps her quiet; "she suppressed the daughters, as he suppressed them" (*TIW*, 175). The harsh language of subordination brings its own corrective. One of the daughters appears at the end of the novel to spur Ellerton to a new opinion of women and to fulfill Judith's dream of making the land a productive enterprise.

The generational gap between the parents and their youngsters who grew up during the war is a troubling concern. Judith is not an old-fashioned mother herself; she wants to be the best of mothers and believes that she has the closest of relationships with her son until she begins to discover that he simply will not discuss some things with her. The war is one unmentionable subject, she tells Ellerton, as if to ask whether all this silence about something so important is really worse than talking about it. When he is disturbed about the ever-present hostilities in the world, she communicates her own sense of peace with him in a political observation; peace does not have to be trumpeted loudly. As a result he becomes convinced that his writing is an effective means of influencing public policy.

The man and woman who seemed determined to face their own aging independently come to admit to each other that their friendship is precious. They both despise the idea of remarriage, but the neighborhood quickly and thoroughly misrepresents their friendship. Judith's son tells her that gossip has made them lovers. They themselves overhear a servant couple joking about their liaison. Their first response is fear and resentment. After a nightlong struggle with her conscience, Judith arrives at Ellerton's manor house to propose marriage to him. In a very deliberate inversion of sexual roles, Robins portrays Judith's visit as an intrusion upon Henry's private space. Judith defies the servant who refuses to admit her, and when she senses that the grand room dressed with Indian tapestries and artifacts does not represent the Ellerton whom she knows, she insists on seeing his workroom. She discovers that his chair is placed so that he looks out toward her house. "So it's like that" (*TIW*, 339), she comments, and later asks with some irony when she sees his field glasses whether he has a love for watching birds. The discoveries give her courage to propose to him that they can save their friendship and "*call* it a marriage" (*TIW*, 342) to please the community. Earlier, Judith had spoken of marriage as a "capitulation . . . to old age" (*TIW*, 327). Now they both welcome the union as their fulfillment.

Judith's direct sharing of Henry's work is more conspicuous than his willingness to become part of her efforts in the orchard. She tells him what she feels—that his presence is soothing. The reader grows closer to her unspoken thoughts than to his, and Judith reflects on the difference between men and women in their needs for each other. It is considered part of their unconventionality that they decide to move to her little house, and she promises, as they enter the house together for the first time as man and wife, to neglect him very much. She comes to regret that it takes her so long to break that promise. She assists him as a co-worker in his effort to complete his book on India; for her it represents not a sacrifice of her own independence but a fulfillment of interests long held. In her exploration of the reasons why Henry cannot reciprocate this sharing and take more than a passing interest in her agricultural project, she comes to a sudden understanding: "Men have too little chance for practice here. All the woman work they've known about has been tributary to some man's work. This [recultivating her orchard] wasn't tributary in any sense a man could yet accept" (*TIW*, 364).

In these sentences Robins presents the thesis of her forthcoming political tract, *Ancilla's Share*. Judith subsequently convinces Henry that all women's work is *not* secondary to man's. She uses the uncanny happenstance of his daughter's return, in the company of her partner Kate Duff, to persuade him to rent Rhodes Hall as agricultural center and training camp for "surplus women." The two young women gained their experience from their work during the war. Mary Ellerton had discovered she was no good as a nurse in the ambulance detail, so she became an accomplished horse trainer for the Remount Corps. Her friend turned her family's farm into a training camp for women to work the land. Judith questions their finances and their seriousness of commitment, but she learns that they have a network of independent women who will support their plan. When she predicts that Mary will get married, Mary replies with an emphatic "No." Judith understands that the word "carried the conviction of an oath" (*TIW*, 366); the young woman has no intention of dissolving her partnership with Kate.

Ellerton's unwillingness to allow the women to try out their scheme prompts another reflection. For Judith, as for Robins herself, the denial of the opportunity is a haunting thought. In a moving diary entry (June 11, 1919), Elizabeth Robins had recorded her impressions of the wide contrast between David Scott's ease of existence at Oxford and Octavia Wilberforce's struggle to prepare for a profession.

The final three chapters of *Time Is Whispering* deal with Judith's recollection, at Ellerton's deathbed, of the events in the years since her marriage. He fades in and out of consciousness and calls to her repeatedly, "Are you there?" (*TIW*, 375). While Judith sustains him now simply by her reassuring presence, she reflects upon their joys and the sorrow of her not having found more complete fulfillment with him: "If her mind swerved now—it was to measure the loneliness he had saved her from, by the loneliness he was committing her to" (*TIW*, 376). Without sentimentality, and with the use of a stylistic technique that more closely approaches modernism than anything Robins wrote, the ending of the book conveys, with Judith's stream-of-consciousness thought and with contractions of language and events, the sense that years have passed in an instant.

The passages are more realistic than the "Time Passes" section of Virginia Woolf's *To the Lighthouse* and less poetic than Woolf's equation between a day's time on the seashore and the passing of the life stages of six friends in *The Waves*. Nevertheless, Robins to some degree anticipates Woolf in her breaking away from conventional narrative. We cannot be sure, for instance, that Robins's ostensibly realistic narrative has not compressed time. Nor can we be sure that the prolonged vigil is one of hours, days, weeks, or even years; this last possibility would cast the last section of the novel into a future time. In her reflection upon events, Judith suggests that more years have passed than might be expected. The younger women's farming enterprise has graduated many workers, developed a reputation, endured many changes. Ellerton's book has made Rhodes a place of pilgrimage; thus, the vaguely defined Indian crisis, founded as it was on Robins's knowledge of contemporary events and advised by William Archer's brother Charles, seems to stand for Robins's future prediction of such a crisis. Likewise, Robins implies that the idyllic life as represented by Kate Duff and Mary Ellerton is yet to be fully achieved.

Robins needed the hypothetical resolution possible in fiction in order to anticipate political and social advances that were painfully slow in coming. While she devised a fruitful relationship between her older couple and a practical solution to equal opportunities for women, she (to borrow the language of her April 11, 1922, diary entry, which in turn echoes the language in Hamlet's soliloquy) looked "before" on a personal life of missed relationships and looked "after" at a present world that was more and more eager to force women back into a subservient position. The English edition of *Good Housekeeping* bought her series of articles on this theme, which she had called in her notes "the projected series against the Prostitute Mind, the Painted Woman &c."[23] She best described the pressures put on women to go back to their prewar roles by illustrating how the women's volunteer army had been disbanded by the force of public opinion, for after the war was over every woman in uniform became the target of a hissing campaign. In one of the articles, "She Loves to Sew," Robins mocked women's habit of taking up their needles whenever they were thwarted in their real work. In so doing she was able to attack the self-destructive aspect of their overcommitments and to suggest that women's fatigue was an issue worthy of attention.[24]

Ancilla's Share, 1924

Ancilla's Share: An Indictment of Sex Antagonism is arguably the political counterpart to *Time Is Whispering*. It states more forcefully the novel's conviction that woman's natural tendency is to work "with the man"[25] and that, when they are denied this opportunity, women must work in concert with each other. The circumstances were urgent, Robins adds, for the future of civilization was at stake.

Despite the reprinting of *Ancilla's Share* in 1976 and despite discussion and analysis of Robins's argument by feminist scholars Dale Spender and Jane Marcus, Elizabeth Robins's contribution to postwar feminism and pacifism has been all but forgotten today. The obscurity of Robins's treatise derives in part from the fact that the book was of specific relevance to contemporary policy and that it can be best understood in the context of Robins's own personal circumstances. Robins's education beyond secondary school came from her own reading; she developed her philosophy from her responses to the day-to-day accounts of women's issues and war policy, debated in Congress and Parliament, and discussed in the press. Rather than draw on Marxist theory, she identified her socialist ties more closely with the current issues of the Labour Party. Rather than invoke earlier antiwar theorists or the feminist thinkers with whom she was familiar, she used her own life as an actress and writer; responded to the most recent literature, social conditions, and press accounts; and constructed a timely argument.

Robins had somewhat different motives for seeking anonymity in publishing *Ancilla's Share* than she had had previously. Although she again sought an unbiased hearing for this book, she speaks in the voice of a woman of an older generation, and the reader of this book can recognize landmarks in her lifetime of work on behalf of women. The veil of anonymity in fact broadens the book's scope, as if she had spoken as Everywoman. In passages where Robins might well have made clear that "I" or "this author" experienced the events described or that the writer herself had interviewed a respected official, she adopted a third-person point of view. For instance, she placed her interview with Ernest Budge at the British Museum on a heightened fictional plane by giving herself the persona of "the visitor," the "inquirer," and the "loiterer," while Budge remained an unspecified "Authority." Virginia Woolf adopted a similar strategy in her use of "Mary Beaton, Mary Seaton, Mary Carmichael," in *A Room of One's Own*, and her fictionalized visit to the British Museum has come to represent any woman's encounter with male privilege, especially in academia. Elizabeth Robins's intentions were no doubt similar; in assigning experiences to a myriad of third-person female archetypes, she sought to generalize and make universal the conditions of man's discriminating attitudes that had denied women equitable status.

By adopting the persona of the anonymous woman, Robins presents her readers with extreme challenges, however. She trusts us to accept her indictment of Henry James's attitude toward women without revealing an essential component, that she knew him personally and could have claimed, with first-hand knowledge, "something touching in his letters of affection, something singularly appealing in his personal relations." Man's view of woman, Robins concluded, was seeing only what he wanted to see, and for James, as for others, this notion meant that woman would never possess any characteristic more conspicuous than her "resigned inferiority."[26] The Elizabeth Robins who was James's friend sought his advice and respected the artistry of the "Master." While she honored him by adopting some of his themes, however, she found ways to break away from his limited vision of women's social position.

Other sections of *Ancilla's Share* demonstrate the distancing effect that her anonymity prompted. Robins cites for readers the complete text of Senator William Borah's Resolution on the Outlawry of War, but she does not tell us that she corresponded closely with Borah's chief political adviser, her own brother Raymond Robins, or that Raymond Robins and Borah were part of an influential lobby which kept the Outlawry of War movement before the people.

Robins also impersonalizes the text when she analyzes the misfortune of the Pankhursts' move to sever the Pethick-Lawrences from the WSPU leadership. Without telling us that she was there when it happened, Robins asserts that autocracy in the WSPU led to the disastrous policy of physical force (*Ancilla*, 245).

Robins disguises her own experiences in her third-person account of the

Endell Street Hospital and her tribute to Flora Murray. It was Murray who organized the transformation of a warehouse into wards and the conversion of partially trained and untrained staff into an effective, mostly volunteer, women's organization. As she called her previous chapter, about the demise of the WSPU leadership, the "Waste of Rarer Human Material," she calls this "The Waste of Commoner Human Material," stressing here that Murray's enterprise proved how often the "latent powers of women" are never tapped (*Ancilla*, 254).

In the world at large, Robins's signature certainly meant something. Rhondda wanted to reprint and circulate her *Times* letter which identified health as a woman's issue. When Robins wrote to Edith Wharton through Wharton's publisher, Appleton, to praise her writing, both Appleton and Edith Wharton asked Robins for permission to quote the compliment in advertising. In a private notation, Robins records the request as "my opinion of her powers." In *Ancilla's Share*, Robins's more critical analysis of Wharton's near-greatness is unsigned. Similarly, her tributes to the actress Mrs. Patrick Campbell and to the achievement of Mrs. Humphrey Ward lose their potential effect because Robins withholds her identity as one who knew and worked with these women. Fragments of her speech to the Women Writers' Suffrage League found their way into one section. Thirteen years earlier, she had urged women to write the lives of other women with the remark, "Would that George Eliot had found her Gaskell!" (*Ancilla*, 62). Here she used the same phrase to stress that men regularly ignored distinguished women.

These and other instances demonstrate that Robins spoke from her own experience without revealing her authorship. Her motive was more complicated than her desire not to disclose her identity; the book is more than an exposé of attitudes. "The theme is not ordinary life," she writes at the opening of the twenty-fifth chapter, having admitted that all her pages to this point have discussed the ordinary life, in the hope "that their appeal might thereby be wider."

"The theme is threatened war," she continues (*Ancilla*, 257). Even more than in previous chapters, at this point she stresses how thoroughly this pacifist argument is woman centered: "The precedent to a secure peace is the mobilisation of womanpower" (*Ancilla*, 274). Her "Introductory," which updated the analysis that she had begun in 1919, described in detail the threatened buildup of arms. In the final chapters, she sets forth both the theories behind a needed philosophy of protest and the urgency of reform. She identified the efforts women made to earn degrees as nothing more consequential than what in other ages would be equivalent to "the exquisite art of homemaking." Not to do more than complete a course of study, she warned, was inviting more "shock of war and new orgies of sex-domination" (*Ancilla*, 272).

Robins calls upon the women to claim their place as leaders and organizers and members of councils. She indicts the governing bodies and councils who work for peace but who exclude women from their executive boards. She deplores the fact that the most recognized body working for peace, the League of Nations, had not one woman participant and that its office had no man able to answer her question about a pamphlet written on the work women are doing for peace. Her single-sentence paragraph, asserted repeatedly, with slight variations, throughout the text, serves as a refrain: "Wars will cease when women's will-to-peace is given equal hearing out in the world, and equal authority in council, with man's will-to-war" (*Ancilla*, 300, 308).

The presence of still more women in decision-making positions does not automatically bring more lovers of peace and a more peaceful world: "No mistake could be more tragic in its consequences than to suppose women immune from that war-poison which has destroyed men and empires" (*Ancilla*, 282). War does indeed pervert women's values. Robins asks why the young woman whom Mrs. Ward interviewed and who had reveled in her job as a maker of bombs saw her work as having a "purpose" and declares that the purpose of home building has been thwarted by low wages and degrading conditions. She declares that women, during the war, became violently wrenched from their natural state: "The very life-sources of compassion were tainted. The mothers, instead of fosterers, became the furies, thirsting for the blood of other women's sons" (*Ancilla*, 282).

Robins's anonymity had ambiguous results. Her publisher, Hutchinson, contacted her after the book had been released and pleaded with her to disclose her identity; only three hundred copies had sold. She wrote in her diary that her brother Raymond had "pooh-poohed" her conviction that women were more committed to peace than men. Nevertheless, she overheard, at one of Lady Astor's receptions, many people talking about the book with more interest because they did not know who had written it.

When Robins did release her name, the "second large edition" was announced in the *Times*. People told Robins privately that a year ago they would not have been receptive to her argument but that now they were persuaded. Hutchinson assured Robins that H. G. Wells's attack on the book would help sell copies, and the publisher negotiated a contract which gave her an advance for her next novel.

Perhaps the remark which most affirms the part *Ancilla's Share* played in establishing Robins's status in the feminist movement was made by fellow American and feminist Crystal Eastman, who, writing of the formation of the

British Advisory Group in 1925, described *Ancilla's Share* as a "profound satirical study of the position of women through the ages, which is rapidly becoming the feminist 'Bible.'"[27] Another American feminist, Alice Paul, helped to bring the advisory group into being in order to stress the need for an international equal rights policy. Robins later credited Paul with bringing *Ancilla's Share* to the attention of American publishers.

Inevitably, however, Robins was perceived by a new generation of feminists as the "old-time woman" that she had labeled herself. Virginia Woolf observed in her review of Robins's 1920 collection of short stories that they represented, regrettably (despite the inclusion of "The Tortoise-Shell Cat"), a decidedly prewar world.

H. G. Wells's attack upon *Ancilla's Share* was further evidence of a lack of support for Robins's viewpoint. He dismissed her work, in part by suggesting that the book was not entirely her own, and declared, "Disarmament is manifestly a question of minor importance to women."[28] Most revealing of Wells's statements is his charge that "Miss Robins thinks she is at war with men; she is really at war with sex." Certainly she was at war with the view of sex that Wells, a womanizer, faulted her for lacking. Robins had long before attacked his advocacy of sexual freedoms to further man's dominance of woman, but in the 1920s, the Wells view was too much in the ascendancy for his ridicule of her not to have some force.

It is unfortunate that even the current generation of feminists tends to classify Robins as a woman not in touch with her sexuality. (She was shocked at the physicality of Rodin's sculpture and rejected what she knew of Freud's theories.) Nor is it appropriate to see her primarily in the roles of muse and madonna, images which she may have appeared to her admirers to have cultivated but actually just as thoroughly rejected. Unlike Dorothy Richardson's *Pilgrimage*, Robins's subjective and close-focused autobiographical trilogy regarded an earlier era from a feminist perspective. She stood in contrast to her fellow expatriate writers partly because her active involvement in feminist politics informed her artistic response to her self-exile. In *Camilla*, she used her personal convictions to criticize Edith Wharton's satire on American marriage; in *The Messenger*, she did the same with typical Jamesian themes. If there is not a feminist critical language capable of acknowledging Robins for the myriad of achievements, unfinished agendas, and ambiguities in her life, perhaps it is time to invent one.

Robins had deplored the lack of biographies of women when she addressed the Women Writers' Suffrage League in 1911 and again in *Ancilla's Share*. "To posterity the biography is indeed the life" (*Ancilla*, 62), she stated in 1924, almost as a prediction that her own life would wash into insignificance unless her personal achievement was somehow recorded. The Ibsen centennial in 1928 clarified one primary concern of her last years, that of writing about her position in the theater; and Virginia Woolf (whose Hogarth Press published *Ibsen and the Actress*) urged Robins to continue her autobiography beyond the years covered in *Both Sides of the Curtain*.

Robins pursued other projects as well. The novel she began in 1924, *The Secret That Was Kept*, took her two years to complete, first because she hoped she could sell the film scenario, and then because she fell ill. It centers on a woman who murders her abusive husband in order to have a child by the man she loves. The novel was published without critical attention in 1926 because the newspapers that usually carried reviews were on strike.

In 1927, she took up, with firmer command of her material, the novel based on records that her father kept—what Henry James had called a "rich storehouse" of material—and turned it into another female bildungsroman by mingling her father's crisis at the hands of financial swindlers with her heroine's determination to be an actress in spite of his regrets; but this six-hundred-page novel, "Rocky Mountain Journal," never found a publisher.

Robins faced another personal crisis, the six weeks' disappearance of her brother Raymond in 1932, by returning to her 1900 diary and writing his memoir. The year and more she spent writing *Raymond and I* turned to bitter disappointment after Raymond forbade her to have the book published during his lifetime. The political crisis of the Second World War further disrupted work on her autobiography and forced her to return to America, a country that she no longer recognized. Ultimately, the complications of travel during wartime destroyed the part of her autobiographical portrait that she had completed. Her trunks were rifled at the docks in Liverpool when she returned to England in 1945, and her missing manuscripts were never recovered.

Throughout the years in which she struggled to work on her memoirs and became distracted by more immediate projects—especially by reminiscences of those she knew, including Annie Besant, Alice Duër Miller, Oscar Wilde, W. T. Stead, and Dorothy Yates Thompson—she held to the vision of her brass bar, the singing curtain rod in her garret room in New York that had first echoed back her dramatized voice. Just as Robins had discovered the artistic strength in speaking with two voices, she also found greater self-expression in the successive clashes among the many personae she became: widow in mourning, actress devoted to Ibsen, pseudonymous author, independent theater manager striving for artistic excellence, sister to the brother who could only disappoint her, adventuresome traveler in Alaska, feminist playwright and militant suffragette, mother substitute, Anglophile critical of American wartime neutrality, expatriate forced to reestablish American citizenship, lover of peace, frequent invalid, and lobbyist for women's health care. Her many pursuits and feminist perceptions affirm the values of her most personal writing, not only when she confessed to dramatizing her true self even to her most intimate associates, but also when she preserved, carefully annotated, and turned into fiction her autobiographical sources.

Epilogue

If I write when I am too old to act, my best capital next to sympathetic observation and an unaffected style would be a diary of my own life. . . . I will try to write the real happenings within and without—excusing myself to myself for lack of complete frankness by calling my silences self reverence, a dignified reserve, a 19th century shrinking from the nude. And yet since I take the trouble (and very great trouble it is) for my own future guidance let me leave as little dark as I can with decency reveal. As I write I feel sure I'll forget "decency" and all self consciousness in its narrow sense as soon as I am interested in what I'm putting down.

—Elizabeth Robins, Diary, August 21, 1891

The kind of writer I am has a view and purpose which are inseparable from her work. It is, briefly, to represent a phase of life, not to hop, skip, and jump over the years, picking out the exceptional incidents which other people might select as worth recording. This last is also a method, and no doubt marketable. But my way in this particular instance has found such response as no other work of mine ever approached.

—Elizabeth Robins to Earl Balch of Putnam's Sons, August 28, 1940

BIOGRAPHER [ESTABLISHING THE SCENE]: A private room at the Vassar College Alumnae House, May, 1942.[1] Remnants of morning tea, at about 1:00 P.M. Fresh flowers in a vase. Ink, pens, pencils, and all of a writer's paraphernalia. Elizabeth Robins, in her eightieth year, sits at a writing desk cluttered with papers and books, today's mail, old diaries and manuscripts, and a new typescript that she is marking. An open trunk reveals more of the same. She opens a package from Chinsegut, postmarked Brooksville, Florida, that contains her book, *Ibsen and the Actress*. She reads the letter enclosed.

Raymond Robins, confined at Chinsegut because of an injury to his spinal cord seven years earlier, writes Elizabeth at Vassar that he is glad she has found a place where she can work. He offers to pay for a secretary and encloses the usual check; his payments reflect his awareness that he has deprived Elizabeth of the home they were supposed to have shared, a home that she purchased at great personal cost.

Elizabeth Robins, a late photograph. (*Courtesy of the Fales Library. Reproduced with the permission of Mabel Smith, for the Backsettown Trustees.*)

The war and the American government forced Robins out of Sussex, England, and back to an America she has found difficult to recognize. Encouraged by her Eliot cousins in Pittsburgh that she may stay here at Vassar as a "Resident Guest," she has settled into a routine of dictating, writing, revising, and reading over old notes, yet she never passes up an opportunity to make new acquaintances.

Elizabeth Robins is hunting, finding, and reading bits of her earlier records; she is addressing a gathering at the Alumnae House or recreating an earlier address to her public; she is testing and quizzing her biographer. She is constantly correcting, emending, and critiquing herself as well as speaking to her audience of one, her biographer, whom she presumes, for the most part, to be the young woman hired as her secretary.

ELIZABETH ROBINS. So here is my book from Raymond that I asked for, and here you are, ready to take a few notes. I must get acquainted with you first, so don't mind my rambling. I'm finding my own way around these scraps, pulling out the things that strike me as usable. I shall not give up this effort to continue my memoirs. It may be the last chance, you see. How did I get here, though? You ought to know a few things.

There were so many long years of little chance to work, interruptions by illness, the slight heart attack, and finally, the last insult, being ordered out of England—which had come to be home for me—by the American embassy in the summer of 1940. After an excruciating scene in Lisbon, Portugal, of panic and desperation among those struggling to escape, I arrived in the United States utterly exhausted. Then I set about to crack a rib! Well, people took care of me as best they could. Yet in all my traveling, from New York, to Maine, to Florida, to Pittsburgh, no place felt more conducive to productive work than this at Vassar.

I was all set to write my full autobiography, inspired by the reaction to this little lecture, "Ibsen and the Actress." That was in 1928, at the Ibsen centennial. Leonard Woolf offered to publish the lecture as one of his pamphlets. And Virginia Woolf encouraged me to go on with the full biography, then gave me just the right title, *Both Sides of the Curtain.*

BIOGRAPHER. So, then, you *have* published your autobiography?

ELIZABETH ROBINS. No, no, there is nothing of Ibsen in that whole volume. That is simply a preliminary record. I needed to set the groundwork, to show what life was like for the *struggling* actress, before Ibsen. But, you see, I get distracted by my attempts to write a memoir of Alice Duër Miller, whose "White Cliffs of Dover" has done so much to rouse American sympathy for England's war. We'd known each other decades ago, and now . . . There are years, you see, of these daily records.

BIOGRAPHER. You depend upon these archives of your former activities. That is your distinguishing characteristic.

ELIZABETH ROBINS. And that is why I distrust those sweeping memoirs. *A Backward Glance*, for instance, hardly tells a *life* story. It's a scattered set of impressions without any chronological substance.

BIOGRAPHER. And yet, that volume reveals something, even when it skims over the essence. Edith Wharton continues to have her readers.

ELIZABETH ROBINS [A bit snappy]. Yes, and she will get all the recognition for having Henry James as a friend, despite the way he and I worked together on so many dramatic projects, despite my tribute in *Theatre and Friendship*. . . . [More subdued; the memory of Henry James reminds her of her more intimate friend of James's.] If only I had put to use earlier what I learned from backstage, watching Ruth Draper perform her theater monologues. [ER picks up a fragment and reads] "Amazing simplicity of external equipment," I wrote in my diary: "An object lesson all thro' in her Art, in her theory of life of High Economy. Deep impression made by this. Had I had it 30 years ago what couldn't I have done!" (Diary, December 2, 1927.) It was Ruth Draper who performed her solo pieces as a benefit—to save Backsettown from financial troubles.

BIOGRAPHER. Yes.

ELIZABETH ROBINS. But I am talking about seizing a moment, grasping the essence, knowing when to strike and where to find one's audience. All those missed opportunities. Yes, and I gave to Stella Campbell all the roles that might have established my career. Yet perhaps I had too much faith in them, in Shaw and Pinero, in Constance Fletcher, and Henry James, as playwrights.

BIOGRAPHER. And you were disappointed by Ibsen, in the end.

ELIZABETH ROBINS. One is, when one is hoping for another Hilda. He had ceased to be the Master. His idea of the model giving her life up to that sculptor was repulsive. "Wreckage on a giant scale" is what I wrote about his last play.

BIOGRAPHER. But this [referring to the small pamphlet ER holds in her hand] tells a different story.

ELIZABETH ROBINS [brightening]. Yes, and this is the point of why you are here, isn't it. So let me "set the scene," as we dramatists would say. It is 1928, the series of lectures to commemorate the Ibsen Centennial.

ELIZABETH ROBINS [Picking an already marked passage]. Here, then. [Begins to read, imagining her audience.]

You may be able to imagine the excitement of coming across anything so *alive* as Hedda. What you won't be able to imagine (unless you are an actress in your twenties) is the joy of having in your hands—free hands—such glorious actable stuff. If we had been thinking politically, concerning ourselves about the emancipation of women, we would not have given the Ibsen plays the particular kind of whole-hearted, enchanted devotion we did give. We were actresses—actresses who wouldn't for a kingdom be anything else. We got over that; but I am talking about '89–'91. How were we to find fault with a state of society that had given us Nora and Hedda and Thea?[2]

[ER pauses, considering, and continues, with her own thoughts.] Where to go next. How to shape and reshape this, and the mass of material from the diaries, the letters, the reviews?

BIOGRAPHER. But isn't it "all of a piece," as you would say: your mission to Alaska, your suffrage years, the long career in letters, the many novels, the compulsive record keeping, the abandoned projects? Put together, they are you.

ELIZABETH ROBINS. Oho, here it comes. You want to analyze me. You think I've blotted things out, covered over the embarrassing facts . . . , "suppressed"—

BIOGRAPHER. You've confessed as much yourself.

ELIZABETH ROBINS.—in order to present only the rosiest portrait of myself.

Let me have you hear the story of the curious fate of the two pictures Sir William Rothenstein did of me as Mrs. Lessingham. [Rummages through a few pages, picks it out, and begins to read.]

His two sketches done of me in that role, "The one quite agreeable, the other dreadful. Describing that horrible one at a dinner party at the Bells, I said, 'Nobody would know it. One eye is down there, and the other eye is up here. The mouth is twisted, and the hands like this.' Whereupon Gertrude Bell interrupted, 'You are exactly like that at this moment.'

"The portrait supposed to be exactly like me was so unnerving that when he offered me my choice between the charming, pretty lady, Mrs. Lessingham, and the strange creature which was me, I instantly chose the strange creature. Later, I hung it on the stairs at Backsettown, but I carefully unstuck the frame, and with the deliberate design of putting her out of the way, covered it over before I had it framed with a photograph done of myself by that famous man Katherine Dreier sent to me from Germany. For years, I went up and down the stairs with an occasional chuckle to think of the horror discreetly hidden under the fashionably dressed lady in the photograph.[3]

BIOGRAPHER. You delight in what is "under the surface," what others do not know of you.

ELIZABETH ROBINS [Playfully sarcastic]. Yes, and I pull them into my confidence with charming enticements and flattery and bribes. [She tries one out on the biographer.] I think you will have to help me write this. You will be a collaborator in my scheme to "sometimes suppress, sometimes embroider."

BIOGRAPHER [Trying to steer ER back to her main topic]. Ibsen, you wrote, invited the performer's collaboration.

ELIZABETH ROBINS [Quoting from memory without skipping a beat]. "Make no mistake, you must let Ibsen play you, rather than insist on your playing Ibsen." [She turns quickly to the last page of her essay to complete the remark.]

"'Collaboration.' Maeterlinck has said: '*Il y a une plus haute collaboration que celle de la plume—celle de la pensée et du sentiment.*' One of the highest of all is, surely, this collaboration between playwright and player" (*Actress*, 56). [She flips back a page or two and continues.]

> "Ibsen, more than any author I have known, comes to the rescue of the actor. . . . Practically he "does it" for you. . . . By the power of his truth and the magic of his poetry he does something to the imagination that not only gives the actors an impetus, but an impetus in a right direction. And I do not say *the* right direction. Whatever direction the individual gift and temper of the actor inclines to, the effects that Ibsen leaves him to make are Ibsen's effects. Just as much they are Ibsen's when, in one actor's hands they turn out one thing, and in another actor's something different—different except for their incomparable freshness, their air of startling spontaneity, of being made to fit the player or the player born to play the part. [*Actress*, 46, 54]

BIOGRAPHER. He seems to inspire the poetry in you. You've invested a great deal of energy, in these recent years, in writing tributes, recording memoirs of others. Is this another aspect of your "doubleness," this digressive mode?

ELIZABETH ROBINS [At her most defensive.] The Henry James book was just something to pass the time, as I recuperated and gathered my strength to attack the autobiography. I suppose, if I don't finish *this*, the collection of his letters to me will be thought of as my last word on those years. No, these little portraits—of Oscar Wilde, Annie Besant, William Stead and Bret Harte, of Sir William and Lady Grey and Mrs. Yates Thompson, and the dear Alice Miller—they hardly characterize a psychosis, an inability to confront myself. They were simply called for, given that those people *meant* something to me, that vignettes occur and demand to be recorded.

BIOGRAPHER. And yet, they are not about *you*, your most private sensibilities. How you use the memorials of your husband, for instance . . .

ELIZABETH ROBINS [Quietly]. It saw me through the guilt. [Reading, as if she returned to this often as a litany]: "If I am to make a memorial for you . . . , I must set about it as the mother of a posthumous child sets herself to shield the unborn from the long shadow of her grief. For this memorial made by my blood and some mixing with the essential you will be our child." This I wrote on what would have been our twenty-fifth wedding anniversary. But opening my soul to him then freed me, and allowed me to continue to write. And that forced me to deal with my failings. Here, decades later, in one of many rereadings, I've added the remark [ER peers to read the smaller letters she has long ago penned]: "Am I the mother for such a child? Can I '*bear*' this one any more than the physical child? Must there always be holding back in a sense of unreadiness—the temptation to refuse."[4]

BIOGRAPHER. "To write is to hold judgment over one's self."

ELIZABETH ROBINS [Familiar with the quotation]. Ibsen again! Yes, that is quite appropriate here. You recognize it, no doubt, as the epigraph of *The New Moon*. [Snapping out of her deep contemplation.] I do think we must call an end to this session. You go now, and type up whatever of this [referring to the small pile of clippings and hand-drafted sheets that she has on her desk] you think is usable, and then we'll discuss what comes next. But there is one thing you must look over, so as not to fix any impression of me. Here, the draft of a letter written to Raymond, shortly after I came back to this crude country of my birth, my answer to his asking where I want to be buried, if I die before returning to Sussex.

BIOGRAPHER [Stands up, with the letter, recognizing that this is a dismissal, and turns away from the scene, reading ER's letter aloud].

"I'd like the sheets I die in drawn about me and over my face and so an END. If I were to choose I'd say—don't let fancy play over me—nothing ought to be spent (I write as if I were money-obsessed), that can decently be avoided. But if someone outside wanted to put any shingle, or let us say four words on a wooden stave, the words should be: ⸻ ⸻ ⸻ ⸻" (ER to RR, September 19, 1940).

BIOGRAPHER [Addressing ER]. And here you have cut those four words out of the letter with a razor, but marked the slits with another note: "Forgive the cutting out of a thing of no importance."

[The BIOGRAPHER realizes, too late, that her reading of these words has brought on ER's last disappearing act, that she'll have no one to interview, no one's dictation to take, tomorrow. She slips into her narrator's voice, more detached.]

BIOGRAPHER. Elizabeth Robins lived another ten years, and died in her beloved Sussex in May 1952. She was in a desperate hurry to return to war-torn England in 1945, and on that trip her manuscript was lost. She filed a report on the missing document, but it was never found. Briefly, in moments of better health, she recommitted herself to the autobiographical projects. She took the theater historian Phyllis Hartnoll into her confidence, as her new collaborator. And she had a few physical setbacks, long before the end. She tumbled down a flight of stairs. A doctor came to her bedside: "Miss Robins, you are so very lucky you didn't seriously hurt yourself."

VOICE OF ELIZABETH ROBINS. "*Lucky!*"—"I'm an *actress*! I've been *trained* to know how to fall. Lucky!"

BIOGRAPHER. A few things of substance remain. There are three dwellings still standing and important to the heritage of Elizabeth Robins. They are rich with dignity. In Zanesville, Ohio, her childhood home, the Historical Society knows the significance of their "Stone Academy." Some of its features are preserved in Elizabeth Robins's novel, *The Open Question*. Its public history is just as significant. The trap door to the basement records its use as a stop on the underground railroad. The shelves in the library mark the water line of the great flood of 1913. The lilacs, remembered so well by Raymond, continue to bloom in the spring.

I am moved most by the door knocker at Chinsegut, a heavy brass . . . monstrosity, almost, engraved with a scrolled script, "E. Robins, 1771," belonging to Elizabeth's great-grandfather, the first Ephraim Robins but loved by Elizabeth, because she was "E. Robins," too. The Robins genealogy still hangs in the dining room at Chinsegut. The brass door knocker is screwed firmly into the frame of a door that few people use any more. Raymond and Margaret's mansion—the house Elizabeth paid for and wanted to call "home," but at one point was expressly forbidden to revisit by her beloved, heart-breaking brother. The land surrounding Chinsegut is well used, deeded to the Federal Government in 1932. But the knocker rests, stolidly silenced; the cobwebs creep over its surface, the etched letters are green for tarnish and sadly, prominently, proclaim a heritage that has ceased to be known.

There is another engraved record, an ocean away, of a bright blue plaque with white lettering, one of so many like it in England, heralding some part of a story important to the nation. The town is quieter now; the train station is gone, the tracks taken up. East of High Street, on the far side of town, a long, quiet lane insulates the fourteenth-century brick dwelling from postwar housing developments and pastureland. Backsettown is nestled in a quiet dip in the land, so that its huge slate roof is the first thing one notices. Just to the left of the door frame, high on the red brick wall is the plaque: "Elizabeth Robins, 1862–1952, Actress-Writer, Lived Here." Inside this dwelling is another plaque, on the dining room wall, honoring Octavia Wilberforce. Backsettown was open as a rest haven for women for sixty years; and that honors them both, much more than either etched tribute.

Most of all though, there are the masses of papers; the diaries, the manuscripts, the correspondence. "Why do I keep these things of long ago?" she wrote on the envelope of the writings of her aunt Sarah Elizabeth, the poet-playwright who died so young. "Because they once meant something to the people dear to me." She inherited the instinct for diary keeping and for the value of literary remains from her father and grandmother, even as she inherited their papers and diaries. She had some sense of the lasting worth of her own papers, certainly, and some consciousness of how thoroughly her public image was shaped by her unwillingness to reveal her inner self. She inserted a clause in her will that nothing should be touched for thirty years. Enough to discourage any biographer. Did she bury herself with her own epitaph when she recognized herself as the "old-time woman," when she saw around her so many young minds, "academically equipped"?

No, as long as she wrote with such detail, as long as she preserved what she wrote, as long as one reader finds the thrill of a woman's voice, speaking to other women who have for so long suppressed their own voices, she will find biographers—other critics and other collaborators.

Abbreviations

In quotations from manuscript sources, I follow Elizabeth Robins's practice of expanding the abbreviations she used in longhand when she converted documents to typewritten form, unless passages invite the abbreviated style for rhythm's sake. In her original hand, "would," "should," "through," "and," "etc.," proper names, and other words were represented by abbreviations, the ampersand, or initials. I have silently corrected ER's misspelling of proper nouns. In all her correspondence, ER used English spelling, which I have of course retained in direct quotations from that correspondence.

Biographers tend to regularize their subjects, even to the point of simplifying the many names and nicknames by which they were known. Elizabeth Robins, through her lifetime, was known, in addition, as "Bessie," "Clare Raimond," "Mona," "Lisa," and "Florida." She was "ER" not only in her correspondence but also to some who knew her well. Except when distinguishing her from others in her family, I refer to her as "Robins" in my narrative and as "ER" in my notes and annotations.

Berg Collection	Berg Collection, New York Public Library
CER	Charles Ephraim Robins
ER	Elizabeth Robins
ER Papers	Elizabeth Robins Papers
Fales	Fales Library, New York University
FB	Florence Bell
GBS	George Bernard Shaw
HJ	Henry James
JA	Janet Achurch
JHR	Jane Hussey Robins
JM	John Masefield
MDR	Margaret Dreier Robins
RR	Raymond Robins
WA	William Archer
Actress	*Ibsen and the Actress*
Ancilla	*Ancilla's Share: An Indictment of Sex Antagonism*

BSC	*Both Sides of the Curtain*
"CW"	"The Coming Woman"
"DJH"	"Dedicated to John Huntley"
DL	*A Dark Lantern*
EBook	ER's engagement book or yearly date book
ER "Will"	Statement of March 16, 1895, identified by ER as her "will"
GMH	*George Mandeville's Husband*
"M/AW"	"A Masterpiece the World Never Saw; or, Aphrodite of the West"
Mills	*The Mills of the Gods*
MLS	*My Little Sister*
OQ	*The Open Question: A Tale of Two Temperaments*
"SL"	"The Silver Lotus"
T&F	*Theatre and Friendship*
"Theo"	"Theodora: A Pilgrimage"
TIW	*Time Is Whispering*
"WH"	"Whither and How"
WS	*Way Stations*

Unless otherwise designated, all diaries, correspondence, and unpublished literary materials are housed in the Elizabeth Robins Papers, Fales Library, New York University. When a title alone would not suffice to find a document within this collection, I have supplied additional information in a note to indicate how it is cited in the finding aid.

Notes

Introduction

1. I quote from a document that ER labeled "will" on the envelope, which is filed in the ER Papers, Fales Library, New York University, as "Statement about the accuracy of Elizabeth Robins's account of herself, March 16, 1895."

2. Other full-length studies include: Jane Connor Marcus, "Elizabeth Robins" (Ph.D. diss., Northwestern University, 1973); Gay Gibson Cima, "Elizabeth Robins: Ibsen Actress-Manageress" (Ph.D. diss., Cornell University, 1978); and Mary T. Heath, "A Crisis in the Life of the Actress: Ibsen in England" (Ph.D. diss., University of Massachusetts, Amherst, 1986). Articles by Marcus, Cima, Myron Matlaw, Susan M. Squier, and me appear in the bibliography.

1: "I Was Born in the Superlative"

1. My principal source for the scene, from which the dialogue is adapted, is ER to CER, May 26, 1881; for the title of the chapter, ER to CER, April 22, 1885.

2. The quotation is included on a scrap of paper filed with the manuscript "Theodora," ER Papers, Fales.

3. My visit to Zanesville and talk with Norris Schneider, author of *Y Bridge City: The Story of Zanesville and Muskingum County, Ohio* (Cleveland: World Publishing, 1950), clarified the descriptions of the "Stone Academy" which occur throughout the Robins family correspondence. The building, which provided the setting for Robins's 1898 novel *The Open Question* (discussed in chapter 4), is now owned by the Zanesville Historical Society.

4. Details of ER's association with O'Neill are given in Myron Matlaw's article "Robins Hits the Road: Trouping with O'Neill in the 1880s," *Theatre Survey* 29:2 (November 1988), 173–92. My thanks to him for sharing his material with me before publication.

5. Robins composed this introduction as she began work on the novel in 1897, but it was never published.

6. *Courier*, December 2, 1885, copy in ER's scrapbook, ER Papers, Fales.

2: The Coming Woman

1. The source for the entire scene is chapter 12 of Robins's unpublished autobiography, "Whither and How," pp. 1–6. Several drafts of the typescript (ER Papers, Fales) indicate that at one point "Whither and How" may have been conceived as the

concluding section of Robins's *Both Sides of the Curtain*. I have preserved Robins's capitalization of Theatre, Adaptation, etc.

2. William Archer, "A Translator-Traitor: Mr. Edmund Gosse and Henrik Ibsen," *Pall Mall Gazette*, January 23, 1891, p. 2. As quoted in *The Oxford Ibsen*, vol. 7, edited by James Walter McFarlane (London: Oxford University Press, 1966), 512.

3. Robins, *Both Sides of the Curtain* (London: William Heinemann, 1940), 22.

4. Quotations are from the rejection letter written by George Perry, filed with the holograph copy of "Him and Her," ER Papers, Fales.

5. Clement Scott, *Illustrated London News*, November 16, 1889.

6. ER Diary, February 7, 1890, p. 38.

7. Robins, "Across America with 'Junius Brutus Booth,' " *Universal Review* 7:27 (July 1890), 378.

8. Heath, "A Crisis in the Life of the Actress: Ibsen in England," 80–81, 132.

9. Juliet Blair, "Private Parts in Public Places: The Case of Actresses," in *Women and Space*, edited by Shirley Ardener (New York: St. Martin's Press, 1981), 221.

10. ER to Emma Blandy Carrington, June 11, 1892, ER Papers, Fales.

11. ER Diary, October 30, 1890.

12. Robins's own memoirs include: *Ibsen and the Actress* (London: Hogarth Press, 1928); *Theatre and Friendship* (New York: G. Putnam's Sons, 1932); *Both Sides of the Curtain* (London: William Heinemann, 1940). My article on this period, "Elizabeth Robins and the 1891 Production of *Hedda Gabler*," *Modern Drama* 28:4 (December 1985), 611–19, is based on the unpublished "Whither and How."

13. Clement Scott, review of *Hedda Gabler* in *Illustrated London News*, April 25, 1891, 551–52.

14. HJ to William James, February 6, 1891, in *Henry James Letters*, edited by Leon Edel, vol. 3 (Cambridge, Mass.: Belknap Press, 1980), 329.

15. Henry James, "On the Occasion of *Hedda Gabler*," *New Review*, 4 (June 1891), 530.

16. ER to Emma Blandy Carrington, June 20, 1891, ER Papers, Fales.

17. *Star*, May 12, 1892, copy in clippings file, ER Papers, Fales.

18. Robins, "The Coming Woman," typescript in ER Papers, Fales, 15.

19. ER to Mrs. Patrick Campbell, May 2, 1893, as quoted in Mrs. Patrick Campbell, *My Life and Some Letters* (New York: Dodd, Mead, 1922), 85.

20. Robins, typescript of 1891 diary, November 5, 1891, ER Papers, Fales.

21. Robins, "Study for a Woman of Thirty," 5. Originally filed in the ER to FB correspondence, 1892, ER Papers, Fales. Hereinafter cited as "Study." Pages correspond to the six unnumbered sheets of letter-sized paper and four additional fragments.

22. Robins, *Theater and Friendship* (New York: G. Putnam's Sons, 1932), 81.

3: The Power of Anonymity

1. The dinner and James's telling of his dream taken from ER to FB, January 26, 1895. Blanche Althea Crackanthorpe's intimate friendship with ER described in the BAC correspondence and ER to FB letters, ER Papers, Fales.

2. Alice James, *The Diary of Alice James*, edited with an introduction by Leon Edel (New York: Dodd, Mead, 1964), 211 (June 16, 1891).

3. Elaine Showalter, *A Literature of Their Own: British Women Novelists from Brontë to Lessing* (Princeton: Princeton University Press, 1977), 207.

4. Sydney Pawling correspondence to ER, ER Papers, Fales, August 1895, identifies the submission only as a manuscript by Victoria Cross.

5. Cora Crane to ER, May 8, [1894], ER Papers, Fales.

6. Robins, *Ibsen and the Actress* (London: Hogarth Press, 1928), 40.

7. GBS to ER, February 5, 1893, in *Bernard Shaw: Collected Letters*, edited by Dan H. Laurence (New York: Dodd, Mead, 1965), 1:380. Hereinafter cited as *Letters* I.

8. *Pall Mall Gazette*, February 17, 1893, lvi, 1–2 (reprinted in Michael Egan's *Ibsen: The Critical Heritage* [London: Vision, 1972], 266–69).

9. Robins, *Ibsen and the Actress*, 47, 48 (ER's ellipsis).

10. *Sussex Daily News*, March 31, 1893, copy in clippings file, ER Papers, Fales.

11. Anonymous [Florence Bell and Elizabeth Robins], *Alan's Wife*, with an introduction by William Archer (London: Henry & Company, 1893), 47.

12. Archer also thought it important to demonstrate that the central immoral act, a woman's baptism and murder of her child, was not imitative; he appended a letter from Thomas Hardy proving that his *Tess of the D'Urbervilles* and the original Swedish story arrived at similar actions independently.

13. Independent Theatre clippings, British Theatre Association.

14. RR to ER, April 16, 1893, ER Papers, Fales.

15. *New Review* 10:56 (January 1894), unnumbered preface page.

16. "A Lucky Sixpence," *New Review*, 10:56 (January 1894), 122 (published anonymously). Hereinafter cited in the text as "Sixpence."

17. WA to ER, undated letters identified as related to "A Lucky Sixpence" [1894], ER Papers, Fales.

18. *New Review*, 10:56 (January 1894), "Announcement," unnumbered preface page.

19. Mary Kelley, *Private Woman, Public Stage: Literary Domesticity in Nineteenth Century America* (New York: Oxford University Press, 1984).

20. Page numbers refer to this edition, published in vol. 10 of the *New Review*.

21. C. E. Raimond [Elizabeth Robins], *George Mandeville's Husband* (London: William Heinemann, 1894), 56.

22. C. E. Raimond [Elizabeth Robins], "'Gustus Frederick," in the *New Review* 12:70 (March 1895), 281.

23. Robins note, appended to title page of typescript, "Valentine Cobb," ER Papers, Fales. Hereinafter cited in the text as "VC."

24. Archer's pencilled notes accompanying Robins's typescript, "Valentine Cobb," ER Papers, Fales.

25. Especially in parts of her 1900 Alaska journal, her 1906 Chinsegut Diary, her End of Year Diary, and her diary-letter addressed to George Parks, January 1912.

26. Robins, "An American Actress at Balmoral Castle," typescript in ER Papers, Fales, 31, 26. Michael Jamieson's article "An American Actress at Balmoral," *Theatre Research International*, n.s., 2:2 (February 1977), 117–31, draws principally on ER's typescript.

27. C. E. Raimond [Elizabeth Robins], "Miss de Maupassant," in the *New Review* 13:72 (September 1895), 234. All citations refer to this edition, pp. 233–47.

28. My reading of Robins's relationship with Archer leads me to dispute Thomas Postlewait's conjecture that their liaison was sexual and that she may have borne Archer's child. In his *Prophet of the New Drama: William Archer and the Ibsen Campaign* (Westport, Conn.: Greenwood Press, 1986), Postlewait quotes T. S. Eliot and confesses that he is constructing a "contrived corridor" for reading their relationship, and in fact he overlooks ER's diary evidence that disproves his theory.

29. Robins, "The Silver Lotus," typescript in ER Papers, Fales, Act I, 20.

30. Specific occasions, mentioned in her engagement book, include meetings with Carr on March 2 and 9, with Alexander on March 19 and 20, with Tree on March 28, and with Wyndham on May 1. In a letter to Bell on April 21, she reported, "In an hour and a half I will be reading M— to W.," who according to her engagement book was Herbert Waring.

4: Toward the New Century

1. ER to FB, December 12, 1895. Other sources include Robins's subsequent undated letter to Bell, various remarks in the correspondence to Bell, Robins's notes on "Sister Helen," Fales, and Rossetti's poem "Sister Helen."

2. In the United States, the volume was published as *"The Fatal Gift of Beauty" and Other Stories* (Chicago: Herbert S. Stone, 1896).

3. EBook, May 9, 1896, and subsequent entries.

4. GBS to Ellen Terry, in *Letters* I, 708.

5. JA to ER, December 10, ER Papers, Fales; and quoted by Heath.

6. Shaw, "Ibsen without Tears," *Saturday Review* (December 12, 1896), in *Shaw's Dramatic Criticism*, edited by John F. Matthews (New York: Hill & Wang, 1959), 201.

7. As quoted in *T&F*, 188, 189.

8. Shaw, review of *John Gabriel Borkman* in May 8, 1897, *Saturday Review*. Reprinted in *Our Theatres in the Nineties* (London: Constable, 1932), 123.

9. C. E. Raimond [Elizabeth Robins], "La Bellerieuse," *Pall Mall Magazine* 15:61, 33.

10. I am editing the previously unpublished early stage fiction of Elizabeth Robins in a collection tentatively entitled "Highly Respectable Heroines." The stories, together with "The Coming Woman," are an important source for ER's reflections about her two professions.

11. ER's explanatory note appended to the undated (November 1897) letter to FB.

12. From a notebook entitled "Given me in 1897 by F.B.," ER Papers, Fales.

13. Elizabeth Robins, *The Open Question: A Tale of Two Temperaments* (London: William Heinemann, 1898, 1899; New York: Harper, 1899). The Harper edition of 1899 is cited within the text. Charlotte Goodman, "The Lost Brother, the Twin: Women Novelists and the Male-Female Double *Bildungsroman*," *Novel* 17:1 (Fall 1983), 28–43.

14. William Leonard Courtney, *The Feminine Note in Fiction* (London: Chapman & Hall, 1904), 181.

15. Page numbers to *The Mills of the Gods* (New York: Moffat, Yard, 1908), 98.

16. Page numbers refer to the typescript, ER Papers, Fales.

17. See, for example, Whistler's paintings at the Hunterian Art Gallery, University of Glasgow.

18. From ER's memoir, "Oscar Wilde: An Appreciation," typescript in ER Papers, Fales, 8–9.

5: The Magnetic North

1. Raymond vividly recalled the event during the hardships of his later growing up years. This version of the story is taken from his letter, RR to ER, May 13, 1903. All RR to ER correspondence in the ER Papers, Fales, hereinafter cited within the text.

2. The reunion, described in detail in ER's "June 14th" chapter in *Raymond and I*, renewed the closeness which Raymond had known in childhood.

3. Source is ER to FB, October 20, 1900, and *Raymond and I* (London: Hogarth Press, 1956), 341.

4. With the help of the Alaska Humanities Forum, Victoria Joan Moessner and I are preparing a typescript of the Elizabeth Robins Alaska-Klondike Diary. The parenthetical short form "Alaska diary" differentiates this diary (original in the ER Papers, Fales) from other ER diaries.

5. These and subsequent quotations refer to the thirteen-page typescript version of a journal-letter she kept while traveling, May 21–June 1, 1901. In the ER to FB correspondence, ER Papers, Fales.

6. Vernon Robins to ER, May 29, 1901, ER Papers, Fales.

7. Both earlier stories were published in separate volumes after Robins's success with *The Convert*.

8. Published as "Pleasure Mining," *Fortnightly Review*, o.s., vol. 77 (March 1902), 474–86.

9. *Times*, March 7, 1902, p. 3.

10. Lady Dorothy Grey to ER, April 20, 1902, ER Papers, Fales.

11. It was published at the time the boundary dispute between Canada and the United States was being settled in the English courts, in the *Fortnightly Review* 80 (1903), 792–99.

12. Modern feminists disagree on whether Mitchell's treatment was antifemale. See Ann Douglas Wood, "'The Fashionable Diseases': Women's Complaints and Their Treatment in Nineteenth Century America," and Regina Markel Morantz, "The Perils of Feminist History," reprinted in *Women and Health in America*, edited by Judith Walzer Leavitt (Madison: University of Wisconsin Press, 1984), 222–38 and 239–45.

13. *Angela*, by Lady Florence Bell, was published by Ernest Benn, Ltd., in 1926 and dedicated to Bell's good friend Sybil Thorndike, who performed the role at a single matinée on March 14, 1927. The play has the same plot structure and the same theme as the scenario Robins proposed to Bell in her July letter.

14. ER to FB, from the same undated letter, October [29?], 1904. Stead's "First Impressions of the Theatre" appeared in several parts in the October and November 1904 issues of the *Review of Reviews*, London edition.

15. Robins, *A Dark Lantern* (New York: Macmillan, 1905), 121–22.

16. Lady Dorothy Grey to ER, March [17?], 1905, ER Papers, Fales.

17. Deborah Tannen, *You Just Don't Understand: Women and Men in Conversation* (New York: William Morrow, 1990).

18. Quoted from Jane Marcus, "Art and Anger," *Feminist Studies* 4:4 (February 1978), 96–97. Originally published in the *Guardian* (*Church Weekly*), May 24, 1905, p. 899.

19. Robins, "Chinsegut Diary," 1906, ER Papers, Fales, p. 32. Hereinafter cited in the text as CD.

20. *Journal of Katharine Mansfield*, edited by J. Middleton Murry (London: Constable, 1954), 36, 37, from entry dated "May," in 1908 Journal. My thanks to Tillie Olsen, who alerted me to Mansfield's comments on Robins.

6: Votes for Women

1. ER's remarks to the audience are taken from the text of the speech printed in *Way Stations* (New York: Dodd, Mead, 1913), 28–35.

2. Ray Strachey, *The Cause: A Short History of the Women's Movement in Great Britain* (1928; Port Washington, N.Y.: Kennikat Press, 1969), 310.

3. The command of the WSPU was eventually consolidated in Mrs. Emmeline Pankhurst and her daughter Christabel, to the exclusion of another daughter, Sylvia, of Sylvia's and other prolabor forces, and eventually of the Pankhursts' oldest allies and co-leaders, Frederick and Emmeline Pethick-Lawrence. Robins's position on the WSPU board, her closeness to the Pethick-Lawrences, and her growing distrust of both the autocratic leadership and the violent activities of the WSPU are discussed in chapter 7.

4. Antonia Raeburn, *The Militant Suffragettes* (London: Michael Joseph, 1973), 83.

5. Constance Lytton [and Jane Warton, Spinster], *Prisons and Prisoners* (London: William Heinemann, 1914), 270.

6. Elizabeth Robins, *Votes for Women!*, in *How the Vote Was Won and Other Suffragette Plays*, edited and with an introduction by Dale Spender and Carole Hayman (London: Methuen, 1985), 84. *Votes for Women!* was first published in 1909 by Mills & Boon, Ltd. I restore the exclamation point printed in the Court Theatre program of the production primarily to distinguish ER's play from the WSPU periodical of the same title.

7. ER to Millicent Fawcett, November 1, 1906, Fawcett Library, London.

8. ER to Margaret Dreier Robins, November 9, 1906, in MDR Papers, Women's Trade Union League Papers, Microfilm, reel 20, frames 227–28. The Margaret Dreier Robins Papers were microfilmed for the WTUL series from the originals at the University of Florida Special Collections, Gainesville.

9. ER to MDR, January 19, 1907, MDR Papers, reel 20, frames 301–303.

10. *Times*, April 10, 1907.

11. Sara Jeanette Cotes to ER, April 9, 1907, *Votes for Women* correspondence, ER Papers, Fales.

12. Robins, *The Convert* (1907; reprint, London: Women's Press and Old Westbury, N.Y.: Feminist Press, 1980), 23. Page numbers in text refer to this edition.

13. Robins, "The Feministe Movement in England," republished from *Collier's Weekly* in *Way Stations* (New York: Dodd, Mead, 1913), 40.

14. Elaine Showalter, *A Literature of Their Own*, 222.

15. Robins, "Woman's Secret," in *Way Stations*, 14. Other citations in the text refer to this edition, pp. 1–18. "Woman's Secret" was first published as a pamphlet by Garden City Press, Letchworth, England, 1907.

16. S. L. Clemens to ER, July 30, 1899, ER Papers, Fales.

17. Robins, "Suffrage Camp Revisited," in *Way Stations*, pp. 64–65.

18. Jane Marcus, "Introduction," *The Convert*. "The Divine Rage to Be Didactic" is the title of Marcus's essay, v–xvi.

19. Emmeline Pankhurst to ER, n.d. (summer 1908), quoted from Marcus, "Transatlantic Sisterhood," 752.

20. "Why" appeared in *Everybody's Magazine*, December 1909, in serialized form in *Votes for Women*, and as a pamphlet of the Women Writers' Suffrage League. Citations in the text refer to the *Way Stations* edition, pp. 138–95.

21. ER to MDR, November 13, 1908, in MDR Papers of the WTUL (microfilm reel 20, frames 949–54).

22. Jill Liddington and Jill Norris, *One Hand Tied Behind Us: The Rise of the Women's Suffrage Movement* (London: Virago, 1978).

23. Matt. 16:3 (Authorized Version), as quoted for the epigraph to the published version of ER's speech (*WS*, 99).

24. Ruth Jenkins, "Florence Nightingale's 'Cassandra': Revising the Incarnation Myth" (Paper presented at the Stony Brook Graduate Student Conference on Nineteenth-Century British Literature, November 1986), and Jenkins's remarks about her study of Nightingale.

25. Virginia Woolf, *A Room of One's Own* (New York: Harcourt, Brace, 1929), 79.

26. "A Modern Woman," *Anglo-Saxon Review*, vol. 1 (June 1899), 39–65.

27. Robins, "White Violets," typescript, ER Papers, Fales.

28. Herbert Beerbohm Tree to ER, February 7, 1910, ER Papers, Fales. Included with the "Bowarra correspondence" there is a great deal of information on the prospects of the play for production.

29. Quoted from the corrected proof of the Bath Classics edition of *Uncle Tom's Cabin*, ER Papers, Fales.

7: Political Crises and a Pilgrimage into the Past

1. Source for the scene: ER Diary, February 23, 1913. The order for the gravestone and its inscription is in the ER Papers, Fales. "The Ghost" is collected in Lady Margaret Sackville, *Lyrics* (London: Herbert & Daniel, 1912), 22. The Church of St. Andrew could locate no burial records of the Robins children or Parks. No evidence was found that the gravestone still stands.

2. John Masefield to ER, November 27, 1909, Berg Collection, New York Public Library. John Masefield to Elizabeth Robins correspondence, folder 1, letter 5.

3. JM to ER, January 5, 1910, John Masefield to Elizabeth Robins correspondence, folder 5, letter 4, Berg Collection.

4. JM to ER, February 1, 1910, John Masefield to Elizabeth Robins correspondence, folder 17, letter 4, Berg Collection.

5. JM to ER, February 4, 1910, John Masefield to Elizabeth Robins correspondence, folder 19, letter 4 (dated 5:00 P.M., February 4, 1910), Berg Collection.

6. JM to ER, February 6, 1910, John Masefield to Elizabeth Robins correspondence, folder 20, letter 5 (dated 3:45, February 6, 1910), Berg Collection.

7. Constance Babington-Smith, *John Masefield: A Life* (New York: Macmillan, 1978), 101–5.

8. My thanks to June Dwyer for sharing with me before publication ideas from her book on Masefield: June Dwyer, *John Masefield* (New York: Ungar, 1987). She identifies the affair with Robins as the source for Masefield's portrayal of Mrs. Drummond in *The Street of Today* and argues that the book is his most honest portrayal of relations between men and women.

9. ER's dedication, typescript of "Theo at Home," ER Papers, Fales.

10. Willa Cather, *The Song of the Lark* (1915; reprint, Lincoln: University of Nebraska Press, 1978), 307, 321.

11. Judith Fryer, *Felicitous Space: The Imaginative Structures of Edith Wharton and Willa Cather* (Chapel Hill: University of North Carolina Press, 1986), 331.

12. Dorothy Richardson, as cited in "Foreword" to *Pilgrimage I* (1938; reprint, London: Virago, 1979), 11–12.

13. The quotation is from a note written later and filed with "Theo Book" ("Theo at Home"), ER Papers, Fales.

14. In the late 1940s, Robins still hoped for publication of this later volume of her Theodora series, "Rocky Mountain Journal; or, Kenyon and His Daughter." One of her lifelong problems, that her American stories were not attractive to an English readership (the reverse also applied), prevented Phyllis Hartnoll from approving it for Macmillan's of London.

15. Jane Marcus, in her introduction to the Women's Press edition of *The Convert*, discusses this and the fact that later Robins persuaded a publisher to retract his offer to publish Wells's next novel, *The New Machiavelli*.

16. "A New Art of Travel (An Impression of Gertrude Lowthian Bell's Books *The Desert and the Sown* and *Amurath to Amurath*)," *Fortnightly Review*, vol. 89 (March 1911), 470–99.

17. Raeburn, *The Militant Suffragettes*, 153.

18. The speech is incorrectly dated in the contents and on p. 243 of *Way Stations*. Diary entries confirm that Robins delivered the speech on May 23, 1911, not 1910.

19. DuBois's holograph draft of his remarks to the Lyceum Club is located in the DuBois Collection, University of Massachusetts, Amherst.

20. It was at this benefit, on February 9, 1912, that all 112 of the printed copies of "Under His Roof" sold out and Robins had to order more.

21. As quoted in Raeburn, *The Militant Suffragettes*, 164.

22. *Times*, March 7, 1912, p. 7, col. 4. The letter is quoted as it appears in the *Way Stations* edition, which was printed without this heading.

23. I quote from the American edition, *My Little Sister* (New York: Dodd, Mead, 1913). Page numbers in the text refer to this edition.

24. Robins, "The Girl with a Lamp," typescript in ER Papers, Fales.

25. Katharine Houghton Hepburn, *Woman Suffrage and the Social Evil* (New York: National Woman Suffrage Publishing, n.d. [1913?]).

26. Paul Reynolds Account Books, Paul Reynolds Papers, Columbia University.

27. Robins, "Christabel," *Harper's Weekly*, December 27, 1913, 6–8.

28. Jane Gallop, "Writing and Sexual Difference: The Difference Within," in *Writing and Sexual Difference*, edited by Elizabeth Abel (Chicago: University of Chicago Press, 1982), 289.

29. Susan Gubar, "'The Blank Page' and Female Creativity," in *Writing and Sexual Difference*, 77.

30. JM to ER, February 25, 1910, 6:11 P.M., John Masefield to Elizabeth Robins correspondence, folder 30, letter 2, Berg Collection.

31. Thomas Wells to ER, October 18, 1915, ER Papers, Fales.

32. Personal notes, from Kenneth Burke, guest at class seminar, Amherst, 1981.

8: "My Share in Graver Business"

1. Source for the Scene: ER's diary of this date and the chapter in *Ancilla's Share*, "College Women," 158–68.

2. I quote statements made during the Sir Alfred Keough interview from ER Diary, July 22, 1915.

3. Robins, "Stretcher-Bearing for Women," *Daily Mail*, August 18, 1915.

4. Robins, *Theatre and Friendship* (New York: G. Putnam's Sons, 1932), 291.

5. "Conscription for Women," *Contemporary Review* 111 (April 1917), 478–85.

6. "Women at Home and Beyond the Seas," *Nineteenth Century* 81 (March 1917), 640–50.

7. Robins, "The Tortoise-Shell Cat," in *The Mills of the Gods and Other Stories* (London: Thornton, Butterworth, 1920), 295.

8. R. W. B. Lewis, *Edith Wharton: A Biography* (London: Constable, 1975), 393.

9. Robins, *The Messenger* (New York: Century, 1919), 335. Citations in text refer to pages in this edition. First published in the *Century Magazine*, serialized November 1918 to July 1919.

10. Virginia C. Fowler, *Henry James's American Girl: The Embroidery on the Canvas* (Madison: University of Wisconsin Press, 1984) explores the motif in James's major novels.

11. Robins, "A New View of Country Life," *Nineteenth Century* 85 (March 1919), 585.

12. Robins, "The Main Peace Asset," undated proof, ER Papers, Fales.

13. *Time and Tide*, July 18, 1924, 692–94.

14. "Women Doctors: Lord Knutsford's Charge," *Sunday Times*, March 12, 1922, p. 9.

15. Octavia Wilberforce, "The Eighth Child," Fawcett Library, 201 (typescript). The autobiography has been edited by Pat Jalland as: *Octavia Wilberforce: The Autobiography of a Pioneer Woman Doctor* (London: Cassell, 1989). Because the pub-

lished version omits (or relegates to short excerpts used as introduction) those sections important to my argument, my quotations are from the typescript, hereinafter cited in the text as "Eighth Child."

16. It is not true that Robins adopted David Scott and other children.

17. ER to MDR, May 31, 1920, reel 26, frame 142, Women's Trade Union League Papers.

18. Reeves to ER, *Time and Tide* correspondence, ER Papers, Fales, February 2, 1920.

19. Quotations are from the proof copy, "Woman Comes of Age—Throwing over the Traces of Paternalism," ER Papers, Fales.

20. Waldo Frank, *Our America* (New York: Boni & Liveright, 1919), 109.

21. Marcus, "Art and Anger," *Feminist Studies* 4:4 (February 1978), 69–97.

22. *Time Is Whispering* (New York: Harper, 1923), 85.

23. In her diary, she called one piece "Face Painting." The essays which survive in manuscript in the ER Papers at the Fales are "She Loves to Sew," "Reaction," and "Temptation."

24. Robins, "She Loves to Sew," manuscript copy, ER Papers, Fales, 8.

25. ER used the phrase earlier to express the same idea in the letter that the *New York Times* published in 1913.

26. Robins, *Ancilla's Share: An Indictment of Sex Antagonism* (1924; reprint, Westport, Conn.: Hyperion, 1976), 80, 81.

27. Crystal Eastman, "International Co-operation," in *Equal Rights*, May 9, 1925; reprinted in *Crystal Eastman on Women and Revolution*, edited by Blanche Wiesen Cook (New York: Oxford University Press, 1978), 166.

28. Wells, "Sex Antagonism: An Unavoidable and Increasing Factor in Modern Life," collected in *A Year of Prophesying* (London: T. Fisher Unwin, 1924), 256. This review of Robins's book first appeared on August 30, 1924.

Epilogue

1. Sources for the scene: ER Diary, RR to ER, and ER to RR correspondence.

2. Robins, *Ibsen and the Actress* (London: Hogarth Press, 1928), 31–32.

3. ER's memoir of Sir William Rothenstein, typescript in ER Papers, Fales.

4. Robins, "To G.R.P." [January 12], 1912, ER Papers, Fales, 19.

Bibliography

General References

Ammons, Elizabeth. *Edith Wharton's Argument with America*. Athens: University of Georgia Press, 1980.

Archer, Charles. *William Archer: Life, Work, and Friendships*. London: Allen & Unwin, 1931.

Archer, William. *The Old Drama and the New*. Boston: Small, Maynard, 1923.

——. *Study and Stage: A Yearbook of Criticism*. London: Grant Richards, 1899.

——. *The Theatrical World for 1893–1897*. London: W. Scott, 1894–98.

Astor, Lady Nancy Witcher (Langhorne). *My Two Countries*. Garden City, N.Y.: Doubleday, Page, 1923.

Babington-Smith, Constance. *John Masefield: A Life*. New York: Macmillan, 1978.

Bashkirtseff, Marie. *The Journal of Marie Bashkirtseff*. Translated with an introduction by Mathilde Blind. 2 vols. London: Cassell, 1890.

Bell, Lady Florence. *Angela*. London: Ernest Benn, 1926.

——. "Elizabeth Robins: An Appreciation." *Time and Tide*, May 14, 1920, 7–8.

——. *The Heart of Yorkshire*. London: A. L. Humphreys, 1923.

Blair, Juliet. "Private Parts in Public Places: The Case of Actresses." In *Women and Space*, edited by Shirley Ardener. New York: St. Martin's Press, 1981.

Bradbury, Nicola. *Henry James: The Later Novels*. Oxford: Clarendon Press, 1979.

Campbell, Mrs. Patrick. *My Life and Some Letters*. New York: Dodd, Mead, 1922.

Carter, Huntly, ed. *Women's Suffrage & Militancy*. London: Frank Palmer, n.d.

Cather, Willa. *One of Ours*. New York: Vintage Books, 1971.

——. *The Song of the Lark*. 1915. Reprint. Lincoln: University of Nebraska Press, 1978.

Cima, Gay Gibson. "Discovering Signs: The Emergence of the Critical Actor in Ibsen." *Theatre Journal* 35 (March 1983), 5–22.

——. "Elizabeth Robins: The Genesis of an Independent Manageress." *Theatre Survey* 21 (November 1980), 145–63.

——. "Elizabeth Robins: Ibsen Actress Manageress." Ph.D. Diss., Cornell University, 1978.

Collis, Maurice. *Nancy Astor: An Informal Biography*. New York: E. P. Dutton, 1960.

Courtney, William Leonard. *The Feminine Note in Fiction*. London: Chapman & Hall, 1904.

Crackanthorpe, Blanche Althea. *Milly's Story (The New Moon)*. Pioneer Series, vol. 8. London: William Heinemann, 1895. (The author is incorrectly identified in the *British Museum General Catalogue of Printed Books* as C. E. Raimond.)

Crackanthorpe, David. *Hubert Crackanthorpe and English Realism in the 1890s.* Columbia: University of Missouri Press, 1977.

Cunningham, Gail. *The New Woman and the Victorian Novel.* New York: Barnes & Noble, 1978.

Dangerfield, George. *The Strange Death of Liberal England.* 1935. Reprint. London: MacGibbon & Kee, 1966.

Dreier, Mary E. *Margaret Dreier Robins: Her Life, Letters, and Work.* New York: Island Press Cooperative, 1950.

Dwyer, June. *John Masefield.* New York: Ungar, 1987.

Eastman, Crystal. "International Co-operation." In *Crystal Eastman on Women and Revolution,* edited by Blanche Wiesen Cook. New York: Oxford University Press, 1978.

Edel, Leon. *Henry James.* 5 vols. Philadelphia: Lippincott, 1972.

Egan, Michael. *Henry James: The Ibsen Years.* London: Vision, 1972.

———, ed. *Ibsen: The Critical Heritage.* London: Routledge & Kegan Paul, 1972.

Ehrenreich, Barbara, and English, Deirdre. *For Her Own Good: 150 Years of the Experts' Advice to Women.* Garden City, N.Y.: Anchor Press/Doubleday, 1978.

Fawcett, Millicent Garrett. *What I Remember.* London: T. Fisher Unwin, 1924.

———. *The Women's Victory—and After: Personal Reminiscences, 1911–1918.* London: Sidgwick & Jackson, 1920.

Fowler, Virginia C. *Henry James's American Girl: The Embroidery on the Canvas.* Madison, Wis.: University of Wisconsin Press, 1984.

Franc, Miriam. *Ibsen in England.* Boston: Four Seas, 1919.

Frank, Waldo. *Our America.* New York: Boni & Liveright, 1919.

Fryer, Judith. *Felicitous Space: The Imaginative Structures of Edith Wharton and Willa Cather.* Chapel Hill: University of North Carolina Press, 1986.

Gallop, Jane. "Writing and Sexual Difference: The Difference Within." In *Writing and Sexual Difference,* edited by Elizabeth Abel. Chicago: University of Chicago Press, 1982.

Gates, Joanne E. "Elizabeth Robins and the 1891 Production of *Hedda Gabler.*" *Modern Drama* 28:4 (December 1985), 611–19.

———. "Elizabeth Robins: From *A Dark Lantern* to *The Convert*—A Study of Her Fictional Style and Feminist Viewpoint." *Massachusetts Studies in English* 6:3 & 4 (1978), 25–40.

———. "*Hedda Gabler,* 1980: A Narrative of the Production." M.F.A. thesis, University of Massachusetts, Amherst, 1981.

———. Introduction to Elizabeth Robins, "The Herstory of a Button." *American Voice,* no. 19 (Summer 1990), 35–38.

———. "Stitches in a Critical Time: The Diaries of Elizabeth Robins, American Feminist in England, 1907–1924." *Auto/Biography* 4:2 (3–4) (Winter 1988), 130–39.

Gilman, Charlotte Perkins. *The Yellow Wallpaper.* 1891. Reprint. Old Westbury, N.Y.: Feminist Press, 1973.

Goodman, Charlotte. "The Lost Brother, the Twin: Women Novelists and the Male-Female Double *Bildungsroman.*" *Novel* 17:1 (Fall 1983), 28–43.

Gubar, Susan. "'The Blank Page' and Female Creativity." In *Writing and Sexual Difference,* edited by Elizabeth Abel. Chicago: University of Chicago Press, 1982.

Hamilton, Cicely. *Marriage as a Trade*. New York: Moffat, Yard, 1909.

Heath, Mary T. "A Crisis in the Life of the Actress: Ibsen in England." Ph.D. diss., University of Massachusetts, Amherst, 1986.

Heilbrun, Carolyn G. *Writing a Woman's Life*. New York: Norton, 1988.

Hepburn, Katharine Houghton. *Woman Suffrage and the Social Evil*. New York: National Woman Suffrage Publishing, n.d. [c. 1913].

Holledge, Julie. *Innocent Flowers: Women in the Edwardian Theatre*. London: Virago, 1971.

Ibsen, Henrik. *Hedda Gabler, The Master Builder*, trans. Edmund Gosse and William Archer. New York: Scribner's, 1907.

———. *Little Eyolf, John Gabriel Borkman, When We Dead Awaken*. Introduction by William Archer. New York: Scribner's, 1908.

———. *The Oxford Ibsen*. 8 vols. Translated and edited by James Walter McFarlane. London: Oxford University Press, 1961.

James, Alice. *The Diary of Alice James*. Edited with an introduction by Leon Edel. New York: Dodd, Mead, 1964.

James, Henry. *The Bostonians*. 1886. Reprint. New York: New American Library, Signet, 1980.

———. *The Complete Plays of Henry James*. Edited by Leon Edel. London: Rupert Hart-Davis, 1949.

———. *Essays in London and Elsewhere*. New York: Harper, 1893.

———. *Letters*. Edited by Leon Edel. Vols. 3, 4. Cambridge, Mass.: Belknap Press, Harvard University Press, 1980, 1984.

———. "On the Occasion of *Hedda Gabler*." *New Review* 4 (June 1891), 530.

———. *The Sacred Fount*. New York: Grove Press, 1953.

———. *Shorter Masterpieces, Vol. I*. Edited by Peter Pawlings. Totowa, N.J.: Barnes & Noble, 1984.

———. *The Tragic Muse*. 2 vols. 1890. Reprint. New York: Scribner's, 1908.

Jamieson, Michael. "An American Actress at Balmoral." *Theatre Research International*, n.s., 2:2 (February 1977), 117–31.

Jenkins, Ruth. "Florence Nightingale's 'Cassandra': Revising the Incarnation Myth." Paper delivered at the Graduate Student Conference on Nineteenth-Century British Literature, State University of New York, Stony Brook, New York, November 1986.

Kelley, Mary. *Private Woman, Public Stage: Literary Domesticity in Nineteenth-Century America*. New York: Oxford University Press, 1984.

Kenney, Annie. *Memories of a Militant*. London: E. Arnold, 1924.

Kolodny, Annette. *The Land Before Her: Fantasy and Experience of the American Frontiers, 1630–1860*. Chapel Hill: University of North Carolina Press, 1984.

Leavitt, Judith Walzer. *Women and Health in America: Historical Readings*. Madison, Wis.: University of Wisconsin Press, 1984.

Lewis, R. W. B. *Edith Wharton: A Biography*. London: Constable, 1975.

Liddington, Jill, and Norris, Jill. *One Hand Tied Behind Us: The Rise of the Women's Suffrage Movement*. London: Virago, 1978.

Lovering, Joseph P. *S. Weir Mitchell*. New York: Twayne, 1971.

Lytton, Constance (and Jane Warton, Spinster). *Prisons and Prisoners*. London: William Heinemann, 1914.

Macaulay, Rose. *Noncombatants and Others*. London: Hodder & Stoughton, 1916.

Mackenzie, Midge. *Shoulder to Shoulder*. New York: Alfred A. Knopf, 1975.

Mammen, Edward William. *The Old Stock Company School of Acting: A Study of the Boston Museum*. Boston: Trustees of the Public Library, 1945.

Mansfield, Katherine. *Journal of Katherine Mansfield*. Edited by J. Middleton Murry. London: Constable, 1954.

Marcus, Jane. "Art and Anger." *Feminist Studies* 4:4 (February 1978), 69–97.

———. "Introduction." *The Convert*. Old Westbury, N.Y.: Feminist Press, 1980.

———. "Transatlantic Sisterhood: Labor and Suffrage Links in the Letters of Elizabeth Robins and Emmeline Pankhurst." *Signs*, Spring 1978, 744–55.

Masefield, John. *Complete Poems*. New York: Macmillan, 1962.

———. *The Street of Today*. New York: E. P. Dutton, 1911.

Matlaw, Myron. "Robins Hits the Road: Trouping with O'Neill in the 1880s." *Theatre Survey* 29:2 (November 1988), 173–92.

Meiburger, Sister Anne Vincent. *Efforts of Raymond Robins toward the Recognition of Soviet Russia and the Outlawry of War, 1917–1933*. Washington, D.C.: Catholic University of America Press, 1958.

Meyer, Michael. *Henrik Ibsen*. 3 vols. London: Rupert Hart-Davis, 1971.

Mitchell, David. *Queen Christabel: A Biography of Christabel Pankhurst*. London: MacDonald & Jane's, 1977.

Murray, Janet Horowitz. *Strong Minded Women and Other Lost Voices from Nineteenth-Century England*. New York: Pantheon Books, 1982.

Orme, Michael [Alix Augusta Grein]. *J. T. Grein: The Story of a Pioneer, 1862–1935*. London: John Murray, 1936.

Pankhurst, E. Sylvia. *The Life of Emmeline Pankhurst: The Suffragette Struggle for Women's Citizenship*. Boston: Houghton Mifflin, 1936.

———. *The Suffragette Movement*. London: Lovatt, Dickson & Thompson, 1931.

Peters, Margot. *Bernard Shaw and the Actresses*. Garden City, N.Y.: Doubleday, 1980.

———. *Unquiet Soul: A Biography of Charlotte Brontë*. Garden City, N.Y.: Doubleday, 1975.

Pethick-Lawrence, Emmeline. *My Part in a Changing World*. 1938. Reprint. London: Hyperion, 1976.

Phillips, Stephen. *Paolo and Francesca*. A Tragedy in Four Acts. London: John Lane, Bodley Head, 1900.

Postlewait, Thomas, ed. *William Archer on Ibsen: The Major Essays, 1889–1919*. Westport, Conn.: Greenwood Press, 1986.

———. *Prophet of the New Drama: William Archer and the Ibsen Campaign*. Westport, Conn.: Greenwood Press, 1986.

Raeburn, Antonia. *The Militant Suffragettes*. London: Michael Joseph, 1973.

———. *The Suffragette View*. New York: St. Martin's Press, 1976.

Repington, Lieut.-Col. C. à Court. *The First World War, 1914–1918: Personal Experiences*. 2 vols. Boston: Houghton Mifflin, 1920.

Rhondda, Viscountess [Margaret Haig]. *Notes on the Way*. London: Macmillan, 1937.

————. *This Was My World.* London: Macmillan, 1933.

Richardson, Dorothy. *Pilgrimage I.* London: Virago, 1979.

Rosen, Andrew. *Rise Up, Women!* London: Routledge & Kegan Paul, 1974.

Rossetti, D. G. "Sister Helen." In *Poems and Translations, 1850–1870.* London: Oxford University Press, 1968.

Ryan, Kate. *Old Boston Museum Days.* Boston: Little, Brown, 1915.

Sharp, Evelyn. *Rebel Women.* 2d ed. Introduction by Elizabeth Robins. London: United Suffragists, 1915.

Shaw, George Bernard. *Bernard Shaw: Collected Letters.* Edited by Dan H. Laurence. Vol. 1. New York: Dodd, Mead, 1965.

————. "Ibsen Without Tears." In *Shaw's Dramatic Criticism*, selected by John F. Matthews. New York: Hill & Wang, 1959.

————. *Our Theatres in the Nineties.* 3 vols. London: Constable, 1932.

————. *The Quintessence of Ibsenism.* London: W. Scott, 1891.

Shorter, Clement K. *Charlotte Brontë and Her Sisters.* London: Hodder & Stoughton, 1905.

Showalter, Elaine. *A Literature of Their Own: British Women Novelists from Brontë to Lessing.* Princeton: Princeton University Press, 1977.

Sinclair, May. *Feminism.* London: Women Writers' Suffrage League, 1912.

————. *The Three Brontës.* Port Washington, N.Y.: Kennikat Press, 1967.

————. *The Three Sisters.* New York: Macmillan, 1914.

Spender, Dale, ed. *Time and Tide Wait for No Man.* London: Pandora Press, 1984. (Reprints ER's "Six Point Group Supplement Introductory" from *Time and Tide*, January 19, 1923.)

Squier, Susan M. "The Modern City and the Construction of Female Desire: Wells's *In the Days of the Comet* and Robins's *The Convert.*" *Tulsa Studies in Women's Literature* 8:1 (Spring 1989), 63–75.

Steiner, George. *Language and Silence: Essays on Language, Literature, and the Inhuman.* New York: Atheneum, 1967.

Strachey, Ray. *The Cause: A Short History of the Women's Movement in Great Britain.* 1928. Reprint. Port Washington, N.Y.: Kennikat Press, 1969.

Strouse, Jean. *Alice James.* Boston: Houghton Mifflin, 1980.

Tannen, Deborah. *You Just Don't Understand: Women and Men in Conversation.* New York: William Morrow, 1990.

Trevelyan, George Macaulay. *Grey of Fallodon.* London: Longmans, Green, 1937.

Ward, Mary Augusta (Mrs. Humphrey). *Eleanor.* New York: Harper, 1900.

————. *Harvest.* New York: Dodd, Mead, 1920.

Wells, H. G. *Ann Veronica.* 1909. Reprint. New York: Peter Smith, 1932.

————. *The New Machiavelli.* New York: Duffield, 1910.

————. *A Year of Prophesying.* London: T. Fisher Unwin, 1924. (Chapter 52, "Sex Antagonism," 255–58, reviews *Ancilla's Share.*)

Wharton, Edith. *The Collected Short Stories of Edith Wharton.* Edited by R. W. B. Lewis. 2 vols. New York: Scribner's, 1968.

————. *The Custom of the Country.* New York: Scribner's, 1913.

————. *Glimpses of the Moon.* New York: Appleton, 1922.

————. *A Son at the Front*. New York: Scribner's, 1923.

Wilberforce, Octavia. "The Eighth Child." Fawcett Library, London. Typescript.

Wood, Ann Douglas. " 'The Fashionable Diseases': Women's Complaints and Their Treatment in Nineteenth Century America." In *Women and Health in America*, edited by Judith Walzer Leavitt. Madison: University of Wisconsin Press, 1984.

Woolf, Leonard. *The Journey Not the Arrival Matters*. New York: Harcourt, Brace & World, 1970.

Woolf, Virginia. *A Room of One's Own*. New York: Harcourt, Brace, 1929.

————. *Three Guineas*. New York: Harcourt, Brace, 1938.

————. *The Voyage Out*. New York: Harcourt, Brace, 1920.

Yeazell, Ruth Bernard. *The Death and Letters of Alice James*. Berkeley: University of California Press, 1981.

Works by Elizabeth Robins

Published Novels, Plays, and Collections of Stories

Alan's Wife [with Florence Bell]. London: William Heinemann, 1893.

Camilla. New York: Dodd, Mead, 1918.

Come and Find Me. New York: Century, 1908.

The Convert. 1907. Reprint. Old Westbury, N.Y.: Feminist Press, 1980.

A Dark Lantern. New York: Macmillan, 1905.

"The Fatal Gift of Beauty" and Other Stories. Chicago: Herbert S. Stone, 1896. (Published in the United Kingdom as *"Below the Salt" and Other Stories*. Contents: "The Fatal Gift of Beauty," "The Portman Memoirs," "Below the Salt," "Confessions of a Cruel Mistress," "Vroni")

The Florentine Frame. New York: Moffat, Yard, 1909.

George Mandeville's Husband. London: William Heinemann, 1894.

The Magnetic North. 1904. Reprint. Upper Saddle River, N.J.: Gregg Press, 1969.

The Messenger. New York: Century, 1919.

The Mills of the Gods. New York: Moffat, Yard, 1908.

The Mills of the Gods and Other Stories. London: Thornton Butterworth, 1920. (Contents: "Miss Cal," "The Derrington Ghost," "Under His Roof," "Monica's Village," "The Threlkeld Ear," "The Mills of the Gods," "The Tortoise-Shell Cat")

My Little Sister. New York: Dodd, Mead, 1913. (Published in the United Kingdom as *Where Are You Going To?*)

The New Moon. New York: D. Appleton, 1895.

The Open Question: A Tale of Two Temperaments. New York: Harper, 1899.

Prudence and Peter [with Octavia Wilberforce]. New York: W. Morrow, 1928.

The Secret That Was Kept. New York: Harper, 1926.

Time Is Whispering. New York: Harper, 1923.

Under the Southern Cross. New York: Frederick A. Stokes, 1907. (Begun 1889; completed 1899)

Votes for Women[!]. In *How the Vote Was Won and Other Suffragette Plays*, edited by Dale Spender and Carole Hayman. London: Methuen, 1985.
Where Are You Going To? London: William Heinemann, 1913. (Published in the United States as *My Little Sister*)

Uncollected Short Stories

"La Bellerieuse." *Pall Mall Magazine* 15:61, 20–33.
"Dedicated to John Huntley." *New Review* 10 (July 1894), 746–58.
"Embryo Americans." *Harper's Monthly*, September 1901, pp. 598–602.
"The Father of Lies." *Chapman's Magazine*.
"The Frog Baby." *Woman's Leader*, 1920, February 6, pp. 14–15; February 13, 36–37; February 20, 60–61; February 27, 84–86.
" 'Gustus Frederick." *New Review* 12:70 (March 1895), 270–81.
"The Herstory of a Button." *American Voice*, no. 19 (Summer 1990), 35–38. (Composed in 1875 while ER was a student at Putnam Female Seminary; introduction by Joanne E. Gates)
"Lady Quassia." *Century Magazine* 48 (September 1905), 721–28.
"Lost and Found." *Harper's Monthly* 131 (September 1915), 500–511.
"A Lucky Sixpence." *New Review* 10:56 (January 1894), 105–26.
"Miss de Maupassant." *New Review* 13:72 (September 1895), 233–47.

Nonfiction

"Across America with 'Junius Brutus Booth.'" *Universal Review* 7:27 (July 1890), 375–92.
"The Alaska Boundary." *Fortnightly Review* 80 (November 1903), 792–99.
"Among My Books: The British Merlin." *Literature*, January 21, 1899.
Ancilla's Share: An Indictment of Sex Antagonism. 1924. Reprint. Westport, Conn.: Hyperion, 1976.
"Anglo American Understanding: A Talk with Mr. Otto H. Kahn." *Time and Tide*, July 30, 1926, pp. 241–42. (Unsigned)
"Bolt Seventeen." *Fortnightly Review* 107 (January 1920), 71–76.
Both Sides of the Curtain. London: William Heinemann, 1940.
"Christabel." *Harper's Weekly*, December 27, 1913, pp. 6–8. (Sketch of Christabel Pankhurst)
"Conscription for Women." *Contemporary Review* 111 (April 1917), 478–85.
"Dr. Flora Murray: Reminiscences of Her War Work." *Observer*, August 5, 1923.
"Elizabeth Robins at Cape Nome." *Seattle Post Intelligencer*, August 19, 1900. (Publication of ER's Alaska letters provisionally entitled "The Court Arrives" and "Living Under Martial Law")
"The First Woman M.D. of London." *Time and Tide* (July 18, 1924), 692–94. (Review of the autobiography of Dr. Scharlieb)
"The Gold Miners of the Frozen North: A Visit to Cape Nome." *Pall Mall Magazine* 23 (January 1901), 55–65. (With photographs)
Ibsen and the Actress. London: Hogarth Press, 1928.

"Introduction" to Evelyn Sharp, *Rebel Women*. 2d ed. London: United Suffragists, 1915.

Letter to the *Times*, March 25, 1919. Reprint. London: Ministry of Health, Women's Consultative Council, 1919. (Broadside)

"The Main Peace Asset," *Chronicle*, February? 1919.

"A Modern Woman Born 1689." *Anglo-Saxon Review* 1 (June 1899), 39–65. (Commentary on Lady Mary Wortley Montagu)

"A New Art of Travel." *Fortnightly Review* 89 (March 1911), 470–99. (An impression of Gertrude Lowthian Bell's books, *The Desert and the Sown* and *Amurath to Amurath*)

"A New View of Country Life." *Nineteenth Century* 85 (March 1919), 584–92.

"On Seeing Madame Bernhardt's Hamlet." *North American Review* 171 (December 1900), 908–19.

"Pleasure Mining." *Fortnightly Review* 77 (1902), 474–86.

Portrait of a Lady: or, The English Spirit Old and New. Letchworth: Hogarth Press, 1941. (Memoir of Elizabeth A. M. Thompson)

Raymond and I. London: Hogarth Press, 1956. (Written in 1933–34)

"Sir Herbert Austin." *Time and Tide* 14 (September 30, 1933), 1149. (Letter to the editor)

"The Six Points and Their Common Centre." In *Time and Tide Wait for No Man*, edited by Dale Spender. London: Pandora Press, 1984.

"Some Personal Opinions on the National Theatre, Elizabeth Robins." *Drama*, December 1929, p. 41.

"Stretcher-Bearing for Women." *Daily Mail*, August 18, 1915.

Theatre and Friendship: Some Henry James Letters with a Commentary by Elizabeth Robins. New York: G. P. Putnam's Sons, 1932.

"The Very Latest Gold Field in the Arctic Circle." *Review of Reviews*, London ed., 22 (October 1900), 343–45. (Letter from Grantley Harbor, Alaska)

"War Service at Home." *Nineteenth Century* 76 (November 1914), 1113–22.

Way Stations. New York: Dodd, Mead, 1913. (In addition to the commentaries included in the "Time Table" sections separating each entry, *Way Stations* includes the following essays, speeches, and published letters: "Woman's Secret," WSPU pamphlet printed by Garden City Press [Letchworth, England, 1907]; "The Prisoners' Banquet" [Savoy Hotel, December 11, 1906]; "The Feministe Movement in England" [*Collier's Weekly*, June 29, 1907]; "The Suffrage Camp Revisited" [Portman Rooms Lecture, March 1908]; "The Meaning of It" [*Daily Mail*, June 22, 1908]; Speech at Newcastle Town Hall [September 1908]; "Signs of the Times" [*Votes for Women*, March 1909]; "To the Women Writers Suffrage League" [Waldorf Hotel, May 4, 1909]; "The Hunger Strike" [*Westminster Gazette*, July 21, 1909]; "Why," a WSPU pamphlet; "Shall Women Work?"; "Mr. Partington's Mop" [*Votes for Women*, August 12, 1910]; "The Women Writers at the Criterion" [May 23, 1911]; "Come and See" [*Westminster Gazette*, June 16, 1911]; Speech at Crowborough, Sussex [October 23, 1911]; Letter to the *Times* [March 7, 1912]; "The Perfidy of Sympathizers" [*Votes for Women*, March 22, 1912]; Speeches at the Albert Hall [March 28, June 15, 1912]; "Sermons in Stones" [*Contemporary Review*, April 1912]; "Woman's War" [*McClure's Magazine*, March 1913, 41–52].)

What Can I Do? London: Lady Chichester Hospital for Women and Children, n.d. (Pamphlet)

"Why Suffragettes Go to Jail." *Hearst's Magazine*, September 1913, 487–89.

"Woman's Place in the New Order: Purpose of Militancy." Letter to the Editor. *Times*, May 4, 1921.

"Women at Home and Beyond the Seas." *Nineteenth Century* 81 (March 1917), 640–50.

"Women Doctors: Lord Knutsford's Charge." *Sunday Times*, March 12, 1922.

Unpublished Plays

"Benvenuto Cellini" (1899–1900)
"Bowarra" (1909)
"Evangeline" [1914]
"Judith" (unfinished, 1906)
"The Mirkwater" (1895)
"The Old Woman of the Sea" (Pre-1895)
"Over a Cup of Tea" (Pre-1895)
"The Silver Lotus" (1895–96)
"Where Are You Going To?" (two versions, 1913, 1914)

Unpublished Fiction

"The Centaur," story (c. 1916)
"Clare and Jerry" (Story)
"The Coming Woman" (Novella, 1892)
"Discretion" (Story and play, 1912)
"An Egyptian Necklace" (Story; alternate title: "Pergarnack's Necklace")
"Go to Sleep Stories" (Story series, c. 1905)
"Him and Her" (Story, 1888)
"An Incident of Travel" (Story)
"Jessamine Gardens" (Story)
"A Lost Opportunity" (Story)
"A Masterpiece the World Never Saw or, Aphrodite of the West" (Story, 1900)
"Newtimber Tale" (Fragment)
"Poppy and Mandragora" (Story)
"The Pleiades" (Novel based on CER's Colorado records [1914])
"Rocky Mountain Journal; or, Kenyon and His Daughter" (Autobiographical novel, 1927–30)
"Scenes Behind the Scenes" (Story collection, 1897–98. Includes: "Maria McMurdo," "A Highly Respectable Heroine," "A Manager's Mistake," "How to Succeed On the Stage")
"A Separable Friend" (Story)
"Sixes and Sevens" (Story, c. 1912)
"Stall B.25" (Story)

"Theodora at Home" (Autobiographical novel, first version, 1910)
"Theodora; or, The Pilgrimage" (Autobiographical novel, subtitled "A Study in Egoism," 1910–11)
"Valentine Cobb" (Novella, 1895)
"White Violets" (Novel, "A Study in Isolation; or, Great Powers," 1909–10)

Unpublished Nonfiction: Memoirs, Political Essays, and Speeches

"An American Actress at Amergau" (Oberammergau, 1890)
"An American Actress at Balmoral Castle; or, A Close up View of Queen Victoria and the English Stage" (1895)
"Annie Besant"
"The Book of Revelations" (1920–21)
"Bret Harte and Madame Van de Velde"
"The Caribou Stand"
"Catching the Train for North America"
"Christabel Pankhurst and White Slavery; or, The Girl with the Lamp" (1913)
"Dorothy Grey" (Selections quoted in *Dorothy Grey*, by Louise Creighton, 1907)
"An Education Act"
"Edward VIII"
"Gertrude Bell" (BBC radio broadcast, 1927)
"Gertrude Lowthian Bell"
"Heights and Depths" (Continuation of "Whither and How," (?)1940)
"Henrik Ibsen: The Drama of Ideas, a Determined Originator"
"Ibsen" (BBC talk, 1928)
"Kaomi" (Unpublished preface, *The Magnetic North*, 1901)
"Memoir of W. T. Stead" (1948)
"The Old England and the New"
"Oscar Wilde: An Appreciation"
Preface to *Uncle Tom's Cabin*, corrected proofs (scheduled for publication in *Author*, 1908)
"Reaction"
"She Loves to Sew"
"Some Aspects of Henrik Ibsen"
"The Spirit of the People"
"Temptation"
"To the Home-Keepers in America from the Home-Keepers in England"(1940)
"Whither and How" (Continuation of *Both Sides of the Curtain*, (?)1939–40)
"Woman Comes of Age: Throwing Over the Traces of Paternalism" (Proofs)
"The Woman Juror" (To the editor of the *Morning Post*, proofs)

Index

Wilberforce, William, 199

Wilde, Oscar, 29, 30, 57, 64, 84, 253, 260; discusses theater of the future with ER, 48; ER influenced by his recitation of "The Artist," 114–15; model for Maurice Neill, 50

Wilhelm Meisters Lehrjahre (Goethe), 190, 193

Wilson, Woodrow, 225, 233

Wings of the Dove (James), 231

Wirt, Rev. Loyal L., 122, 124, 128

Wollstonecraft, Mary, 167, 178

"Woman Comes of Age—Throwing over the Traces of Paternalism" (Robins), 240–41

Woman of Genius, A (Austin), 194

"Woman's Secret" (Robins), 166–68, 172, 178

"Women at Home and Beyond the Seas: An Anomaly" (Robins), 228

Women's Coronation Pageant, 198

Women's Institutes, 233–34

Women's Peace Party, 230

Women Writers' Suffrage League, 159, 181, 194, 197–98, 234, 250, 252

Woodhull, Victoria, 7

Woolf, Leonard, 239, 257

Woolf, Virginia, 75, 143, 167–68, 178, 193, 221, 236, 247, 249, 252, 253, 257. *See also titles of individual works*

Wreckage (Crackanthorpe), 87

"Writing a War Story" (Wharton), 229

WSPU (Women's Social and Political Union), 156–59, 161, 163, 165, 166, 175–76, 195, 198, 201, 204, 205, 206, 207; ER sends resignation, 208; dissolution of Board of Directors, 211–12, 272 (n. 3)

Wyndham, Charles, 46–47, 61, 80, 82, 90, 136

Yellow Book, The, 87

"Yellow Wallpaper, The" (Gilman), 136

You Just Don't Understand: Women and Men in Conversation (Tannen), 143

Zanesville, Ohio, 5, 7–8, 14, 17, 18, 104, 262

JOANNE E. GATES is Associate Professor of English at Jacksonville State University.